I0214521

THE HISTORY OF

THE ROYAL NORTHUMBERLAND FUSILIERS

IN THE SECOND WORLD WAR

1. Captain J. J. B. Jackman, V.C., killed in action with the 1st Battalion on the 25th November 1941.
From a portrait by S. P. Kendrick

THE HISTORY OF THE ROYAL NORTHUMBERLAND FUSILIERS

IN THE SECOND WORLD WAR

By

Brigadier C. N. BARCLAY, C.B.E., D.S.O.

Produced under the direction of the

REGIMENTAL HISTORY COMMITTEE
ROYAL NORTHUMBERLAND FUSILIERS

Published for the

Regimental History Committee, Royal Northumberland Fusiliers

by

WILLIAM CLOWES AND SONS LIMITED

Little New Street, London, E.C.4

First published 1952

DEDICATION

THIS book is dedicated to the memory of those Officers, Warrant Officers, Non-Commissioned Officers and Fusiliers of the Royal Northumberland Fusiliers who gave their lives for their King, Country and Regiment in the campaigns of the Second World War of 1939–1945.

CONTENTS

APPENDICES

STATEMENT OF CONTENTS BY BATTALIONS

NOTE: A table of contents in this form has been included for the benefit of those readers who may wish to follow the activities of any particular battalion.

MAPS

MAPS WHICH FOLD OUT

Facing page

MAPS IN THE TEXT

Page

ILLUSTRATIONS

Facing page

FOREWORD

By

MAJOR-GENERAL H. DE R. MORGAN, D.S.O.

The Colonel of The Regiment

THE main aim of a writer of history of war may be either to paint a word picture of life under war conditions—as, for example, was that of John Masefield in writing his epic *Gallipoli* which boasted no accuracy of detail; or it may be limited to producing a faithful record of operations. By recalling events which are still vivid in their memory, the first will appeal to those who shared the experiences related; the second may be the more valuable to posterity. Granted the space, the historian, by combining these requirements, may be able to satisfy both purposes.

The task committed to the present historian was one of peculiar difficulty. Within the narrow limits of one book he was required to record the inter-war history of the Regiment and the war history of its several units in the various theatres in which they were engaged. These units, moreover, were not only fulfilling a variety of roles, but by their nature were often required to disperse their sub-units over a wide field of operations.

Recognizing these difficulties I have been impressed by the amount of personal detail which Brigadier Barclay has found it possible to include in the fine and accurate record he has produced. In this book, which I have read with great interest, I feel that many like myself will for the first time obtain a full idea of the services rendered by the Regiment as a whole, which personal distraction and the fog of censorship during the war years made impossible.

Never before have we suffered so many changes and reorganizations, and yet through all these pages one is aware of that great spirit which inspired all—the name and fame of the Regiment. The ranks were often replenished by men who had no county or Regimental connection, but who, carried along by that indefinable sentiment which is indomitable and eternal, were prepared to face any odds in their pride for the ancient traditions which it was their privilege to maintain.

The recital of the deeds and a description of the character of the war conditions in which they achieved them cannot therefore but inspire those who come after them in the battalions of the Fifth Fusiliers; so that should they too in their generation be called on to pass through the ordeal they also may in the faith of their fathers pass through unshaken to final victory.

Lastly, on behalf of all who have served in the Regiment, I wish to record our gratitude to Colonel B. Cruddas, without whose generous guarantee this history could not have been produced, and to Colonel O. B. Foster, M.C., D.L., for the additional financial support he has given in memory of his son, the late Lieut.-Colonel Kingsley Foster, D.S.O.

H. DE R. MORGAN.

Llandefaelog House, Brecon.
February 1952.

AUTHOR'S PREFACE

THIS record of the Royal Northumberland Fusiliers covers the years 1919 to the end of 1945, although in one or two cases the period has been extended into 1946 in order to complete a phase or incident. All units of the Regiment have been included. Just before going to press it was decided to include a list of casualties suffered by, and honours awarded to, the 1st Battalion in Korea, up to October 1951 and these will be found in Appendix E.

The story has been written almost entirely from accounts and notes compiled by members of the Regiment. In nearly every case these were written by officers, and others, present at the time, and in a substantial number of cases I have recorded the narrative in their own words. It may be said, therefore, that, with very few exceptions, this record of events is an 'eye-witness' account. In this connection I must place on record the valuable assistance obtained from the many excellent accounts which have appeared in the Regimental journal—the *St. George's Gazette*.

In order to compress the activities of eight battalions over a number of years into one volume, the accounts of peace-time and non-operational phases in war have been reduced to the minimum. For the same reason many notable and gallant actions by small parties and individuals have, of necessity, been omitted.

In general the book is set out in chronological order, although there is some departure from this in detail. This is due partly to campaigns, and other events, overlapping, and partly to the desirability of giving some degree of continuity to the story of each battalion.

I have aimed at providing sufficient background to enable the reader to fit the various details of Regimental activities into the general picture of the war and the appropriate campaigns. The events leading up to the Second World War are described in Chapter 1, and local background is provided throughout the text as considered necessary. I have not hesitated to include events on the grounds that they are well known or even elementary. I feel that happenings which are common knowledge today may be unfamiliar in a few years' time, and that future generations of readers may welcome these brief descriptions of matters in the wider field. In order to make each chapter self-contained, as far as possible, some slight repetition of background has been unavoidable.

I wish to express my thanks to Major-General H. de R. Morgan, D.S.O., the Colonel of the Regiment; to Brigadier H. R. Sandilands, C.M.G., D.S.O., to Lieut.-Colonel B. Tarleton, and many others, for their advice and assistance during the course of my work.

Lieut.-Colonel Tarleton was originally responsible for collecting the script and notes, and as a basis for writing the history I found these most comprehensive and complete. Later this work was taken over by Brigadier Sandilands, who provided additional matter, checked my original drafts, and gave me the full benefit of his unique experience of Regimental matters and as author of the history of the Fighting Fifth in the First World War. I cannot over-emphasize his part in the production of this book. Although my name appears as author his contribution has certainly been no less than mine.

In spite of my wish to avoid mentioning too many names I feel that I cannot omit that of Major D. L. Lloyd, M.C. (the Secretary, Regimental History Committee), who checked, and rewrote, much of the chapters dealing with the 1st Battalion in North Africa and Italy.

In addition I wish to thank the publishers, Messrs. William Clowes and Sons Ltd., for their advice, help and consideration, and the Imperial War Museum for permission to publish official photographs.

Finally, I would like to record my pride and satisfaction in having been given the opportunity to write the story of this famous Regiment during, perhaps, the most momentous years in its history.

C. N. BARCLAY,
Brigadier.

Wylye, Wiltshire.
November 1951.

GLOSSARY

Abbreviations, Technical and Colloquial Terms

NOTE: This Glossary includes some abbreviations and terms which are well known. They have been included because as time passes they may be less frequently used, and less perfectly understood by future generations of readers.

A.A. Anti-Aircraft.

A.T. Anti-Tank.

'*Bazooka.*' A hand gun which can be operated by one man to destroy tanks.

Bde. Brigade.

Armd. Bde. Armoured Brigade.

Inf. Bde. Infantry Brigade.

B.E.F. British Expeditionary Force. The term was not used after the evacuation of the B.E.F. from Dunkirk in May 1940.

B.G.S. Brigadier, General Staff.

Bn. Battalion.

'*Buffaloes.*' Amphibious vehicles of American design, capable of carrying thirty men, or small vehicle and eight men, over rough country and moderately calm water. Bullet and splinter proof.

Carrier (or *Bren Carrier*). Small tracked vehicles, used mainly as the tactical vehicle in M.G. units and by infantry as a mobile reserve. Bullet and splinter proof. Also used by artillery and other arms—mainly for transporting wireless personnel and sets.

C.D.L. Tanks. Canal Defence Light Tanks. Tanks equipped for producing artificial light by means of searchlights.

C.G.S. Chief of the General Staff.

C.I.G.S. Chief of the Imperial General Staff—the senior military member of the Army Council.

Coy. Company.

'*Crocodiles.*' Flame-throwing tanks.

D.D. Tanks. Amphibious tanks.

Div. Division.

Armd. Div. Armoured Division.

D.Ps. Displaced Persons. The term applied to persons of the conquered and occupied countries who were removed by the Germans from their homes for forced labour elsewhere—mostly in Germany.

'*Dumping.*' The process of collecting ammunition near gun, mortar, machine-gun, etc., positions, prior to an attack. Also occasionally applied to stores and rations.

E.N.S.A. Entertainment National Service Association. The organization which provided concert parties, and other entertainments, for the Fighting Services.

F.D.Ls. Forward Defended Localities. The most advanced posts in a defensive position.

'*Flails.*' Tanks equipped with special chains for destroying mines by beating the ground in front of them.

F.O.O. Forward Observing Officer. Usually applied to artillery officers who go forward with the leading infantry and communicate with their guns by wireless or field telephone.

'*Fortress Europe.*' A term used by the Nazis for that portion of Europe occupied by German troops in the Second World War.

G.O.C. General Officer Commanding.

G.O.C.-in-C. General Officer Commander-in-Chief.

Harassing Fire. Intermittent fire directed at localities, roads, cross-roads, etc., behind the enemy's front, where his troops or vehicles are known, or likely, to be. Employed by artillery, machine-guns and mortars.

'*Jeep.*' A small and very robust motor vehicle of American design, with very high horsepower and an exceptional cross-country performance. Used extensively in the British Army.

'*Kangaroos.*' Armoured personnel carriers. Sherman tanks with the turret removed. Used for carrying infantry in the forward areas. Splinter, bullet and partially shell proof.

L. of C. Lines of Communication.

L.S.T. Landing Ship, Tanks.

M.G. Machine-gun.

M.T. Mechanical Transport.

O.P. Observation Post.

'*Piat Gun.*' Personal Infantry Anti-tank Gun. A weapon about the same size as a rifle and easily carried by one man. Fires a small bomb with a flat trajectory and range of about 100 yards. Issued mostly to infantry platoons.

Pl. Platoon.

P.R.I. President, Regimental Institutes.

Reservists—Class A. Specially selected reservists, who accepted liability to recall in an emergency not involving general mobilization—such as the Shanghai Defence Force (1927) and the Arab Rebellion in Palestine (1936). In the infantry Class A Reservists were limited to twenty-five per regiment.

R.T.R. Royal Tank Regiment.

Sec. Section.

Sqn. Squadron.

Tp. Troop.

Waterproofing. The process of making vehicles, wireless sets, etc., partially impervious to water. Employed during amphibious operations, prior to river crossings and in marshy country.

CHAPTER 1

BACKGROUND

The events which led up to the Second World War

THIS history of the Royal Northumberland Fusiliers covers, in outline, the period between the wars, when for most of the time it was a normal infantry regiment, and in greater detail the war years, from 1939 to 1945, when it was a machine-gun regiment—although, as recorded later, several of its units were given other roles.

Those who have served in the Regiment or been associated with it are justly proud of its fine record. Nevertheless, the part played by the units of any single regiment was obviously a small one in events as a whole. A mere chronicle of the comings and goings and deeds of the several units would be difficult to assimilate intelligently. It is essential for the reader to possess some knowledge of the wider fields in which the activities of the Regiment were framed. It is true that today these events are well known; but in a few years a generation will have grown up to whom they are less familiar, and who will welcome this introduction to Regimental history. It is the purpose of this opening chapter to supply this background.

I. THE LEAN YEARS

With the collapse of Germany and her allies in the autumn of 1918 the thoughts of the whole country turned to the tasks of demobilizing the armed forces, the transfer of industry from a war to a peace footing and a general return to the conditions of 1914. With no previous experience as a guide it was almost universally accepted that this could be brought about in a comparatively short time.

The demobilization arrangements for the forces had been planned in considerable detail in advance, and on the whole they worked smoothly. The process was somewhat retarded by irksome 'incidents,' such as wars in Afghanistan and North Russia, unsettled conditions in distant parts of the Commonwealth and open rebellion in Ireland. These were not, however, regarded as serious compared to the great events which had just terminated, and by 1923 the Army had returned to an almost pre-war footing in strength and organization. This meant a return to the Cardwell system, with *theoretically* half the Army at home and half abroad—for most regular infantry regiments one battalion at home and one abroad. In practice this ideal was not always possible, and there were frequent occasions when both regular battalions of an infantry regiment were serving overseas.

The newly formed Regular Army had to overcome serious difficulties. The rates of pay compared unfavourably with those in civil life. Even with lowered physical and medical standards it was difficult to attract recruits in sufficient numbers.

Politicians coined a new catch-phrase, 'No major war for ten years.' This not only had a detrimental effect on recruiting, but also on the Army Estimates—which were reduced annually as a matter of routine.

In industry the war-time factories were closed down and the blue-prints and experimental equipment designed for the campaigns of 1919–20 were pigeon-holed or discarded. The Army was not, therefore, provided with the latest arms and equipment, but with that which happened to be in use—and of which there was a good reserve—when the war ended.

The shortage of regular recruits was felt more seriously by units stationed at home than by those overseas. Unsettled conditions in India and elsewhere made it necessary to maintain overseas garrisons at full strength, and this could only be done at the expense of their linked units in the United Kingdom. For a considerable period in the 1920s and 1930s it was not uncommon for a regular infantry battalion at home to be reduced to a strength of 300. A strength of 500 was exceptional. Under these circumstances training, above a company level, became extremely difficult—sometimes farcical. On higher training only one or two companies per battalion could be mustered at full strength, the remaining sub-units being represented by flags.

These conditions naturally had an effect on the supply of officers—whose rates of pay, although considerably higher than in 1914, were nevertheless well below those for equivalent employment in civil life. Families with an Army tradition had been hard hit by the rising cost of living, income tax and death duties. Many could no longer afford to put their sons to a profession which did not pay an economic wage and which discarded them at a comparatively early age without prospects of well remunerated civil employment. On the whole the quality among officers remained high, but for many years there was a deficiency in numbers.

In the Territorial Army conditions became even worse. There was some economic reason for joining the Regular Army, which in times of serious unemployment at least provided a living. With the reiteration of the phrase 'No major war for ten years' only the most ardent and patriotic citizen could be expected to join a force which existed mainly for participation in a major conflict, and to serve in which was likely to result in financial loss, to both officers and men. The results achieved in some units, in face of financial stringency, lack of equipment and shortages of men, were truly remarkable. It was due almost entirely to the small devoted bands of officers and N.C.Os.—which seemed to exist in nearly every Territorial Army unit—whose enthusiasm overcame every difficulty. The Nation owes these men a debt of gratitude: it was they who kept the Territorial Army 'alive' in the lean years.

Since 1914 another factor had arisen which produced serious problems, particularly in the infantry, which were not solved until the Second World War. By 1918 industry had become highly specialized—due mainly to the high organization and tempo of war production. Tradesmen, such as fitters and electricians, were highly paid in civil life and men in that capacity in the now more mechanized Army expected correspondingly high rates of service pay. In addition the Army invented trades of its own—wireless operators, drivers, clerks, etc.—who received preferential financial treatment. This popularized recruiting in arms which had a preponderance of these specialists—to the detriment of the infantry, who only had a few. In the infantry

2. Major-General Sir Percival S. Wilkinson, K.C.M.G., C.B., Colonel of the Regiment 1915–1935. *From a portrait by Edward Halliday*

arm itself the specialists and tradesmen tended to acquire a superior status to the ordinary fighting man in a rifle section. This outlook continued till after Dunkirk in 1940. It took the very mobile campaigns which followed to establish the fighting infantryman as a high-grade technician—perhaps the greatest 'specialist' of all.

Summarized it may be said that within three years of the Armistice of November 1918 the British Army had been reduced overseas to a well-disciplined police force, and at home to a nucleus force on which a modern army might be built up over a period of years. This condition continued until the rise of Hitler in 1933; but so great was the leeway to be made up that even by the late summer of 1939 our Army was still deficient of equipment regarded as essential in modern war.

So far this brief account of the lean years has been a dismal one; but not all was on the debit side. There were a few good signs and features to set against the frustrations and disappointments. Many young officers who had served in the war displayed remarkable aptitude for the military profession. Some remained on as regular officers, and a proportion of these, together with new entries, showed an enthusiasm which could not be stifled. In the late 1920s and 1930s competition for entry to the Staff Colleges was extremely keen, in some years as many as 500 candidates competing for fifty-odd vacancies. Some who found monotony in home soldiering, sought refuge in periods of secondment to the King's African Rifles, the West African Frontier Force and similar colonial forces. Others secured attachments to foreign armies or went abroad on language study. A good proportion of these officers attained high rank and distinction in the Second World War, and the policy undoubtedly paid a handsome dividend. In addition the Commonwealth built up a fine corps of officers in the old Indian Army and in the Dominion forces.

Between the wars there was also a remarkable amount of military writing—not only in the service journals, but in the national daily and weekly press. Many of the authors were retired senior officers, but civilians with military experience in the 1914–18 war also contributed. Much of this writing was unorthodox and revolutionary; but it provided material for thought and to some extent kept service matters before an otherwise apathetic public.

II. REARMAMENT

Early in 1933 the Nazi Party assumed control of Germany and Herr Hitler became head of the German Reich. Although the main plank in his policy was the repudiation of the Versailles Peace Treaty—particularly the clauses limiting German armaments—the Nazi assumption of power did not, in itself, cause any alarm or zeal for military preparedness in this country. Unlike Mr. Winston Churchill, who from the outset sounded the alarm, the average citizen was unmoved. By a process which later became known as 'wishful thinking,' he assumed that the Nazis would confine their activities to within the Reich. A modest programme of rearmament was started, confined almost entirely to the Royal Air Force. The event did, however, effectively silence the catch-phrase 'No major war for ten years'—which had been extended long beyond the period from its inception.

As always in a democracy, Government action was limited by public opinion. It took a long time to educate the man in the street to the idea of another war with Germany. The process was hardly accelerated by the Italian invasion of Abyssinia in October 1935—although this demonstrated only too clearly the impotence of the League of Nations as an instrument to prevent aggression.

The few with inside knowledge were not, therefore, surprised when the Nazi rise to power was followed by the reoccupation of the Rhineland in March 1936 and by the march into Austria in March 1938, but even these violations of the Peace Treaty failed to produce any serious reactions on the majority. They were warnings to be on the alert, but little more.

By the summer of 1938 Germany was exerting ever-increasing pressure on Czechoslovakia for the return of the Sudetenland; and in the early autumn this led to events which at last brought the British people to a realization of their danger.

In September 1938 Mr. Neville Chamberlain held his series of conferences with Herr Hitler, which terminated with that at Munich on the 30th September. These negotiations, which some thought had just a chance of averting war, were followed at once by the first stage in the dismemberment of Czechoslovakia. Mr. Chamberlain was criticized by a few at the time, and by many more later, when his efforts failed to secure peace. The question of the wisdom of his conduct at these meetings is likely to remain highly controversial; but it is at least possible that the extra year of preparation which they gave saved us from defeat. It is not unreasonable to hold the view that Hitler's suicide and the complete ruin of Nazi Germany in 1945 were attributable to the Munich Conference of 1938—painful and degrading as it was at the time.

Mr. Chamberlain's views on the likelihood of the success of his talks with Herr Hitler were reflected in his action on his return from Munich. Almost at once he announced a rearmament programme which was without parallel in times of peace. Unfortunately there was to be a big gap between the announcement of the programme and even its partial fulfilment. Nevertheless, the British Commonwealth was on the warpath, and the measures which the Government announced received the unanimous support of the British people.

March 1939 saw the occupation of Czechoslovakia by German forces and the country declared a German protectorate. Having attained his ends in this direction Herr Hitler switched his policy to one of pressure on Poland for the return of Danzig to the Reich and other concessions. It became clear that his appetite was insatiable and that only a miracle could preserve peace.

Early in 1939 the Government announced the doubling of the Territorial Army—a policy attributed to Mr. Hore-Belisha, the then Secretary of State for War, without consultation with his military advisers. By the majority this was acclaimed at the time as a master stroke. In fact it had little *immediate* effect on our military preparedness. Although it produced some extra manpower it did not result in a doubling of the total strength of the Territorial Army. For every reasonably efficient unit it substituted two ill-organized, weak and ill-trained units. In the long run, however, this measure—together with conscription, which was introduced for the first time in our history in peace in May 1939—provided the framework of the army which, with the other services, brought us victory in the Second World War.

This period also saw the conversion of a number of infantry regiments—of which the Royal Northumberland Fusiliers was one—into machine-gun regiments.*

It will be seen that by May 1939 provision had been made for the necessary man-power, and the organization, to fight a major war on land. It remained to equip and train the forces now in being. Unfortunately the provision of equipment lagged far behind the organization and recruitment of personnel, and without the arms, vehicles and other impedimenta of a modern army the troops could not be properly trained.

Apart from the Royal Arsenals and a few private firms who supplied arms mainly as a subsidiary activity, we had no industries for the mass production of war materials.

Up to the end of 1938 the turnover of industry from peace to war production had proceeded in a leisurely fashion—all concerned being more imbued with the hope of averting war than with co-operating in the modest rearmament programme of pre-Munich days. When the signal was given for an all-out production drive we discovered, to our cost, that neither the service departments responsible for experiment and design nor civil industry were capable of producing early results. So drugged had we been by the victory of 1918, and our hopes in the League of Nations to maintain peace, that no proper plans, designs or knowledge existed with which to implement the orders for war material which all now admitted to be essential to national security. Moreover, by the spring of 1939 the claims on our armament industry had grown to colossal proportions. In addition to our own fighting services, regular and non-regular, urgent requests for war equipment came from the Dominions, India and our Allies and friends all over the world. The latter had been greatly increased by the Government policy of 'guaranteeing' almost every small nation in Europe against German or Italian aggression. The expectations of purchasing commissions from Poland, Turkey, Roumania and other countries in imminent danger of attack were pitiful to those who knew the extent of our own deficiencies.

In spite of our really great efforts from Munich onwards the fact remains that the small British Expeditionary Force which went to France in October 1939 was equipped mainly with the weapons of 1918—although in transport and other administrative impedimenta it had, to some extent, kept pace with the trend in civil life.

The inventors of the tank could not muster a single efficient armoured division by the spring of 1940. The 4·5-in. gun-howitzer, although part of the establishment of the artillery, was not ready in sufficient quantities by the opening of hostilities and many batteries went to war equipped with the obsolete 18-pr. gun. Infantry battalions possessed only two anti-tank guns, these being of French manufacture and issued to units of the B.E.F. only a few days before they crossed to France.

On the 31st March 1939 the British Government had announced an agreement with Poland, guaranteeing that country against aggression.

---

* This major change in infantry organization—which has such an important bearing on this history—and the subsequnt changes in the role and organization of machine-gun battalions are dealt with in detail in Chapter 2.

On the 1st September 1939 Herr Hitler's armies invaded Poland, and two days later, at 11.15 a.m., the Prime Minister—Mr. Neville Chamberlain—announced over the wireless to the Nation that the British people were once again at war with Germany.

It was in this setting that the units of the Royal Northumberland Fusiliers embarked on the Second World War.

CHAPTER 2

MACHINE-GUNS AND MACHINE-GUN BATTALIONS

A general survey of their organization, equipment and role

THE Maxim gun, invented by Sir Hiram Stevens Maxim, and demonstrated by him in 1884, was the first automatic small-arms weapon to be used in the British Army. Some doubt exists as to whether it was the first weapon of its kind to be produced; but it was certainly the first to be used effectively on the battlefield.

By the time of the First World War the Maxim gun had been superseded, or was in process of being superseded, in the British Army by the Vickers machine-gun, which although differing in detail embodied the fundamental principles of the original invention. Similarly the Vickers gun in use today differs only in detail, and in certain accessories which have been added from time to time, from the original models. Unlike the internal-combustion engine and other mechanical devices, the first machine-guns of sixty-five years ago were little less efficient mechanically than those in use at the present time, although the technique of firing, their tactical handling and their transportation have advanced out of all recognition.

In the Boer War and in other colonial campaigns the machine-gun had been used only in small numbers, and its potentialities under modern conditions, between armies equipped and trained to European standards, were not at first realized. It was not until the First World War of 1914–18 that the machine-gun took its place as the greatest 'killer' in use on the battlefield. It was this weapon, protected by concrete and earth and used in large numbers, more than any other, which brought about the stalemate of trench warfare and the huge casualty lists of 1915–17. It remained operationally dominant until the advent of the tank in the latter years of the war.

The British Expeditionary Force which went to Flanders in 1914 was equipped on a scale of two machine-guns per infantry battalion. It soon became apparent that this was inadequate, and steps were taken to increase the numbers—first by adding to those with battalions, then by forming machine-gun companies in each brigade, and finally by incorporating all machine-guns into a new arm of the service, the Machine Gun Corps. The last organization gained flexibility in the employment of this important weapon, and—owing to the introduction of the lighter (but less accurate and less efficient for sustained fire) Lewis gun—the fire-power of the infantry battalion was not seriously reduced.

The new Corps not only improved the firing technique of the weapon—by innovations such as indirect and overhead fire, night firing on fixed lines, etc.—but greatly improved its tactical handling, both in defence and attack.

The Machine Gun Corps' organization proved so satisfactory that many were surprised when, soon after the termination of hostilities, the Corps was disbanded and machine-guns reverted to infantry battalions—in the form of one machine-gun platoon per battalion. The reasons for this apparently retrograde step were as follows:

(a) *Financial.* The victorious conclusion of the war resulted in a nation-wide demand for drastic economies in the armed forces.

(b) *Manpower.* The retention of the Machine Gun Corps would have entailed a reduction in the number of infantry battalions and machine-gun units were regarded as less efficient for overseas garrison duties, which it was contemplated would be mostly of an internal security nature.

(c) *In view of the scattered locations* of the Regular Army overseas it was obviously more convenient to decentralize machine-guns than to retain them in large self-contained units—which presupposes large concentrated forces under centralized control.

(d) *The introduction of the tank* was considered not only to render the machine-gun less effective in defence, but also to have provided a good vehicle for its use in an offensive role.

Of these considerations (a) and (b) undoubtedly carried most weight, and although more centralized organizations were reintroduced later, it is probable that in view of the conditions at the time, the disbandment of the Corps was a wise and indeed inevitable step.

Later the decision was made to increase the number of machine-guns in the infantry and include a machine-gun company in each battalion.

By 1935—the Nazi Party having been in power in Germany for two years, and the Italian invasion of Abyssinia being in progress—the authorities began to give thought to the modernization of the armed forces for possible participation in a major conflict. The country was not, as yet, in the mood to shoulder heavy additional expenditure and such reforms as were considered had to be within the slender financial resources available. One of the problems which had been exercising the General Staff and Commanders was the increasing number of weapons which the infantry soldier had to learn. This, together with the high standard of tactical skill which modern war demands of the foot soldier, was considered to place an undue burden on the infantryman. The multiplicity of weapons was perhaps acceptable in the comparatively long-service Regular Army, but was considered too much to demand of the part-time Territorial. As it was an accepted principle that the two should be organized and equipped on similar lines there was no question of altering one without the other.

Consequent on this point of view—about which there could be little doubt as far as the Territorial Army infantry was concerned—it was proposed to re-equip the battalions of twelve infantry regiments as machine-gun units, to a modified organization of the Machine Gun Corps of the war years. It was calculated that this would provide machine-gun battalions on a scale of approximately one per infantry brigade—both Regular and Territorial.

The theoretical adjustment of this organization took some time to reach finality; but the scheme was actually in process of fulfilment when other views were put forward. By 1938 the German attitude had become so clearly aggressive that the British Army's role had changed completely from that of an overseas police force to that of a force likely to be engaged in highly mobile operations in Europe or the Middle East against an enemy equipped on modern lines. Mr. Hore-Belisha, who had become Secretary of State for War, with General Lord Gort as Chief of the Imperial General Staff, was by this time engaged in the task of thoroughly modernizing the Army—a task in which financial considerations began to play a less important part.

It was considered that an army which would operate in Divisions—grouped in Corps at the outset, and later in Armies and perhaps Army Groups—required its machine-guns organized not on a brigade but on a divisional basis. Moreover, the transfer of the battalions of twelve infantry regiments to a machine-gun role would have made it impossible to provide a sufficient number of normal infantry battalions for the European Expeditionary Force which was being planned.

Another reason for continuing the reorganization in a modified form was that the Army had recently been issued with the Bren gun, a much more efficient weapon than the Lewis. As this weapon possessed many of, although not all, the characteristics of the Vickers, the withdrawal of the latter did not seriously diminish the fire-power of the infantry.

The decision was made, therefore, to rescind the previous instructions and to confine the re-equipment to four infantry regiments instead of twelve. This gave an allotment of approximately one machine-gun battalion per Division, with a few over as Corps and Army troops. In practice it did not work out quite correctly for the Territorial Army, and later a few isolated Territorial battalions were re-equipped as machine-gun units.

The four regiments selected for transfer were: the Royal Northumberland Fusiliers, the Cheshire Regiment, the Middlesex Regiment and the Manchester Regiment.

At the same time the Vickers machine-gun became known officially as the 'medium machine-gun,' to distinguish it from the Bren light automatic.

It is interesting to note that at the time of the original project to convert twelve regiments all infantry regiments were invited to state their wishes in the matter. In most—including the Royal Northumberland Fusiliers—there was considerable difference of opinion as to the wisdom of 'electing' for conversion. In the modified form, however, the four regiments were given no option in the matter.

These regiments—with numerous exceptions in the cases of individual battalions—continued in the machine-gun role throughout the Second World War. They, however, experienced many alterations in organization, equipment, nomenclature and tactical doctrine, which often differed in nature and in the time of change according to the theatre of operations in which a unit happened to be serving.

In order to avoid frequent reference to this chapter when reading later chapters, it is not proposed at this stage to describe in detail the various minor changes brought about by general requirements and operational demands in the various theatres. These will be dealt with when describing the activities of each unit of the Regiment. It will, however, be convenient to record here the general trend of changes in organization and equipment which affected machine-gun regiments as a whole.

In 1936 when machine-gun battalions were first formed the guns and crews were given 15-cwt. trucks. This was operationally unsatisfactory, as the trucks had a poor performance across country, except in the desert. It was, however, a necessary expedient due to the shortage of Bren carriers—the vehicle which it had originally been intended to provide. The losses of equipment at Dunkirk further delayed the provision of the proper vehicle, and it was not until the spring of 1941 that carriers began to be issued to machine-gun battalions.

At the commencement of hostilities in 1939 machine-gun battalions were organized as follows:

H.Q. company
4 machine-gun companies—each of 3 platoons of 4 guns each

Soon after the arrival of the British Expeditionary Force in France the Commander-in-Chief, Lord Gort, asked for additional machine-gun battalions, and as a result of this request the number was approximately doubled during the winter of 1939–40, by the despatch of Territorial machine-gun battalions.

After Dunkirk, however, the decision was made to provide machine-gun battalions on a scale of one per division in all theatres of operations and to include them as part of the divisional organization.

As a result of experience at Dunkirk, and in the early operations in North Africa, it became apparent that modern conditions had, to some extent, reduced the usefulness of the machine-gun as a defensive weapon. It was of very limited value against tanks and other armoured vehicles. The fluid nature of operations gave little opportunity for the construction of concrete emplacements and elaborate earthworks, which had been so extensively utilized to protect machine-gun detachments in 1914–18. Moreover, the highly efficient Bren gun performed many of its duties in defence, whilst in some roles machine-guns mounted in tanks were preferable to those operated from the ground.

Nevertheless, throughout the war the machine-gun, used as a battalion weapon, remained an essential factor in the organization of any defensive position. The general trend of experience and thought led, however, to two modifications in the original design for machine-gun battalions—one tactical and the other concerned with organization—namely:

(*a*) Increased training in the use of machine-guns in an offensive role. The high performance of their vehicles (Bren carriers) and increased speed and fluidity in modern warfare gave full scope for their employment offensively.

(*b*) With the development of new weapons the problem was constantly arising as to the arms of the service in which they should be incorporated. It was felt that machine-gun battalions might well carry one or more additional weapons of a type suited to their normal lay-out in a machine-gun role.

As a result, early in 1942 machine-gun battalions in the United Kingdom were issued with 4·2-in. heavy mortars—a weapon hitherto employed by chemical warfare units, R.E. At the same time all medium machine-gun battalions were converted into divisional support battalions, consisting of a headquarters and three brigade support groups—each made up of headquarters, a machine-gun company of twelve carrier-borne machine-guns, a heavy mortar company of two platoons each of four 4·2-in. mortars and a light anti-aircraft company. Although support battalions remained divisional units, each support group normally worked with its own infantry brigade and was in fact regarded as part of the brigade. In practice the support battalion commander became primarily a supervisor of training.

In the winter of 1943/44 General Montgomery took command of the 21st Army Group in the United Kingdom, with the task of completing its training and organization for the invasion of North-West Europe. His belief in overwhelming fire-power as a battle winner—and no doubt his appreciation that heavy artillery and air support (if weather conditions were bad) might be lacking in the initial stages of the invasion —induced him to make a further change in the machine-gun and heavy mortar organization. Under the new organization the unit reverted to its old name of 'Divisional Machine-Gun Battalion' and consisted of headquarters, three machine-gun companies and a heavy mortar company of eight platoons. The main features of this change were the increased tactical control of the battalion by divisional headquarters and the doubling of the number of 4·2-in. mortars. This organization was not adopted in other theatres of operations.

It is interesting to record that the machine-gun battalions of 21st Army Group were provided with a very much reduced light scale of transport for the initial invasion, which it was proposed to increase as the operation progressed inland. It proved so satisfactory, however, that the additions were never made and the machine-gun battalions of 21st Army Group finished the war on the light scale.

With the arrival of peace very much the same arguments were used for discontinuing machine-gun battalions as were used at the end of the First World War for disbanding the Machine Gun Corps. Within a very short time of the cessation of hostilities all machine-gun regiments had reverted to the role of normal infantry—with a machine-gun company as part of the establishment.

Without going into details of changes of a temporary nature to meet special conditions, the above paragraphs give the main alterations in medium machine-gun organization—other than in the Royal Armoured Corps—between 1914 and 1945.

NOTE: Although officially a machine-gun regiment during the period 1936 to 1945, some battalions of the Royal Northumberland Fusiliers were given other roles; in some cases permanently, in others temporarily.

The following statement shows the roles of all field force battalions during the period of the war:

Bns.	*Dates*		*Role*
	From	*To*	
1st	Sept. 1939	1945	Machine-gun
2nd	Sept. 1939	Dec. 1943	Machine-gun
	Dec. 1943	Dec. 1944	Support battalion
	Dec. 1944	1945	Infantry
4th	Sept. 1939	Aug. 1940	Motor-cycle reconnaissance battalion
	Aug. 1940	Dec. 1942	Reconnaissance battalion
	Jan. 1943	Apr. 1944	Support battalion
	Apr. 1944	1945	Three independent machine-gun companies

Bns.	*Dates*		*Role*
	From	*To*	
5th	Sept. 1939 March 1945	Mar. 1945 1945	Searchlight regiment, R.A. Infantry
6th	Sept. 1939	1945	Two battalions of the Royal Tank Regiment
7th	Sept. 1939	Sept. 1944 (disbanded)	Machine-gun
8th	Sept. 1939 Nov. 1940	Nov. 1940 1945	Motor-cycle reconnaissance battalion Reconnaissance battalion
9th	Sept. 1939	Feb. 1942 (captured at Singapore)	Machine-gun

CHAPTER 3

THE INTER-WAR YEARS

The Royal Northumberland Fusiliers during the period 1919 to 1939

I. GENERAL

THE Armistice with Germany on the 11th November 1918, which terminated hostilities in the First World War, was followed at once by public demands for the release of all men in the armed forces who were serving on war-time engagements. 1918–1919

The heavy casualties and wastage of more than four years of total war had reduced the Regular Army to little more than a cadre of senior officers. The problem of the Government and Army Council was, therefore, the formation of a new Regular Army of young soldiers to replace the national war-time army of 1914–18 as quickly as possible. It had been decided that the reconstituted Regular Army should be on the same pattern and approximately the same size as the pre-war army. The extent of Germany's defeat made it unnecessary to provide heavy equipment on an extensive scale: an army for overseas garrison duties, and for occasional 'colonial wars,' was all that was necessary.

Nevertheless, the urgency of the problem was soon made apparent by disturbances in India and elsewhere abroad, open rebellion in Ireland and the persistent, although mostly orderly, demands of the war-time soldiers to be sent home and released from military service.

This was the setting in which the Regular Army was hastily reformed in 1919, followed by the much more leisurely rebirth of the Territorial Army. This chapter describes, very briefly, the process of reforming, the difficulties of the years of financial stringency up to 1933 and the rearmament which followed the rise of Hitler—as they affected the battalions of the Royal Northumberland Fusiliers.

II. THE 1ST AND 2ND BATTALIONS—1918–19

The signing of the Armistice had found the 1st and 2nd Battalions in close proximity in France, separated only by the Forêt de Mormal. Exactly one month later, on the 11th December, the 1st Battalion had crossed the frontier of Germany, but in April 1919 it was withdrawn to Wargnies Le Grand, in France, where the 2nd Battalion had been located since the previous January. Though both at this time were in process of being reduced to cadre strength, while a nucleus of each was being formed in England for the reorganization of the Regiment, this union of the two battalions—the fifth only that had occurred throughout the long history of the Regiment *—was

* Holland [1799], Salamanca [1812], Gibraltar [1896] and the Ypres Salient with the 28th Division [1915].

1919–1922 a notable event. On the 10th April, in the temporary absence of Lieut.-Colonel Hardman-Jones, the singular honour fell to Lieut.-Colonel Cruddas of assuming command of both battalions. It is, however, with the nucleus battalions in England that the future history of the Regiment is concerned and to which it is, therefore, now necessary to turn.

III. THE 1ST BATTALION

On the 9th July 1919 the nucleus of the new 1st Battalion left the Depot at Newcastle-on-Tyne under the command of Bt. Lieut.-Colonel A. C. L. Hardman-Jones for Durrington Camp, Salisbury Plain, where they were to take over additional personnel of the 3rd (Special Reserve) Battalion. On arrival a Colour Party—consisting of Captains T. F. Ellison, M.C., and C. B. Carrick, M.C., C.S.M. A. Graham and Privates T. Norwich and S. P. Poole—was sent with the Colours to Paris to take part in the Victory March on the 14th July, and returned thence for a similar ceremony held in London five days later.

On the 21st July Bt. Colonel C. Yatman, C.M.G., D.S.O., assumed command of the Battalion.

In September the Battalion moved to Guadaloupe Barracks, Bordon, and became part of the Fusilier Brigade. This was to be the unit's home for nearly two years.

On the 1st November they assisted in lining the streets of London on the occasion of the visit of the Shah of Persia.

1920 and the first half of 1921 were occupied in training and the normal periodical ceremonial occasions of peace soldiering—an inspection by the Secretary of State for War, the Rt. Hon. Winston S. Churchill, in January 1920, a review at Aldershot by His Majesty King George V in May.

In April 1921 they moved to a tented camp in Victoria Park, London, in anticipation of the Coal Strike then in progress becoming a General Strike. For this duty the Battalion was made up to a strength of 800 by reservists, who were themselves mostly miners. By the 20th April the situation had eased and they returned to Bordon.

On the 4th June orders were received to proceed to Ireland. That country was by then in a condition of open rebellion. Dublin was almost in a state of siege: the murder of loyal citizens and police, attacks on troops, the burning of houses and sabotage of railways and other public services had become everyday occurrences.

The Battalion moved to Ireland on the 13th June, and was quartered at Curragh Camp in County Kildare. Later they moved in company detachments to County Carlow.

On the 27th August 1921 Colonel Yatman vacated command on promotion, and was succeeded by Lieut.-Colonel A. C. Hardman-Jones.

In February 1922 the Battalion left Ireland and returned to Bordon, preparatory to joining the British Army of Occupation in Germany.

In April and May a number of officers and senior N.C.Os. joined the Battalion from the disbanded Royal Dublin Fusiliers and a disbanded battalion of the Royal Fusiliers.

1922–1928

The move to the Rhine was delayed and it was not until the night of the 12th/13th July that they left Bordon in two trains to relieve a battalion of the Black Watch in Cologne.

The British Army of the Rhine, commanded at that time by General Sir Alexander Godley, was a comparatively small force, consisting of one regiment of cavalry, one brigade of Royal Artillery and two infantry brigades (each of four battalions). With the exception of one battalion at Solingen all the troops were quartered in Cologne and its suburbs. Throughout its three and a half years' service in Germany the permanent quarters of the 1st Bn. Royal Northumberland Fusiliers were the Marienburg Barracks, Cologne. During the summer and autumn months, however, much of the time was spent at musketry, and other forms of training, away from barracks. There were also excellent facilities for recreation—cricket, football, hockey, a nine-hole golf-course, shooting, race meetings and an annual horse show. The British garrison of Germany on the whole fared better, both as regards training and amenities, than the garrisons at home and elsewhere overseas. The rate of exchange being favourable, money had much greater purchasing power than in most places, although at times the sharp fluctuations of the mark caused difficulties.

In 1923 and 1924 the Colours of the Battalion were trooped on St. George's Day, the Colonel of the Regiment, Major-General Sir Percival S. Wilkinson, K.C.M.G., C.B., attending in 1923.

Such was military life in occupied Germany in the early 1920s.

On the 23rd November 1925 Lieut.-Colonel A. C. Hardman-Jones completed his period of command and was succeeded by Lieut.-Colonel W. N. Herbert, C.M.G., D.S.O. Lieut.-Colonel Hardman-Jones had had the unique experience of full-time command of both regular battalions—the 2nd Battalion 1915 to 1919 and the 1st Battalion 1921 to 1925.

In February 1926 the Battalion left the Rhine Army for Ballykinlar in Northern Ireland. By this time the garrison of Ireland was confined to the North, British troops having vacated the South in 1923.

This first tour of duty in Northern Ireland was a short one. By May 1926 the General Strike—the biggest and most serious strike in British history—had commenced, and the Battalion moved to Glasgow as a precautionary measure against lawlessness. There they remained for an uneventful five months, but in October they returned to Ballykinlar.

The remainder of the Northern Ireland tour was one of normal routine soldiering; but was notable for the Battalion's remarkable series of successes at sport, which included the following:

Boxing:	Winners Northern Ireland District Tournament 1926, 1927, 1928.
Athletics:	Winners Northern Ireland District Team Sports 1926, 1927, 1928.
Cross Country:	Winners Northern Ireland District Championship 1927, 1928.

In October 1928 the Battalion moved from Ballykinlar to York, where they formed part of the 15th Infantry Brigade.

1929–1936 The St. George's Day parade celebrations in 1929 were attended by the Lord Mayors of York and Newcastle.

The summer of 1929 was mainly occupied with the Northern Command Tattoo—military tattoos in the larger garrisons having by this time grown to formidable proportions and being the chief means of supporting the various Army charitable funds.

In November Lieut.-Colonel W. N. Herbert vacated command, being succeeded by Lieut.-Colonel R. M. Booth, D.S.O.

There were no outstanding incidents during the Battalion's three years at York.

On the 13th September 1931 they embarked at Southampton on H.M.T. 'Lancashire' for Bermuda and Jamaica, where they relieved the 2nd Bn. the West Yorkshire Regiment. Two companies and the Band were in Bermuda and the rest of the Battalion in Jamaica. The splitting of the Battalion in this manner was not a very satisfactory arrangement. In Bermuda training facilities were very poor. In both places sport and recreation were difficult to arrange for the rank and file, although the officers were more fortunate, polo, golf, tennis and cricket being available.

In October 1933 Lieut.-Colonel Booth handed over command to Lieut.-Colonel J. F. Chenevix-Trench, D.S.O., and in January 1934 the Battalion left Jamaica and Bermuda for Egypt.

In the spring of 1933 Herr Hitler and the Nazi Party came into power in Germany. This event resulted in some revival of thought on military matters among the more responsible British people and some slight measure of rearmament; but it was to be some years before these took practical or concrete form in infantry units of the overseas garrison.

The Battalion travelled to Egypt in the troopship 'Dorsetshire,' calling at Southampton en route. On arrival they were quartered first in The Citadel at Cairo and later at Hilmi Barracks, Abbassia. The first eighteen months in the new station were uneventful; but in September 1935 Lieut.-Colonel J. F. Chenevix-Trench vacated command and was succeeded by Bt. Colonel J. G. des R. Swayne. The new Commanding Officer had previously served in the Somerset Light Infantry; but before leaving England to take up his new command he took the opportunity to visit the Depot at Newcastle-on-Tyne and meet Major-General W. N. Herbert, C.B., C.M.G., D.S.O., who had in the previous July succeeded Major-General Sir Percival S. Wilkinson, K.C.M.G., C.B., as Colonel of the Regiment. Under Colonel Swayne training went on apace, being given added impetus, and greater reality, by the Italian invasion of Abyssinia and the possible Italian threat to Egypt.

In March 1936, owing to further deterioration in the international situation, the Battalion moved to Mersa Matruh in the Libyan Desert, with one company further west at Sidi Barrani. Here they remained for four months and, in spite of frequent sandstorms, thoroughly enjoyed the experience. St. George's Day was celebrated by various forms of sporting contests.

In June 1936 they returned to Abbassia, and in December moved to Helwan in the Desert, where three weeks' very realistic training was carried out. The march back to Abbassia—some twenty-five miles—was normally carried out in two days, but on this occasion the 1st Bn. Royal Northumberland Fusiliers did it in one.

Towards the end of 1936 information was received that the Battalion was shortly 1936–1939
to be converted into a machine-gun battalion. Officers and N.C.Os. were sent to England for courses on the new weapon, and the unit's very fine horsed transport was replaced by mechanized vehicles. The men proved apt pupils in M.T. driving and maintenance and the conversion to the new role was carried out with enthusiasm.

Early in March 1937 Colonel Swayne left Egypt to take up the appointment of a senior instructor at the Staff College, and Major T. C. L. Redwood assumed temporary command. On arrival in England Colonel Swayne met Lieut.-Colonel E. E. Dorman-Smith who was to succeed him in command and to whom the main task of conversion to the machine-gun role was to fall.*

The rearmament programme was by this time producing practical results within units, and in consequence the issue of equipment for the new role was on a comparatively lavish scale, and included some 120 new M.T. vehicles. Lieut.-Colonel Dorman-Smith was an officer of progressive ideas, and many interesting and novel exercises were carried out under his direction. Within twelve months a high standard of training had been achieved, and by the time Lieut.-Colonel J. H. Hogshaw took over command in May 1938 the Battalion was in every way a thoroughly battleworthy machine-gun unit.

But before the year was out the Battalion was required to revert to an infantry role on being moved to Lone Tree Camp, at Sarafand in Palestine, in order to assist in winding up the Arab rebellion, which, though nominally over, had left the country in a very disturbed state. The Battalion lived behind heavily guarded barbed-wire, and outside the camp perimeter there were many irksome restrictions on movement. For his conduct during one of the small, but nevertheless sharp, incidents which occasionally occurred Captain S. Enderby was awarded the Military Cross. The citation read as follows:

Captain S. Enderby, 1st Bn. The Royal Northumberland Fusiliers

'On 26th February 1939 a reconnaissance party was fired on by rebels near Shuqba. Captain Enderby in charge of two Sections moved in pursuit and found himself exposed on forward slopes, and under fire from the enemy rear party from positions of cover. He seized a rifle from the first man who came up and, advancing on the enemy, himself killed two and wounded the third. The leadership displayed, and the cool action of this officer under fire, were entirely responsible for the success of this operation.'

There were, however, no other incidents of note during the stay in Palestine, and by the outbreak of war in September 1939 the Battalion had returned to Cairo and to its orthodox role of a machine-gun battalion.

IV. THE 2ND BATTALION

By June 1919 the Battalion had been reduced to cadre strength and on the 8th it 1919
was brought home to Newcastle-on-Tyne and absorbed by the nucleus. Thus the

* For further details concerning the conversion of infantry battalions to machine-gun battalions see Chapter 2.

1919– post-war 2nd Battalion was formed, under the command of Lieut.-Colonel E. M.
1920 Moulton-Barrett, D.S.O.

The news that they were to proceed to Mesopotamia was welcomed by the recently joined young soldiers; but was not so well received by the older married men, many of whom had seen a lot of overseas service and fighting in the war. The Battalion embarked at Liverpool on H.M.T. 'Derbyshire' on the 7th September. Reaching Bombay on the 2nd October they transhipped to H.T. 'Shuja'—a native-owned pilgrim ship—and in company with the 4th Bn. Royal Fusiliers proceeded to Basra. On arrival they moved by river steamer to Baghdad, thence by rail to Shergat and completed the journey to Mosul, the final destination, by a seventy-mile march, arriving in the middle of November. Here they formed part of the 54th Indian Infantry Brigade, of the 18th Indian Division.

The early months at Mosul were mostly uneventful. The only incident of note was the arrival of the married families—in spite of strong representations by the Battalion that they should not be sent. Their lot was a most unhappy one. They were accommodated in tents a hundred miles south of Mosul, and their feeding, health, welfare and protection were to prove a serious embarrassment.

In May 1920 there were rumours of unrest being fomented among the Arab tribes by members of the family of the Sheriff of Mecca; and the Political Officer at Tel-a-Far, a town of some 8,000 inhabitants, forty miles west of Mosul, reported his anxiety over the attitude of the local Arabs. In response to his representations, a machine-gun manned by one N.C.O. and one man of the Rifle Brigade was sent as a somewhat slender reinforcement to the Arab gendarmerie, on whose doubtful protection the Political Officer was dependent. At the end of May vague reports were received that a force of Sheriffian troops, estimated at 500 strong, was approaching Tel-a-Far, with the intention of raising the tribes and attacking Mosul. At 4 a.m. on the 3rd June, Lieut. Clive Smith, M.C., of The Fifth, attached to 14th Light Armoured Motor Battery, was despatched with two armoured cars and four Ford vans, carrying spare parts, to reconnoitre towards Tel-a-Far. His instructions were not to enter the town if found hostile. Included in the party were Fusiliers Booth, Kennedy, Greenwood and Wilson of The Fifth. As the party failed to return, an aeroplane was sent out, and reported that one car had been observed on fire outside the town and the remainder, apparently derelict, inside. Further reports were received that the Political Officer, Major Barlow, and the gendarmerie officer had been assassinated, the latter by his own men. The sole survivor of the reconnaissance party was the officer's Mohammedan servant, whose life had been spared by his co-religionists, but on whose account of how the disaster had occurred little reliance could be placed. It was established that one of the armoured cars had broken down in attempting to cross a drift some little distance from the town. Clive Smith had on many occasions shown himself a young officer of great courage and resource. Evidence showed that the two men of the machine-gun detachment had put up a long and gallant defence at the Political Officer's house before being killed, and it is thought that, finding these men still holding out, he determined to disregard his orders and attempt their rescue. By the death of Lieut. Clive Smith the Regiment lost a brilliant young officer, whose deeds in the preceding war had won for him the Military Cross and bar.

3. Major-General W. N. Herbert, C.B., C.M.G., D.S.O., Colonel of the Regiment 1935–1947

On the 5th June a punitive column of all arms was sent out. After some slight opposition on the 8th, the column reached Tel-a-Far on the following day, and recovered the bodies of those who had been killed. A garrison of all arms was left in the town, of which one company of the Battalion formed part. 1920–1926

By December 1920 the Arab rebellion was at an end and the country in a condition of comparative tranquillity.

On the 4th January 1921 the Battalion embarked at Basra on S.S. 'Chakdara' for Bombay, where on arrival it entrained for Dinapore in Behar. Dinapore was a one-battalion station, with one company at Muzaffapore; but compared with the discomforts of Mosul the amenities appeared luxurious and the facilities for sport and recreation good. Major-General T. A. Cubitt, the commander of the Presidency and Assam District, which included Dinapore, had had a lifelong association with The Fifth through his father, who had served as an ensign in the Regiment during the Indian Mutiny (1857) and was at this time in his eighty-eighth year.

In January 1922 Lieut.-Colonel H. R. Sandilands, C.M.G., D.S.O., assumed command of the Battalion in succession to Lieut.-Colonel Moulton-Barrett, and in the following November the 2nd Bn. Royal Northumberland Fusiliers moved to Fyzabad. This was an exceptionally good station for an infantry battalion, being sufficiently far removed from higher authority to be given a large degree of independence, whilst affording good facilities for military training and recreation. Again the District Commander was an old friend—Major-General C. J. Deverell (later to become a Field Marshal and C.I.G.S.). He had had the 1st Battalion under his command for over two years (1916–18) and took a great personal interest in the Regiment.

Whilst at Fyzabad the Battalion more than held its own in sport. In 1924 it won both the 19th Brigade Football League and Athletic Championship. In 1924 its polo team was narrowly beaten (4–3) in the semi-final of the Infantry Tournament, and in 1925 won the Lucknow Junior Tournament. But perhaps its main success during these years was in boxing. It won the open boxing tournament at Ranikhet in 1924 and 1925, and in the latter year Bandsman T. Anderson was bantamweight champion of Eastern Command, while Fusilier R. Hosker was flyweight champion of All India.

On the 15th September 1925 Lieut.-Colonel Sandilands vacated command on promotion, and was succeeded by Lieut.-Colonel S. H. Kershaw, D.S.O.

In November 1926 the Battalion moved to Nowshera, near the North-West Frontier. During the inter-war years the turbulent, but in many respects likable, tribesmen of the independent mountain territory on India's North-West Frontier were in an almost continuous state of war. Their inhospitable country was incapable of supporting the tribes, and in consequence their chief means of livelihood was by plunder and border raiding. At times they came into conflict with the Government of India as a result of disturbances fermented by religious fanaticism.

As a result of these conditions the troops stationed at Peshawar, Nowshera and other places on the Frontier had to be highly trained in mountain warfare and in instant readiness for active operations.

On arrival in Nowshera the Royal Northumberland Fusiliers—already a well-trained and seasoned unit—set about the task of acquiring the somewhat specialized

1926–1931 technique of frontier mountain warfare of that time. An old friendship with the Corps of Guides was renewed and a new one made with the 3/1st Punjab Regiment. So close was this that in the words of Lieut.-Colonel Kershaw—'The Jemadar-Adjutant of the Guides thought nothing on manœuvres of coming up and saying, "Colonel-Sahib, we want your Machine-Gun Company: you can have ours when it comes up."'

It so happened that during the Battalion's tour on the Frontier no large-scale operations took place, and they were never actively engaged. The years 1927–28 passed without any major incidents and early in November 1928 the Battalion moved to Lahore.

While at Lahore the Commanding Officer received a letter from Mr. Rudyard Kipling recalling his happy time with the Regiment in Lahore in the 'nineties. Another incident of note was a visit to the Battalion by the famous French general Gouraud—the Lion d'Argonne. On the whole, however, the period at Lahore was one of normal training and routine.

It is interesting to recall that on St. George's Day 1928 the Commanding Officer of the 2nd Battalion, who was at home on leave, had the unique distinction of taking the salute on the march past of the 1st Battalion, then at Ballykinlar, as he was the senior 'Old Fifth' officer present.

Lieut.-Colonel Kershaw relinquished command in October 1929 and was succeeded by Lieut.-Colonel O. B. Foster, M.C.*

In March 1930 the Battalion moved to Dagshai, where the Colours were trooped and the usual celebrations carried out on St. George's Day, soon after arrival.

This was soon followed by a move back to Lahore at short notice. At this time widespread communal disturbances had broken out all over India and Lahore was one of the chief centres of trouble. Here they remained until October, when the Battalion (less two companies which remained at Lahore) returned to Dagshai. However, owing to the continuance of trouble they again concentrated at Lahore a month later.

In January 1931 orders were received for a move to Shanghai, and on the 7th February all families embarked on H.T. 'Lancashire' for England. The Battalion left Karachi in H.T. 'Neuralia' on the 2nd March, and travelling via Colombo, Singapore and Hong Kong reached Shanghai on the 21st March, where they were quartered at Kiaochow Camp. On St. George's Day the Colours were trooped in front of a crowd of 15,000 spectators, including representatives of American, Russian and Japanese units.

In June the unit was visited by Major-General J. W. Sandilands, G.O.C.-in-C. Far East (and brother of Brigadier H. R. Sandilands, an ex-Commanding Officer of the Battalion).

By July there were signs of trouble in the Far East and much time was spent in strengthening the defences of Shanghai.

On the 24th November 1931 the Battalion embarked on H.T. 'Neuralia' for

* Lieut.-Colonel O. B. Foster's son, Lieut.-Colonel K. O. N. Foster, O.B.E., was killed in action in 1951, when in command of the Fighting Fifth in Korea.

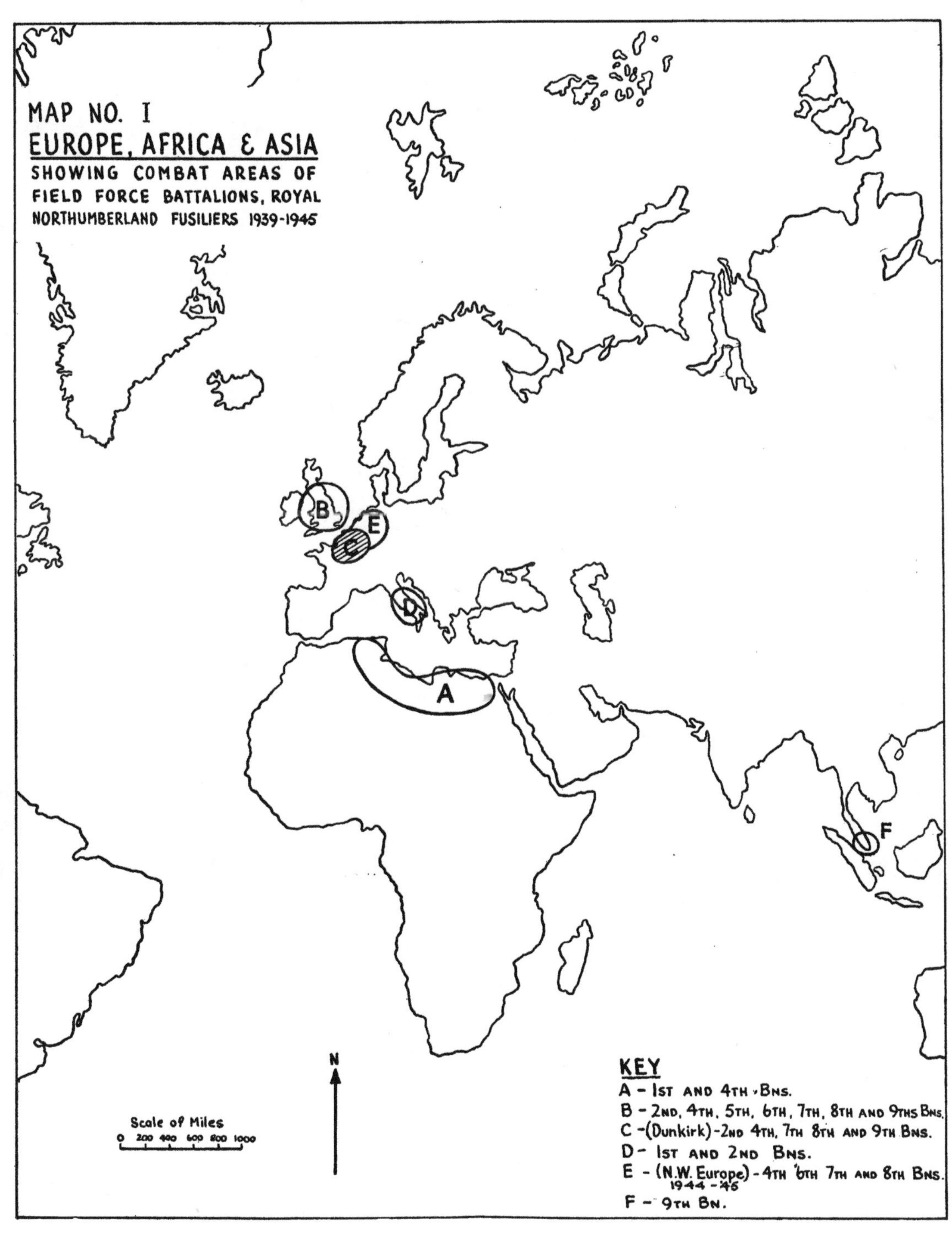
MAP NO. I
EUROPE, AFRICA & ASIA
SHOWING COMBAT AREAS OF
FIELD FORCE BATTALIONS, ROYAL
NORTHUMBERLAND FUSILIERS 1939-1945
A
B
C
D
E
F
N
Scale of Miles
0 200 400 600 800 1000
KEY
A - 1st and 4th Bns.
B - 2nd, 4th, 5th, 6th, 7th, 8th and 9ths Bns.
C - (Dunkirk) - 2nd 4th, 7th 8th and 9th Bns.
D - 1st and 2nd Bns.
E - (N.W. Europe) 1944-'45 - 4th 6th 7th and 8th Bns.
F - 9th Bn.

England, arriving at Southampton on the 29th December. On the following day they marched into barracks at York—in tropical kit in a snowstorm. 1931–1936

About 400 men were due for discharge and some 500, after proceeding on leave, were drafted to the 1st Battalion. Consequently the muster on the St. George's Day parade of 1932 was a very small one.

In January 1933 the old custom, dating from 1762, of displaying on the St. George's Day parade the banner which is a replica of that captured from the French at Wilhelmstahl (1762)—in addition to carrying the King's Colour and Regimental Colour—was regularized. His Majesty King George V was graciously pleased to give formal approval for this ancient custom.

On the 15th September of this year Lieut.-Colonel O. B. Foster relinquished command and was succeeded by Lieut.-Colonel A. P. Garnier, M.B.E., M.C.

At York the Battalion was part of the 15th Infantry Brigade, and during its stay there carried out the normal routine of garrison life and duties at home. At this time the organization was as follows:

Battalion H.Q.
H.Q. Wing.
3 Rifle Coys.
1 Machine-Gun Coy.

This was a very clumsy organization from a tactical point of view, and unsatisfactory because of the multiplicity of weapons and technical equipment within the unit. This had been recognized for some time, and when more funds became available consequent on the rearmament programme, the decision to convert some infantry regiments to a machine-gun role was made.

In the autumn of 1935 the Battalion moved to Bordon, and almost immediately received instructions for conversion into a machine-gun battalion, and at the same time transfer from a horse-drawn to a mechanized basis of transport. The conversion did not work very smoothly owing to lack of equipment, particularly M.T. vehicles, and to delays in deciding the final organization for machine-gun battalions.

During a divisional exercise in the late summer of 1936 the Battalion received orders to return to barracks and mobilize on an infantry battalion basis for service in Palestine. Class A reservists were recalled to the Colours, and on the 12th September the unit embarked on H.M.T. 'Dorsetshire' at Southampton under command of Lieut.-Colonel H. de R. Morgan, D.S.O.,* who had been selected to succeed Lieut.-Colonel Garnier. The new Commanding Officer had not previously served with the Regiment, having been transferred to command from The Buffs. The move to Palestine was occasioned by the Arab rising in that country, which necessitated the despatch of a division from the Aldershot Command as reinforcements.

The voyage was without incident, and on disembarkation at Haifa the Battalion moved by train to Bethlehem, where they were accommodated in buildings.

Arab methods and tactics were similar to those adopted by most eastern 'guerrillas' —the setting up of road blocks, sniping, ambushes and raids by day and by night, the

* Now Major-General H. de R. Morgan, D.S.O., the Colonel of the Regiment since 1947.

1936–1939 derailing of trains and general sabotage. His hostility was directed more against the Jews than against the British troops in their efforts to restore order.

Counter measures by British troops consisted of escorting trains and lorries, active patrolling, the setting up of piquets and offensive operations against located bodies of armed Arabs.

Four or five weeks after the arrival of the Battalion a so-called 'armistice' was arranged, and the troops, whilst remaining on the alert, were less energetically employed. Much more time was devoted to sport and recreation.

After three months in the country the Aldershot Division was brought home; the 2nd Bn. Royal Northumberland Fusiliers arrived back at Bordon on New Year's Eve 1936.

They remained at Bordon throughout 1937, being again converted into a machine-gun battalion.

1938 saw the Battalion at Dover as the machine-gun battalion of the 3rd Division.

During the summer of 1939 the Regiment's reservists were called up for training, and many familiar faces were seen in barracks. This call-up proved very valuable, as reservists were, of course, mostly unfamiliar with the machine-gun and entirely unfamiliar with army mechanical transport.

After mobilization in the early days of September 1939 the Battalion moved into camp near Shorncliffe, prior to proceeding to France.

V. THE TERRITORIAL ARMY BATTALIONS

1920 When the Territorial Force was reconstituted after the First World War it was given the new title of 'Territorial Army,' and henceforth its units wore the badges of their corps and regiments in exactly the same form as the regular units.

The Territorials were destined to play a much more important part in our defence structure after the War than they had done in the years which preceded it.

The 149th (Northumberland) Infantry Brigade, comprising the 4th, 5th, 6th and 7th Bns. Royal Northumberland Fusiliers, was reconstituted to form part, once again, of the 50th (Northumbrian) Division, in the early months of 1920.* It was fortunate that, despite casualties suffered in the war, many officers and other ranks who had served with one or other of the four battalions had not only survived but had retained a keen regimental spirit—and were natives of Northumberland. Accordingly, very soon after recruiting for the new Brigade was opened, large numbers of those with war service with the old Brigade joined up—for a period of four years on the active list of the Territorial Army, followed by one year on the T.A. reserve. Within a few weeks a strong nucleus was in existence in each of the four battalion areas.

Before the 1914 war the Territorial Force engagement was for Home Defence only, but the new Territorial Army exacted an obligation for overseas service in the event of general mobilization.

* The 149th Infantry Brigade had been the first Territorial infantry brigade to go into action as such, in the war of 1914–18.

1920–1921

Brigadier-General E. P. A. Riddell, C.B., C.M.G., D.S.O., who had been the original Adjutant of the 7th Battalion in 1908, and who had commanded the Brigade during the latter part of the war, was appointed Brigade Commander, with the new rank of Colonel Commandant. Major W. Anderson became the first Brigade Major. Major-General Sir Percival S. Wilkinson, K.C.M.G., C.B., the Colonel of the Regiment, who had commanded the 50th Division for a long stretch during the war, was appointed to command the new Division.

Headquarters of the four battalions and the first post-war Commanding Officers were:

4th Battalion, Hexham (later to be moved to Newburn-on-Tyne):
Lieut.-Colonel J. R. Robb.
5th Battalion, Walker-on-Tyne:
Lieut.-Colonel A. Irwin, D.S.O., T.D.
6th Battalion (The City Battalion), St. George's Drill Hall, Newcastle-on-Tyne:
Lieut.-Colonel E. Temperley.
7th Battalion, Alnwick:
Lieut.-Colonel N. I. Wright, D.S.O., T.D.

(NOTE: The names of subsequent Commanding Officers are given in Appendix A.)

Lieut.-Colonel B. Cruddas, D.S.O., who had the honour of commanding both 1st and 2nd Battalions at different periods of the war, came back as Second-in-Command of the 4th Battalion, of which he had been Adjutant in peace-time and for the first two years of the war.*

Apart from a minimum of twenty 'drills' per annum, or forty in the case of recruits during their first year's service, and the Annual Weapon Training Course, the great event in the Territorial Army year was the fifteen days' Annual Training in camp.

The first post-war Brigade camp was located on the racecourse at Scarborough during the middle of August 1920; and here the four battalions 'shook down' and took stock; and the foundations of the new 149th Infantry Brigade were well and truly laid. The War Office policy was that Annual Training and the places for camp should follow a regular cycle, and in a four-year period the Brigade was scheduled to visit first Ripon (Yorks), next a sea-side resort, then Ripon again—followed by a Divisional concentration at Catterick. This excellent arrangement was upset, however, by the Coal Strike of 1921, which started just as summer training was commencing. Mr. Lloyd George's Government called for volunteers from the Territorial Army to serve for a maximum period of ninety days in a special Defence Force to meet the national emergency. The response was excellent, and, based on their respective company and battalion drill halls, the four battalions were virtually mobilized for three months, during which time fortunately they were not called upon for any drastic action, although many guards were found and much valuable training carried out.

The stand-down came in July; and in view of the fact that many who had already done three months' service could not afford the time for the recognized fifteen days'

* Lieut.-Colonel Cruddas sat as National Conservative M.P. for the Wansbeck Division of Northumberland from 1931 to 1940.

1921–1933 camp period, there was no Brigade Camp that year; but each battalion organized its own annual training for those who could spare the time to attend—on a purely voluntary basis.

The peace-time establishment of a Territorial battalion was but 60 per cent. of war establishment; and by the end of 1921 the 149th Infantry Brigade was almost up to strength—and, indeed, in numbers the 50th Division always ranked amongst the foremost of the fourteen Territorial divisions of those days.

Normally the camp period was made to coincide with 'Race Week'—when Tyneside takes a holiday for a few days—and hence Annual Training took place during the last two weeks of June. This was an excellent time of year, as usually the weather was fine—and the days were long. The troops settled down astonishingly quickly on arrival at camp, and the policy was that nothing in the way of training that could be done at home, or in or around the local drill halls, was permissible at camp. Platoon and company training was started immediately, followed by battalion training, and at least one Brigade Field Day. When at Ripon, the 'middle Sunday' saw a Brigade Ceremonial Church Parade service at the Cathedral, followed by a march past the Brigade or Divisional Commander. The massed drums beat Tattoo on two or three occasions each year.

A feature of these inter-war years was the very real and close liaison between the Regular Battalions, the Regimental Depot and the Territorial Battalions. All T.A. officers became honorary members of the Depot Mess at Fenham Barracks, and warrant officers and sergeants of the Sergeants Mess. Each year the Depot, or the Regular Battalion serving at home, attached a 'Demonstration Platoon' and a number of 'specialists' officers and N.C.Os. to the 149th Infantry Brigade for the fifteen days' training in camp, and much was taught and learnt in this way. Above all a keen regimental spirit was fostered among all ranks of all battalions. *Esprit de corps* was of the highest order. The first 'Demonstration Platoon' was commanded by Lieut. L. C. Thomas,* and even in those distant days, when he was a young officer, many prophesied that he would go far in the Army—as indeed proved to be the case.

One of the 'great occasions' of the years between the wars was in June 1930, when five battalions of the Regiment—the 1st, 4th, 5th, 6th and 7th—were all under canvas together, at Wathgill, near Catterick Camp. Another very interesting event was the presentation of the first Colours to the 4th Battalion—by Major-General Sir Percival S. Wilkinson, Colonel of the Regiment, at Newburn, in 1929.

The late 1920s and early 1930s were very difficult times for the whole Army—the Territorial Army in particular. Financial stringency reached its peak during this period, and was reflected in economies which seriously affected efficiency. Thus after the General Strike of 1926 the annual camp was cancelled, as it was again in 1933 because of the financial crisis. Nevertheless, much solid progress was made—by means of week-end camps for musketry and tactical training—and the strength of units was maintained at a high level.

The location of Brigade Camps was varied from year to year and included Ripon

---

* Now Major-General L. C. Thomas, C.B., C.B.E., D.S.O.

(on several occasions), Marske in Yorkshire, Pwllheli in North Wales and Halton near Lancaster. 1938–1939

In 1938 it was decided to break up the 149th Infantry Brigade, this being part of a general scheme for the reorganization of the whole Territorial Army. Under this plan the designations and roles of the units were as follows:

4th Bn.—Motor Cycle Reconnaissance Bn., 50th (Northumbrian) Division
5th Bn.—Searchlight Regiment, Royal Artillery
6th Bn.—43rd Bn. of the Royal Tank Regiment
7th Bn.—Machine-Gun Bn.

When in the spring of 1939 conscription was introduced, and it was decided to double the size of the Territorial Army, the following additional battalions were formed:

8th Bn. (duplicate of 4th Bn.)—Motor Cycle Reconnaissance Bn. of the reconstituted 23rd (Northumbrian) Division
9th Bn. (duplicate of 7th Bn.)—Machine-Gun Bn.—also in the 23rd Division
49th Bn. Royal Tank Regiment—formed from the 6th Bn., as a duplicate of the 43rd Bn. Royal Tank Regiment.

The 5th (Searchlight) Battalion was not duplicated, but its strength was nearly doubled.

Thus in September 1939 the Royal Northumberland Fusiliers mobilized eight Territorial Army battalions in varying roles—the 4th, 5th, 6th, 7th, 8th and 9th, with two tank battalions formed from the 6th.

Subsequent changes in role and organization will be found in the appropriate chapters dealing with the various phases of the war.

CHAPTER 4

THE DUNKIRK PHASE

September 1939 to June 1940

2nd, 4th, 7th, 8th and 9th Battalions

(*See Maps Nos. II and III*)

1. GENERAL

Sept.–Oct. 1939 THE British Expeditionary Force which went to France in October 1939 consisted of four regular divisions (grouped in two Corps) and numerous Army and L. of C. troops. Prior to the 10th May 1940 the British troops were not actively engaged, being separated from the enemy by the neutral countries of Holland and Belgium. The troops were employed on work extending the Maginot Line to the sea along the Franco-Belgian frontier.

The only battalion of the Royal Northumberland Fusiliers to proceed with the original force was the 2nd, which was a machine-gun battalion—2nd Corps troops allotted to the 4th Division.

During the winter of 1939/40 several Territorial Army divisions joined the B.E.F., and with them other battalions of the Royal Northumberland Fusiliers—namely:

4th Bn.—Motor Cycle Reconnaissance Bn., 50th (Northumbrian) Division
8th Bn.—Motor Cycle Reconnaissance Bn. } 23rd (Northumbrian) Division
9th Bn.—Machine-Gun Bn. }
7th Bn.—Machine-Gun Bn., 51st (Highland) Division

In the early spring of 1940 it became evident that the Germans were contemplating an advance through Holland and Belgium. In this eventuality the French Armies of the North and the B.E.F. planned a rapid advance into Belgium to the line of the River Dyle. This was known as 'Plan D' and had been worked out in the very greatest detail.

When the German attack came on the 10th May 1940 the 2nd, 4th, 8th and 9th Battalions of the Regiment were with their respective Divisions in Northern France—the 2nd and 4th in a fighting role near the Belgium frontier: the 8th and 9th engaged on airfield construction.

The 7th Battalion was with the 51st Division in the Saar area of the Maginot Line, where it was attached to the French Army in order to gain battle experience in contact with the enemy.

As is well known the affairs of the Franco-British armies did not prosper. By the first week in June 1940 the greater portion of the B.E.F. had been evacuated from Dunkirk and the French armies, and nation, were on the point of collapse.

It was a matter of importance that throughout this brief campaign the weather remained fine and warm—except on the 28th May, which was dull and wet. Had it not been for this fine spell it is doubtful if the withdrawal and embarkation of the B.E.F. could have been accomplished successfully.

The remaining sections of this chapter give a detailed account of the activities of the five Royal Northumberland Fusilier battalions with the B.E.F. in France and Flanders in 1939–40.

II. THE 2ND BATTALION

Prior to the outbreak of hostilities the Battalion had been earmarked as the machine-gun battalion of the 4th Division of the B.E.F.

Mobilization was completed to schedule by the 10th September 1939, when the Battalion left Connaught Barracks, Dover, for camp at Dibgate, near Folkestone—where they remained until the 1st October.

During this period much valuable training was carried out, particularly with reservists—a proportion of whom were unfamiliar with, or rusty in, modern machine-gun technique and tactics. A portion of the Battalion went on forty-eight hours' leave.

The vehicle party, under Major T. C. L. Redwood, embarked at Southampton on the 27th September, the main body of the Battalion following on the 1st October. Disembarkation took place at Cherbourg on the 2nd October.

After short halts at other places the Battalion arrived in the small town of Dourges, in the Lens mining district, on the 7th October. Two days later they moved to the nearby village of Attiches and thence to Billy Montigny, a suburb of Lens. During their stay here the time was occupied in constructing defences at Mons en Pevele.

On the 13th November, as a result of a false alarm of German activity, a move was made to the French frontier town of Tourcoing, where they were destined to remain until the 10th May 1940—when the 'phoney' war ended and active operations commenced. The stay at Tourcoing was a pleasant one. The bulk of the Battalion was employed constructing defences along the Franco-Belgian frontier, but two weeks were spent at Dannes, near Le Touquet, for the purpose of carrying out field firing and one week on field training near St. Pol. From December onwards one company at a time visited the Saar area of the French front and occupied positions in the Maginot Line.

On the 12th February 1940 Lieut.-Colonel H. de R. Morgan left the Battalion on promotion to command the 148th Infantry Brigade. He was succeeded by Major T. C. L. Redwood, with Major R. W. H. Fryer, M.C., as Second-in-Command.

Early in April the Battalion became closely associated with the 4th Battalion of the Regiment, the two battalions being given similar roles in the event of active operations.

Plans for the advance of the B.E.F. into Belgium—known as 'Plan D'—were by this time fully matured. In the initial move forward to the River Dyle the 2nd and 4th Bns. Royal Northumberland Fusiliers had been given the task of protecting and regulating the routes by which the B.E.F. was to move. The duties included the guarding of vulnerable points, anti-parachute duties and the control of traffic and

May–June 1940

refugees. The 2nd Battalion was allotted the eastern sector and the 4th Battalion the western.*

The Battalion first heard the news of the German invasion of Holland and Belgium from the 7 a.m. B.B.C. news summary on the 10th May—although enemy air activity during the night had indicated that something unusual was afoot.

The following statement shows the 'key' appointments in the Battalion when it arrived in France in October 1939, changes which had taken place by the 10th May 1940 being indicated in brackets:

Commanding Officer . .	Lieut.-Colonel H. de R. Morgan, D.S.O.† (Lieut.-Colonel T. C. L. Redwood)
Second-in-Command .	Major T. C. L. Redwood (Major R. W. H. Fryer, M.C.)
Adjutant	Captain C. R. M. Threlfall (Captain H. R. M. Wilkin)
Quartermaster . . .	Captain J. H. Rowsell (Lieut. W. R. E. Brown)
Regimental Sergeant-Major	R.S.M. W. Greaves
O.C. A Coy. . . .	Captain R. S. N. Clarke
" B "	Major H. A. Ingledew
" C "	Captain W. P. Fryer-Jones (Captain C. R. M. Threlfall)
" D "	Major R. W. H. Fryer, M.C. (Captain J. Cox-Walker)
" H.Q. Coy. . .	Major C. R. Freeman, D.S.O., M.C.

On the morning of the 10th May the Battalion moved to its pre-arranged rendezvous at Templemars. At 0615 hrs. on the 11th they crossed the Franco-Belgian frontier en route for their allotted sector—from Borsbeke to Vilvorde (north-east of Brussels), a distance of about 25 miles. An additional duty was the defence of Brussels airfield against air attack.

Some delays in the forward move were occasioned by damage to the route caused by earlier enemy air action, but these were not serious. By 1600 hrs. the column had reached its destination (with Bn. H.Q. at Merchtem) and the various detachments had assumed their duties.

In this situation the Battalion remained for the next six days—under conditions of increasing difficulty, as refugees became more numerous.

On the 16th May it became known that the enemy had broken through on the front of the 9th French Army, south of Namur. The B.E.F. had experienced little difficulty in holding its positions on the River Dyle; but the serious situation on the French front made it inevitable that they should conform to the general withdrawal which had been ordered.

---

* See also Section III of this chapter, which deals with Route Regulation by the 4th Battalion.

† Now (August 1951) Major-General H. de R. Morgan, D.S.O., the Colonel of the Regiment.

The Battalion's role of 'Route Regulation' came to an end at 1800 hrs. on the 16th, and they then withdrew to Kirxken, west of the Dendre Canal, behind which the B.E.F. had taken up new positions.

On the 17th May the Battalion reverted to command of the 4th Division (Major-General D. G. Johnson), from whom they had been detached since the commencement of active operations on the 10th May.

Meanwhile the situation in Northern France was deteriorating rapidly and on the morning of the 18th the Battalion received orders to move behind the River Escaut. This move commenced at 1330 hrs. and, after a change of destination, the Battalion arrived late that night at Ooteghem, some 7 miles east of Courtrai. The column was much delayed by traffic, and by being misdirected to an area occupied by other troops.

On the 19th the Battalion deployed in the front of the 4th Division along the line of the River Escaut—A and B Coys. in support of the 10th and 11th Infantry Brigades respectively in the Front Line, and C and D Coys. in support of the 12th Infantry Brigade on the Reserve Line. Bn. H.Q. remained in the vicinity of Ooteghem. The enemy first made contact with this position at about 0800 hrs. on the 20th. Pressure increased on the 21st and by that evening the Germans had gained a firm lodgement on the front of the 44th Division on the left. This necessitated numerous adjustments in the 2nd Bn. Royal Northumberland Fusiliers' dispositions. Some fine shoots at long range took place on this day.

During the night of the 22nd/23rd May the 4th Division withdrew to the line of the Franco-Belgian frontier defences—which had been constructed by the B.E.F. during the winter and spring. The Divisional sector was in the salient north of Tourcoing, with the 12th Infantry Brigade on the right, about Roncq and the 10th Infantry Brigade on the left near Halluin, opposite Menin. C Coy. was in support of the 12th Infantry Brigade, and A in support of the 10th—C Coy. having the advantage of being on their 'home ground' in occupation of the sector which they had helped to construct. H.Q., B and D Coys. were in reserve at Bousbecq on the River Lys, south-west of Halluin. During the occupation of this position Captain R. S. N. Clarke (O.C. A Coy.) was wounded.

These positions, with minor modifications, were occupied until the 25th, when news was received that the Belgian Army's defences between Menin and Courtrai had been penetrated and that the 5th British Division on the left flank, north of the River Lys, was in danger of encirclement. In consequence of this B Coy. was withdrawn from a position near Roncq and moved to an area about Wervicq Sud, on the Lys—where it arrived on the morning of the 26th.

By this time the decision to evacuate the B.E.F. from Dunkirk had been made. Although this was known to senior officers it had not yet been communicated to the rank and file. To the latter the course of events was somewhat bewildering. They were ordered to retreat almost daily, yet so far they had not been very heavily engaged and could have held every position they had occupied for an indefinite period—or so it seemed to them. There were not many who realized that within ten days the survivors of the Battalion would be in England planning, in some haste, the defence of their country with the scanty equipment left to them.

May–June 1940

About this time the Germans commenced firing propaganda pamphlets and maps into the British lines. These were very accurate and provided useful information as to the general situation.

This phase of operations terminated, for the time being, the 2nd Bn. Royal Northumberland Fusiliers' connection with the 4th Division. After many orders and counter-orders, and a move, mainly by side roads, full of minor irritations and difficulties, the Battalion eventually arrived on the line of the Yser Canal, north of Ypres soon after midday on the 27th May. The sector to be held was occupied by the French Division Légère Méchanique, who were about to be relieved by the 151st Infantry Brigade of the 50th (Northumbrian) Division. The position was occupied at once by A Coy. right, D Coy. centre and C Coy. left, with Bn. H.Q. at Brielen and B Coy. in a reserve position in front of Brielen. The 151st Infantry Brigade did not, however, start arriving until late that evening, and consequently the fire plan was not properly co-ordinated until the morning of the 28th May—although forward elements of the enemy had reached the canal the previous evening. The Germans were not, however, very active during that night.

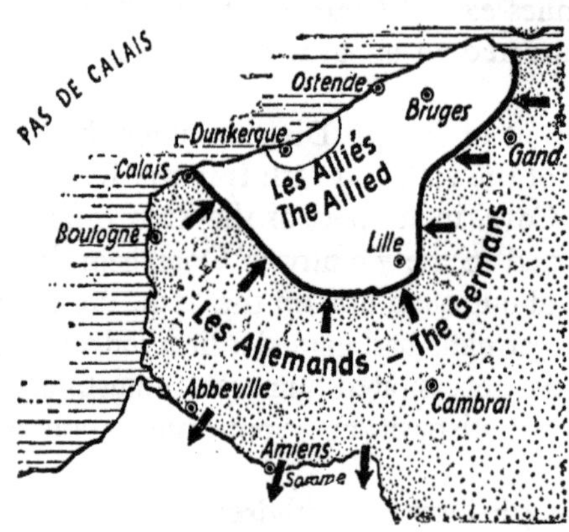

Camarades!

Telle est la situation!
En tout cas, la guerre est finie pour vous!
Vos chefs vont s'enfuir par avion.
A bas les armes!

British Soldiers!

Look at this map: it gives your true situation!
Your troops are entirely surrounded — stop fighting!
Put down your arms!

The 28th May, unlike the days of the previous three weeks, was dull and wet. Apart from exchanges of artillery fire there were no incidents of particular note.

On the night of the 28th/29th May the 50th Division withdrew under orders to a rearguard position facing south-west, with its right on the north-eastern outskirts of Poperinghe and its left at Woesten. In this position A and B Coys. supported the 150th Infantry Brigade on the right and C and D Coys. the 151st Infantry Brigade on the left. At about 1700 hrs. orders were received to hold this position until 2000 hrs. and then withdraw to positions on the Bergues–Furnes Canal, which was part of the outer defences of the Dunkirk perimeter.

The enemy were in close contact and this withdrawal was not carried out without difficulty. Moreover, the route of withdrawal was a very complicated one, mostly up narrow lanes. On crossing the canal traffic congestion became acute. By the early morning of the 29th the Battalion had arrived at Moeres, where companies took up positions in support of the same brigades as in the previous area. These positions were maintained during the 30th, which was a comparatively quiet day.

The German advanced guards appeared in front of the position early on the 31st and a considerable amount of shelling took place, which continued throughout the day. During the afternoon the enemy made determined attempts to penetrate the position on the front of the 151st Infantry Brigade. During this engagement the Battalion was heavily involved and suffered severe casualties. Captains Threlfall and Johnson of C Coy. were both killed by shell-fire, Captain Cox-Walker of D Coy. was wounded and a number of other ranks became casualties. Captain G. W. Thornton took over command of C Coy. and Captain R. M. Pratt D Coy. May–June 1940

A very grave situation was restored by a most gallant counter-attack by a battalion of the Grenadier Guards.

At 1800 hrs. on the 31st May the command of the B.E.F. passed to the Ist Corps, who formed the rearguard. The embarkation of the 2nd Corps proceeded throughout the night of the 31st May/1st June and it was the intention to embark the whole of Ist Corps on the following night. With this aim in view the 50th Division received orders to withdraw to the coast on the night of 31st May/1st June.

The destination of the 2nd Bn. Royal Northumberland Fusiliers was Bray Dunes, about 8 miles east of Dunkirk. It should be mentioned that only essential fighting personnel remained, as all administrative personnel had left for Dunkirk for embarkation twenty-four hours previously. By the morning of the 1st June all companies had arrived in, or were in process of moving to, the area. As the position was uncertain various local protective measures were taken in hand in conjunction with other troops of the 50th Division.

At about 1500 hrs. that portion of the Battalion with 151st Infantry Brigade (i.e. the Battalion less A and B Coys.) received orders to march to the Mole at Dunkirk. Before leaving all remaining transport and machine-guns were destroyed. The party arrived at Dunkirk at dusk and embarked after dark without incident.

This is a fitting place to pay tribute to the fine work of the Light Aid Detachment, under Lieut. D. B. A. Moore, R.A.O.C., by whose tireless efforts the impressed vehicles were kept on the road with remarkable efficiency.

Meanwhile A and B Coys., who had been with the 150th Infantry Brigade, arrived at the point near Bray Dunes where transport was to be destroyed—at about 0400 hrs. 1st June. In the absence of orders they assumed that they were to embark from the nearby beaches and spent several hours in slit trenches awaiting instructions. At about 1700 hrs. they were called upon to take up a defensive position (in the role of rifle companies), to meet a possible enemy threat towards Zuydecoote—a threat which did not materialize. This position was held until 2145 hrs., when the two companies marched to Malo-les-Bains (about one mile east of Dunkirk Mole), where they were to receive orders to embark. They reached their destination soon after midnight, B Coy. having suffered some 14 casualties from shell-fire as they moved along the water-front. On arrival they were informed that the last boat would leave at 0230 hrs.: on enquiry at the Mole it was discovered that the last ship from there had already left. Eventually A Coy., and about half B Coy., managed to embark in some empty boats which had apparently been overlooked. The rest of B Coy. had to wait until the following night, when they were conveyed in a destroyer from the Mole.

Thus by the 3rd June the survivors of the Battalion had arrived at various ports in the south of England, having suffered 140 casualties. Although they had been almost continuously on the move for three weeks, under most exhausting conditions, it cannot be said that the Battalion had been very heavily engaged in battle, except on

May–June 1940

the 31st May. Nevertheless, the casualties had amounted to more than 25 per cent. of the original strength, which demonstrates the disproportionate losses which occur during a retreat.

The Battalion assembled at Willsworthy Camp, in Devon, where they quickly reorganized to play their part in the Battle of Britain.

III. THE 4TH BATTALION

Sept. 1939–May 1940

After embodiment on the 1st September 1939 the 4th Bn. Royal Northumberland Fusiliers spent the first few weeks at its drill halls in West Northumberland.

The Battalion was a motor-cycle reconnaissance battalion and a divisional unit of the 50th (Northumbrian) Division (Major-General G. Le Q. Martel).

At the end of September the Battalion concentrated in billets in the Newburn area. Here they completed their organization, absorbed new personnel and drew up the balance of the somewhat scanty scale of equipment available in those days. By the middle of October training was in full swing.

On the 15th October the Battalion Colours were deposited with due ceremony in Hexham Abbey.

On the 20th they moved to the Divisional concentration and training area in Warwickshire, being located near Stratford-on-Avon as follows:

Bn. H.Q. H.Q. Coy.	Admington Hall
X Coy.	Quinton
Y ”	Ilmington
Z ”	Halford

In this area the Battalion was gradually made up to a more generous scale of equipment, and during its three months' stay there much valuable training was carried out.

Early in the new year the 50th Division received orders to prepare to join the B.E.F. in France. In consequence of this the 4th Bn. Royal Northumberland Fusiliers was made up to a strength of 570 other ranks, and received their balance of war equipment, transport and stores.

In the middle of January, a few days before departure, the Battalion was inspected by His Majesty The King, the ceremony taking place in the main street of Broadway.

The Battalion embarked at Southampton on the 21st January and landed at Cherbourg on the following day. This was followed by a rail move to a billeting area between Le Mans and Alencon.

On the 26th February there commenced a road move which terminated on the 29th at Fontaine Bonneleau, south of Beauvais. They remained there until the 29th March, when they moved to La Bassée.

At the end of April a further move forward was made—to Lannoy, south of Roubaix on the Belgian frontier. Here the Battalion was occupied in improving the defences of this, as yet incomplete, portion of the Maginot Line. They were still located in this area when the whole scene was transformed by the German invasion of Holland and Belgium on the 10th May 1940.

May–June 1940

On this date the Battalion state was as follows:

Commanding Officer . .	Lieut.-Colonel R. Wood, T.D.
Second-in-Command .	Major J. Clark
Adjutant	Lieut. C. L. Stephenson
Quartermaster . . .	Captain C. H. Makeham, M.B.E.
Regimental Sergeant-Major	R.S.M. J. Chapman
O.C. H.Q. Coy. . .	Captain A. D. Smith
" X Coy. . . .	Captain H. B. Portnell
" Y "	Major K. A. Clark
" Z "	Major J. T. Lisle

As explained at the beginning of the chapter a German invasion of Holland and Belgium was to be followed immediately by the advance into Belgium of the B.E.F., and French Armies of the North, to the line of the River Dyle. In this initial move the Battalion had been given an important role in connection with the protection and control of the routes forward. At this time a number of officers and other ranks were on, or proceeding to and from, leave in the United Kingdom. Among these were the Commanding Officer, Lieut.-Colonel R. Wood, and the Second-in-Command, Major J. Clark—leaving Major K. A. Clark in command.

The tasks of the Battalion in the advance were as follows:

(*a*) To provide motor-cycle patrols and contact between the static control posts.
(*b*) To protect certain bridges and other vulnerable points. A.A. and A.T. personnel were used for this purpose.
(*c*) To protect the routes against airborne attack. The two scout car platoons performed this task.
(*d*) Refugee control. Performed mainly by motor cycles.

The area of advance between the Franco-Belgian frontier and the River Dyle was divided into two sectors—east and west—with a dividing line running approximately north and south through Alost. The 4th Bn. Royal Northumberland Fusiliers were responsible for the western sector and the 2nd Battalion (M.G. Bn. to the 4th Division) was by a fortunate coincidence responsible for the eastern sector. Both units were controlled by H.Q. 3rd Division (Major-General B. L. Montgomery)—the 4th Battalion being thus temporarily detached from the 50th Division, which was in G.H.Q. reserve.

This task required the various detachments of the Battalion to be in position before the leading troops began to use the routes. Actually the Battalion was packed up and ready to move within one hour of receipt of orders. Owing to a delay in the arrival of the 12th Royal Lancers, who were to cover the advance, the B.E.F. was in fact led into Belgium by the 4th Bn. Royal Northumberland Fusiliers, who claim to have been the first major unit to cross the Belgian frontier.

Bn. H.Q. was established at Petegem, with X Coy. in the area east of Audenarde, Z Coy. west of Audenarde and Y Coy. in reserve at Escanaffles.

Space does not permit a detailed account of the activities of each detachment. The general picture was one of almost clockwork timings and precision in the early

May–June 1940

stages, with difficulties gradually increasing—due mainly to uncontrolled civilian motor and horse-drawn traffic, and an increasing number of refugees moving west. The scene was enlivened by periodical air attacks, rumours of airborne landings and reports of 'fifth column' activities. It can be said that the Battalion fulfilled its role well and played an important part in the successful advance of the B.E.F. to the Dyle position.

On the 11th May Major J. Clark returned from leave and took over command, and on the 15th Captain A. D. Smith (O.C. H.Q. Coy.) and 90 other ranks rejoined. By the 15th May the advance of the B.E.F. had been completed, but the Battalion remained in position with the tasks of protecting and keeping the routes open.

On the 17th Lieut.-Colonel R. Wood rejoined from leave and resumed command of the Battalion.

By the 18th refugee traffic had greatly increased and road congestion became a very serious problem. Increased enemy air activity, the sounds of battle moving gradually westwards and the increasing amount of British and French transport moving in the wrong direction indicated that the affairs of the Franco-British armies were not going entirely according to plan. In fact the B.E.F. was in process of withdrawing. On this day, and during the night of the 18th/19th, the Battalion was responsible for traffic control on the route of withdrawal of the 3rd and 4th Divisions.

By the morning of the 19th the last British troops had crossed the River Escaut and the enemy was shelling the line of the river. The Battalion was then ordered to cease route regulation and rejoin the 50th Division. They moved to an area known as Bellegham Bosch Wood, near Courtrai. Before the whole battalion could be concentrated, however, orders were received to move to Wavrin. This move was completed by about 1900 hrs.

Early on the 20th May orders were received to move at once to undertake the defence of Vimy Ridge—facing south towards Arras, from which direction a serious German threat was developing. By the afternoon this position (with a three-mile front from Givenchy to Thelus) had been taken up, the Battalion having under its command one battery 65th A.T. Regt., 151st Infantry Brigade A.T. Coy., two companies Royal Engineers acting as infantry and one platoon of the 8th Bn. Durham Light Infantry.

During the night of the 19th/20th orders were received to withdraw into reserve on some high ground south of Avion. While this move was in progress verbal orders were issued to the Commanding Officer in connection with an attack to be carried out by the 50th Division to the west and south of Arras on the 21st May.

This attack was carried out by 151st Infantry Brigade supported by two battalions of tanks. Its general direction and the scope of the operation are shown on Map No. II. Detailed orders were as follows:

> The Right Column (blue), consisted of the 8th Bn. Durham Light Infantry, with Z Coy. and No. 12 (Scout) Pl., 4th Bn. Royal Northumberland Fusiliers, in support.
>
> The Left Column (red), consisted of the 6th Bn. Durham Light Infantry with Y Coy. and No. 11 (Scout) Pl. in support.
>
> The Battalion (less Y and Z Coys. and two Scout Pls.) was in reserve near Vimy.

4. Captain C. R. M. Threlfall, first officer of the Regiment to be killed in the war on the 31st May 1940

5. Officers of the 2nd Battalion at Tourcoing, March 1940. Captain H. R. M. Wilkin, Lieut. D. B. A. Moore, R.A.O.C., Lieut. W. R. E. Brown, Lieut. A. B. Fountain, R.A.M.C., Lieut. D. R. Holderness-Roddam, Lieut. H. B. Van der Gucht, Lieut. W. P. S. Hastings, Captain G. W. Thornton, Captain J. Cox-Walker, Lieut. F. Gray, Lieut. J. A. Matthewson, Lieut. J. A. G. Ward, Captain R. S. Clark, Captain R. H. Pratt, Captain L. Johnson, Major C. R. Freeman, Lieut.-Colonel T. C. L. Redwood, Major R. W. H. Fryer

6. 4th Battalion at Fontaine Bonnelieu, March 1940

7. 4th Battalion, leading the advance to the River Dyle, crosses the Belgian frontier at Lannoy, the 10th May 1940

Owing to the fact that the Battalion was on the move considerable difficulty was experienced in carrying out these orders. Z Coy. on the right was somewhat late, but followed up closely along the route.

The attack started at 1400 hrs. In its initial stages it met with considerable local success and undoubtedly had the effect of checking the Germans in the Arras area—with possibly far-reaching results on operations as a whole. By this time, however, the German columns were advancing rapidly in other areas and the battle for Northern France and the Channel ports was already all but lost. The French attack from the south, which was planned to link up with that of the 50th Division, did not materialize. Towards evening the advancing troops were attacked in strength by German dive-bombers, which caused the infantry to lose touch with their supporting tanks. Many casualties to personnel and vehicles were suffered. The attack lost impetus and the troops were eventually ordered to withdraw.

The right column made good initial progress, and Z Coy. was heavily engaged in the latter stages. Two platoons were surrounded by the enemy, but were eventually extricated by the enterprise and courage of 2/Lieut. G. W. Anderson—who was later awarded the Military Cross. No. 12 (Scout) Platoon suffered heavily and lost 6 of its 11 scout cars.

Y Coy. and No. 11 (Scout) Platoon acted as advanced guard to the left column and had a heavy day's fighting. Early in the advance the Company successfully attacked parties of enemy seen debouching from the outskirts of Arras, and captured 40 prisoners. 2/Lieut. T. D. Fairhead played a leading part in this action, and also distinguished himself later in the day during the withdrawal. After this the advance continued for some miles round the western outskirts of Arras. It was at this stage that the enemy dive-bombing attack took place and soon after orders to withdraw were received.

Y Coy. was ordered to cover the withdrawal and for this purpose two platoons were deployed, a section of scout cars being allotted to each. Soon after assuming these dispositions the Company was subjected to a tank attack supported by heavy artillery fire. One enemy tank was destroyed in a sunken road, which brought the attack to a temporary halt. Later the tanks advanced again, supported by infantry. This attack was repulsed with heavy losses to the enemy. The enemy renewed his efforts towards dusk, when his infantry again advanced, this time supported by flame-throwers. Y Coy. suffered numerous casualties in this encounter. Lieut. T. Bland was severely wounded and died later in enemy hands, two other ranks were killed and about 12 wounded. The Germans continued to press forward until it was almost dark, but the Company held doggedly to its positions. Cpl. T. G. Winder, although wounded in both legs, continued to command his section—a fine example of devotion to duty.

A further attack by enemy tanks made it clear that any organized withdrawal was impracticable and the Company Commander (Major K. A. Clark) issued orders for the Company to withdraw by twos and threes, or if necessary individually. Soon after issuing this order Major Clark was wounded and taken prisoner.

Although a few individuals escaped, the bulk of the two leading platoons (Nos. 4 and 5) and No. 11 (Scout) Platoon were either killed or captured. No. 6 Platoon, which had not been deployed in the final position, escaped and rejoined the Battalion.

May–June 1940

This was a fine operation, worthy of the best traditions of the Regiment. During this battle Bn. H.Q. and X Coy. were not engaged.

The Battalion casualties were:

Officers

Missing (later reported died of wounds): 2/Lieut. T. Bland; Missing (later reported prisoners of war): Major K. A. Clark, Lieut. E. W. I. Johnson and 2/Lieut. T. D. Fairhead	4

Other ranks

Killed, wounded and missing 166

These losses represented more than half of the Battalion fighting personnel. In addition Y Coy. had lost all its vehicles, Z Coy. about half and out of 21 scout cars only 5 remained.

On withdrawal the Battalion organized a defensive position on the high ground south of Avion.

Early on the morning of the 22nd May the 4th Bn. Royal Northumberland Fusiliers were ordered to reoccupy the Vimy Ridge—this time on a much shorter front on the left flank. In this position the troops were attacked by dive-bombers throughout the day.

On the afternoon of the 23rd the Battalion moved to a position at Givenchy Wood to protect the right flank. Here they remained until the early morning of the 24th May. Enemy dive-bombers were again active and although German tanks and infantry made several appearances no actual assault was launched. It became apparent, however, that the whole position was gradually being enveloped by strong enemy forces.

In the early hours of the 24th the Battalion commenced to withdraw—an operation which was not unaccompanied by anxiety, but which was carried out without further loss. By midday the Battalion had arrived at Barques.

This brought to a close the gallant action of the 50th (Northumbrian) Division at Vimy. They had suffered heavy casualties, and the survivors had only just succeeded in withdrawing through the narrow corridor left open to them.

The Battalion remained in Barques during the whole of the 25th May—their first period of rest for fifteen days. It is interesting to record that while at Barques the 8th Battalion, and elements of the 2nd Battalion, were in close proximity. To complete the Regimental picture the Colonel of the Regiment, Major-General Herbert (commanding the 23rd Division), arrived in a car with his G.S.O.1.

On the morning of the 26th a move to Erquinghem, a small village on the Lys Canal, was made, followed on the 27th by a further move to Elverdinghe.

On the 28th May the Battalion came under orders of the 150th Infantry Brigade and moving to the Dickebusche area took up a defensive position on the right flank facing Kemmel. At dusk they withdrew to a wooded area near Westvleteren.

During the preceding days of intense activity officers and men were absorbed in their own affairs and had little opportunity to consider or listen to news of the general situation. There had been rumours, but it was not until he attended a conference at H.Q. 50th Division about midday on the 29th that the Commanding Officer was officially informed of the decision to evacuate the B.E.F. from Dunkirk. In fact the evacuation had, of course, already commenced. May–June 1940

On the evening of the 29th the Battalion commenced a move to Moeres—on the Belgian frontier and within the Dunkirk perimeter. The route was heavily congested by French transport—all making for Dunkirk—and frequently attacked by hostile aircraft. Just before reaching the Bergues–Furnes Canal, which was the line of the perimeter outer defences, the column was directed to an area where all but a small proportion of the transport was to be destroyed. This dismal task was soon completed, except that all remaining scout cars, motor cycles and one 15-cwt. truck per platoon were retained.

At Moeres the Battalion was given the task of Divisional mobile reserve. They also organized the area of a nearby cross-roads into a defended locality.

On the 30th May all administrative personnel moved to La Panne under Captain S. A. Johnson for embarkation.

On the 31st detachments from the Battalion moved forward with the object of closing certain gaps in the canal defences; but late that evening orders were received to withdraw and move to Bray Dunes.

On the evening of the 1st June orders were issued to abandon and destroy all remaining vehicles and move to Dunkirk. This entailed a march along the beach of about 8 miles, which was harassed by machine-gun fire from enemy low-flying aircraft and spasmodic shelling.

The Battalion eventually embarked from Dunkirk Mole on the 'Medway Queen'—a small pleasure boat which had given splendid service throughout the evacuation of the B.E.F. The boat left Dunkirk at 2350 hrs. and the Battalion disembarked at Margate at 0630 hrs. on the 2nd June 1940.

The Battalion assembled at Knutsford, in Cheshire, to reorganize and refit.

IV. THE 8TH AND 9TH BATTALIONS

As explained earlier the 8th and 9th Battalions were part of the 23rd (Northumbrian) Division which had been formed in the spring of 1939 as a 'duplicate' Division of the 50th (Northumbrian) Division, when the decision was made to double the Territorial Army. Sept. 1939–March 1940

The Division was commanded by Major-General W. N. Herbert,* a distinguished Fifth Fusilier officer and Colonel of the Regiment.

As both battalions were Divisional units—the 8th a motor-cycle reconnaissance battalion and the 9th a machine-gun battalion—it will be convenient to give an account of their activities during this phase of the war in one and the same section of this chapter.

On embodiment on the 1st September 1939 they were both considerably under strength, deficient of trained junior leaders and sadly lacking in essential weapons, modern equipment and transport. Units of the 23rd Division had been given little opportunity to train, except on the most elementary lines in their drill halls in the

---

* Major-General Herbert died on the 25th April 1949.

Sept. 1939–March 1940

evenings, although the 8th and 9th Bns. Royal Northumberland Fusiliers had each attended camp for fourteen days in June, near Catterick Camp, Yorkshire. Summarized it may be said that they were two enthusiastic bodies of fine potential soldiers —eager to learn, but as yet almost entirely untrained and lacking all but the simplest equipment.

8th Battalion

Embodiment took place at Prudhoe and the Battalion was immediately called upon to provide guards for various nearby 'vulnerable points.'

Between October 1939 and January 1940 some 200 militiamen (conscripts) were received direct from civil life. These were followed by all the unfits and immatures from the 4th Battalion when that unit proceeded overseas. In April 1940 further reinforcements were received—170 other ranks from No. 2 Motor Training Battalion and about 80 from the Queen's Westminster Rifles. Although the establishment of vehicles was 230 none of these were forthcoming during the winter of 1939/40 and the training of drivers had to be carried out with a few trucks borrowed from the 4th Battalion.

It had been laid down that individual training was to be completed by 30th April 1940. Actually this programme was considerably behind schedule and the Battalion moved to France a few days before the target date.

9th Battalion

The 9th Battalion was embodied with its various components located as follows:

Bn. H.Q. . . .	At 7th Bn. Drill Hall, Alnwick.
W Coy. . . .	Morpeth
X ,, . . .	Ashington
Y ,, . . .	Amble
Z ,, . . .	Berwick

Each detachment provided numerous local guards, the men living mostly in their own homes.

Early in December the Battalion was concentrated at Gosforth Park. Individual training continued throughout the winter, but was hampered by an almost total lack of essential equipment. It is almost incredible, but true, that up to the end of 1939 this machine-gun battalion possessed only two machine-guns—these being German weapons captured in 1918 and acquired by an officer of the Regiment. Each man had a rifle and there was one Bren gun in the Battalion. Transport consisted of three hired 5-ton lorries, two or three hired cars and a varying number of hired motor cycles.

From time to time the Battalion received drafts of militiamen, straight from civilian life, to bring it up to strength; and immediately before proceeding overseas, five officers from the Regimental Depot.

From the foregoing account it will be apparent that by the spring of 1940 neither battalion was in any sense battleworthy. They had learnt something of administration and done some individual and elementary tactical training; but lack of weapons and transport had given little scope for technical or collective training. They had, however, become well-disciplined troops and had acquired the spirit of camaraderie and *esprit de corps* for which the Regiment is famous.

In the spring of 1940 it was decided to send certain 'duplicate' Territorial Army divisions to France to join the B.E.F. The 23rd (Northumbrian) Division was among the divisions selected to join the B.E.F. in April 1940. Its primary role was to be the construction of airfields, the plan for each week's activity being four days' work on the airfields, two days' training and one day's rest. After three months, by which time it was estimated that the airfields would have been completed, it was intended to bring the Division back to England to complete its training. As the role was a working and not a fighting one the Division proceeded on a much reduced scale of weapons, equipment and transport. The Divisional Artillery and Signals remained at home, and only one field ambulance went to France. On arrival, towards the end of April, units of the Division were dispersed over a very wide area to the aerodrome sites on which they were to work.

8th Battalion

The road party, with the Battalion's 53 vehicles, sailed for France in the middle of April, followed by the main body which embarked at Southampton on St. George's Day. Disembarkation took place at Cherbourg on the 24th April and the Battalion reached its final destination—Diéval (between St. Pol and Bethune) on the evening of the 29th, the road party having arrived the previous day.

Accommodation was in a tented camp adjoining the airfield, on which they commenced work on the 2nd May—on the basis of four-sevenths of the Battalion working, two-sevenths training and one-seventh resting.

9th Battalion

Prior to embarkation the Battalion had received a skeleton scale of equipment, consisting of six service and eighteen D.P. Vickers guns, ten 15-cwt. trucks, three 30-cwt. trucks, one water truck, one orderly room truck, the C.O.'s car and one motor cycle; together with a few Bren guns and one anti-tank rifle.

The Battalion embarked at Southampton soon after midday on St. George's Day. Cherbourg was reached in the early hours of the 24th April 1940, and after an uncomfortable train journey, which included a long halt at Caen, eventually detrained at La Hutte. Headquarters, W and X Coys. went into billets in the nearby village of Piacé, while Y and Z Coys. were about a mile distant at Juilliet. The Battalion transport had already reached Piacé, having arrived at Cherbourg on the 20th April and moved by road.

During the short stay in this area preparations were made for commencing work on the airfields, conferences were held and lectures delivered—in fact the usual routine consequent on arrival in a theatre of war.

On the 28th April the move was continued, the Battalion entraining at La Hutte for Diéval—the detraining station for the airfield site. In this move the 9th Battalion was accompanied by the 8th, which travelled on the same train—an exceptionally long one.

April–June 1940

Thus by the end of April 1940 the 8th and 9th Bns. Royal Northumberland Fusiliers were both assembled in France, the 8th at Diéval and the 9th at Monchy Breton, with the primary task of airfield construction.

All plans for the employment of the 23rd Division on airfield construction were, however, upset on the 10th May 1940, when the Germans invaded Holland and Belgium. The Anglo-French Armies of the North immediately advanced into Belgium to occupy the line of the River Dyle, in accordance with the carefully prepared 'Plan D.'

The suddenness of the attack, and the speed of the German advance through Holland, Belgium and France, made it necessary for the Division to assume a fighting role at very short notice—ill-equipped and unprepared as it was for such a task.

It was in this setting that the 8th and 9th Battalions of the Royal Northumberland Fusiliers first met the enemy in the Second World War.

8th Battalion

On the 10th May 1940 the Battalion was still located at, and around, Diéval, the key appointments being as follows:

Commanding Officer	Lieut.-Colonel F. B. Clarke
Second-in-Command	Major J. Challoner
Adjutant	Major K. A. Seth Smith
Quartermaster	Captain Milne
Regimental Sergeant-Major	R.S.M. J. Lenham
O.C. A Coy.	Captain D. Portnell
„ B „	Captain N. Nicholson
„ C „	Major N. B. Pigg, D.S.O., M.C.
„ H.Q. Coy.	Lieut. C. Mitchell

The Battalion had been made responsible for providing what was known as 'Column E' in the L. of C. defence scheme—the area allotted being Merville–Bethune–Lens–St. Pol—with a possible expansion to include Lille. On the 15th May this area was extended to include the coastal belt from the Belgium frontier as far south as Le Touquet, this being the Boulogne sub-area. Actually the Battalion never operated in the 'Column E' role.

Early on the 17th May H.Q. 23rd Division issued orders for the protection of certain crossings of the Canal du Nord with 70th Infantry Brigade right and 69th Infantry Brigade left. The 8th Bn. Royal Northumberland Fusiliers were to be in reserve at St. Leger; Divisional H.Q. at Cherisy.

The Battalion commenced leaving Diéval at about 1600 hrs., moving via Houdain–Ecurie–Roclincourt–St. Laurent-Blangy–Tilloy les Moufflins. Before the whole Battalion had reached St. Leger, however, the destination was changed to Croiselles, with C Coy. at Cherisy for duties with Divisional H.Q. This move was made very difficult by an acute shortage of transport. When the destination was changed it became necessary to impress a number of civilian vehicles. By 0400 hrs. 18th May all troops had arrived in the area Croiselles–Cherisy. About 1030 hrs. Bn. H.Q. and B Coy. joined C Coy. at Cherisy, leaving H.Q. Coy. and A Coy. at Croiselles.

A further move was made during the night of 18th/19th May, the whole Battalion accompanying H.Q. 23rd Division to the village of Monchy-le-Preux.

Later orders were received to the effect that the Battalion would be responsible for traffic control during the night of the 19th/20th May, when the whole Division would move north to a defensive position north of the La Bassée Canal. Soon after the commencement of this move an order was received cancelling it and ordering the construction of defensive positions and anti-tank obstacles, roughly in an area from the north-east to south-west of Arras. As a result the Battalion proceeded during the night to the airfield at Thélus in expectation of being given a day's rest, but were immediately given the task of constructing anti-tank obstacles in the neighbourhood of Lens.

At about 0900 hrs. orders were received to move at once to Arras and come under command of 'Petreforce.' At this time 'Petreforce' consisted of the 1st Bn. Welch Guards, various Artillery and Engineer units, a few light tanks, a small party of French troops armed with anti-tank guns and the 8th Bn. Royal Northumberland Fusiliers. On the 21st May the 5th Bn. The Green Howards joined 'Petreforce.' The task of this force was the close defence of Arras.

The 8th Battalion occupied a sector of the Arras defences until the night of the 23rd/24th May, when just after midnight, orders were received from 'Petreforce' to withdraw and proceed with all possible speed to Douai. The move started soon after receipt of orders and by dawn all companies were clear of the town. The conditions of urgency under which this move was made had left little time for the issue of proper orders, and the Battalion left Arras in small parties rather than as a complete unit. There was a considerable congestion on the roads due to a demolished viaduct over the railway about two miles outside Arras. Confusion increased soon after dawn when the German Air Force came into action along the route. Soon after this German infantry, crossing to the north of the River Scarpe, intercepted the column, which was caught in most unfavourable conditions and suffered heavily. The Battalion casualties were 5 officers and about 120 other ranks—mostly prisoners, including the Commanding Officer, Lieut.-Colonel F. B. Clarke. Had it not been for a heavy mist, which enabled men to by-pass the Germans, casualties would have been much heavier.

After much confused fighting, and movement, the survivors broke contact with the enemy and the Battalion eventually assembled in a small wood about 10 miles west of Douai.

On the 25th a move to Seclin was made and here Major J. Challoner assumed command, with Major N. B. Pigg as Second-in-Command. 2/Lieut. N. Gill became O.C. C Coy.

By this time the decision to evacuate the B.E.F. from Dunkirk had been made, and the next five days were spent in moving towards the coast.

The withdrawal to the coast was carried out by march route and was uneventful. Moving via the outskirts of Lille, Hazebrouck and Poperinghe, the Battalion eventually reached the dunes between Dunkirk and La Panne just before midnight on the night of the 30th/31st May—having covered over a hundred miles since leaving Arras.

April–June 1940

Great difficulty was experienced in embarking owing to the shortage of small craft to convey the troops from the beaches to the destroyers and other ships lying offshore. Eventually this was accomplished in small parties, the bulk of the Battalion travelling in a destroyer to Dover. Here trains left at intervals of twenty minutes, conveying troops to various transit locations in the south of England—irrespective of their unit or eventual destination.

After a stay of twenty-four or forty-eight hours in the transit locations men of the Battalions were sent to Launceston in Cornwall, which was the assembly area for the 23rd Division.

9th Battalion

The Battalion was still at Monchy Breton when the German offensive started on the 10th May 1940, the key appointments in the Battalion being held as follows:

Commanding Officer . .	Lieut.-Colonel L. C. Thomas, O.B.E., M.C.
Second-in-Command .	Major F. B. Cowen, M.C., T.D.
Adjutant	Major W. N. C. Crawhall
Quartermaster . . .	Lieut. (Q.M.) J. W. M. Purcell
Regimental Sergeant-Major	R.S.M. P. Magee
O.C. H.Q. Coy. . .	Lieut. C. Wilkinson
„ W „ . .	Lieut. A. Ainslie
„ X „ . .	Captain E. B. L. Hart
„ Y „ . .	Captain B. Berey
„ Z „ . .	Captain R. W. Armstrong

The first task allotted to the Battalion was the defence of Monchy Breton and the immediate locality. On the 12th May anti-parachute patrols were instituted. These were intensified on the 14th when rumours of frequent enemy parachute landings—large and small—began to be circulated. Actually no parachute attacks developed.

On the 15th May the Divisional Commander visited the Battalion and gave the first hints that all was not going well for the Anglo-French armies. Orders for the occupation of various points in the Lillers–Seclin area were issued and in the afternoon the Commanding Officer and his O. Group made a detailed reconnaissance.

On the following day the Battalion moved to occupy these positions. For the purpose of the move they were allotted some vehicles of a troop-carrying section R.A.S.C., but the number provided was insufficient and the move had to be carried out in two stages—the last vehicles not leaving Monchy Breton until about 0900 hrs. on the 17th May. The move was much hampered by refugees who thronged the roads. By the afternoon of this day Bn. H.Q. was installed at Lillers and all companies were in occupation of their positions, which in general terms constituted an all-round defence of the town of Lillers.

On the 18th news reached the Battalion of the German break-through and the consequent threat to the right flank and rear of the B.E.F. The Second-in-Command made a reconnaissance of the railway line between Bethune and Avion, with a view to locating additional defensive posts if necessary.

On the 19th the news was more serious. The Germans were reported to be closing in on Arras—a domestic repercussion being that the Commanding Officer's car, which was in that town for repairs, had to be abandoned. A trifling incident perhaps, but a serious loss to a unit on such a low scale of transport.

At 1600 hrs. orders were received for the Battalion to concentrate at Lestrem and this move was completed by 0700 hrs. 20th May.

On the 21st the nearby airfield at Merville was heavily attacked, and in the evening news was received that the Battalion would shortly move to the Seclin area, where the 23rd Division was to concentrate. This move was never executed, as a little later orders were issued for the Battalion to come under command of the 46th Division (Major-General H. O. Curtis) with the task of defending Merville. At the same time the Battalion, in company with other forward units of the B.E.F., was placed on half rations—an order which had little practical effect, as ample food was procurable in the deserted villages and farms.

The last company reached Merville at about 0100 hrs. on the 22nd May and the Battalion immediately commenced the construction of road blocks and other defences.

Later in the day X Coy. was sent to guard the crossings of the canal between St. Momelin and Blaringhem, a frontage of 10 miles which included the town of St. Omer in the centre. Before moving off, this Company was allotted a large proportion of the Battalion's meagre equipment of Vickers and Bren guns. No. 6 Platoon was put into position to guard the bridge at St. Momelin, and the Company, less this platoon, moved on to St. Omer, which, unknown to them, had already been occupied by the enemy. French soldiers in the streets, thought to be directing the traffic, waved the Company on. Later the entire Company was ambushed and after a short and sharp engagement all were taken prisoner. Captain E. B. L. Hart, the Company Commander, was shot by the Germans as he was being marched with his troops into captivity.

Merville was heavily attacked by German aircraft—using bombs and machine-guns—on this day.

The early hours of the 24th May found the Battalion moving into Steenbecque. They received orders at 0330 hrs. to reoccupy the canal bridges between St. Omer and Thiemes, assisted by the Cavalry Regiment * (The Inniskilling Dragoons) of the 46th Division. At 0500 hrs. Lieut.-Colonel Thomas issued orders for the following dispositions to be taken up:

W Coy. . . . To Boeseghem to cover the occupation of the bridges at Thiemes, Aire and Wittes.
Z „ . . . To Les Ciseaux to make contact with the Cavalry Squadron already in position.
Y „ . . . To remain at Steenbecque, with one platoon to Sercus to contact the Divisional Cavalry already there.
H.Q. Coy. . . To remain at Steenbecque.

These dispositions were not taken up without incidents. No. 2 Platoon of W Coy., which was directed on the bridge at Aire, was ambushed and took up a position in a

* Divisional Reconnaissance Regiments, although fully mechanized, were at this time still known as 'Cavalry.'

April–June 1940

farm. They were heavily mortared and machine-gunned, but the platoon was eventually extricated. Z Coy. were unable to find the Cavalry Squadron Headquarters, but sighted and engaged some Germans from positions on the high ground between La Belle Hostess and Les Ciseaux. Captain T. V. H. Beamish of Y Coy. ran into five enemy tanks with his truck. He 'turned about' and was pursued by the enemy, but made good his escape.

In accordance with orders the forward companies withdrew to Steenbecque in the afternoon. This move was accomplished successfully, except that No. 2 Platoon of W Coy. failed to return and 2/Lieut. W. T. Hook and his 27 other ranks were reported missing.

Later, when the tanks of the cavalry withdrew, the enemy became bolder and the Battalion positions round Steenbecque were heavily mortared and shelled, and also came under direct fire from enemy tanks.

About 1600 hrs. W Coy. and part of Z Coy. commenced to withdraw, under the impression that an order to withdraw had been given. No such order had been issued by Bn. H.Q. The troops involved were intercepted by the Second-in-Command and they reoccupied their original positions.

The enemy continued to fire on the positions until about 2000 hrs.; but no actual assault was delivered.

During the night of the 24th/25th May the Battalion withdrew to Morbecque by march route, where they went into bivouac in a field with the Divisional Cavalry Regt.

During the action of the 24th May the Battalion casualties, apart from No. 2 Platoon, had not been heavy; but among the wounded were Captain R. W. Armstrong and 2/Lieut. J. D. L. Bastable. Captain Armstrong died in hospital the next day.

During the withdrawal part of the transport became detached from the Battalion and these trucks, and their valuable loads, were lost.

On the 25th a move was made to La Motte, where Y and H.Q. Coys. were deployed to fill gaps in the line. In the course of the afternoon the following message was received from the G.O.C. 46th Division.

25th May 1940.

> Well done. If you had not held the Steenbecque Ridge against tanks and infantry for 48 hours the Bosches might now be in Dunkerque. The ninth have enhanced the traditions of the Fighting Fifth.
>
> (sgd.) H. O. Curtis,
> Major-General, 'Pol Force.'

The next move was to Doulieu, which was reached about 0300 hrs. on the 27th May. By this time the seriousness of the general situation was apparent to all—although the decision to evacuate the B.E.F. had not, as yet, been communicated to the troops.

After a difficult march the Battalion reached Berthen, where the companies occupied a series of small copses near the main road. This area was very heavily bombed and some neighbouring units suffered heavy casualties and damage to vehicles. The 9th Bn. Royal Northumberland Fusiliers were fortunate and suffered neither casualties or damage.

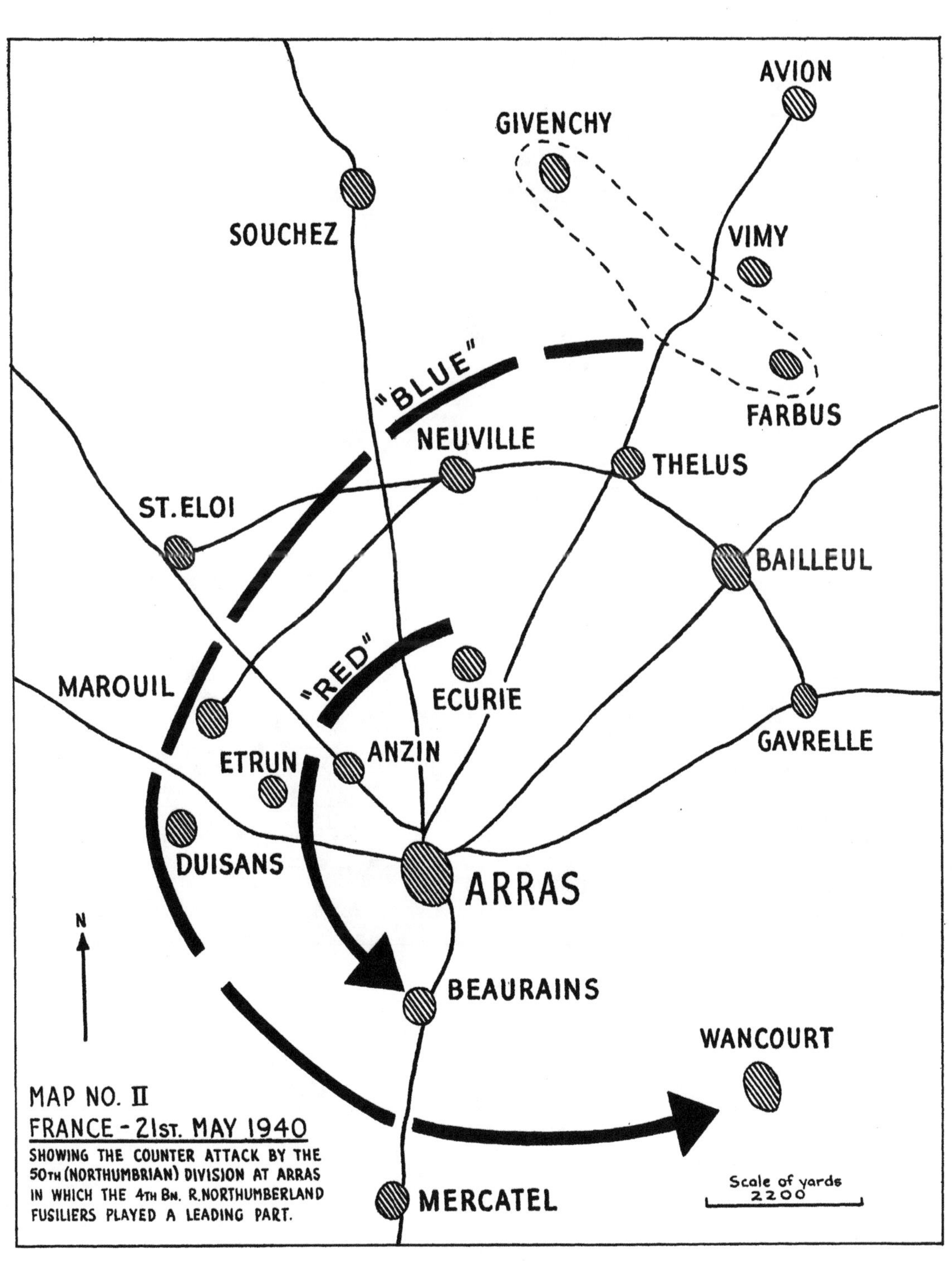

MAP NO. II
FRANCE - 21ST. MAY 1940
SHOWING THE COUNTER ATTACK BY THE 50TH (NORTHUMBRIAN) DIVISION AT ARRAS IN WHICH THE 4TH BN. R. NORTHUMBERLAND FUSILIERS PLAYED A LEADING PART.

At about 1530 hrs. on the 28th the Battalion marched from Berthen. Watou was reached at 1800 hrs. Here the Commanding Officer secured some lorries, which enabled a proportion of the men to be ferried back to Teteghem. By the evening of the 29th Oest Dunkirk Bains had been reached. Here the Battalion came under the orders of the 4th Division and was given a sector of the Dunkirk perimeter to hold. Apparently it was thought that the 9th Battalion was a fully equipped machine-gun battalion. Apart from minor patrol activities there was no engagement with the enemy. April–June 1940

In the early hours of the 31st May orders were received to move forthwith to La Panne for embarkation to England. On arrival at the beach thousands of men were found to be awaiting embarkation. The prospects were far from bright. Plenty of ships were anchored off the coast, but owing to the shortage of small craft the process of conveyance from the beach was an extremely slow one.

Later it was decided to march along the beach to Dunkirk and embark from the pier. This involved a march of 12 miles along the beach, during which the Battalion was subjected to shelling and numerous machine-gun attacks from the air. The Commanding Officer and Adjutant went on ahead by road and organized a 'ferry service' of trucks. On arrival French troops were also embarking; but the Battalion eventually completed embarkation, mostly on the destroyer H.M.S. 'Malcolm,' from Dunkirk Mole at about 1800 hrs. on the 31st May 1940—reaching Dover at 2030 hrs. Small parties of the Battalion arrived in other ships at other British ports.

The numbers which finally assembled at Launceston in Cornwall—the assembly area for the 23rd Division—were:

22 officers
31 warrant officers and sergeants
462 rank and file

Thus ended the first phase of active operations for the 8th and 9th Bns. Royal Northumberland Fusiliers in the Second World War. It may be said that they participated in the Dunkirk campaign by accident; but they acquitted themselves well in difficult circumstances and gained much valuable experience.

V. THE 7TH BATTALION

Soon after embodiment on the 1st September 1939 the Battalion concentrated at Gosforth Park, near Newcastle-on-Tyne. Almost immediately about 50 per cent. of the men who were miners were sent back to the pits and replaced by militiamen. This entailed much reorganization and considerably hampered early training. Sept. 1939–Feb. 1940

In December a move to the south of England was made, the Battalion going into billets at Alton in Hampshire, where they came under IIIrd Corps. Individual training was continued, as well as useful collective training, which included several exercises of two or three days' duration.

At Alton the Battalion received a generous allotment of most equipment, including its full complement of machine-guns, anti-tank rifles and vehicles. This enabled specialist training—especially the training of M.T. drivers (including reserve drivers) to go on apace.

March–June 1940

In March 1940 the Battalion proceeded to France as IIIrd Corps troops, being later attached to the 51st (Highland) Division (Major-General Victor Fortune) as machine-gun battalion. This Division, being a first-line Territorial division, was in a much higher state of training, and more generously supplied with modern equipment, than the 23rd (Northumbrian) Division mentioned in Section IV of this chapter. Whereas the latter proceeded to France to increase the labour force on airfield construction, and with the intention that it should return to the United Kingdom to complete its training, the 51st Division went in a fighting role—albeit with the hope of improving its standard of training before active mobile operations commenced.

The Battalion landed at Le Havre and, after a short stay near the port, moved to Strazeele, near Bethune.

In April the 51st Division moved south to the French sector of the Maginot Line near Metz. Here they occupied a portion of the front in contact with the Germans. Although a quiet sector it gave valuable experience in patrolling, concealment and other accomplishments which were lacking in the north—where the opposing armies were separated by many miles of neutral territory.

Thus when the German invasion of Holland and Belgium took place on the 10th May 1940 the 51st Division was on the Saar Front of the Maginot Line, with the 7th Bn. Royal Northumberland Fusiliers located roughly as follows:

Bn. H.Q. . . .	D'Ebervillers	
One coy. . . .	Front Line	Inter-Coy. reliefs were carried out frequently
One coy. . . .	Support	
One coy. . . .	Reserve	

At this time the key appointments were held as follows:

Commanding Officer . .	Lieut.-Colonel G. E. Fenwicke-Clennell
Second-in-Command . .	Major I. J. Kilgour
Adjutant	Captain D. V. Brims
Quartermaster . . .	Captain C. J. J. Samwell
Regimental Sergeant-Major .	R.S.M. W. E. Wasse
O.C. A Coy. . . .	Captain W. S. Sanderson
" B " . . .	Captain C. R. I. Besley
" C " . . .	Captain J. Fawcus
" D " . . .	Major W. C. W. Potts
" H.Q. Coy. . .	Major W. P. Fryer-Jones

As soon as active operations commenced plans were made for the relief of the 51st Division by French troops and its return to the B.E.F. in the north. By the 17th May the general deterioration in the position of the Anglo-French armies made the completion of this move a matter of urgency.

The withdrawal of the Battalion commenced on the 20th May and by the evening of the 21st the whole Battalion (less D Coy. and one platoon of C Coy.) had moved from D'Ebervillers to Amanvillers, north of Metz. D Coy. and the one platoon of C Coy. remained in position in front of the Maginot Line, assisting to cover the withdrawal of the 51st Division. Some difficulties were experienced in withdrawing the guns of the forward platoons, as the positions were very exposed and vehicles could not be employed in daylight. The problem was solved by the co-operation of an Indian Pack (Mule) Transport Coy. May–June 1940

By the evening of the 23rd May the whole Battalion had assembled at Lanhères near Etain—which was the concentration area for the 51st Division. By this time the general situation was very serious. It was now not so much a question of the Division rejoining the B.E.F. as avoiding destruction, or surrender, with the general collapse of the French armies which was now becoming increasingly apparent. By this time, or soon after, the decision to evacuate the B.E.F. from Dunkirk had been made; but it was clear that the chances of the 51st Division reaching Dunkirk were remote. It was, therefore, tentatively arranged for the Division to move via the neighbourhood of Paris to Le Havre, where it was hoped they might be able to embark. As will be seen, these plans were subject to many alterations and eventually failed.

The move via Paris was soon abandoned and a billeting party from the Battalion sent to Pacy (north-west of Paris) was not seen again until the 29th.

By daybreak on the 25th May the Battalion had reached Cornay, near Varennes, where they remained until the evening of the 26th. The move during the night of the 24th/25th May was a particularly anxious one. The route was difficult to find and the roads congested with French transport and refugees.

The move north continued until the 29th May—mostly by night and under conditions of continuous traffic congestion, orders and counter-orders. On this day the Battalion arrived at Preuseville, near Abbeville on the Somme.

(NOTE: Details of the latter stages of the move are shown on accompanying Map No. III.)

By this time the evacuation of the B.E.F. from Dunkirk was nearing completion; but it was still hoped to stabilize a line covering Paris along the Rivers Aisne and Somme, from Reims to Amiens and thence to the sea north-west of Abbeville. The 51st Division was in the area of the 10th French Army, consisting of three armoured divisions, three cavalry divisions and eight infantry divisions. These troops were, however, in various stages of disorganization and their ranks sadly depleted. It soon became apparent that this line was unlikely to hold, and the enemy had little difficulty in establishing bridgeheads over the Somme at Abbeville and St. Valery-sur-Somme.

On the evening of the 29th, A Coy. came under orders of 154th Infantry Brigade and moved to Millbosc, and B Coy. moved to Forêt D'Eu under 152nd Infantry Brigade. H.Q., C and D Coys. remained with Bn. H.Q. at Preuseville.

During the next few days much confused fighting took place and many minor tactical adjustments were made. Companies and isolated platoons of the Battalion were in action daily, and numerous casualties were suffered.

On the early morning of the 4th June the 51st Division made an attack on Abbeville, but failed to reach their objectives.

On the 7th, A Coy. were in action on the River Bresle; and by the evening of that day the whole Battalion (less A Coy.) had withdrawn to the St. Aignan area, where they immediately put the village in a state of all-round defence.

On the 9th June the Commanding Officer was informed that it was the intention of the 51st Division to fight a rearguard action to Le Havre and embark there.

June 1940

This move was to be covered by 154th Infantry Brigade, occupying the line Fécamp–Bulbec.

On the 10th June the Battalion (less A and C Coys., who were under 153rd Infantry Brigade) left La Chaussée, where they had moved on the night of the 8th/9th, for Ambrumesnil.

On the night of the 10th/11th June A and C Coys. moved on Cany, but found it occupied by the enemy and turned back. Meanwhile Bn. H.Q. and the other companies were in process of destroying all their surplus kit, in accordance with orders received from H.Q. 51st Division.

It now became clear to all that the French armies of the North were disintegrating rapidly and were offering little resistance to the German panzer divisions in their sweep towards Rouen, Le Havre and the lower Seine. It was obvious that the only alternatives for the British troops were early embarkation, destruction or surrender.

During the 11th June Divisional H.Q. moved into St. Valery, where it was hoped to find shipping for the Division to embark. All hope of reaching Le Havre had by this time been abandoned.

On the afternoon of the 11th orders were received for the Battalion to destroy all vehicles and machine-guns and then to march to St. Valery—timing their move so as to arrive at 0300 hrs. 12th June. On arrival the Commanding Officer was informed that no ships were available, or likely to become available, and he thereupon marched the Battalion out of the town under cover of a sunken road fringed with trees. Here the bulk of the Battalion was eventually assembled, B Coy., which had been allotted tasks in the dock area, joining later. In the early hours of the morning rumours of a possible surrender were received. At 0800 hrs. the French troops surrendered and at 0940 hrs. the Battalion—acting on orders received from H.Q. 51st Division—reluctantly conformed.

Thus this good Territorial Army battalion—together with the bulk of Scotland's famous Highland Division—went into captivity within five weeks of the commencement of active operations. They were swamped by events over which they had no control; but very soon a new 7th Bn. Royal Northumberland Fusiliers was to be formed in England. Their subsequent achievements worthily upheld the traditions of their comrades whose fighting careers ended under such tragic circumstances at St. Valery.

This ends the story of Dunkirk and the account of the activities of the five Royal Northumberland Fusiliers battalions which took part in the campaign.

The 2nd, 4th, 8th and 9th were soon to be reorganized to play their part in the Battle of Britain. The 7th—which had to be completely reformed owing to losing all its personnel at St. Valery—took longer.

The further activities of these battalions are related in subsequent chapters of this history.

(NOTE: Much of the 'background' of this section has been obtained from Mr. Winston Churchill's book *The Second World War*, Vol. II, pages 130–135, and the accompanying maps.)

CHAPTER 5

NORTH AFRICA

September 1939 to December 1941
1st Battalion

(*See Maps Nos. IV and V*)

PRIOR to the outbreak of war with Germany on the 3rd September 1939 the 1st Bn. Royal Northumberland Fusiliers were stationed at Cairo in Egypt. Tension had existed between Britain and Italy since the latter's unprovoked invasion of Abyssinia in 1935, but her probable attitude in the early days of the war was a matter for speculation. As events turned out she did not openly join her Axis partner until June 1940, when the fall of France gave Mussolini what he regarded as an opportunity for plunder too good to be missed. Sept. 1939–Feb. 1940

Before the war the 1st Battalion had made a careful reconnaissance of defensive positions at Mersa Matruh on Egypt's western frontier adjoining the Italian colony of Libya. As soon as hostilities with Germany commenced they left Cairo for this area, where—in company with other troops in the Western Desert—they spent the next few months in strengthening the frontier defences and making other preparations to meet Italian participation in the war.

At Mersa Matruh the Battalion was quartered in tented camps by companies in rear of their sectors—not the best conditions with the approach of winter. Contrary to popular belief the Western Desert can be quite cold and very wet in winter. There was much work digging and wiring, and hard training on innumerable exercises. Conditions were made somewhat irksome by frequent sandstorms and periodic heavy rains. There were, however, good facilities for bathing and sport; leave parties to Cairo were also organized. For a short period a number of Australian officers and N.C.Os. were attached to the Battalion to gain experience of Middle East conditions.

The Battalion state at the start of the war was as follows:

Commanding Officer . .	Lieut.-Colonel J. H. Hogshaw, M.C.
Second-in-Command . .	Major G. J. W. Gatehouse
Adjutant	Captain G. P. Hobbs
Quartermaster . . .	Lieut. O. C. Dipper, D.C.M.
Regimental Sergeant-Major .	R.S.M. C. Dalby
O.C. W Coy. . . .	Major R. F. Forbes-Watson
,, X ,, . . .	Major D. E. F. Waight, M.C.
,, Y ,, . . .	Major E. O. Martin
,, Z ,, . . .	Major E. H. Butterfield
,, H.Q. Coy. . . .	Major R. H. Yorke

March–June 1940

In early March the Battalion left the Western Desert for Moascar on the Suez Canal. Their farewell to the 2nd Bn. Scots Guards and the Welch Regiment, with whom they had been closely associated at Mersa Matruh, was lightened by finding themselves quartered near old friends—the Durham Light Infantry—in the new station. Here conditions were extremely good, with peace-time barracks and excellent amenities in the form of canteens and facilities for sport.

The period of rest and comfort at Moascar was short-lived and soon after the German attack in the west, the Battalion was rushed up to the Alexandria area to carry out anti-parachutist duties on aerodromes along the coast. This entailed being widely dispersed between Amyria, just south of Alexandria, and Daba, some hundred miles westwards. This role was not destined to last for long and a few days later when all companies had just settled down and perfected their plans to deal with surprise landings by unknown numbers of parachutists, orders were received to concentrate at Sidi Bishr. The Battalion had been selected to take part in an operation to occupy the island of Crete, in certain eventualities. Actually the operation never materialized as planned at that time, but preparations for it kept the Battalion fully occupied for some weeks. Lieut. Colbeck and the M.T. staff spent many weary hours in the Dockyard experimenting with loading vehicles as deck cargo on the cruisers which were to transport the Battalion.

On the 11th June 1940 Mussolini's Fascist government declared war on France and Britain. This news was received by the Battalion during a concert at Sidi Bishr given by Mrs. Barker and her concert party, who were to entertain the Battalion so often later in the war during periods of rest out of the desert. By this time General Sir Archibald Wavell's Middle East Headquarters at Cairo had assumed responsibility for any operations which might take place in the Middle East proper, in other parts of the African continent and the Mediterranean. Although during the winter of 1939/40 reinforcements—in the form of Australian, New Zealand and Indian divisions—had joined his command, the forces at his disposal were dangerously small for such a vast theatre of possible operations.

Soon after the Italian entry into the war Marshal Graziani, the Italian commander in North Africa, commenced preparations for the invasion of Egypt. These included the extension and improvement of the road and railway from Tripoli to the Libya-Egyptian frontier about Bardia and the concentration of a large army between there and Tobruk, together with vast supplies of munitions and stores. These preparations were carried out in a very ponderous and leisurely manner.

During the summer and autumn of 1940 officers and men became somewhat impatient of the inactivity prevailing in the Middle East; but they had not long to wait. Events were shaping which were to give the Battalion all the fighting it wanted for many months to come. For—in the autumn of 1940—General Wavell, who rightly judged the Italian troops to be of doubtful efficiency, commenced preparations for an offensive of his own, which resulted in one of the most audacious and brilliant campaigns in the history of war.

Just before the Italian advance into Egypt, W Coy. under Major R. F. Forbes-Watson moved up to join the 3rd Bn. Coldstream Guards which was part of a light covering force. Their plan was to withdraw in front of Marshal Graziani's army until

Army Form C.2128.

MESSAGE FORM

Serial No.

CALL AND INSTRUCTIONS		No. of Groups.	OFFICE DATE STAMP
	IN	GR.	
	OUT		

(ABOVE THIS LINE IS FOR SIGNALS USE ONLY.)

TO 9. RNF.

FROM General H O Curtis Pol Force

Originator's Number | Date | In Reply to Number

WELL DONE. If you had not held the STEENBECQUE ridge against tanks & inf for 48 hrs the Boches might have been in DUNKERQUE. The 9th have entered the traditions of the Fighting 5th.

H O Curtis Maj Gen

This message may be sent AS WRITTEN by any means.

If liable to be intercepted or fall into enemy hands, this message must be sent IN CIPHER.

Originator's Instructions Degree of Priority 25/5/40

Time of Origin

Signed

Signed

(BELOW THIS LINE IS FOR SIGNALS USE ONLY.)

T.H.I.

System In	Time In	Reader	Sender	System Out	Time Out	Reader	Sender	System Out	Time Out	Reader	Sender

T.O.R.

Forms C2128/13. Wt. 36168/1798. 1,000m. pads. 12/38. B.& S. Ltd. 51-5237.

8. Congratulatory message to 9th Battalion

June–Dec. 1940

the latter came up against the main defences round Mersa Matruh and Garawla. However, the Italian advances never got further into Egypt than Sidi Barrani. W Coy. took up intermediate positions on the escarpment above Sollum, astride Halfaya (Hellfire) Pass, from which many offensive patrols were carried out. Eventually the Italians made a further advance. It was a magnificent spectacle, rather like a large-scale advance in review order—lines of motor cycles, tanks and vast quantities of heavy lorries. They came in perfect straight lines offering wonderful targets for the machine-guns of W Coy. and for the Gunners. The covering force maintained contact for the next two or three days with the Italians halted on the Sidi Barrani line. Shortly after this W Coy. rejoined the Battalion at Garawla.

General Wavell's offensive at first only envisaged the destruction of the most easterly troops of Graziani's army. Later, owing to the remarkable initial successes, it was extended in scope and eventually led to the almost complete annihilation of the Italian forces in North Africa. Control of the operation was in the hands of General Sir Maitland Wilson, the executive commander being Major-General R. N. O'Connor.

By the autumn of 1940 the 1st Bn. Royal Northumberland Fusiliers were located at Naghamish, a few miles east of Mersa Matruh, and formed part of the 4th Indian Division, with whom they carried out innumerable exercises in the Desert. In August the Italian troops carried out a small advance to Sidi Barrani, which was destined to be the first objective in the offensive planned to commence in December.

The measures taken to ensure secrecy for the opening stages of this offensive were, to most participants, a novelty and resulted in some slight confusion, but this was infinitesimal when compared to the surprise from which the Italians never really recovered.

The rehearsal for the battle was carried out some fourteen days in advance as a normal exercise, though live ammunition was used. After this exercise a Divisional conference was held at which officers were told that various faults had occurred as a result of which a similar exercise would be held ten days later. Meanwhile the Divisional and Corps Commanders went on leave and were seen about frequently in Cairo, lesser persons being content to take a breather before the next 'exercise,' which came to be known as 'No. 2.' Normal leave continued, and in fact things seemed so quiet that Colonel Hogshaw despatched his Adjutant off on a somewhat overdue seven days' leave. Preparations for Exercise No. 2 took their leisurely course until forty-eight hours before its commencement, when Commanding Officers were let into the secret, paybooks were withdrawn (a measure which subsequently caused great confusion and was not repeated) and all secret documents were ordered to be left behind. This last order made the Colonel painfully aware of the absence of his Adjutant, but Division sternly forbade the latter's recall by telegram.

Thus it happened that the Battalion set off to meet the enemy with all the plans for the defence of Egypt in the 'office truck.' But as darkness began to fall at the end of the first day of the approach march the Adjutant, still in his shore-going kit, cast up and, discovering the enormity, despatched the provost sergeant back to Naghamish with the offending documents.

Dec. 1940

The Battalion state at this time was as follows:

Commanding Officer . .	Lieut.-Colonel J. H. Hogshaw, M.C.
Second-in-Command . .	Major E. O. Martin
Adjutant	Captain E. E. Williams
Quartermaster . . .	Lieut. O. C. Dipper, D.C.M.
Regimental Sergeant-Major .	R.S.M. J. Tulip
O.C. W Coy. . . .	Major R. F. Forbes-Watson
„ X „ . . .	Major R. H. Yorke
„ Y „ . . .	Captain R. F. B. Hensman
„ Z „ . . .	Captain H. Holmes

The initial deployment of the Battalion was as follows:

W Coy.	detached—with Arthurforce
X Coy. (less two platoons) .	with Bn. H.Q.
Y Coy.	with 11th (Indian) Infantry Brigade
Z Coy.	with 5th (Indian) Infantry Brigade
D Coy. 1st Cheshire Regt. .	with 16th (British) Infantry Brigade

Owing to a shortage of transport drivers X Coy. had to make good the deficiency and only mustered one fighting platoon. This was made good by the attachment to the Battalion of D Coy. 1st Cheshire Regiment.

The night before the attack went in, the Air Force kept up an all-night shuttle service over the Italian positions. Being short of bombs these were supplemented with empty bottles, and between the whining of the descending 'empties' and the detonation of the 'lives' the enemy had a most disturbed night and had only just about got off to sleep when the initial artillery bombardment opened on the most southerly enemy camp at Nibeiwa.

The advance of some 180 miles commenced on the morning of the 19th December. The columns were widely dispersed and elaborate precautions were taken to ensure surprise. Although at that time they possessed superiority in the air the Italians remained in complete ignorance and were taken unawares.

The attack on the most southerly enemy camp at Nibeiwa was carried out by the 11th (Indian) Infantry Brigade, with Y Coy. in support, on the morning of the 21st, and by 1000 hrs. all opposition had been overcome. The attack on the next position, at Tummars, by the 5th (Indian) Infantry Brigade with Z Coy. in support, was then launched. Progress here was much the same and by dusk all resistance was at an end. A somewhat half-hearted counter-attack was easily repulsed, mainly by fire from a platoon of Z Coy. Fusilier J. Barnes was awarded the Military Medal for his part in this action.

By evening on the following day Barrani had fallen. Here more resistance was encountered and D Coy. 1st Cheshire Regiment suffered some casualties among personnel and vehicles. The first phase of the offensive was now over: 40,000 Italians had been captured and many killed. At this stage W Coy., which had been operating in a detached role along the coast, rejoined the Battalion. This detached role consisted of being in support of a small force which was to carry out a feint attack on Maktila,

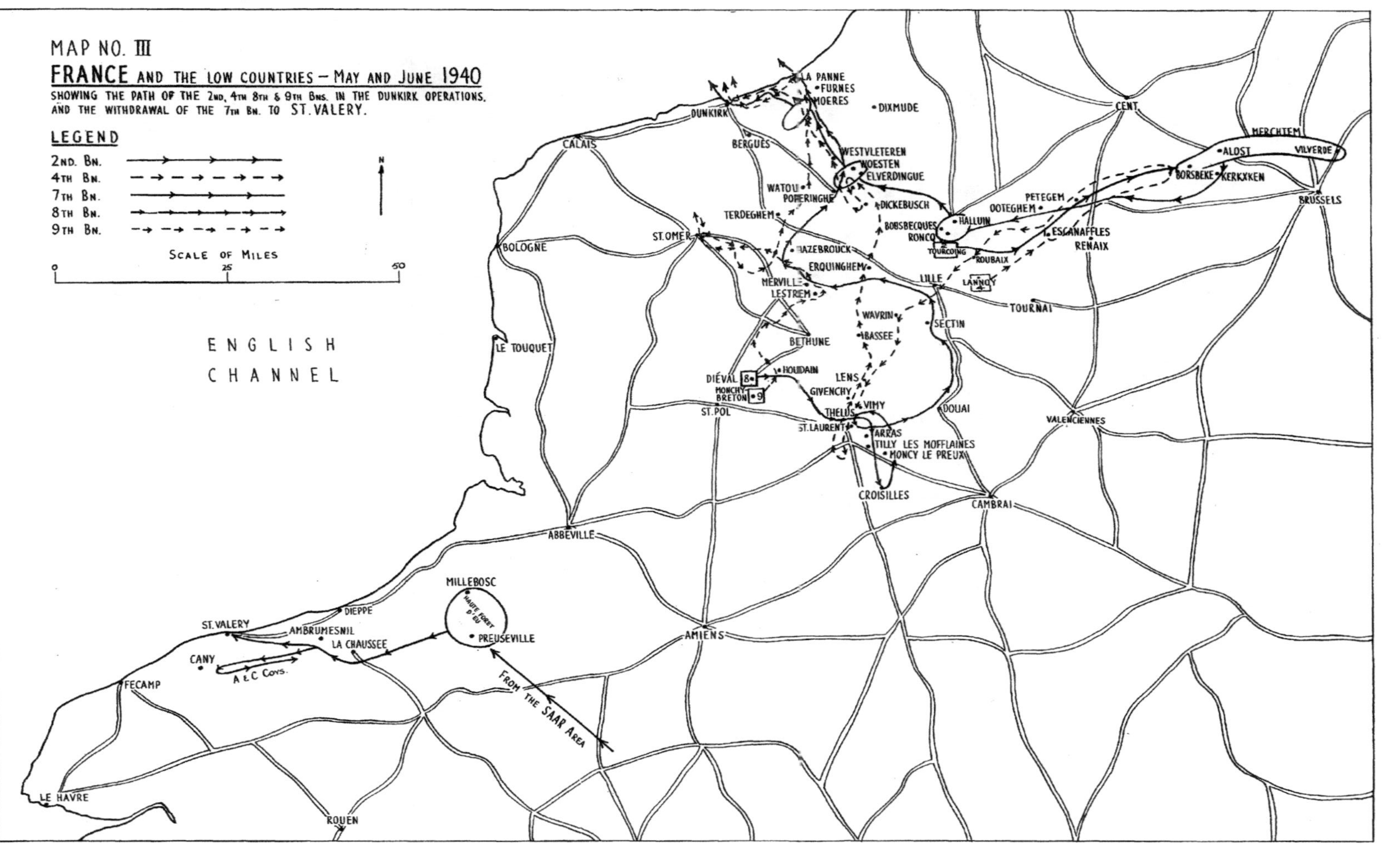
MAP NO. III
FRANCE AND THE LOW COUNTRIES – MAY AND JUNE 1940
SHOWING THE PATH OF THE 2ND, 4TH 8TH & 9TH BNS. IN THE DUNKIRK OPERATIONS, AND THE WITHDRAWAL OF THE 7TH BN. TO ST. VALERY.
LEGEND
2ND. BN.
4TH BN.
7TH BN.
8TH BN.
9TH BN.
N
SCALE OF MILES
0
25
50
ENGLISH CHANNEL
LA PANNE
FURNES
MOERES
DIXMUDE
DUNKIRK
CALAIS
BERGUES
WESTVLETEREN
WOESTEN
ELVERDINGUE
WATOU
POPERINGHE
DICKEBUSCH
TERDEGHEM
ST. OMER
BOLOGNE
HAZEBROUCK
ERQUINGHEM
MERVILLE
LESTREM
BOBSBECQUES
RONCQ
TOURCOING
HALLUIN
ROUBAIX
LILLE
LANNOY
TOURNAI
CENT.
MERCHTEM
ALOST
VILVERDE
BORSBEKE
KERKXKEN
BRUSSELS
PETEGEM
OOTEGHEM
ESCANAFFLES
RENAIX
WAVRIN
BASSEE
SECTIN
BETHUNE
LE TOUQUET
DIÉVAL
8
MONCHY BRETON
9
HOUDAIN
LENS
GIVENCHY
VIMY
THELUS
ST. POL
ST. LAURENT
ARRAS
TILLY LES MOFFLAINES
MONCY LE PREUX
DOUAI
VALENCIENNES
CROISILLES
CAMBRAI
ABBEVILLE
MILLEBOSC
HAUTE FORET D'EU
PREUSEVILLE
DIEPPE
ST. VALERY
AMBRUMESNIL
LA CHAUSSEE
AMIENS
CANY
A & C COYS.
FECAMP
FROM THE SAAR AREA
LE HAVRE
ROUEN

the most easterly Italian camp. The enemy, however, withdrew rapidly westwards before contact was made. Dec. 1940–Feb. 1941

The next movement was the investment of Bardia. For this and subsequent operations the Battalion came under command of 6th Australian Division. The Battalion was not fully committed to defensive positions round the perimeter of the Fortress until after Christmas and though conditions were by no means ideal every effort was made to observe the occasion in the traditional manner. Y Coy. was camped in a small wadi at the top of Halfaya Pass, while Bn. H.Q. and the remainder of the Battalion made themselves comfortable in the broken ground at the foot of the pass.

The assault on Bardia began on the 2nd January 1941. Y Coy. supported the leading Australian Brigade while Z Coy. initially took part in a diversionary attack on a strong point to the east of the actual break in and then moved into the fortress in support of their parent Australian Brigade. The operation was completed in three days, two of stiff fighting and one of mopping up. The Battalion casualties were fortunately not heavy, though W Coy. had three men killed. P.S.M. Bell and Fus. Ryles (both of W Coy.) were awarded the Military Medal, the latter continuing to keep his gun in action after being wounded twice. The total bag of prisoners was about 45,000.

No sooner had Bardia fallen than the Battalion moved on for a similar operation against Tobruk. The attack was launched on the 21st January and, as in the case of Bardia, was completed in two days. The Battalion had no casualties and when fighting had finished took the opportunity of adding some excellent Italian lorries to their now much depleted transport. It is of interest to note that during the investment stage of the operation all companies operated on ground which they were to fight over again during the siege and breakout of Tobruk, thus gaining invaluable knowledge.

The next move was to Derna, where the problem was a somewhat different one, as the enemy defences were less well-prepared and more ill-defined. The country was, however, intersected by a number of deep wadis, which made it necessary to abandon the use of transport and resort to manhandling. The attack on Derna was in consequence more methodical than the earlier operations, and this resulted in most of the Italian garrison escaping.

This operation was followed by the pursuit of the now fast retreating Italians to the west. The Battalion by-passed Benghazi and eventually halted at Soluch to the west. A week of bad weather had now set in which considerably added to the difficulties of movement. Much time had to be spent retrieving, and repairing, vehicles which became bogged in the desert mud. This operation resulted in driving the remaining Italian troops into the arms of British armoured columns which had made a wide detour to the coast west of Benghazi to cut them off. A further 16,000 prisoners were captured, including General Bergonzoli and several other Italian commanders of high rank. Benghazi fell on the 5th February. Since December 133,000 Italian prisoners and 1,300 guns had been captured.

About this time the Commanding Officer, Lieut.-Colonel J. H. Hogshaw, left the Battalion on promotion, being succeeded by Lieut.-Colonel E. O. Martin.

After a few days at Soluch the Battalion moved into the newly built Duke of Aosta Barracks in Benghazi, where they were given the task of guarding some 17,000 Italian prisoners and arranging for their move back to base P.O.W. camps. Soon

Feb.–April 1941

after arrival Y Coy. (Captain R. F. B. Hensman) departed for El Agheila, where the most westerly British troops were located, to come under command of the Support Group of the 2nd Armoured Division. At this stage it will be convenient to leave the Battalion to give a brief account of the general situation in the Mediterranean and in Africa, followed by the activities of the detached Y Coy.

While these events were going on along the North African coast the Italian Empire in other parts of the continent was being liquidated. On the 20th January 1941 the Emperor Haile Selassie re-entered Abyssinia and on the same day British forces invaded the Italian colony of Eritrea; but these operations consumed large numbers of troops and equipment and left General Wavell's forces in North Africa perilously weak. Meanwhile reports were accumulating of German preparations for a Balkan campaign. By early March these apprehensions amounted to almost certainty and General Wavell—on instructions received from the Government—was in process of still further weakening his Desert Army by the despatch of a considerable force to Greece.

By this time Germany had also decided to take a hand in the North African campaign. Information to this effect had already reached General Wavell, who appreciated—wrongly as it turned out—that the German troops would not be ready for operations until May. Their intervention actually commenced on the 31st March and with it the entry on the African scene of one of the most remarkable and colourful figures of the war—Erwin Rommel.

On arrival in the forward area, Y Coy. was placed under command of the Tower Hamlet Rifles, the only infantry unit apart from a small French contingent now left in the Support Group. Their task was to hold a defensive position on a ridge astride the Tripoli–Benghazi road in the area of the village of Mersa Brega. Here the road runs parallel to and some two miles from the coast. The village of Mersa Brega itself lies at the northern end of the ridge, while the ground to the south of the road west of the ridge is marshy. Some 2,000 yards forward of the position was a small rocky hill, known as Cemetery Hill, which gave good observation over all forward posts on the position itself. The Company was of necessity deployed on a broad front and more emphasis was placed on the ground to the south of the road, which was perfect machine-gun country, than on the more undulating ground nearer the coast.

The German advance began on the 1st April and first news of it was brought by a patrol of the K.D.Gs. Shortly after this, at about 0900 hrs., the outpost company on Cemetery Hill, which was supported by No. 12 Platoon (Lieut. Wells) less one section, saw enemy armour advancing and were shelled. After a short time this force withdrew to the main position according to plan. Shortly after this the main position was heavily dive-bombed and machine-gunned and one of the Coy. H.Q. 30-cwt. trucks was put out of action. From then on, enemy pressure increased and at 1600 hrs., after another air attack, small groups of enemy were seen infiltrating along the road and along the coast among the sand-dunes. These were engaged at ranges of about 1,600 yards. The enemy continued to close, especially on the right flank, where the broken ground near the coast gave good cover. Cpl. Harrison's section (No. 12 Platoon) were soon heavily engaged, and although they succeeded in halting the enemy infantry for a time, they were unable to deal with the tanks which appeared in support. After a chapter of accidents, including running out of ammunition, they were eventually overrun. Cpl. Harrison was mortally wounded but spent the last minutes of his life directing the burial of his locks and the spare parts of his guns in the sand.* April 1941

The Mersa Brega position was evacuated at last light and the force moved back to an intermediate position some 10 miles back, once again on a ridge astride the Tripoli road. The enemy did not follow up quickly, and by the morning of the 2nd April, the Company was again deployed in support of the motor companies of the Tower Hamlets. The day was quiet and warm and the only incident was an air attack in the evening, which caused some casualties in the No. 12 Platoon area just north of the road. The enemy gained contact early on the 3rd April and by midday the situation had become unpleasant. At this stage, too, the water situation had become acute and Captain Neilson was sent back to Agedabia with some of Coy. H.Q. and No. 11 Platoon (Sgt. Lynch) to reconnoitre the next position and fill all available water containers. Nos. 10 and 12 Platoons again withdrew with their parent companies, but unfortunately the former (Lieut. Maclennan) were attacked by tanks at close range while negotiating a marsh and all but a few individuals were either killed or captured.

The next position on the high ground north of Agedabia was not destined to be held for long. The enemy followed up quickly and No. 12 Platoon, who were responsible for the left flank, had hardly moved into position before armoured cars were seen advancing south of them. The order to abandon their position never reached Coy. H.Q. and the first intimation they received was the general withdrawal of all other units at speed. All platoons became dispersed and it was only by luck that it was discovered that Antelat was the next goal. By evening the Company had concentrated in this area, and it was not till then that No. 10 Platoon's fate was known. On arrival at Antelat, Cpl. Laverick (No. 12 Platoon), who had been severely wounded at the intermediate position but could not be evacuated, died and was buried by his Platoon.

On the 4th April the force continued its withdrawal northwards along the edge of the escarpment. At Scaledeima, a halt was called and the Company was ordered to come under command of 2nd Armoured Brigade. Unfortunately the map reference of the H.Q. of that formation was incorrect, and after searching for an hour without success, and having no wireless to check the instructions, the Company moved northwards again and caught up with the Support Group towards dusk.

This, for the time being, ended the Company's contact with the enemy, and the next two days (4th and 5th April) were spent in movement eastwards, attempting to locate and rejoin the rest of the Battalion. They eventually joined up at El Abiar and were immediately deployed for action in the wooded heights above Barce.

It will now be appropriate to return to the main body of the Battalion, located in and around Benghazi. As transport was a major problem, Italian diesel lorries were used as far as possible and some Italian drivers co-opted. Our own unit transport (mainly Morris 15-cwt. trucks), the shortage of which had necessitated the greater

* These were found in 1943 when British troops were again in occupation of the area and one of them is now in the Regimental Museum.

April 1941

part of X Coy. being left out of the Sidi Barrani operations, had since been virtually unreplenished, all eyes in Egypt being at this time focussed on Greece. The most serviceable transport was handed over to Y Coy. for their mobile role with the 2nd Armoured Division. Lack of transport and the prisoners precluded any training other than N.C.Os.' cadre courses.

Less than a week before Rommel struck, the Battalion despatched the last of its prisoners to Barce, where a transit camp had now been established. Colonel Martin immediately moved the Battalion out of Benghazi to an area in which training could be carried out, a few miles to the south. At the same time, as a result of a visit to H.Q. Cyrenaica Command, under whose direct command the Battalion came, it transpired that, in the event of a strong counter-offensive necessitating the withdrawal of 2nd Armoured Division from the Agedabia area, the Battalion was to come under command of the 9th Australian Division. Its role was to garrison Cyrenaica and it had been given until the end of April to equip and train in readiness for the expected offensive in May. Benghazi was not to be defended, but its harbour installations and airfields were to be demolished, and the Battalion was to find escorts to assist H.Q. Benghazi Sub-Area and its demolition parties to get away afterwards.

It had been decided that, if it became necessary, the Australians would hold the line of the escarpment from Barce to Er Regima, a line some twenty-five miles in length and running approximately along the line of most probable enemy advance. They were but two brigades strong, the third still being in the Tobruk area, on its way west. In the event of 2nd Armoured Division withdrawing there appeared to be every likelihood of the 9th Australian Division's positions being turned or by-passed. After some discussion it was decided that the Battalion should strengthen the left flank by taking up positions from Er Regima eastwards, covering a very probable line of enemy advance. For this independent role they were to be allotted an Australian anti-tank company.

Very soon there was disquieting news of the 2nd Armoured Division. The extent of their defeat was uncertain, but rumour was rife, and spread by stragglers in vehicles who passed rapidly through Benghazi northwards.

One disadvantage of moving out of Benghazi was that the Battalion was no longer in touch by telephone with the Sub-Area H.Q. (unit wireless was not envisaged at this time). Information had to come, therefore, from the front and this was unreliable.

Meanwhile elements of 2nd Armoured Division had begun to come through El Abiar, and early the next morning Y Coy., now at half strength, rejoined. Earlier X and Z Coys. had rejoined, so the Battalion was together once again.

The 9th Australian Division now withdrew to the next escarpment immediately east of Barce, the Battalion acting as rearguard during this move.

On arrival at Barce the whole Battalion was placed under command of 20th Australian Infantry Brigade and took up positions overlooking the town. That evening the enemy attacked rather half-heartedly. Some machine-gun platoons, and in particular Z Coy., opened fire and the attack was beaten off. Though the Battalion did not know it at the time, the German Afrika Korps was by-passing them across the base of the Cyrenaican peninsular—as the 7th Armoured Division had done in reverse two months earlier. Once this was realized by higher authority a general withdrawal was ordered to positions about 150 miles eastwards, which a year later came to be better known as the 'Knightsbridge' area. April 1941

The withdrawal continued, the Battalion still doing rearguard. Early next morning they halted to refuel and feed a few miles west of Derna on the coastal plain. On checking up, several vehicles, including all the reserve of ammunition, were found to be missing. Weeks later the occupants were reported captured.

In Derna a traffic jam occurred that would have warmed the heart of any hostile airman, but fortunately the Luftwaffe did not appear. The congestion was caused by German armoured cars which had reached the road to the east. However, some British artillery units restored the situation and the withdrawal continued.

By that evening the Division was in position along a low escarpment in the Knightsbridge area. The Battalion, which had been finding rearguard throughout the withdrawal, was told to rest, and accordingly withdrew to a secluded wadi and prepared for a good night's sleep—the first for nearly a week. During the night a great deal of transport was heard moving eastwards and the Commanding Officer sent an officer to investigate. This officer returned to report that the position had been evacuated. The Battalion was immediately roused and moved off, again doing rearguard, but this time solely by reason of having been forgotten. Early the next morning they found an Australian infantry brigade in position astride the road about 20 miles west of Tobruk. They joined it and took up positions in support. X Coy., however, was detached to join the other brigade in Tobruk and took up positions on the western perimeter, from which subsequently they were largely instrumental in repulsing a determined enemy attack. Had this been successful the Fortress might well have fallen before the garrison had had time to organize its defences.

After a mild artillery duel and some air straffing the remainder of the Battalion withdrew into Tobruk, on the night of the 9th/10th April 1941, where it was destined to remain for eight long months.

The state of the Battalion at this time was as follows:

Commanding Officer	Lieut.-Colonel E. O. Martin
Second-in-Command	Major R. F. Forbes-Watson
Adjutant	Captain E. E. Williams
Quartermaster	Lieut. O. C. Dipper, D.C.M.
Regimental Sergeant-Major	R.S.M. J. Tulip
O.C. W Coy.	Captain H. Holmes
" X "	Major R. H. Yorke
" Y "	Captain R. F. B. Hensman
" Z "	Captain J. J. B. Jackman

Meanwhile Rommel, who had commenced this operation as a reconnaissance in force with only modest objectives, came to a quick decision. He had met with unexpected initial success and resolved to convert the operation into a full-scale offensive. Strategically conditions were favourable, as by this time some 60,000 men, with armoured units, had been detached from General Wavell's forces in North Africa and sent to Greece—which was invaded by the Germans on the 6th April. The British forces in North Africa were hustled eastwards, confusion being intensified by the

April 1941

chance capture by a German patrol of Lieut.-General P. Neame (who had recently taken command in the Western Desert) and Lieut.-General Sir Richard N. O'Connor (who in view of his local knowledge had been sent forward to assist General Neame). Benghazi fell on the 3rd April and Sollum on the 28th, the British forces finally making a stand along the Egyptian frontier. General Wavell had made the decision to hold Tobruk as an advanced strong-point on the flank of the advancing enemy columns, and in the seven and a half months' defence of that place the 1st Bn. Royal Northumberland Fusiliers were to play a leading part. Communications to the garrison were, of course, entirely by sea.

To add further to General Wavell's difficulties a revolt had broken out in Iraq on the 3rd April, and a force from Palestine had to be sent to Baghdad to protect British interests.

The garrison of Tobruk consisted of the 9th Australian Division, a Brigade Group of the 7th Australian Division, a small armoured force and sundry miscellaneous units—all under command of General Morshead. The 1st Bn. Royal Northumberland Fusiliers were attached to the 9th Australian Division.

The first few days were full of intense activity, the defenders making desperate efforts to organize a properly co-ordinated defence before the enemy could launch a strong attack. Although they probed the defences the enemy had so far outrun their communications as to be unable to mount any considerable offensive. Z Coy. had successfully engaged enemy advancing in vehicles and A.F.Vs. on the 10th April. This was complicated by a thick heat haze.

The Italians had fortified an area round the small town and fine natural harbour, which extended some 20 miles wide and 10 miles deep. The perimeter was surrounded by an anti-tank ditch and barbed wire. Many concrete emplacements had been built for the forward troops, but, though these afforded ample space below ground, they did not permit of all personnel using their weapons at one time, a defect which had largely contributed to its capture by a greatly inferior force three months earlier. Fire positions in the F.D.Ls. therefore had to be extended and defence in depth organized, with minefields within the perimeter, before the Fortress could be efficiently defended.

The defences were divided into three sectors, west, centre and east. 9th Australian Divisional H.Q. was located in caves in the escarpment below Fort Solaro. One infantry brigade was retained in Divisional reserve, usually located in the area of Fort Airente. Brigade positions were held in as great a depth as the ground to be covered allowed, but the chief depth was afforded by the machine-guns. The machine-gun plan was made on a Divisional basis and, though companies were occasionally placed under command of brigades or battalions for a specific operation, such as a counter-attack or other offensive operation, they were normally in support and not under command of the brigades in whose area they were located. The area to be covered did not permit of any machine-guns being held in reserve; but to afford a degree of rest companies relieved one another from time to time and platoon positions were often relieved within companies. Initially Bn. H.Q. was located near Fort Pilastrino; but this becoming rather an over-populated area, and receiving marked attention from dive-bombers and artillery, they moved back behind the next escarpment, nearer to Divisional H.Q.

In the air the Luftwaffe had almost complete air superiority throughout. An R.A.F. fighter squadron was present in the early days; but suffered such severe casualties that the few remaining planes and personnel were evacuated. A tactical reconnaissance squadron continued until all its planes became unserviceable, when its remaining personnel were also evacuated. The Royal Navy made a gallant attempt to maintain a footing in the harbour, but without air cover ships were quickly sunk, and the garrison had to be maintained thereafter solely by destroyers entering and leaving the harbour the same night.

April 1941

Water was severely rationed in the early days, but as arrangements matured for distilling sea water this situation was soon improved though never entirely removed, the shortage being most apparent during the hot summer months. Food, though never really short, was far from plentiful and was very monotonous. There was practically no fresh food during the eight months' siege, and meals were made up of biscuits, bully beef, bacon or cheese with an occasional tin of stew as a luxury. To make up for the lack of fresh vegetables all ranks had to take ascorbutic acid tablets—Vitamin C. The health of the garrison remained remarkably good, though there was some dysentery, particularly amongst the forward troops, and jaundice became rather common, but usually in a mild form.

Everyone lived in dugouts, skilfully camouflaged against air attacks which were all too frequent (three or four a day during the worst period). These were mostly Stuka dive-bombing raids of anything from 20 to 100 aircraft. They were usually directed against the harbour and town, which suffered heavily, as did the hospital which was on the outskirts. If any positions were spotted by aircraft, they could be certain of receiving a severe shelling or a bombing raid. Each morning, therefore, after ration parties had been up in the night, casualties and sick evacuated or reliefs completed, the troops would recamouflage their positions, smoothing over the sand on the tracks made by walking troops (these show up very clearly in air photographs, like chalk lines on a blackboard), and they would spread bits of scrub and camel thorn round and over the dugouts.

Recreation was a serious problem, bathing being the only readily attainable form. The Commanding Officer started a rest camp near the sea where troops out of the line could sleep as long as they liked, and swim and lie in the sun as often as Stukas would let them. Troops in forward positions had a very different life. Reading material was desperately short, and they had to lie in their dugouts, which were usually roofed with corrugated iron covered with sand, during the hours of daylight. They were tormented by flies, against which there was no protection: mosquito nets were not issued and such things as flit-guns and fly-whisks were not available. The hot sun beating down on the metal-roofed dugouts produced an effect like an oven inside, and this together with the flies made life almost intolerable and caused a great strain on the men. A few succumbed to the 'desert madness' or *cafard*, one was found trying to shoot flies with a revolver, but the remarkably high morale and good discipline throughout the Battalion made such cases rare.

During the first few days of the siege the enemy made several determined but small-scale attacks which were easily repulsed. In its turn the garrison made several raids in strength and captured a good number of prisoners; but as the enemy positions

April–May 1941

became better organized these became too costly and, after the first month, were discontinued. Thereafter active patrolling, at which the Australians became most adept, not only kept the enemy always on the alert but also gave valuable information of his intentions. To this machine-gun platoons added frequent harassing shoots, both by night and in the early dawn.

Early in May the Germans launched their first full-scale attack on the southern sector. Breaches were made in the perimeter astride the El Adem road and some enemy tanks penetrated almost to the first escarpment, but the Australians held their ground and, after some fierce fighting and with good artillery support, managed to close the gaps. By that time the enemy had had enough and after some further fierce hand-to-hand engagements they withdrew, leaving many dead and wounded and some burnt-out tanks behind them. The situation was completely restored by nightfall.

Some weeks later they made another attempt to capture the Fortress and this time gained some success. An evening attack was launched on the prominent feature Ras El Medauuar, which overlooked a large portion of the west and central sectors. That night the situation was confused and next day, to add to the fog of war, a sandstorm blew up. By midday the Germans were believed to have captured the hill and it was not known what infantry were still opposing them. There was a danger of a break-through. It was at this stage that Major Yorke (X Coy.), accompanied by an Australian infantry officer, went forward from one of his platoon positions to contact some troops seen to be digging about 500 yards east of the hill. These proved to be Germans and Major Yorke was captured (X Coy. being taken over by Captain Colbeck); but our troops then awoke to the fact that the enemy was virtually unopposed and reinforcements were brought up to plug the gap. Counter-attacks were launched on that and following days; but, though the enemy positions were to a certain extent squeezed out, the defenders were never able to recapture Ras El Medauuar, which in course of time the enemy fortified so strongly that this sector became the 'hot' one, and conditions rather akin to the trench warfare of the First World War. The Italians, however, preferred to keep their distance, and in sectors opposed by them it was usually possible to move about with reasonable freedom.

Life in Tobruk now became one of routine: delivery of rations to platoons by night, harassing shoots and routine reliefs being the main activity. The Colonel, constantly visiting the platoons in the forward areas, set a fine example to all commanders and kept the morale of the men at a high level. Our relations with the Australians were excellent, particularly at the lower levels, where our men soon came to identify themselves wholeheartedly with the 'Diggers.' In fact the Geordie (for they were still at this time 95 per cent. so) had much in common with the Australian soldier, both possessing an independence of character and rugged disposition which make them particularly intolerant of 'red tape.'

Before long, however, minds were kept occupied by a system of major reliefs and reinforcements which took place. The Polish Brigade, commanded by General Kupanski, was the first to arrive. These fine troops had but one ambition, namely to kill Germans. Some coolness arose when they found they were facing Italians, and they announced that they were not at war with Italy; but they were eventually persuaded to put in some practice on Italians! X Coy. was initially in support of this brigade, and despite the language difficulty, excellent liaison was maintained. May–Nov. 1941

Towards the end of June General Sir Claude Auchinleck had succeeded General Sir Archibald Wavell as Commander-in-Chief, Middle East.

By mid-October most of the Australians in Tobruk had been relieved by the 70th British Division, the 1st Bn. Royal Northumberland Fusiliers joining the new formation.

The state of the Battalion was now as follows:

Commanding Officer	Lieut.-Colonel E. O. Martin
Second-in-Command	Major R. F. Forbes-Watson
Adjutant	Captain H. Holmes
Quartermaster	Captain O. C. Dipper, D.C.M.
Regimental Sergeant-Major	R.S.M. J. Tulip
O.C. W Coy.	Major C. C. G. Milward
" X "	Major E. E. Williams
" Y "	Captain R. F. B. Hensman
" Z "	Captain J. J. B. Jackman

In the autumn of 1941 plans were being made to take the offensive, aimed at the destruction of the forward troops of Rommel's German–Italian Army and the occupation of a substantial part of North Africa. The advance of the main British forces from the Egyptian frontier was to be accompanied by offensive operations by the Tobruk garrison, with the object of containing enemy forces and seizing tactical features which would help the main army in its westward movement. As the latter came abreast of Tobruk the two forces were to join up.

The Battalion carried out an intense programme of harassing shoots which formed part of the plan for the break-out, except Z Coy., who did special training, as they were cast for a leading role and destined to play a distinguished part. The plan for the Battalion was as follows:

One platoon of Y Coy. (under Lieut. MacManners, later Adjutant) was to go forward to help consolidate an enemy position to the east after it had been captured. The remainder of Y Coy. and W and X Coys. were in a holding role on the perimeter.

Z Coy. (Captain J. J. B. Jackman) was to be under command of the 32nd Army Tank Brigade, together with one squadron of the King's Dragoon Guards, a battery of anti-tank guns and the 1st Bn. Essex Regiment. The task of this force was the capture of an important feature on the El Adem escarpment known as Ed-Duda—about eight miles south of Tobruk.

The first thrust forward was made on the 19th November 1941, and the attack on the first three objectives was successful. In the evening Z Coy. was called upon to assist in the consolidation of the most southerly of these, which had been captured by the Black Watch, who suffered severe casualties. Later one platoon was sent to help defend another captured locality. The enemy reacted by shelling the positions heavily.

Next morning the Company, less Nos. 13 and 15 Platoons who were still required in the defence of previously captured positions, supported an attack by the 1st Bn.

Nov. 1941

York and Lancaster Regiment and a squadron of tanks against a further enemy defended locality which flanked the approach to Ed-Duda, the final goal of the break-out forces. This position was held in approximately battalion strength and was supported by many anti-tank guns and machine-guns, the whole area being surrounded by wire and mines. The attack met with heavy opposition and was halted. Captain J. J. B. Jackman, on seeing this, made a quick and bold decision. He led No. 14 Platoon, under 2/Lieut. F. Ward, off to the south and then swung away in a wide circle and came in on the enemy's right flank. Although they had to go through some heavy shell-fire, they got on to the objective and took some prisoners. The drill for getting into action off vehicles had been perfected and No. 14 Platoon were very soon firing hard from the captured positions while their vehicles were being driven away to safety.

The enemy counter-attacked shortly afterwards: preceded by heavy shelling they drove up in lorries protected by light tanks. The shelling forced the infantry off the positions, as they were not yet dug in; but one machine-gun section of No. 14 Platoon was well placed to deal with the attack, which they proceeded to do in no uncertain fashion. After firing practically all their ammunition and suffering considerable damage from shells and small-arms fire, the section by their stubborn resistance beat off the attack. For his personal gallantry and leadership, Sgt. D. McKay, the Section Commander, was awarded the D.C.M.

This battle is a remarkable tribute to the efficacy of machine-guns boldly and skilfully handled by highly trained men.

On the conclusion of this engagement Z Coy. reverted to command of the 32nd Army Tank Brigade from whom they had been temporarily detached.

These preliminary operations resulted in the formation of a thin wedge-shaped penetration into the enemy position. X and Y Coys. were brought forward to form the framework of the defence of this salient. Plans were now made for the capture of the final objective—Ed-Duda; but owing to the enemy's stubborn resistance the attack was not carried out until the 26th November.

The advance on Ed-Duda was led by two regiments of tanks, Z Coy. following in rear in open formation. The tanks were held up by very heavy shelling and mortar fire; but Captain Jackman, repeating his previous tactics, led the Company forward at high speed, regardless of enemy fire. On reaching a prearranged line each platoon moved off to its area and came into action, most of the vehicles withdrawing under cover.

Company Sergeant-Major G. Hughes particularly distinguished himself at this time. His task, rehearsed many times before the Company left Tobruk, was to follow Captain Jackman closely in his vehicle, and when the former gave the signal, C.S.M. Hughes was to drive to a high point on the Ed-Duda feature, where he was to get out of his vehicle and wave a large flag to tell the platoons to break formation and drive straight to their positions. It must be remembered that machine-gun companies had no wireless in those days. As platoons came up on to Ed-Duda, C.S.M. Hughes was to signal each one in turn and then point with his flag roughly towards the area where they were to go into action. C.S.M. Hughes carried out this duty to the letter, and in a miraculous way he escaped injury despite extremely heavy shelling over the area by 210-mm. guns. There is no doubt that the sight of this jovial figure calmly waving his flag amid the shell-bursts put great heart into the Company. Nov. 1941

From their positions, all platoons had excellent shooting on to Trigh Capuzzo, which was the enemy's main supply line. Captain Jackman drove round the positions in his vehicle co-ordinating the defence and encouraging his men. For a considerable time he bore a charmed life, but was eventually killed at one of the gun positions. His last moments are best described in the words of No. 4612503, Fus. R. J. Dishman, one of the gun numbers:

> '. . . Captain Jackman came and lay down on the gun line, and began to observe through his binoculars. He then gave us the order to fire on a truck and cyclist. "Give them a burst," he said, and just as these words were said a mortar bomb dropped just in front of our left-hand gun, wounding three and killing Captain Jackman and Corporal Gare instantly. . . .'

For his decisive and gallant part in this action Captain Jackman was given a posthumous award of the Victoria Cross. The citation read as follows:

> *Lieutenant (temporary Captain) James Joseph Bernart Jackman* (69102), The Royal Northumberland Fusiliers (Dunlaoghaire, Co. Dublin).
>
> 'On 25th November, 1941, at Ed Duda, South East of Tobruk Captain Jackman showed outstanding gallantry and devotion to duty above all praise when he was in command of a Machine Gun Company of The Royal Northumberland Fusiliers in the Tank attack on the Ed Duda ridge. His magnificent bearing was contributory in a large measure to the success of a most difficult and hard fought action. As the tanks reached the crest of the rise they were met by extremely intense fire from a larger number of guns of all descriptions: the fire was so heavy that it was doubtful for a moment whether the Brigade could maintain its hold on the position.
>
> 'The tanks having slowed to "hull-down" positions, settled to beat down the enemy fire, during which time Captain Jackman rapidly pushed up the ridge leading his Machine Gun trucks and saw at once that Anti-Tank guns were firing at the flank of the tanks, as well as the rows of batteries which the tanks were engaging on their front.
>
> 'He immediately started to get his guns into action as calmly as though he were on manœuvres, and so secured the right flank. Then standing up in front of his truck, with calm determination he led his trucks across the front between the tanks and the guns—there was no other road—to get them into action on the left flank.
>
> 'Most of the tank commanders saw him, and his exemplary devotion to duty regardless of danger not only inspired his own men, but clinched the determination of the tank crews never to relinquish the position which they had gained.
>
> 'Throughout he coolly directed the guns to their positions and indicated targets to them and at that time seemed to bear a charmed life, but later he was killed while still inspiring everyone with the greatest confidence by his bearing.'

There can be no instance of a more merited award of the Victoria Cross than that to this courageous officer of the Fighting Fifth.

Nov.– Dec. 1941

By dawn the following morning a battalion of the Essex Regiment and a battery of anti-tank guns had arrived on, and consolidated, the Ed-Duda feature. After being heavily and almost continuously shelled for three days the position was attacked on the 29th November by enemy tanks, followed by infantry. The Essex Regiment suffered heavily and Lieut. Langley's platoon of Z Coy. was overrun and practically wiped out. Lieut. Ward's platoon also suffered heavily, and although they were overrun, Sgt. McKay's section were not mopped up and managed to hold out. British tanks counter-attacked towards evening, but without success. Much confused fighting took place on and around the position. An Australian infantry battalion was, however, moved forward at dusk to assist in the defence. That night the main British forces coming from the east began to influence the Tobruk battle and the enemy tanks withdrew. The Australian battalion then drove out the enemy infantry and by dawn the position had been satisfactorily stabilized.

Shortly after this Z Coy., who had lost one and a half platoons in this engagement, were relieved by W Coy. and withdrew to Tobruk for a short rest. Later they assisted a battalion of the Durham Light Infantry to capture El Adem, but no outstanding incidents occurred during this operation.

Meanwhile the rest of the Battalion had been in a holding role. They did useful and essential work, but were overshadowed by the brilliant and spectacular exploits of Z Coy. Officers and men of this company were awarded the following decorations:

Victoria Cross	Captain J. J. B. Jackman
Military Cross	Captain D. L. Lloyd Lieut. F. Ward
Distinguished Conduct Medal	C.S.M. G. Hughes Sgt. D. McKay Cpl. J. McCloy
Military Medal	Cpl. R. Myers Cpl. S. Fram L/Cpl. F. Lloyd Fus. J. Kay Fus. F. Peary Fus. T. E. Preston

The award of so many decorations to the personnel of one sub-unit, for operations lasting only a few days, must be almost unique. That the Company carried out this operation so successfully was largely due to the intense and meticulous training and vehicle drill which the Commanding Officer and the Company Commander had insisted on the Company undertaking for three weeks before the break-out.

By the 3rd December 1941 Tobruk had been relieved, and on the 15th December 1941 the 1st Bn. Royal Northumberland Fusiliers moved to Cairo. It is believed that the Battalion had had a longer continuous spell in the Desert than any other unit. They had left Alexandria in September 1940 and did not return until December 1941 —a period of fifteen months of living under abnormal conditions, during which they had, for most of the time, been in close contact with the enemy.

CHAPTER 6

THE HOME FRONT

The Battle of Britain—June 1940 to August 1943
2nd, 4th, 7th, 8th and 9th Battalions

I. GENERAL

THIS chapter deals with the activities of the five Field Force Battalions of the Regiment who fought with the B.E.F. in the Low Countries and France in 1939–40. It covers the period in the United Kingdom commencing with the conclusion of the Dunkirk campaign and ending in August 1943—the date of the Quebec Conference. It was at this conference that the Allied leaders finally decided in principle on the invasion of North-West Europe. It was, therefore, the end of a phase for all troops quartered at home. The anti-invasion role was no longer the primary one, and preparation for the Normandy campaign took its place. June 1940

This change-over was a gradual one. Only the highest-ranking officers knew that it was taking place, and the date for the invasion had, as yet, not been even approximately fixed.

The evacuation of the B.E.F. from Dunkirk—followed almost immediately by the fall of France—left the British Commonwealth alone in the war against Germany, who was joined by Italy on the 11th June 1940.

The plans of the German High Command were, of course, unknown; but the best military opinion took the view that an early attempt to invade our island, by sea and air, was a very likely course of action. To meet this threat we had the Royal Navy in undisputed control of the surface sea; a highly efficient, but seriously outnumbered, R.A.F.; and an Army which had lost the greater part of its heavy equipment in France and Flanders.

Led and inspired by the Prime Minister, Mr. Winston Churchill, the fighting services and the civil population set about the task of defence against invasion with a spirit of determination and energy which has perhaps never been equalled in our history. The efforts of the home country were matched by those of other Commonwealth nations, and in addition we enjoyed the benevolent neutrality of the United States of America, whose policy included every possible assistance short of actual war.

The plans for defeating invasion were roughly as follows:

(*a*) To bomb the ports of embarkation on the Continent.
(*b*) To destroy as many of the enemy as possible at sea by naval and air action, in the case of airborne forces in the air with fighter aircraft and anti-aircraft fire.
(*c*) To oppose the landings on the beaches, and to counter-attack any forces which got ashore and moved inland.

June 1940

Apart from anti-aircraft formations and units, the Army troops available comprised some twenty-five divisions, including the 1st Canadian Division, a variety of administrative, technical and instructional units and establishments, and the recently formed Local Defence Volunteers (later renamed 'Home Guard'). Of the field divisions not more than about six were in a battleworthy condition from a training point of view, and all were lacking in essential weapons and equipment—particularly artillery and anti-tank weapons. There were reputed to be less than 200 tanks in the country, and the mobility of most units was seriously restricted by lack of transport.

The formations evacuated from Dunkirk were quickly assembled in divisional concentration areas, where the task of reorganizing, absorbing new drafts from the depots and, as far as possible, re-equipping, went on at an amazing tempo. By early July 1940 the whole Army in the United Kingdom had been redeployed with the object of meeting the threatened invasion.

It was in this setting that the Battle of Britain was fought.

The term 'Battle of Britain' is usually associated with the Royal Air Force, and it cannot be denied that the major honours went to the gallant pilots of Fighter Command. In this book, however, the term is used in its wider sense. In fact the Battle of Britain was fought by the entire adult population of the United Kingdom—Army, R.A.F. and civilians, men and women—and by the officers and men of the Royal Navy and Mercantile Marine based on ports in home waters.

II. THE 2ND BATTALION

After its evacuation from Dunkirk the 2nd Battalion (still part of the 4th Division) assembled at Willsworthy Camp in Devon; but only remained there a few days before moving to the area Sturminster Newton–Stalbridge–Marhull, in Dorset.

At this time preparations were afoot to form a 'Second B.E.F.,' under Lieut.-General Sir Alan Brooke, to continue the struggle in Western France. The Battalion received orders to be ready to embark on the 27th June to join this force. In consequence reorganization was carried out at a feverish speed.

The Battalion state, after reorganization, was as follows:

Commanding Officer . .	Lieut.-Colonel T. C. L. Redwood
Second-in-Command . .	Major R. W. H. Fryer, M.C.
Adjutant	Captain H. R. M. Wilkin
Quartermaster . . .	Lieut. W. R. E. Brown
Regimental Sergeant-Major .	R.S.M. W. Greaves
O.C. H.Q. Coy. . . .	Major C. R. Freeman, D.S.O., M.C.
„ A „	Captain J. D. Buckle
„ B „	Major H. A. Ingledew
„ C „	Captain M. Robson
„ D „	Captain R. M. Pratt

With the surrender of France on the 21st June the arrangements for proceeding overseas were cancelled, and the Battalion (less B Coy.) moved to the Isle of Wight, where they came under command of the 12th Infantry Brigade. After a few days at

9. Machine-gun in action at Tobruk—Cpl. Shaw and Fus. Campbell

10. Desert picnic, Tobruk, 1941—Cpl. J. Hall, Fus. E. Newton, Lieut. Stewart-Moore, Fusiliers G. Hutchinson, C. Wright, Shutt

11. Lieut.-Colonel E. H. D. Grimley, commanding 8th Battalion, conducting a tactical exercise in 1941. On his left are Major J. L. Challoner, Captain N. Gill and Lieut. A. S. Gardner

12. A Bren-gun carrier of the 8th Battalion in training near Sturminster-Newton, 1941

Calbourne they moved to the east of the Island and took up coast defence positions between St. Catherine's Point and Bembridge. Bn. H.Q. was established at Brading. June 1940–March 1942

B Coy. was located at Puncknowle, in Dorset, under command of the 50th (Northumbrian) Division.

About this time the Battalion received a welcome reinforcement of officers—19 second-lieutenants.

In September the Battalion (less B Coy.) moved to a camp in Ashurst Wood, near Lyndhurst Road Station, and came under command of the 11th Infantry Brigade. Here the main task was anti-parachute duties within the Brigade area. While in this camp Major R. W. H. Fryer left the Battalion to take command of the 7th Bn. Royal Northumberland Fusiliers, his place as Second-in-Command being taken by Major H. A. Ingledew.

About a month later another move was made to the Lymington area and soon after B Coy. rejoined the Battalion. The stay at Lymington was a very happy one. Reasonable quantities of transport and other equipment were received and several large-scale exercises took place. At this time the 4th Division was commanded by Major-General J. G. des R. Swayne—an ex-Commanding Officer of the 1st Bn. Royal Northumberland Fusiliers—the Commander of the Vth Corps (of which the Division formed part) being Lieut.-General Sir B. L. Montgomery.

In the autumn of 1940 an air raid on London destroyed the whole property of the Officers' and Sergeants' Messes of the 2nd Battalion, which had been placed in Messrs. Pickford's store in Islington, pending its removal to greater safety in the country. Among the articles lost, which included a very fine collection of medals, were a silver St. George centre-piece, in replica of that in possession of the 1st Battalion; a portrait by Edward Halliday of Major-General Sir Percival Wilkinson, exhibited in the Royal Academy prior to the war; an oil painting of the Battle of El Bodon; and a very beautiful silver-gilt Georgian goblet presented to the Regiment in 1898 by its Colonel, Lieut.-General F. A. W. Willis, C.B. The three last-named articles were Regimental property, which were always held by the home battalion.

In the circumstances it was fortunate that, on the 2nd Battalion's disbandment after the Peninsular War, its older treasures had passed to the 1st Battalion.

The unit remained in the Lymington area until November 1941, when they moved to Mandora Barracks, Aldershot. Here training was carried out on much the same lines as before, but with an ever-increasing amount of modern weapons and equipment. Whilst at Aldershot detachments of the Battalion were inspected by His Majesty The King.

By the end of 1941 the U.S.A. had entered the war, and the prospects of the Allied Armies returning to the European continent were receiving consideration. Combined operations—particularly the assault on a defended coast—were to become a feature of training in the United Kingdom. Special craft were designed and constructed for this purpose and soon became available in small quantities for training. Special centres and schools of instruction were established in Scotland, where combined operations were studied, and where whole formations could be practised in this type of warfare.

In March 1942 the 4th Division moved to Scotland, Bn. H.Q. and B Coy. being

March 1942–June 1943 billeted at Dalbeattie, A Coy. at Selkirk, C Coy. at Langholm and D Coy. in Castle Douglas. Each company (except B Coy., which was held in operational reserve)—attached to an infantry brigade of the Division—moved in turn to Inverary in Argyllshire for intensive training in combined operations. The culmination of this training was Exercise 'Dryshod,' held in the late summer of 1942, in which a considerable body of troops put into practice on a large scale the lessons which they had learnt in detail at Inverary.

In October 1942 the Battalion returned to the Selkirk area, and soon after this were reorganized into a Support Battalion. This took the following form:

> Bn. H.Q. and H.Q. Coy. were greatly reduced in strength, the rest of the Battalion being formed into three Brigade Support Companies—A, B and C. D Coy. was disbanded.
>
> Each Brigade Support Company consisted of:
>
> Coy. H.Q.
> A Bde. Defence Pl. (for the local defence of Inf. Bde. H.Q.)
> Two Heavy (4·2-in.) Mortar Pls.
> Two Anti-Aircraft (20-mm. Oerlikons) Pls.
>
> As there were no 4·2-in. mortars or Oerlikon guns available the mortar platoons were given 3-in. mortars and the anti-aircraft platoons retained their Vickers machine-guns in an anti-aircraft role.

This organization was eventually changed, and was never used in battle.

In February 1943 the Battalion moved to the west of Scotland, to Kirkmichael House between Dumfries and Moffat, and about the same time Lieut.-Colonel F. H. Butterfield took over command from Lieut.-Colonel T. C. L. Redwood.

Towards the end of February the 4th Division received orders to embark for French North Africa, which had been successfully invaded by a seaborne Anglo-American force in November 1942. As the reorganization of the Battalion was still incomplete they did not accompany the Division, but moved in April to Bake Camp, near St. Germans in Cornwall, where they came under command of the 55th Division.

In May a further reorganization took place, in which each of the three Brigade Support Companies was converted into a much more formidable unit under the name of Brigade Support Group.*

The unit mobilized for overseas service in the early days of June 1943 and embarked for North Africa on H.M.T. 'Tamaroa' on the 17th June.

III. THE 4TH BATTALION

June 1940 On their return from Dunkirk personnel of the Battalion reassembled at Knutsford in Cheshire, where the initial reorganization of the unit took place.

By mid-June 1940 the redeployment of troops of Home Forces in the south and south-east of England, to meet invasion, had commenced. On the 22nd June the 4th Bn. Royal Northumberland Fusiliers moved to a hutted camp at Yeovil in

* The details of this organization are given in Chapters 2 and 11.

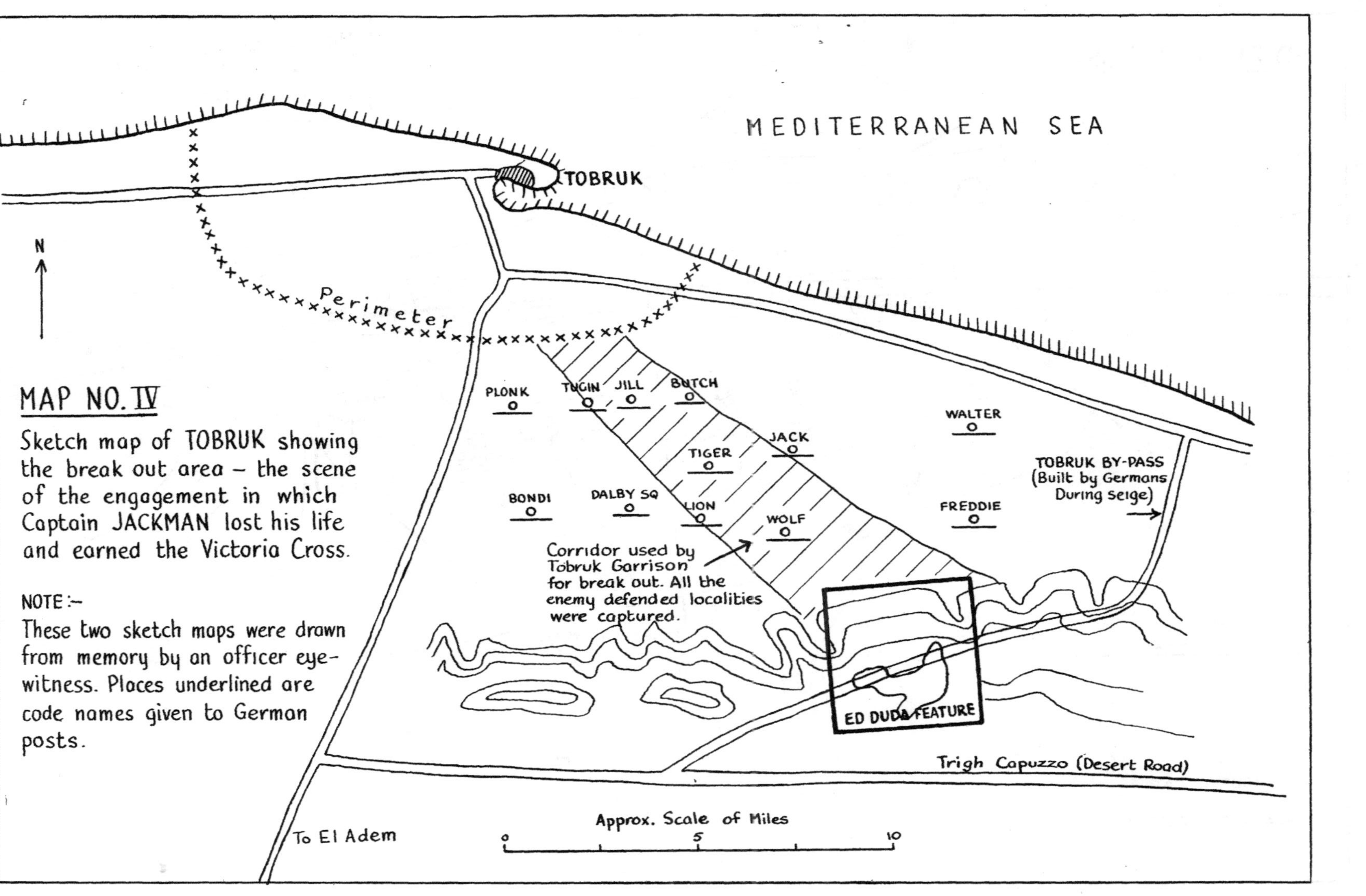

MAP NO. IV

Sketch map of TOBRUK showing the break out area – the scene of the engagement in which Captain JACKMAN lost his life and earned the Victoria Cross.

NOTE:–
These two sketch maps were drawn from memory by an officer eye-witness. Places underlined are code names given to German posts.

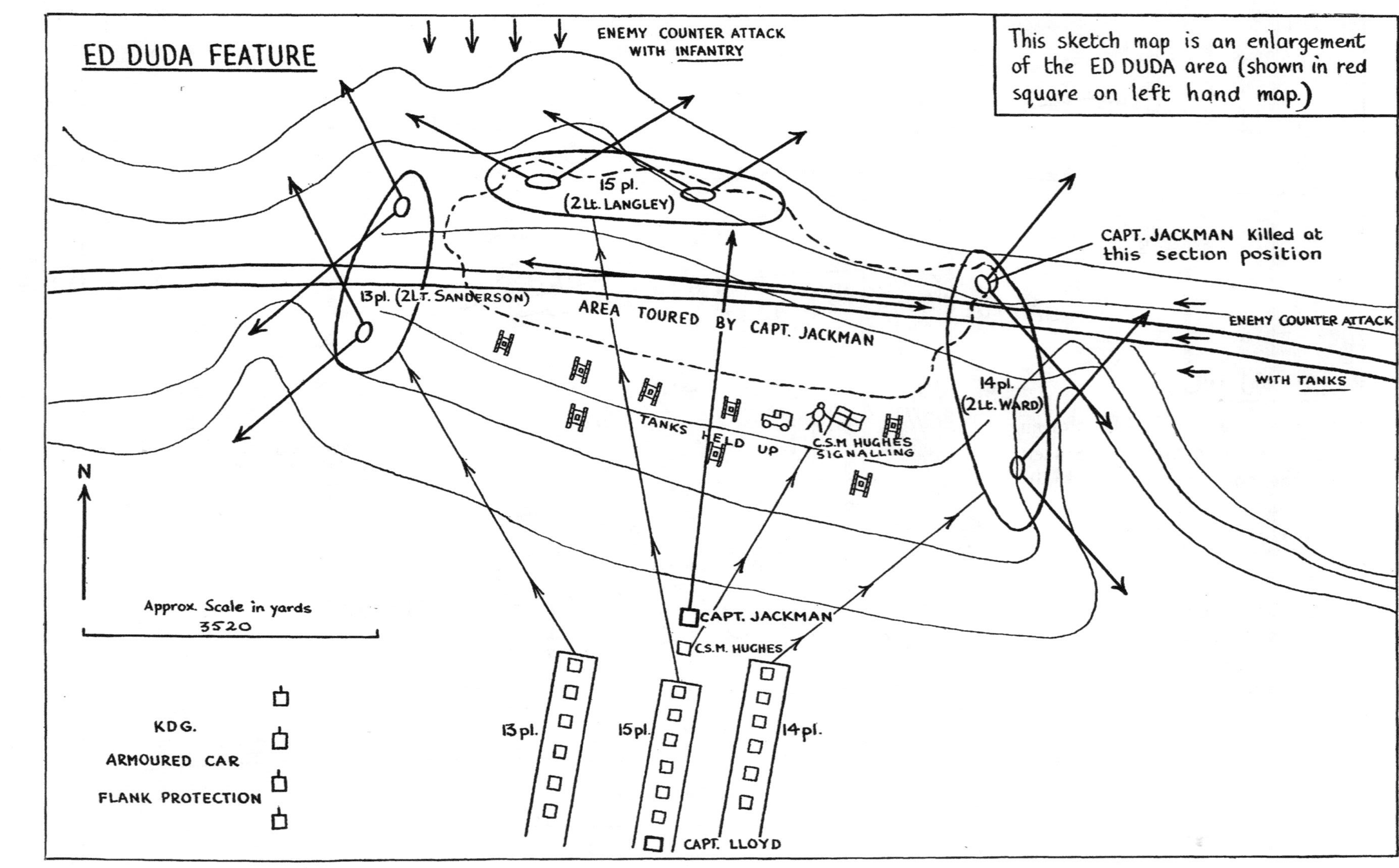
ED DUDA FEATURE
ENEMY COUNTER ATTACK WITH INFANTRY
This sketch map is an enlargement of the ED DUDA area (shown in red square on left hand map.)
15 pl. (2Lt. LANGLEY)
13pl. (2LT. SANDERSON)
AREA TOURED BY CAPT. JACKMAN
CAPT. JACKMAN Killed at this section position
ENEMY COUNTER ATTACK
WITH TANKS
14pl. (2Lt. WARD)
TANKS HELD UP
C.S.M HUGHES SIGNALLING
N
Approx. Scale in yards
3520
CAPT. JACKMAN
C.S.M. HUGHES
13pl.
15pl.
14pl.
CAPT. LLOYD
KDG.
ARMOURED CAR
FLANK PROTECTION

Somersetshire and on the 27th to a tented camp at Piddlehinton, in Dorsetshire. Here the process of reorganization was continued and the unit received a scanty supply of equipment and some vehicles. June 1940–Jan. 1941

On the 12th July they moved to Bournemouth, where they took over the coast defences of the town from some Artillery units. A further issue of assorted vehicles was received. At Bournemouth the duties were indeed varied—including the construction of an anti-tank ditch, mine-laying, the conversion of buildings into strong points, the demolition of two piers and the erection of many hundreds of yards of barbed wire.

On the 4th August the Battalion left Bournemouth, on relief by the 9th Bn. King's Own Royal Regiment, and proceeded to Blandford. An interesting period followed. The unit was directly under H.Q. Southern Command, with the operational task of keeping open communications within the area. Many instructive exercises were carried out with the object of training for desert warfare—as far as this was practicable in England. Scout platoon classes were organized by the Battalion for personnel of the Guards, 3rd, 4th and 50th Divisions, scout cars being one of the few varieties of fighting vehicles available in any numbers at that time.

The Battalion had the honour of being selected to escort Her Majesty Queen Mary to Scotland in the event of invasion. For this purpose a variety of routes to the North were reconnoitred.

By the end of August reorganization as a motor-cycle battalion had been completed; but soon after this the role was changed and the unit became the first 'Reconnaissance Battalion.'* The initial organization was largely experimental and, owing to shortages, the vehicles and other equipments were on an improvised scale. In fact the unit employed its old motor-cycle unit vehicles in the early stages. The new role excited much interest and attention. Numerous demonstration exercises were carried out and photographs taken for the press.

Training in the Blandford area continued until the 3rd November 1940, when a move to Amesbury Abbey was made—the Battalion taking over from an Australian unit.

At the end of December the Battalion reverted to its old Division of Dunkirk days —the 50th (Northumbrian) Division.

On the 16th January 1941 the unit took over billets from the 2nd Bn. Royal Northumberland Fusiliers with Headquarters at Shepton Mallet in Dorsetshire and with companies at Shepton Mallet, Chewton Mendip and Batcombe.

Much concentrated training was carried out in this location and as the supply of equipment increased, and became progressively better, so the Divisional Reconnaissance Battalion, in its final form, gradually began to emerge. The unit at this time consisted of Headquarters and three companies (X, Y and Z), based on the scout car as the primary fighting and reconnaissance vehicle—and with an increasing number of motor cycles and an elaborate system of intercommunication by wireless.

---

* A Reconnaissance Battalion became part of every division, fulfilling much the same functions as the old Divisional Cavalry. Before finality was reached they suffered many changes in organization and equipment.

April 1940–Jan. 1941

On the 18th April the Battalion had a serious accident with a 3-in. mortar bomb, in which 33 casualties were suffered, four proving fatal (Sgt. J. S. Pick, Sgt. T. Bradley, L/Cpl. W. Scott and Fus. T. May). Five officers were wounded—2/Lieut. G. A. Davis very seriously.

St. George's Day 1941 saw a memorable reunion with the 2nd and 8th Battalions of the Regiment. The three battalions attended Church Parade in the morning, took part in football and sports in the afternoon and held a St. George's Day dinner in the evening. On this day Lieut.-Colonel R. Wood relinquished command after five years' tenure of office. He was succeeded by Lieut.-Colonel E. des Graz (Rifle Brigade).

In May the Battalion received preliminary orders for overseas service in the Middle East—whither they were to proceed with the 50th Division. This was followed by a period of intensive training and preparations for embarkation.

The 4th Bn. Royal Northumberland Fusiliers embarked at Newport and sailed on the 'Arundel Castle' on the 24th June 1941. Their part in the Battle of Britain was at an end.

IV. THE 7TH BATTALION

As explained in Chapter 4 the 7th Bn. Royal Northumberland Fusiliers was captured in its entirety, together with the bulk of the 51st (Highland) Division, in France in June 1940.

For some weeks the question of forming a new unit, under the same designation, was in doubt; but in August 1940 it was decided to do so. Immediately after the Dunkirk evacuation 60 additional infantry battalions had been formed, among them the 15th Bn. Durham Light Infantry, which contained some 70 officers and men of the 7th Bn. Royal Northumberland Fusiliers—mostly those who had not been present with the unit at St. Valery, but also a few who had escaped capture.

In September this D.L.I. Battalion was renamed '7th Bn. Royal Northumberland Fusiliers' and came under the command of Lieut.-Colonel R. W. H. Fryer, a Fifth Fusilier.

From the outset the process of reforming and organizing into a machine-gun battalion was a difficult one. The shortage of machine-gun and other technical instructors was overcome with the arrival of a cadre from the Regimental Depot headed by R.S.M. Dalby, with Sgt. Armstrong as M.T. Sergeant. Progress was hampered by an acute shortage of equipment and by very frequent changes among officers—many of the original ones being officers from the Reserve, who were mostly unfamiliar with machine-gun technique and tactics. In these days the Battalion was 'nobody's child.'

The early days were spent at Gosford House, near Edinburgh, where the unit came under Edinburgh Area—a purely administrative Headquarters—but in January 1941 a move was made to Middlesbrough, where they were for a time the Machine-Gun Battalion of the 50th (Northumbrian) Division. This division was, however, destined for the Middle East at an early date, and it soon became apparent that the 7th Battalion could not be made operationally efficient for some time to come. They were, therefore, transferred to the 59th (Staffordshire) Division, with whom they were to remain until it, and the Battalion, were disbanded in France in September 1944. Soon after joining the Division, and while still at Middlesbrough, the unit was given a more generous scale of equipment and transport, which enabled training to proceed on more practical lines. Jan. 1941–1943

It is unnecessary to give details of the activities during the next two years, which followed the pattern of most other units stationed at home during this period. Moves were frequent—to Hawes, Middleton, Barnard Castle and Catterick, with a spell in Northern Ireland. By the late summer of 1943 they had returned to England and were quartered at Shorncliffe in Kent. By this time they had become a well-trained and well-equipped machine-gun battalion, and the 59th Division was definitely part of the 21st Army Group.

It should be recorded that these gratifying results were due very largely to the initiative and untiring energy of the Divisional Commander, Major-General J. S. Steele,* who commanded the 59th Division from the time the Battalion joined it until just before its return to England from Northern Ireland. He was a good friend to the 7th Bn. Royal Northumberland Fusiliers.

V. THE 8TH BATTALION

The 8th Battalion reassembled after its return from Dunkirk at Okehampton in Devon, where it occupied a tented camp. Here the process of reorganization and, as far as supplies permitted, re-equipping went on throughout June 1940. By the end of the month some reinforcements had been received and serious training commenced—primarily in the form of cadre courses for officers and N.C.Os. At nights there were occasional alarms, due to reported enemy parachute landings. June–August 1940

In July, Lieut.-Colonel E. H. D. Grimley took over the Battalion from Lieut.-Colonel J. L. Challoner, who had been in temporary command. The new Commanding Officer recorded that, although only partially trained, the rank and file of the unit provided raw material of the very finest quality.

In August the Battalion was ordered to Start Bay (between Dartmouth and Start Point), where, under command of Headquarters, Plymouth District, they were employed preparing defences against possible seaborne landings. The stay in this area was a short one, as towards the middle of the month they were relieved by other troops, who included the 9th Bn. Royal Northumberland Fusiliers (under Lieut.-Colonel L. C. Thomas), and sent to Falmouth, where they occupied a camp overlooking the harbour. At that time Falmouth was the only port in use on the south coast of England.

At the new location the Battalion had a 'grandstand' view of the almost daily daylight raids made by small formations of enemy bombers on shipping and coastal installations. After a few days the Battalion moved camp to a less conspicuous position near the Falmouth water-supply reservoir. During this period the unit commenced training in the use of motor-cycle combinations, which were then being delivered in

* Later to become General Sir James S. Steele, G.C.B., K.B.E., D.S.O., M.C., Adjutant-General to the Forces.

Sept. 1940–Jan. 1941

reasonable quantities. Although their vehicles were changed they continued in the role of a motor-cycle battalion.

Further changes of location took place early in September. One company was sent on detachment to Plymouth and the rest of the Battalion moved to the area of the Lizard—where it was disposed as follows:

Bn. H.Q. . . .	Prah Sands (later changed to Helston)
H.Q. Coy. . . .	Prah Sands
One Coy. . . .	Helston (later changed to Prah Sands)
One Coy. . . .	Mullion Cove

In those days one move followed another in quick succession and the month of October 1940 found the Battalion at Shepton Mallet in Somersetshire, under direct command of Headquarters, Southern Command.

In November 1940 the 8th Bn. Royal Northumberland Fusiliers joined the 3rd Division (Major-General J. Gammell), of which they were destined to become the Divisional Reconnaissance Battalion. Training in the new role started at once, at first on a very improvised basis—motor-cycle combinations being disguised on exercises to represent armoured cars and Bren carriers.

Up to this time, since the Dunkirk evacuation, the changed circumstances and shortages of equipment had compelled the Army at home to reorganize largely on an improvised basis, to meet the immediate requirements of the times. By the autumn, however, a more long-term policy had begun to take shape and this was reflected in units by less frequent changes of role and organization.

In December 1940 the Battalion moved to Sturminster Newton in Dorset, and immediately began receiving vehicles (armoured cars and carriers) at an almost embarrassing rate of delivery. Fortunately a number of drivers had already been trained for this purpose—although, due to the speed at which this had been carried out, the standard of driving was, as yet, not very high.

There followed a very interesting six months during which the Battalion, through a process of trial and error, evolved a tactical doctrine for a role for which no text-books were provided. This period of evolution was interspersed with large-scale exercises and with frequent changes in equipment, as the original vehicles became obsolete and could be replaced by more suitable types. These changes were not confined to vehicles, but included such items as wireless sets, weapons and cooking gear. During this period the 3rd Division, together with the 4th Division, constituted the Vth Corps, commanded by Lieut.-General Sir B. L. Montgomery. Thus the 8th Battalion and the 2nd Battalion (M.G. Bn., 4th Division) often opposed each other on exercises, although in very different roles.

In the spring of 1941 the Battalion changed its designation to '3rd Reconnaissance Regiment (N.F.)' and like all similar units adopted cavalry terms, such as 'squadron,' 'troop,' etc. This change of name was accompanied by efforts, from outside, to sever the Royal Northumberland Fusilier connection, and in particular to prevent the wearing of the Regimental cap badge. These attempts were most strenuously resisted and, although a year or so later the 'battle of the cap badge' was lost, the unit continued to wear Royal Northumberland Fusiliers shoulder titles until its disbandment after the war.

Progressive training in the new role continued until the end of September 1941, by which time a high standard had been attained, and some degree of 'stability' as regards the scale and types of equipment existed.

In October training was interrupted by the necessity of providing large working parties to erect anti-assault-landing defences in the shallows along part of the Dorset coast. This duty lasted several weeks and often involved working waist deep in the sea for long periods.

In November a move to Berkhampstead was made. This was carried out by night and, in spite of lack of practice in night driving without headlights, only one vehicle suffered damage. About this time Major-General E. C. Hayes took over command of the 3rd Division from Major-General J. Gammell and the Division became part of Home Forces general reserve.

From November 1941 to April 1942 the Battalion enjoyed an almost uninterrupted spell of training in every aspect of its operational role. By the early summer of 1942 it had become a highly efficient and battleworthy unit.

In April 1942 the Battalion staged a very successful demonstration, in reconnaissance regiment methods of operating in the field, for His Majesty The King.

This month also saw the relinquishment of command by Lieut.-Colonel Grimley, who was succeeded by Lieut.-Colonel E. C. Bols. The Battalion owed much to Lieut.-Colonel Grimley's sound training methods and high sense of duty. His influence was not confined to his own battalion. He played a major part in developing ideas for the tactical employment of this new type of unit and much of his teaching was incorporated in the official text-book for reconnaissance regiments which was issued shortly after he gave up command.

During the period at Berkhampstead two other senior officers, Major N. B. Pigg and Major J. L. Challoner, left the Battalion.

Soon after this a succession of moves took place—first to a tented camp at Romsey in Kent, where they remained for about six weeks under very bad conditions; then to Bournemouth and in the late summer back to Kent, to an area between Canterbury and Folkestone. While in this area Lieut.-Colonel Bols relinquished command of the Battalion and was succeeded by Lieut.-Colonel H. H. Merriman.

Training in Kent with the 3rd Division continued under constantly improving conditions as regards method and equipment, until the Battalion moved north to Thornhill Camp in Dumfriesshire in the spring of 1943. This move was accompanied by visible signs, and rumours, that the 3rd Division was preparing for overseas service. Extensive training in combined operations was carried out; but just as the time for embarkation appeared imminent all preparations were stopped and it became clear that the Division was to remain at home for the time being. Actually the Division was being prepared for the assault on Sicily (which took place in July 1943), although the destination was not known at the time. A last-minute decision was made, however, to send a Canadian division instead. The cancellation was a great disappointment to the Battalion, which was destined to remain another year in the United Kingdom before proceeding on active service.

The 8th Battalion was still in Thornhill Camp in August 1943.

VI. THE 9TH BATTALION

June–July 1940

After Dunkirk the Battalion concentrated at Launceston in Cornwall and by the end of June 1940 reorganization, training and a modicum of re-equipment were in full swing. The men were conscious that they had done well in Flanders under difficult conditions and set about their new task, of preparing to resist invasion, with enthusiasm. Substantial reinforcements were received, including some men who had been left behind when the Battalion went to France in April.

After a few days in billets in the town the Battalion moved to a tented camp at Werrington Park, a short distance from Launceston. Here intensive training commenced; but early in July this was interrupted by a sudden move to South Devon with the operational task of defending a long stretch of coast at Slapton Sands. This was a particularly vulnerable part of the coast, affording an easy landing place for tanks. Although the frontage was a very long one it provided excellent fields of fire. Unfortunately the Battalion had not been re-equipped with machine-guns; but the shore establishments of the ever resourceful Royal Navy were able to provide an assortment of weapons. These included Belgian Maxim guns, a few Vickers guns and some other automatics of American design. This was typical of the equipment position in those days. These weapons were soon got into serviceable condition by the Battalion armourers and other personnel.

About this time, consequent on the reorganization of the Army at home to meet the new conditions, the decision was made to disband the 23rd (Northumbrian) Division and the Battalion received orders to move to Norfolk, where it was to become the Machine-Gun Battalion of the 18th Division—a first-line Territorial Army division commanded by Major-General M. Beckwith-Smith, D.S.O., M.C.

Having been relieved by the 8th Bn. Royal Northumberland Fusiliers the Battalion left South Devon at the end of July for Cromer, where it was accommodated in a number of requisitioned hotels. Two nights after arrival the town experienced its first air raid, a few bombs being dropped but little damage done.

On joining the 18th Division the Battalion was issued with equipment on a comparatively lavish scale—including 48 new Vickers guns and a generous number of vehicles. A few days later a move was made to Holt, where the Battalion was accommodated partly in Gresham's School, but with Y and Z Coys. in some nearby billets. Here further supplies of equipment were received. Training in the machine-gun role went forward apace, with operational roles of dealing with enemy airborne landings and defending Holt as a 'nodal point.'

After a few weeks' intensive training at Holt the Battalion was sufficiently battle-worthy to join the 18th Division in its operational defensive role between Yarmouth and Wells. Components of the Battalion moved to the following localities:

Bn. H.Q. W Coy. } . . .	Stiffkey
Z ,, . . .	Yarmouth (54th Infantry Brigade)
Y ,, . . .	Mundesley (55th Infantry Brigade)
X ,, . . .	Sheringham (53rd Infantry Brigade)

July 1940–August 1941

Later Bn. H.Q. and W. Coy. moved to Coltishall, near Norwich, where they were more centrally placed and conveniently near Divisional H.Q. at Sprowston Hall.

In this area the forward companies on the coast dug and occupied many alternative positions, which in course of time were replaced by semi-permanent concrete emplacements. Training continued hand-in-hand with these operational duties. It was a strenuous time for all.

At this time the Battalion state was as follows:

Commanding Officer . .	Lieut.-Colonel L. C. Thomas, D.S.O., O.B.E. M.C.
Second-in-Command .	Major F. B. Cowen, M.C.
Adjutant	Captain W. N. C. Crawhall
Quartermaster . . .	Lieut. (Q.M.) J. W. M. Purcell
Regimental Sergeant-Major	R.S.M. P. Magee
O.C. W Coy. . . .	Captain W. Ainslie
" X "	Major T. Bennett, M.C.
" Y "	Captain B. Berey
" Z "	Captain J. Thornhill

By the end of October 1940 deterioration in weather conditions, and the shortening days, reduced the likelihood of invasion and enabled many useful exercises to be held—some on a brigade and divisional level.

About this time the Adjutant, Captain Crawhall, took over command of H.Q. Coy., and was succeeded as Adjutant by Captain S. L. Sanderson.

Just before Christmas orders were received for the 18th Division to move to Roxburghshire in Scotland, where it was to become G.H.Q. Home Force's mobile reserve.

The advanced party left Norwich by road on the 1st January 1941. During the move north night halts were made at Peterborough and Catterick. The weather was extremely cold, and a heavy fall of snow made road movement difficult. The main body moved by rail a few days later, and by the 6th January the whole Battalion had arrived at Selkirk. Bn. H.Q. and Z Coy. were billeted at Bowhill, the Duke of Buccleuch's residence, and the remaining companies in the town.

The period in Scotland was devoted mainly to collective training on a higher level and a fortnight's field firing, marred by bad weather—snow and mists.

At the end of April the Battalion moved to the Sandbach area of Cheshire, where they were located as follows:

Bn. H.Q. H.Q. Coy. Y Coy. . . .	Sandbach
W "	Holmes Chapel
X "	Bolton
Z "	Neston (Wirral Peninsula)

As the accommodation at Sandbach was unsatisfactory Bn. H.Q., H.Q. Coy. and Y Coy. moved later to Whitchurch (Salop).

Here collective training continued with brigade and divisional exercises of increasing

Aug.–Oct. 1941

duration, and these were continued when, in August 1941, a move to Droitwich was made. In September a machine-gun 'concentration' was held at Trawsfynnid in Wales.

By this time the 18th Division had become a highly trained formation and the 9th Bn. Royal Northumberland Fusiliers—with its battle experience at Dunkirk—a first-class machine-gun unit. During the autumn there were signs that a move overseas was impending. This took the form of increased issues of the latest equipment, the elimination of unfit personnel and a ruthless cut in the age limits for the various key appointments. The last resulted in the departure of Major F. B. Cowen, M.C., the Second-in-Command—who had proved himself such a fine fighting soldier in Flanders—and R.S.M. Magee. New arrivals included Major H. S. Flower (Second-in-Command), Major B. J. Leech (O.C. H.Q. Coy.) and R.S.M. T. Johnson.

Prior to embarkation the Battalion spent a short time at Pettypool, near Northwich in Cheshire. They left there on the 29th October 1941 and embarked at Liverpool on H.T. 'Warwick Castle' on the following day.

The story of how the Battalion (together with the rest of the 18th Division) was diverted from its original destination (the Middle East) to Singapore is described in Chapter 8.

The story of the further activities of the 4th, 7th and 8th Battalions in the United Kingdom—in preparation for the invasion of Normandy—is told in Chapter 13.

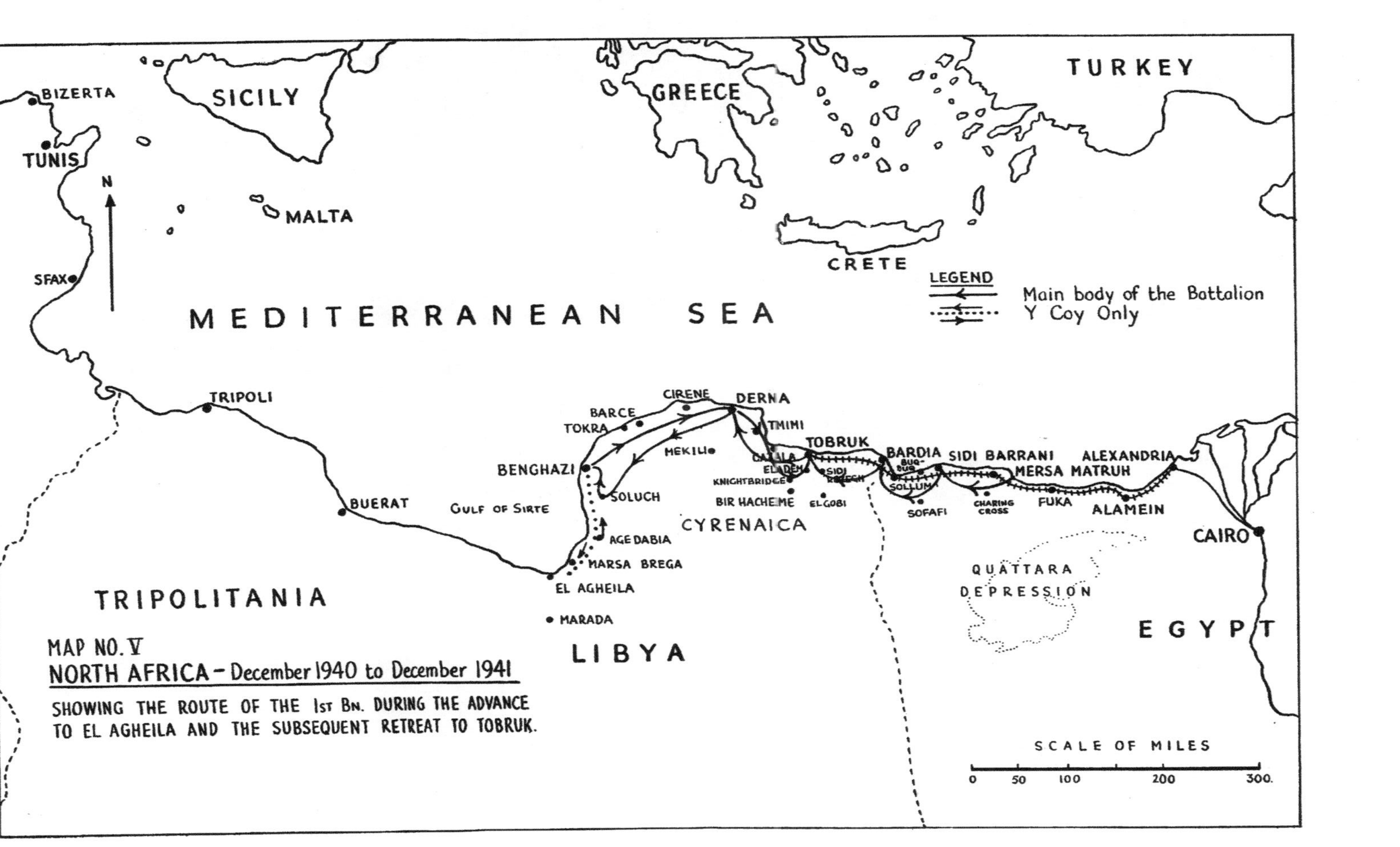

MAP NO. V
NORTH AFRICA – December 1940 to December 1941
SHOWING THE ROUTE OF THE 1st Bn. DURING THE ADVANCE TO EL AGHEILA AND THE SUBSEQUENT RETREAT TO TOBRUK.

CHAPTER 7

NORTH AFRICA

June 1941 to September 1942
4th Battalion

(*See Map No. VI*)

THE 4th Bn. Royal Northumberland Fusiliers sailed from Newport on H.M.T. 'Arundel Castle' on the 24th June 1941. Organized for the role of Reconnaissance Regiment of the 50th (Northumbrian) Division the unit mustered some 800 all ranks, and was destined for the Middle East. Its official designation at that time was 50th Battalion Reconnaissance Corps (4 R.N.F.). June–Sept. 1941

The Battalion state was as follows (names in brackets show changes which had taken place by the beginning of May 1942):

Commanding Officer . .	Lieut.-Colonel E. P. A. des Graz (Rifle Brigade)
Second-in-Command .	Major H. Stepney
Adjutant	Captain C. L. Stephenson (Captain P. H. Hollam)
Quartermaster . . .	Major F. G. Newall, M.B.E. (K.O.Y.L.I.)
O.C. H.Q. Coy. . .	Captain R. C. Porter (Captain D. N. Clark-Lowes)
„ X „ . .	Captain H. Clifford (Major R. C. Porter)
„ Y „ . .	Captain R. H. S. M. Kent (Captain H. Clifford)
„ Z „ . .	Major J. T. Lisle (Major J. Pearson)

Owing to the hazards of the Mediterranean, due to enemy air and submarine activities, the convoy proceeded by the Cape route to Egypt. The trip was uneventful, calls being made at Freetown, Durban and Aden.

It is interesting to record that the Queen and Princesses of Abyssinia travelled as passengers on the same ship en route for their homeland, which had by then been liberated from the Italians.

Some useful individual training was carried out during the voyage. The Battalion disembarked at Tewfik on the 23rd August 1941 and moved at once into camp at Quassasin in the Suez Canal zone.

On the 10th September the Battalion left Egypt to join the 50th Division in Cyprus, disembarking at Famagusta on the 13th. Since the loss of Crete this island had become

Sept. 1941–April 1942

vitally important to our position in the Eastern Mediterranean. This move was followed by others in quick succession, in order to meet the ever-changing political and strategic situation of those times. On the 12th November the Battalion moved by destroyer to Haifa in Palestine; early in December to Bagush near Mersa Matruh in Egypt—in company with the 150th Infantry Brigade of the 50th Division; in early January 1942 back to Haifa, where they joined the 151st Infantry Brigade, and then to Quairsia, near Homs in Syria, where they were quartered in a French cavalry barracks.

These moves were uneventful, but at the end of February 1942 an event of considerable significance took place which had a marked influence on the Battalion's future. This was a move to Sidi-Bishr to become part of the Support Group of the 22nd Armoured Brigade (Brigadier W. Carr) of the 1st Armoured Division (Major-General H. Lumsden). This involved a change in role and organization, the Battalion becoming a Motor Battalion of three Motor Coys. (X, Y and Z, each of three Motor Platoons and one Carrier Platoon) and one Anti-tank Coy. (W, of three Platoons armed with 2-pr. anti-tank guns). Thus with the deepest regret the Battalion severed its connection with the 50th Division with whom they had been associated for over thirty years.

A short stay at Sidi-Bishr was followed in March by a move to Beni-Yusef, near Cairo, where the unit was completely refitted for the new role and commenced intensive training.

The Support Group, which was commanded by Lieut.-Colonel des Graz in addition to his battalion, was organized into three sub-units, each composed as below, for the garrisoning of certain fortified points, termed 'boxes,' designed to form pivots of manœuvre for the mobile armour:

Headquarters
One Battery R.H.A.
One Coy. 4th Bn. Royal Northumberland Fusiliers
Two Troops or Platoons of anti-tank guns (either Northumberland Hussars or 4th Bn. Royal Northumberland Fusiliers)

Companies of the Battalion were usually allotted to the garrisons of the following boxes:

Box No. 1 . . . Z Coy.
Box No. 2 . . . Y Coy.
Box No. 3 . . . X Coy.

(the anti-tank guns of W Coy. being distributed between the boxes). Normally each box served one of the three armoured regiments of the Brigade, though the central control of the Commanding Officer, in this case Colonel des Graz, ensured united action when occasion demanded.

On St. George's Day 1942 the Battalion left the vicinity of Cairo for the Western Desert, and in the early days of May they found themselves near Bir Beleifa, a few miles east of Knightsbridge and behind the great minefield which ran from the sea at Gazala to Bir Hacheim. Since February 1942 the British forces had been holding the line Gazala–Bir Hacheim. By April the Middle East theatre was beginning to lose troops, and have its reinforcements diverted, to meet the Japanese threat in the Far East. Both sides had been preparing to take the offensive in the early summer; but the Eighth Army was awaiting further supplies of equipment—in particular the new 6-pr. anti-tank guns, which were to replace the obsolete 2-prs. This delay enabled Rommel to gain the initiative, and on the 27th May commenced the series of engagements which forced the Eighth Army back beyond the Frontiers of Egypt and resulted in the virtual destruction of the 4th Bn. Royal Northumberland Fusiliers.

April–May 1942

At this time General Sir Claude Auchinleck was Commander of the Middle East theatre of operations and Lieut.-General N. M. Ritchie was in command of the Eighth Army.

On the 25th May the 22nd Armoured Brigade took up a position previously selected to frustrate any attempt by the enemy to cut through the minefield. Boxes 2 and 3 (commanded as a single unit by Lieut.-Colonel des Graz) dug in a few miles south of Knightsbridge facing west; while Box 1, with the armoured regiment it was supporting, took up a similar position further south. This box was somewhat isolated, being about 3½ miles from the other two and some 2 miles from its armoured regiment (Royal Gloucestershire Hussars).

The 26th May was spent improving the positions taken up—digging slit trenches and gun-pits, concealment, etc.

Soon after dawn on the 27th firing was heard to the south, but this occasioned no particular surprise or alarm. About 0800 hrs., however, Lieut.-Colonel des Graz received a message to put Plan A (designed to meet an attack from the south-west) into operation. Lieut.-Colonel des Graz was at Brigade H.Q. at the time, but he proceeded immediately to the position occupied by Boxes 2 and 3, where he assumed command. On arrival he (Lieut.-Colonel des Graz) received news by wireless that Box 1, to the south, had been attacked.

The order to put Plan A into operation had reached Box 1 at 0800 hrs., and about the same time a group of vehicles was observed some 3,000 yards from the position. Visibility made it difficult to identify them; but very shortly they were seen to be armoured vehicles, although Brigade H.Q. stated that they might be British. Nevertheless, the Box Commander ordered O.C. W Coy. (Captain J. McNamara) to despatch an anti-tank platoon to a position some 700 yards south of the box. All doubts as to the identity of the approaching force were soon dispelled when they opened fire on the box—to which the 25-prs. of the R.H.A. replied.

The enemy put down a brief bombardment on the box and on the armoured regiment (Royal Gloucestershire Hussars) behind it, and then, appreciating correctly the weakness of the opposition, swept forward with his armour. All guns except a few 25-prs. and two 2-pr. anti-tank guns had been put out of action by the bombardment and these engaged the enemy until they were overrun. In a short time No. 1 Box had, for all practical purposes, ceased to exist. A few 25-prs. and vehicles made their escape to Nos. 2 and 3 Boxes. The only officers of the 4th Bn. Royal Northumberland Fusiliers to escape were Major H. Stepney (O.C. Box—wounded), Lieut. Smith and Lieut. Biles. Captain McNamara (wounded), Captain Leinster

May–June 1942

(2nd i/c Z Coy.) * and Lieuts. Ashby and McCubbin were captured. The remnants of the box joined up with Boxes 2 and 3.

The general picture was now as follows. The German force had swept round the south of the minefield and then turned north. One column, consisting mainly of the 21st Panzer Division, had come up close to the minefield and liquidated in turn the 3rd Indian Motor Brigade (south of Bir Hacheim) and Box 1 (near Bir El Harmat). By about 1100 hrs. this enemy column was approaching the rest of the 22nd Armoured Brigade, which included Boxes 2 and 3. Other German columns were operating further east towards El Adem and Tobruk. By midday it had become clear that a major enemy offensive had been launched, and that many British formations were operating at a severe disadvantage owing to the non-arrival of the new 6-pr. anti-tank guns.

On receiving news of the losses inflicted on the Royal Gloucestershire Hussars, and the destruction of Box 1, Brigadier Carr ordered the rest of the Brigade to withdraw to the north—to a position just east of Knightsbridge. This was successfully carried out. This position was on the left flank of a well-prepared position occupied by the 200th Guards Brigade (Brigadier J. Marriot). Here the Knightsbridge Box, reinforced by the guns of the 22nd Armoured Brigade Support Group, made a solid pivot round which the armoured regiments could operate freely. Boxes 2 and 3 of the Support Group (under Lieut.-Colonel des Graz) were sited close together facing west and south respectively and located to the east and north-east of Knightsbridge.

Here the Battalion remained for three days—the 27th, 28th and 29th May—with the armoured regiments working with increasing confidence all round them, as the enemy supply position deteriorated and his force became weakened by casualties and wastage. Several enemy attacks were beaten off and the troops had every reason to expect a successful conclusion to the battle.

On the 30th May the enemy commenced to withdraw and on the 31st there was a general lull in the operations. It transpired that the enemy had retreated not south but to the west, into a bulge in the side of the minefield which became known as the 'Cauldron.' Here, protected by the minefield itself, he dug in a formidable line of 88-mm. anti-tank guns along a ridge in front of his position. To dislodge these guns it was decided to attack the ridge with the 9th and 10th Indian Infantry Brigades of the 5th Indian Division. Owing to the distance they had to move and a severe sandstorm, these brigades were not ready to attack until the night of the 4th/5th June.

Meanwhile the enemy had not been idle. His positions had been greatly strengthened by mines, digging and wiring. At dawn on the 1st June he had attacked the 150th Infantry Brigade, the southernmost brigade of the 50th Division, which held the eastern edge of the minefield just north of the 'Cauldron.' By the evening this brigade's ammunition had become exhausted and they were overrun.

This successful attack on the 150th Infantry Brigade turned the scales of the battle. The German general Bayerlein has said of it: 'It all turned on the 150th Brigade Box at Got-El-Valeb. . . . If we had not taken it on June 1st you would have captured the whole of the Afrika Korps. By the evening of the third day we were surrounded

* Captain Leinster escaped a few days later.

and almost out of petrol. As it was, it was a miracle that we managed to get our supplies through the minefield in time.' *

For the attack of the 9th and 10th Indian Brigades on the night of the 4th/5th June the 22nd Armoured Brigade was attached to the 7th Armoured Division (Major-General F. W. Messervy). The Indians' objective was the ridge on which the German 88-mm. guns were sited. Assuming the capture of this, the Support Group was to move forward on to it at dawn, preparatory to supporting the armour—which was to make a semi-circular sweep round the 'Cauldron' area from the south.

The attack opened with a barrage commencing at 0250 hrs. and at 0300 hrs. the infantry crossed the start line. The advance progressed well and they gained their objectives practically unopposed. At first light the Support Group commenced to move forward, but at the same time the enemy launched a powerful counter-attack, supported by heavy artillery fire, which overran the leading troops of the 10th Indian Infantry Brigade. It transpired that the Germans had withdrawn a short distance when the barrage commenced and in consequence had not suffered heavily. This resulted in the Support Group only reaching a subsidiary ridge, which was subjected to a heavy bombardment—being overlooked from the main ridge which the enemy had now recaptured. This fire lasted all day, but the two 'boxes' consolidated and maintained their positions. They were, however, unable to give full support to the armoured units, which at about midday, after suffering heavy losses, abandoned their intended operations and took up positions a short distance ahead of the Support Group. They suffered further losses of Grant tanks later in the day from observed fire from the German 88-mm. guns.

By the evening it was clear that the British attack had failed. Orders were issued for some of the Indian troops and the armour to withdraw; but the Support Group and the remainder of the Indians were instructed to hold their positions.

Soon after dawn on the 6th June the enemy, discovering that the British tanks had withdrawn, began to probe forward with his armour supported by artillery. All frontal attacks on the boxes were beaten off, but the enemy soon began to work round the flanks. At about 0800 hrs. Captain W. Maxwell (O.C. H.Q. Coy.) succeeded in making his way to the boxes with some sorely needed ammunition trucks, but even at that early hour the position was almost surrounded. Attack after attack was beaten off, but the defence was gradually weakened by guns being put out of action and vehicles being set on fire. By 1600 hrs. ammunition was running short, but still the order to stand fast remained.

At about 1730 hrs. the German armour assaulted in strength from the north-west. The surviving guns and their crews failed to stop them. The position was quickly overrun and by dark the 4th Bn. Royal Northumberland Fusiliers had ceased to exist as an effective unit.

In this desperate battle, in which so many played a gallant part, there was one man whose exploits stood out above all others. Lieut.-Colonel des Graz was an inspiration to all throughout the action, and no account of this engagement would be complete

---

* Extract from *Rommel* [page 122], by Brigadier Desmond Young.

June 1942

without an account of the manner of his death. The following is an extract from the account of an officer eyewitness, Lieut. G. F. Thistleton (9th Jats):

> '. . . I had reached my truck when Lieut.-Colonel des Graz appeared over the ridge, standing in a carrier, and drove straight up to a gun. He jumped out and brought the gun into action. The No. 1 of the gun fired two shots, which hit an enemy tank, but failed to penetrate. The tank stopped and opened fire, scoring two hits on the gun shield from a range of about one hundred yards, and silencing the gun. Colonel des Graz was standing immediately behind the 2-pr. and he and two of the gun crew were hit: . . . directly afterwards one of the surviving gun members reported to me that Lieut.-Colonel des Graz and the two gun members had been killed outright.'

NOTE: Another eyewitness, Fus. G. Duff of the 4th Bn. Royal Northumberland Fusiliers, stated that he was informed by Lieut.-Colonel des Graz's batman (Fus. Tiffen) that the Commanding Officer manned the gun himself and knocked out one tank immediately before being killed. It is difficult to say which account is correct.

This gallant officer died as he would have wished, directing the fire of his battalion's weapons at the enemy at close quarters.* His memory will live long in the history of the Royal Northumberland Fusiliers and in that of his parent regiment, The Rifle Brigade.

The action at the 'Cauldron' was followed by a general retreat of the British forces which was to end beyond the Egyptian frontier. Officers and men of the 4th Bn. Royal Northumberland Fusiliers who had survived the previous battles were assembled in the B Echelon area under Major J. T. Lisle and Captain D. N. Clark-Lowes. Here, together with B Echelon personnel, they were organized into an anti-tank company. 6-pr. anti-tank guns had been issued at B Echelon just before the 'Cauldron' battle. Although not used in that engagement they were available for this improvised company and, due to the energy of Captain Clark-Lowes, who had recently returned from hospital, a high proportion of men at B Echelon had been trained in their use. Consequently in the subsequent retreat the remnants of the Battalion were able to give a good account of themselves.

Moving via Tobruk the Company eventually arrived at Sollum on the 15th June, where they joined up with the much depleted 22nd Armoured Brigade. Here they carried out further intensive training in the mechanism and tactical handling of the new 6-pr. guns.

On the 22nd they moved to Bir Enba, whither the Brigade had proceeded a few days earlier. On the 24th a further move was made to a position south of Mersa Matruh. At this time twelve 6-pr. anti-tank guns were available and it was decided to reorganize the Company into three platoons as follows:

No. 1 Pl. (Lieut. R. W. Bedlington) with 10th Royal Hussars
No. 2 Pl. (2/Lieut. A. B. Ryott) with Bde. H.Q.
No. 3 Pl. (Captain P. Leinster) with B Echelon

---

* Lieut.-Colonel des Graz was well known at Bisley and other Army meetings, in peace, as a fine shot with small-arms weapons—particularly with the revolver.

13. Lieut.-Colonel E. P. A. des Graz, killed in action the 6th June 1942

14. H.M. King George VI, accompanied by Lieut.-Colonel L. C. Thomas, inspecting 9th Battalion prior to its embarkation, October 1941 (see chapter 8)

15. The plaque unveiled in the French ship 'Felix Roussel' to commemorate its defence by men of the 9th Battalion (see chapter 8)

Captain D. N. Clark-Lowes and Coy. H.Q. were with No. 2 Platoon. Each platoon consisted of four anti-tank guns.

The attachments of platoons given above did not last long, but changed almost daily—No. 1 Platoon in particular being attached to a variety of units in quick succession.

The next eight days were occupied in carrying out a fighting withdrawal in which the Company, or part of it, frequently acted as rearguard or as a 'screen' to cover the withdrawal of other units. By the 27th June the Company had dwindled from an original strength of four officers and 106 other ranks to less than half that number.

On the night of the 27th/28th and on the 28th an eastward bound of some 50 miles was made. On the 30th June the Brigade column encountered tanks of the 21st Panzer Division, but owing to low visibility, due to dust, gave them the slip—a fortunate escape, as the enemy force was one of considerable size. That evening the Brigade reached the El Alamein line—which although a prepared position fell far short of the expected state of preparedness. Several enemy attacks were repelled in the course of the next few days.

Mention must be made here of 2/Lieut. A. B. Ryott (an officer of the York and Lancaster Regiment, attached to the Battalion) who commanded No. 2 Platoon of the improvised company. Throughout these strenuous days he led his platoon with the greatest courage and energy, and is estimated to have accounted for at least twelve enemy tanks. Unfortunately he was killed on the 1st September 1942 near Hamermat.

By the 4th July the situation along the El Alamein front had become stabilized, with a wide 'no-man's land' between the opposing forces which was patrolled vigorously by both sides.

On the 14th the Company moved forward some four or five miles, where they were able to assist New Zealand and Indian troops who were heavily engaged with German tanks on Ruweisat Ridge.

The Company—together with troops of the 5th Indian Division—remained in this position the following day. During the evening they were heavily and continuously attacked by enemy armour, but this was beaten off with heavy losses. This was Rommel's last attempt, in this phase of the campaign, to break through to Egypt.

A few days later the Company handed over its guns to Australian troops and was withdrawn to Cairo. The officers were posted to the 1st Bn. The King's Royal Rifle Corps, and most of the men to the 1st Bn. Royal Northumberland Fusiliers. Shortly afterwards it was decided that Major Lisle and Captain Clark-Lowes, with a few selected N.C.Os., should return to the United Kingdom to reform the Battalion. The party left Cairo on the 22nd September 1942.

This was the unit's last battle as a battalion in the Second World War. The story of its reforming in England and the exploits of the three independent machine-gun companies into which it was eventually split are told in later chapters of this book. In their two short campaigns—Dunkirk and North Africa—they had the ill luck, on both occasions, to be part of an army which suffered a severe reverse and on both occasions their losses were heavy. They, however, acquitted themselves nobly and fought in the finest traditions of the Regiment.

CHAPTER 8

SINGAPORE—AND CAPTIVITY

October 1941 to September 1945
9th Battalion

(*See Maps Nos. VII and VIII*)

I. THE VOYAGE TO SINGAPORE

Oct. 1941 IN October 1941 the 18th Division (Major-General M. Beckwith-Smith, D.S.O., M.C.), consisting of the 53rd, 54th and 55th Infantry Brigades, was in process of assembling at ports in Great Britain prior to embarking for service in the Middle East. The 9th Bn. Royal Northumberland Fusiliers—the Divisional Machine-Gun Battalion—embarked at Liverpool on H.T. 'Warwick Castle' and sailed on the 30th October. The Battalion M.T. had been loaded on another ship.

At this time the 'key' appointments in the Battalion were held as follows:

Commanding Officer . .	Lieut.-Colonel L. C. Thomas, D.S.O., O.B.E., M.C.
Second-in-Command .	Major H. S. Flower
Adjutant	Captain S. L. Sanderson
Quartermaster . . .	Lieut. (Q.M.) J. W. M. Purcell, M.B.E.
O.C. H.Q. Coy. . .	Major B. J. Leech
,, W ,, . .	Major C. R. I. Besley, M.B.E.
,, X ,, . .	Captain A. E. Hedley, M.B.E., M.C.
,, Y ,, . .	Captain R. Watson
,, Z ,, . .	Captain J. Thornhill
,, R ,, . . (1st Reinforcements)	Captain H. B. Burn
Regimental Sergeant-Major	R.S.M. T. Johnson
Chaplain	Rev. E. W. B. Cordingley, R.A.Ch.D.
Medical Officer . .	Captain H. Silman, R.A.M.C.

The total strength (including 54 first-line reinforcements) was 36 officers and 795 other ranks.

The convoy was escorted by the cruiser H.M.S. 'Cairo' and four destroyers, its first port of call being Halifax, Nova Scotia. On the 4th November it met an eastbound convoy escorted by twelve American warships, including the battleship U.S.S. 'Tennessee' and an aircraft carrier. On meeting, the two convoys exchanged escorts. Although the U.S.A. were still nominally at peace they had accepted the responsibility of escorting 'lease-lend' material a proportion of the distance across the Atlantic,

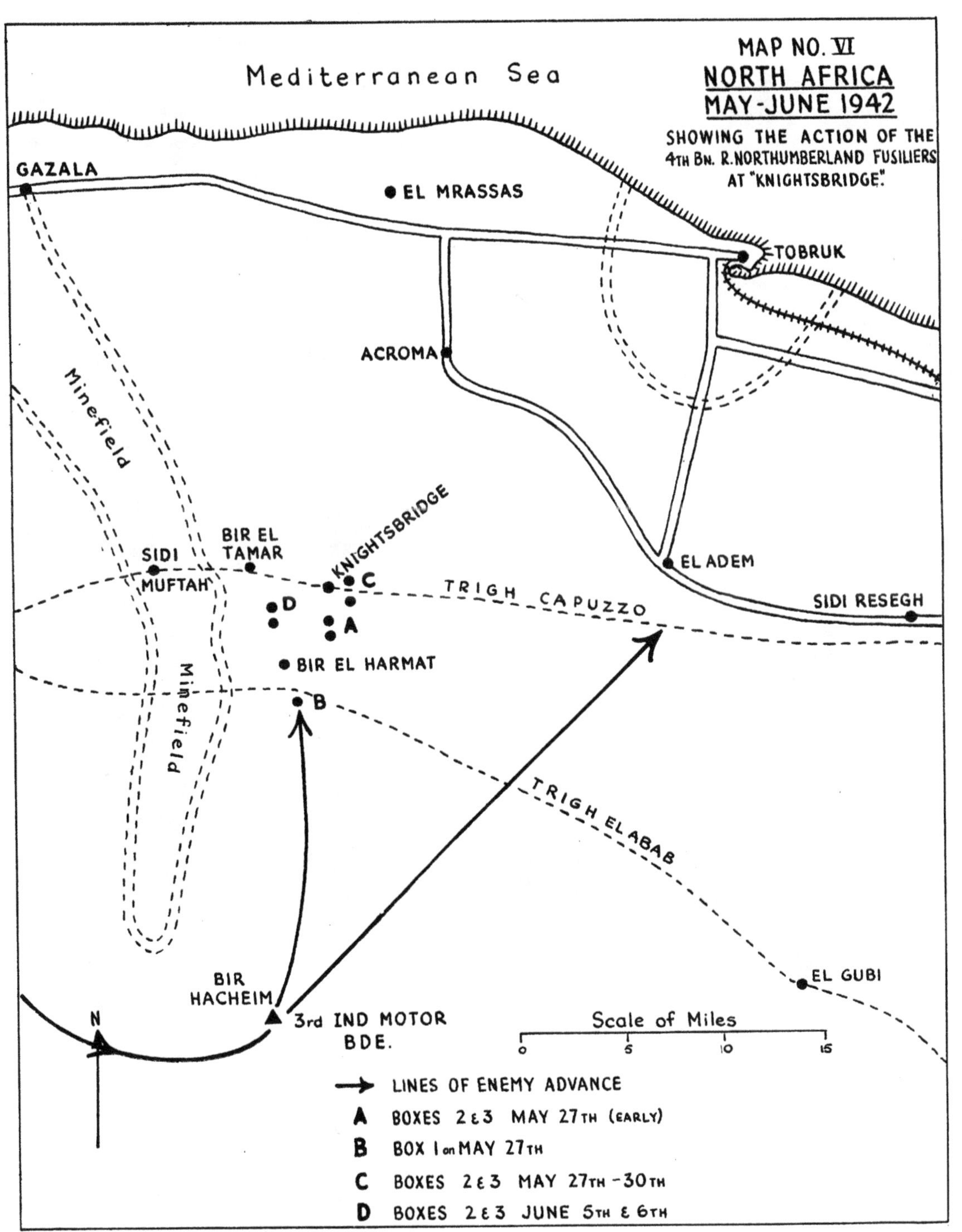
MAP NO. VI
NORTH AFRICA
MAY-JUNE 1942
SHOWING THE ACTION OF THE 4TH BN. R. NORTHUMBERLAND FUSILIERS AT "KNIGHTSBRIDGE".
Mediterranean Sea
GAZALA
EL MRASSAS
TOBRUK
ACROMA
Minefield
KNIGHTSBRIDGE
BIR EL TAMAR
SIDI MUFTAH
C
D
A
TRIGH CAPUZZO
EL ADEM
SIDI RESEGH
BIR EL HARMAT
B
Minefield
TRIGH EL ABAB
EL GUBI
BIR HACHEIM
3rd IND MOTOR BDE.
N
Scale of Miles
0 5 10 15
LINES OF ENEMY ADVANCE
A BOXES 2 & 3 MAY 27TH (EARLY)
B BOX 1 on MAY 27TH
C BOXES 2 & 3 MAY 27TH - 30TH
D BOXES 2 & 3 JUNE 5TH & 6TH

Nov. 1941–Jan. 1942

and many other obligations which conformed to her policy of benevolent neutrality —which in practice amounted to every assistance short of war.

On arrival at Halifax on the 9th November the Battalion re-embarked on U.S.S. 'Orizaba' (Captain Gulbranson). The all-American convoy, again with a powerful escort, left Halifax on the 11th November and arrived at Cape Town, South Africa, on the 9th December. In accordance with American practice the 'Orizaba' was a 'dry' ship, but for most this was fully compensated by the low cost, and plentiful supply, of cigarettes.

The news of the Japanese attack on Pearl Harbour on the 7th December 1941 was received on the wireless on the following day. In a night the British Commonwealth and the United States of America had become allies at war with Germany, Italy and Japan. The whole balance and strategy of the war were to undergo radical changes. Although she had acquired a new and formidable enemy the Commonwealth was no longer fighting alone. Nevertheless, as a result of the new situation she was to suffer the loss of all her Far Eastern territories—as were her American and Dutch allies.

The convoy remained at Cape Town for four days. Shore leave was granted and the troops were able to enjoy the truly overwhelming hospitality of the South African people.

From the 22nd to 29th December the 'Orizaba' lay off the port of Kilindini, near Mombasa, where they were visited by Lieut.-General Sir William Platt—an ex-officer of the Fifth Fusiliers who was then commanding in East Africa.

About this time, owing to the entry into the war of Japan, the decision was made to divert the 18th Division to the Far East. The 53rd Infantry Brigade proceeded direct to Singapore and the rest of the Division to Bombay en route for the same final destination.

On arrival at Bombay on the 6th January 1942 the Battalion went into camp at Deolali (near Bombay). The news from the Far East recorded an unbroken succession of Japanese successes and the next fortnight was devoted to intensive training, acclimatization to Eastern conditions and to the overhauling of M.T. and other equipment.

It is interesting to record that in spite of strict security measures Sandal & Sons, the old Regimental Contractors, sent a wire from Mhow offering their services, and later Chamru, the old 2nd Battalion 'durzi' (tailor) and shoemaker, arrived in person.

On the 21st January the 9th Bn. Royal Northumberland Fusiliers embarked at Bombay on H.T. 'Felix Roussel' flying the Free French flag, and thus began the final stage of their long journey.

It will be convenient here to give a short résumé of the condition and battleworthiness of the 18th Division in general, and the 9th Bn. Royal Northumberland Fusiliers in particular, as the ships approached Singapore at the beginning of February 1942. The Division as a whole was, by the standards of those days, well trained and well equipped. The troops had confidence in their leaders and morale was excellent. Nevertheless, by the end of 1941, no formations in the British Army had attained the high level of staff work and battle-craft—or received the lavish supplies of modern equipment—which characterized the campaigns of 1944 and 1945. Moreover, the journey from England had taken fourteen weeks, most of which had been spent in the confined space of a crowded troopship. Only the most elementary training had been possible and inevitably the men had become somewhat soft. This—combined with the lack of experience of most officers and men of Eastern conditions—placed

Feb. 1942 units at a serious disadvantage when they disembarked at Singapore and went into battle immediately.

On the morning of the 4th February the Battalion had its first encounter with the Japanese, who carried out a high-level bombing attack as the convoy passed through the Banka Straits. The A.A. fire of the escorting cruiser, H.M.S. 'Exeter,' kept the enemy out of range for accurate bombing and the ships suffered no damage.

As they approached Singapore at dawn on the 5th they saw black columns of smoke coming from the destroyed oil tanks of the Naval Base. At 1030 hrs. when near the island the convoy was attacked by 27 enemy aircraft. Two bombs struck the 'Felix Roussel,' killing Fusiliers J. H. Ryan and G. Errington and three men of the R.A.S.C. In addition about 14 men were wounded. Men of the Battalion manning anti-aircraft guns put up a most spirited defence and claimed to have brought down three Japanese planes.*

The 'Empress of Asia,' which was further astern in the convoy, was hit, caught fire and later sank. Her complement were nearly all rescued by small craft from the shore.

II. OPERATIONS ON SINGAPORE ISLAND

At dusk on the 5th February 1942 the 'Felix Roussel' moved into Keppel Harbour, Singapore, and the Battalion disembarked in the dark. They moved at once to the northern slopes of Hill 85 on the north-east side of the Island. The ship containing the unit transport had returned to India without unloading and on the 7th and 8th they were issued with a reduced scale of impressed civilian lorries. These consisted of 10 cars, 86 trucks and 6 motor cycles, mostly of doubtful reliability.

By this time the Japanese had overrun the entire mainland of Malaya, and their troops were preparing to assault across the Johore Straits—the narrow stretch of water which separates the mainland from Singapore Island.

The troops at the disposal of the G.O.C.-in-C. Malaya, Lieut.-General A. E. Percival, for the defence of the Island were the equivalent of about four weak divisions—namely:

11th Indian Division (in which was incorporated the remnants of the 9th Indian Division which had suffered very heavily during the fighting on the mainland)
8th Australian Division (two infantry brigades only)
18th Division
Other troops amounting to the equivalent of about a division

The total strength had been estimated at 85,000 men, many of whom were non-combatants and only about 70,000 of whom were properly armed and equipped.

The battleships 'Prince of Wales' and 'Repulse' had been sunk on the 10th December 1941 and most of our aircraft destroyed early in the campaign. Japanese command of the sea and air was complete.

---

* In 1943 the 'Felix Roussel' was again at Liverpool and, with due ceremony, a plaque was unveiled on the ship inscribed: 'To the glory of God and in remembrance of the men of the Royal Northumberland Fusiliers who gave their lives defending this ship.'

Captain Hindmarch (Malaya Police), whose home was at Felton in Northumberland, was attached to the Battalion as Liaison Officer, and remained with it until the 15th February. His local knowledge was invaluable. Feb. 1942

On the 7th February X Coy. took up position in support of the 54th Infantry Brigade between the River Seletar and Punggol Point, and Y Coy. in support of the 55th Infantry Brigade from Punggol Point to the River Tampinis. W Coy. was also placed under command of the 55th Infantry Brigade; and on the 8th occupied positions in the Wireless Station just south of Seletar airfield.

On the 8th the Battalion, less W, X and Y Coys., received orders to form a strong point in the area north-east of the Mental Hospital, with the object of preventing infiltration along Punggol Creek. The position was never occupied, however, as new orders were issued almost at once.

After a series of delays, due to the poor communications on the Island, Z Coy. was placed under command of the 28th Indian Infantry Brigade of the 11th Indian Division and at about 0100 hrs. on the 9th the Company moved to the Naval Base.

On the night of 8th/9th February the Japanese crossed the Johore Straits and established a bridgehead on the north-west corner of the Island. This area was held by troops of the 8th Australian Division. The defence was greatly hampered by dense undergrowth which limited the field of vision and fire to a few yards, and by the fact that no defence works had been constructed or obstacles erected.

By the morning of the 10th February the situation had deteriorated considerably. The Japanese had extended their bridgehead and occupied part of the Naval Base, where the 28th Indian Infantry Brigade, with Z Coy. in support, were hard pressed. On this day R Coy. (1st Reinforcements) was placed under orders of H.Q. 18th Division for protective purposes and Bn. HQ. withdrew, under orders, from Hill 85 to a jungle area just west of Paya Lebar.

In the meantime Lieut.-Colonel Thomas (with Major Leech as his Staff Officer) had assumed command of a composite force known as 'Tom Force' to operate towards the west with the object of pushing back the enemy in the Bukit Timah area. This plan was not successful, as by that time the enemy was firmly established and supported by tanks. Lieut.-Colonel Thomas and Major Leech returned to the Battalion on the 13th.

By the 12th the situation had become very grave and the decision was made to form a perimeter on the south of the Island covering the City, into which all troops were to be withdrawn. This line ran approximately from the Civil Airport—north to Paya Lebar village—west to Macritchie Reservoir—Adam Road—Holland Road—Reformatory Road. At 1400 hrs. on this day the Battalion commenced to withdraw within the perimeter and by midnight had taken up the following positions:

Bn. H.Q. . Malcolm Road
W Coy. . Just east of Macritchie Reservoir Broadcasting Station
X „ . East end of Malcolm Road
Y „ . The 125 feature on Whitton Road
Z „ . Bukit Timah Road about ¾ mile west of Newton Circus

On the 13th enemy gun, mortar and small-arms fire and bombing continued

Feb. 1942 throughout the day. In the afternoon Bn. H.Q. and H.Q. Coy. moved to Chancery Lane within 18th Division H.Q. perimeter and manned the north and west faces, and R Coy. (1st Reinforcements) formed a strong-point at the junction of Thompson and Whitley Roads.

Up to now the morale of the troops had remained high and casualties only slight, but on this day it became apparent to all that the situation was desperate and that there was little chance of a successful sustained defence of the Island. The enemy's complete superiority in the air, the fact that he now occupied the major part of the Island and had succeeded in landing tanks and artillery—combined with the confusion due to congestion and the breakdown in civil administration—all gave the impression that the end was only a matter of days.

The Battalion had lost many of its vehicles owing to enemy action and mechanical defects. Most of the heavy baggage had been abandoned, including the folding altar, with the Regimental crest, presented to the Battalion after Dunkirk.

At about 2200 hrs. on the 13th the Commanding Officer was called to Divisional H.Q. and ordered to proceed on a secret mission in company with one other officer and six other ranks of the Battalion—to be selected by him. As time was short there was no alternative to making the selection from those in the immediate vicinity of Bn. H.Q. The names were:

Major B. J. Leech (O.C. H.Q. Coy.)
R.S.M. T. Johnson (H.Q. Coy.)
C.S.M. G. McQuade (H.Q. Coy.)
Cpl. A. Sidey (W Coy.)
Fus. A. Casey (Y Coy.)
Fus. T. Bennett (H.Q. Coy.)
S/Sgt. W. Rides (attd. from R.A.O.C.)

At the time the purpose of this mission was not known. Later it was revealed as part of a decision, made at the highest level, to evacuate a few representative individuals from each unit. In due course this party, together with similar parties from other units, arrived in India.* Lieut.-Colonel Thomas's departure was keenly felt by all ranks. His coolness in action and inspiring leadership had been of the highest order. Had the decision to remain with the Battalion or proceed on his 'mission' been left to him no one doubted as to what his answer would have been.

Major H. S. Flower assumed command of the Battalion and Captain A. Veitch took command of H.Q. Coy.

On the 14th February the Battalion took up positions forming the framework of the defensive line of the Mount Pleasant Road from inclusive Thomson Road to inclusive Bukit Timah Road. On this line there were troops of various units, including the 4th Suffolk Regt., 18th Reconnaissance Regt. and some anti-tank gunners.

* On arrival at the docks it was discovered that there was only sufficient official shipping for certain selected senior officers. Lieut.-Colonel Thomas, acting under a direct order, embarked on one of the official ships. Other members of the Battalion party were given the option of rejoining their unit or of attempting to escape under their own arrangements. They chose the latter and their adventures are described in Appendix A.

W Coy. were on the right, Y Coy. centre and Z Coy. on their left, with X Coy. covering the Bukit Timah Road area. In addition to their defensive duties all companies formed collecting posts for stragglers entering the perimeter, who were given food and drink and organized into small battle-groups for action on the spot. Feb. 1942

On the 15th enemy pressure, from both ground and air, was intensified. The Battalion continued to hold the line of the Mount Pleasant Road and dealt with a continuous stream of stragglers and civilian refugees making their way to the City.

By this time the Japanese held all the water reservoirs and orders were issued for the strictest economy in the use of water. Very little was known of the situation outside the Battalion area, but it was clear to all that it was desperate, and deteriorating hourly. Many small isolated engagements took place along the front, in the course of which heavy casualties were inflicted on the enemy.

The front was still holding firmly when at 1330 hrs. a message was received from H.Q. 18th Division stating that an agreement had been made with the enemy that firing should cease at 1600 hrs. and that at that hour all troops were to stand fast in their positions. Some confusion arose regarding the interpretation of this agreement, owing, it is thought, to the difference between local Singapore time and Tokio time, which the Japanese used. At about 1800 hrs. Major Flower went forward, under cover of a white flag, to a part of the front where Japanese troops continued to advance and were taking prisoners. After a lengthy discussion with an enemy regimental commander Major Flower was allowed to march the men back to their own lines.

Many Japanese dead were lying about and many more wounded. They appeared to have no medical equipment with them and were most eager to get hold of British field dressings. Many unwounded Japanese were extremely exhausted: one of their men who could speak a little English fainted twice when acting as interpreter during Major Flower's discussions.

It was revealed later that had the armistice not taken place the Battalion front would have been attacked by two fresh Japanese divisions, supported by tanks, who were in process of forming up for the final assault on the City.

The night of the 15th/16th February was spent by both sides in rest and sleep: there were no incidents.

This ends the dismal story of the campaign in Malaya and Singapore. Many doubted the ability of the Commonwealth forces to hold the Fortress indefinitely, but there were few who expected such a quick Japanese victory. When the defences of Singapore were planned, and constructed, it had been assumed that a formidable fleet would be based there and all the defensive arrangements were made on that supposition. It may be said that the fundamental cause of failure was the early Japanese assumption of complete superiority on the sea and in the air and the inadequacy of the land forces in numbers, equipment and in some cases in training. Nevertheless, it is surprising that so little was done towards the digging of earthworks, the construction of wire and other obstacles and the clearance of fields of fire to meet an attack across the Johore Straits. With the huge civil population on the Island it should have been possible to do much in this direction while the battle on the mainland was still in progress.

Feb.–March 1942

For the 9th Bn. Royal Northumberland Fusiliers the capitulation was indeed a tragic climax to their twenty months' hard training after Dunkirk.

III. CAPTIVITY

In the Russo-Japanese War, and other campaigns in which they were engaged in recent times, the Japanese observed the laws and customs of war punctiliously, and their treatment of prisoners was beyond reproach. There was every reason to expect, therefore, that the Singapore garrison would receive chivalrous and generous treatment at their hands. Unfortunately this was not to be. For some reason, difficult to explain, the Japanese in the Second World War treated their captives with a harshness which often amounted to barbarism—although there were isolated exceptions.*

On the 16th February all weapons were collected and taken over by the Japanese, who also removed unit M.T. vehicles and much other equipment.

At midday on the 17th orders were received for all European troops to move to Changi that day. About three hours later the move commenced, but as everybody had to carry his own blankets and other personal kit, progress was slow and very few troops arrived before dark. The Battalion was fortunate in its quarters. All officers, H.Q. and X Coys. were in permanent barracks, Y Coy. in huts and W and Z Coys. in 160-lb. Indian pattern tents.

All rations were pooled and for a week the troops lived on British rations, the first Japanese food being issued on the 24th February. This consisted of 12 oz. rice, $1\frac{3}{4}$ oz. meat and $\frac{1}{6}$ oz. tea per man per day.

Contact with the Japanese was rare, all orders being issued through the normal British channels of command—Malaya Command, Southern Area, 18th Division, etc.

The following acting unpaid promotions were made to replace casualties:

Major H. S. Flower . .	to Lieut.-Colonel
Captain H. B. Burn . .	to Major
Lieut. T. Fairbairn . .	to Captain
Lieut. J. Brooks, D.C.M. .	to Captain
R.Q.M.S. Mosgrove . .	to R.S.M.
C.Q.M.S. J. Redfern . .	to C.S.M.

About a fortnight after the capitulation, orders were received that each group—the 18th Division forming a group—was to be wired in and nobody allowed outside the enclosure without a white flag. Only four such flags were allowed and this greatly restricted the amenities and put a stop to bathing.

Towards the end of March a party consisting of 450 men of the 9th Bn. Royal Northumberland Fusiliers and 400 men of the 18th Reconnaissance Regt., all under Lieut.-Colonel Flower, marched into Singapore City on a ten-day tour in a camp in Farrer Park. There conditions were extremely bad. The wired-in enclosure only measured about 150 yds. by 200 yds.; tentage was inadequate and of poor quality

* This matter is discussed in *Broken Thread*, by Major-General F. S. G. Piggott, C.B., D.S.O. (Gale & Polden Ltd.), who spent many years in Japan.

and sanitary arrangements extremely primitive. The hardships were increased by heavy rain. Working parties were employed clearing debris and burying corpses. April–Oct. 1942

Prior to this Captain McCreath, with about 100 men of Y Coy. and some selected tradesmen of other companies, had gone to River Valley Road Camp.

On St. George's Day all ranks wore improvised red and white roses, and attended service in St. George's Church, formerly the mosque of the Hong Kong/Singapore Artillery, which Padre Cordingley and a band of helpers had converted into a beautifully equipped place of worship. The service included the Regimental Hymn.

Before the service the Divisional Commander, Major-General Beckwith-Smith,* addressed the Battalion and afterwards took the salute at a march past. By some miraculous means the Quartermaster, Lieut. Purcell, produced a tot of rum for every man's dinner on this day. It is interesting to record that throughout their captivity officers and men of the Battalion never failed to remember St. George's Day and hold some small ceremony of celebration—as circumstances permitted.

Early in May a new camp was formed at the east end of Keppel Harbour. In addition to 444 all ranks of the Royal Northumberland Fusiliers there were men of 18th Divisional Signals, 1st Cambridgeshires, 1/5th Foresters, 1/5th Beds and Herts and 18th Reconnaissance Regt.—a total of about 1,000, all under command of Lieut.-Colonel Flower. Accommodation was in three 'go-downs,' in which were low wooden platforms for sleeping purposes. Other smaller sheds were converted into cook-houses, a hospital, latrines, etc. There was electric light and a piped water supply.

The Battalion was to remain in this camp until the end of October 1942, the men being employed mainly on building work connected with the conversion of Robinson Road Police Station into a Japanese Army Headquarters.

Rations were very poor and deficiency diseases became general. At one time more than 25 per cent. of the prisoners in camp were unfit for work owing to running sores.

Late in June working pay was issued at the rate of 25c. (7d.) per officer, 15c. per W.O. and N.C.O. and 10c. per fusilier per day. A local purchase party was permitted to leave camp about every ten days. In August officers' pay was granted at the same rate as in the Japanese Army. Thus a lieutenant-colonel received, in theory, #220 per month although only #30 per month was handed over in cash—deductions being made for food, clothing, toilet paper, etc.

On the 18th July General Percival, the G.O.C. Malaya, was allowed to visit the camp for a few minutes, prior to being removed to Formosa in company with all other British officers above the rank of lieutenant-colonel.

About this time the Japanese insisted on all prisoners of war signing a parole certificate to the effect that they would not attempt to escape. After many protests, and much ill-treatment of those who refused, Lieut.-Colonel E. B. Holmes, M.C. (The Manchester Regiment, and senior British officer), gave permission for all ranks to sign. Major H. B. Burn was one of the last to sign and only did so after ill-treatment which resulted in a severe attack of fever.

On the 31st October all personnel (777 out of the original 1,000) in Keppel Harbour

* Major-General Beckwith-Smith died as a prisoner of war in Japanese hands.

Oct. 1942– Jan. 1945

Camp were moved to River Valley Road Camp, about the largest prisoners-of-war camp in Singapore.

This initial period of captivity has been described in some detail, as up to this time the Battalion had to some extent been kept together. It will be appreciated that as time passed the unit became more dispersed and numbers decreased. This was due to deaths, the removal of technicians and tradesmen for special work and to the fact that seriously sick men who were sent to hospital did not always return on recovery. The rest of the story is, therefore, in less detail. It is written to give a general impression of life as a prisoner in Japanese hands, rather than a day-to-day, or even month-to-month, account.

On the 7th November 335 officers and men of the 9th Bn. Royal Northumberland Fusiliers, together with some 300 of other units, left Singapore in a train for Siam. This was the main body of the Battalion, although smaller parties, totalling about 413 officers and men, left on other dates also for Siam (fourteen of them for Japan). After many halts the party arrived at Chungkai, about 60 miles west of Bangkok, on the 5th December.

During April 1943—fourteen months after the fall of Singapore—the first mail arrived and a few lucky members of the Regiment received letters.

During the summer the Japanese became very anxious about cholera. At Tarso, where the Battalion moved early in June, a few cases occurred. Fus. J. P. Smith (Z Coy.) died from the disease and three other cases recovered. A few primitive precautions were taken, including inoculation with Japanese-made serum of doubtful efficiency.

The months passed by and as the railway pushed ahead camp was moved frequently—to Touchan South (late June 1943), Kinsiok (late July 1943), Pramkasi (middle of August 1943), Tomajo (23rd September 1943), Namajo (31st October 1943) and back to Tomajo (14th November 1943).

It would make tedious reading to give a detailed catalogue of every move which occurred during the next two years. It will be sufficient to record that as bad food and exposure gradually lowered the men's resistance to disease the death and sickness rate increased. The total number of deaths during the war among those employed on the Burma–Siam Railway has been estimated at:

British and Australian	12,000
Dutch	6,000
Coolies	100,000

The various moves of the main body of the Battalion are shown in detail on Map No. VIII.

By the autumn of 1944 the Battalion had become considerably scattered, but the largest contingent was at Tamuang Camp. This camp contained about 3,000 prisoners of war—British, Australian, Dutch and a few Americans, of whom about 17 officers and 130 other ranks belonged to the Royal Northumberland Fusiliers.

In January 1945 the Japanese decided to separate officers and other ranks and all officers were sent to a camp at Kamburi about 50 kilometres away.

As the year 1945 advanced, and Allied successes increased, the Japanese became

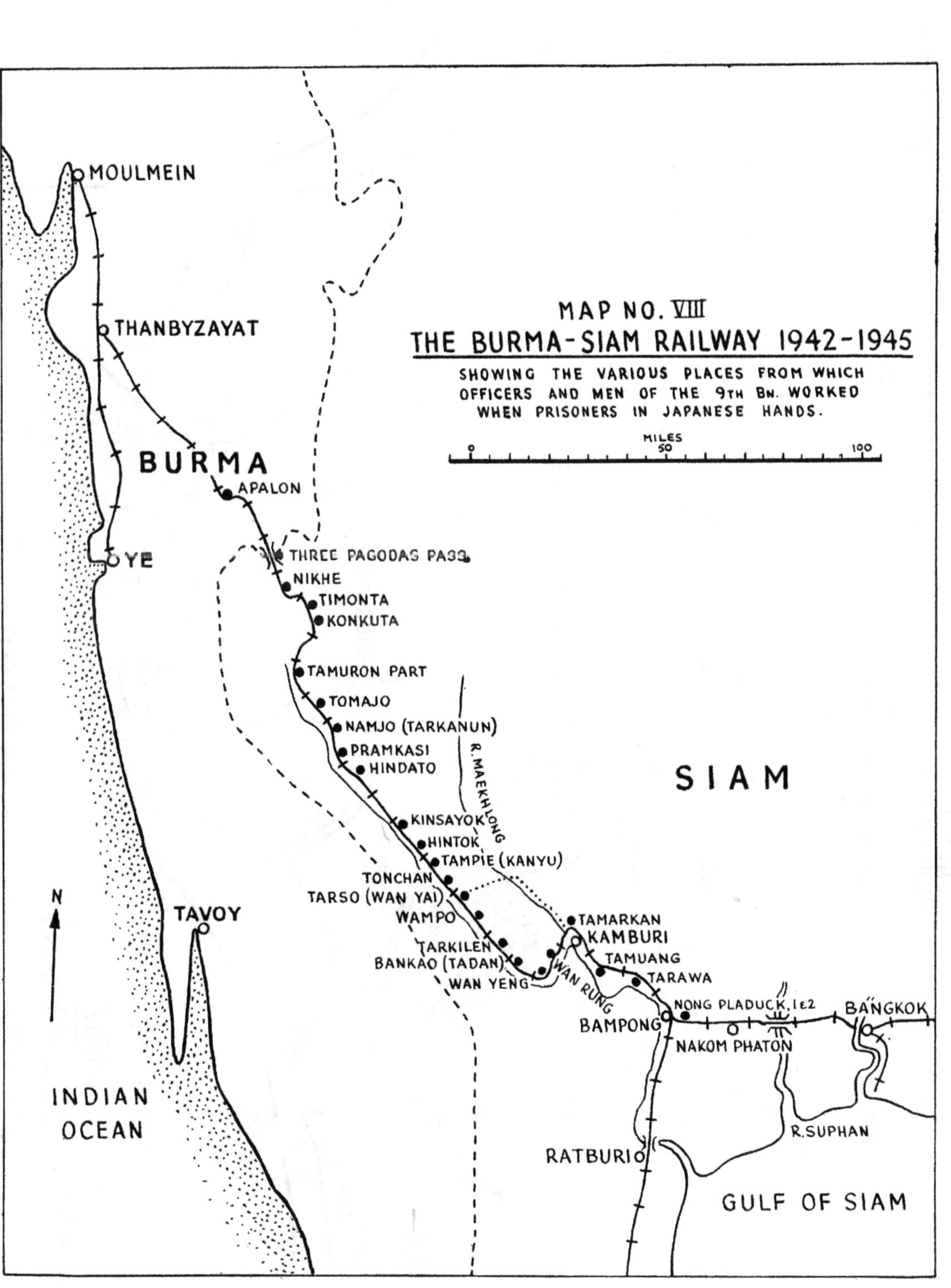
MAP NO. VIII
THE BURMA-SIAM RAILWAY 1942-1945
SHOWING THE VARIOUS PLACES FROM WHICH OFFICERS AND MEN OF THE 9TH BN. WORKED WHEN PRISONERS IN JAPANESE HANDS.
MILES
0
50
100
MOULMEIN
THANBYZAYAT
BURMA
APALON
YE
THREE PAGODAS PASS
NIKHE
TIMONTA
KONKUTA
TAMURON PART
TOMAJO
NAMJO (TARKANUN)
PRAMKASI
HINDATO
R. MAEKHLONG
SIAM
KINSAYOK
HINTOK
TAMPIE (KANYU)
TONCHAN
TARSO (WAN YAI)
WAMPO
TARKILEN
BANKAO (TADAN)
WAN YENG
WAN RUNG
TAMARKAN
KAMBURI
TAMUANG
TARAWA
NONG PLADUCK, 1 & 2
BAMPONG
NAKOM PHATON
BANGKOK
R. SUPHAN
RATBURI
GULF OF SIAM
N
TAVOY
INDIAN OCEAN

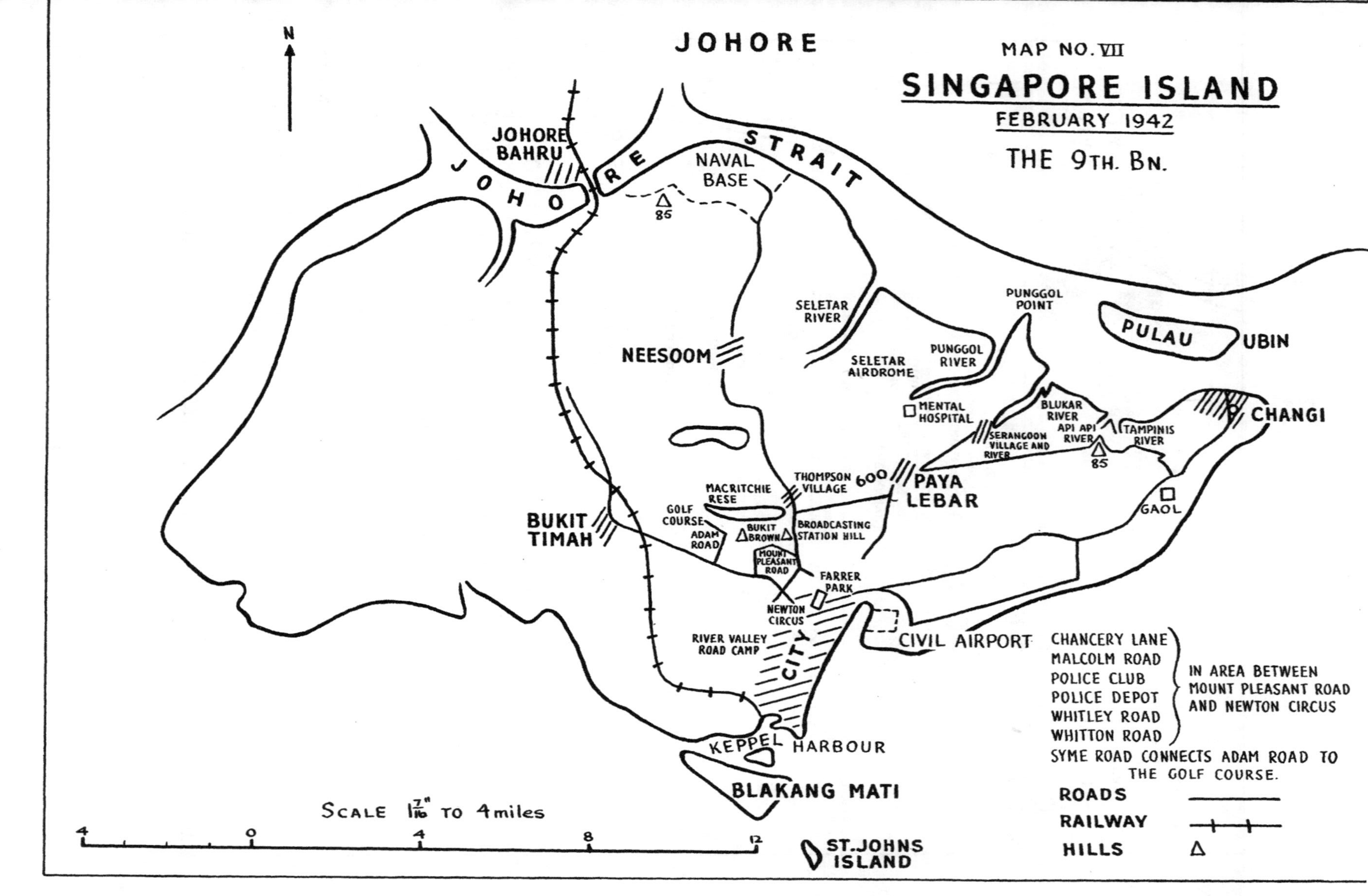
MAP NO. VII
SINGAPORE ISLAND
FEBRUARY 1942
THE 9TH. BN.
N
JOHORE
JOHORE BAHRU
JOHORE STRAIT
NAVAL BASE
85
SELETAR RIVER
SELETAR AIRDROME
PUNGGOL POINT
PUNGGOL RIVER
PULAU UBIN
NEESOOM
MENTAL HOSPITAL
BLUKAR RIVER
API API RIVER
SERANGOON VILLAGE AND RIVER
TAMPINIS RIVER
85
CHANGI
THOMPSON VILLAGE
600
PAYA LEBAR
MACRITCHIE RESE
GOLF COURSE
ADAM ROAD
BUKIT BROWN
BROADCASTING STATION HILL
BUKIT TIMAH
MOUNT PLEASANT ROAD
FARRER PARK
NEWTON CIRCUS
GAOL
RIVER VALLEY ROAD CAMP
CITY
CIVIL AIRPORT
KEPPEL HARBOUR
BLAKANG MATI
ST. JOHNS ISLAND
SCALE 1 7/16" TO 4 miles
4 0 4 8 12
CHANCERY LANE
MALCOLM ROAD
POLICE CLUB
POLICE DEPOT
WHITLEY ROAD
WHITTON ROAD
IN AREA BETWEEN MOUNT PLEASANT ROAD AND NEWTON CIRCUS
SYME ROAD CONNECTS ADAM ROAD TO THE GOLF COURSE.
ROADS
RAILWAY
HILLS

restive and imposed additional restrictions and irritations on their prisoners. Pay was reduced from 30 to 20 baht. per month; walking-sticks were only permitted for the very sick; all valuables had to be handed in; beatings became more frequent and new barbarous forms of punishment were invented. Pencils and writing paper were forbidden. June–Sept. 1945

In June and July 1945 rumours of the German surrender began to filter through, and there were signs that things had gone badly for the Japanese in Burma. The news of the Japanese surrender reached most camps about the 17th August, in the majority of cases by means of the clandestine wireless sets which had been installed. At Nakom Nayok, where several Royal Northumberland Fusilier officers had been moved from Kamburi, the Japanese Camp Commandant informed the senior officer that his Emperor had decided that the war was only causing endless destruction and that he was therefore stopping it.

No sooner was the news received than the conditions of life for the prisoners completely changed. Wireless sets came out into the open, news bulletins were posted up and Allied flags hoisted. National anthems were sung and thanksgiving services held. Parties of officers were sent off to other camps to contact other ranks and a prisoner-of-war headquarters was established at Bangkok.

Some prisoners were flown out on the 1st September, nearly all being sent initially to Rangoon. By the end of September every man of the 9th Bn. Royal Northumberland Fusiliers had been accounted for, the final figures for fatal casualties being:

	Officers	*Other Ranks*
Killed in action	4*	11
Died of wounds	—	7
Died as prisoners of war	—	151
Total	4	169

These figures represent 19·5 per cent. of the strength of the Battalion on embarkation at Liverpool on the 30th October 1941.

All the survivors were suffering from disease in one form or another, mostly deficiency diseases, and some from injuries resulting from ill-treatment by the Japanese.

All available evidence shows that throughout their long captivity the morale and bearing of all ranks of the Battalion remained at the highest standard. They worthily upheld the reputation of the Royal Northumberland Fusiliers, and earned the admiration of their fellow-prisoners and the respect of their Japanese guards.

After the Japanese surrender Major-General Thomas (the Battalion's Commanding Officer prior to the capitulation in February 1942) was in Burma as Inspector-General Burma Army, and saw most of the survivors as they passed through Rangoon

* Officers killed in action were: Major C. R. I. Besley, M.B.E., M.C., Captain R. Watson, Lieut. M. Ward, 2/Lieut. G. B. Willis. Major Besley, taken prisoner with the 7th Bn. in 1940, had escaped from Germany.

Sept. 1945 after their liberation. The following is an extract from a letter which he wrote at the time:

> 'In September the majority of the 9th Battalion passed through here and I met nearly all the officers and many of the men, which led to many happy reunions. It is a delight to get their letters giving descriptions of their arrival home.
>
> 'From all sides—not only in the Battalion—I have heard how simply marvellous they were in captivity. Nothing, simply nothing, broke their spirit and they even won the admiration of the Jap, and held their St. George's Day Parades. When they came through here every man still had his cap badge, which was polished as for Ceremonial Parades. I don't think I have met a finer Battalion either before or since.'

This ends the story of the captivity of the officers and men of a unit which formed part of the largest force ever to surrender to the enemy in the history of the British Army. It must be emphasized, however, that no individual in the Battalion played any part whatever in the surrender negotiations. They were swamped by the general trend of events—events which were outside their power to control.

CHAPTER 9

NORTH AFRICA

January 1942 to May 1943
1st Battalion

(*See Map No. IX*)

By the middle of December 1941 the British offensive in North Africa had resulted in the relief of Tobruk and the capture of Benghazi. By the 8th January 1942 Rommel had withdrawn his forces westwards from Cyrenaica, roughly to the position El Agheila–Marada. The German-Italian Army had suffered a severe defeat, but it had withdrawn in good order and had not suffered devastating casualties. For the British forces the advance had brought an uplift in morale; but also a long and difficult line of supply. Dec. 1941–June 1942

On the relief of Tobruk the 1st Bn. Royal Northumberland Fusiliers moved to Egypt, into barracks at Abbasia, near Cairo. Arriving on the 22nd December 1941, they were able to enjoy a reasonably festive Christmas after their hard life of the previous months.

It will not be necessary to describe the next few months in detail. The time was spent in refitting and training, with the object of becoming a thoroughly battleworthy unit again in the shortest possible time. The task was made somewhat difficult by the general shortage of equipment—particularly transport—and the necessity for guard and other duties in Cairo and elsewhere. Moves were frequent and the Battalion gravitated between Cairo and Alexandria—performing the varying tasks which are normally imposed on a unit at rest in a theatre of operations—and rarely concentrated as a battalion. The 4th Battalion of the Regiment was also in Egypt, and the two units saw much of each other, having first met quite by chance in the Desert when the 1st Battalion was returning from Tobruk to Cairo.

So the time passed until St. George's Day 1942, when the Battalion carried out a very impressive ceremonial march through Cairo and attended a service in the Cathedral. For the only time during the war the Battalion paraded with the Colours. The salute was taken by Sir Miles Lampson, the British Ambassador to Egypt.

The first week of June 1942 was to see the opening of a new German-Italian offensive, which, once again, was to drive the British and Commonwealth forces back into Egypt with heavy losses in men and equipment.

Soon after Rommel commenced his advance the Battalion was ordered back to the Desert; but owing to shortages of equipment W and Z Coys. were left behind in Alexandria—most of their transport and other equipment being handed over to X and Y Coys.

The exact destination was not known, but after passing a night in Tobruk, the Battalion (less two companies) was ordered forward to a rendezvous at a point some 10 miles south-west of Knightsbridge.

June 1942

That night plans were laid for an attack to be made the following day by an Indian brigade supported by the 4th Royal Tank Regiment and X Coy. The objective was a feature well inside the turmoil of the 'Cauldron.' The object was to end the deadlock and try to prevent any further offensive action by the Germans.

Although the primary objective was reached, no further progress was made that day. In this attack Major T. F. C. Hamilton, who was commanding X Coy., particularly distinguished himself in the calm and fearless handling of his company.

Later in the day Y Coy. (Captain R. S. Ferguson) was despatched to join the 4th Battalion of the Regiment under Lieut.-Colonel des Graz and a regiment of artillery, with the object of forming a defensive box. That evening the position was attacked by an overwhelming force of tanks. The gunners fired over open sights, the 4th Battalion, who had as anti-tank weapons the virtually useless 2-pr. guns, fought gallantly, while Y Coy. fired belt after belt at the attacking tanks; but it was all of no avail, and the position was overrun and the order given to withdraw. Part of Y Coy. managed to get away in trucks and conceal themselves in a wadi, hoping to get away when things were quieter. Unfortunately they were spotted by German tanks and had no option but to surrender.

During the evening German armoured cars broke through and carried out a most successful raid on the Divisional H.Q. and B Echelon areas. Bn. H.Q. withdrew hastily and spent the night with the 7th Armoured Divisional Headquarters near Tobruk. The following day, 7th June, the Indian Brigade and X Coy. were withdrawn to El Adem south of Tobruk, where XXXth Corps H.Q. were established. They found another defensive box, which as usual was soon being fiercely attacked, though in this case the defenders managed to withdraw by night.

Amongst the casualties sustained during this battle Captain R. Mitchell, Second-in-Command Y Coy., 2/Lieut. Gatfield, platoon commander Y Coy. and C.S.M. Smith of X Coy. were killed.

By mid-June the Eighth Army had lost the Battle of 'Knightsbridge' and Rommel was advancing on Egypt.

On the 15th June W and Z Coys. moved by train to Sollum to rejoin the rest of the Battalion. This journey took three days and, being carried out in cattle trucks in midsummer, was a most uncomfortable one. The night of the 18th/19th June was spent in Sollum Transit Camp. The next morning they joined the rest of the Battalion in defensive positions round the Sollum perimeter.

A few days later it was decided to vacate Sollum and the Battalion (less Z Coy.) withdrew to Mersa Matruh. Z Coy. and a battalion of the Mahratta Light Infantry remained at Sollum as rearguard, where they had some good shooting at advanced enemy troops. After twenty-four hours this force also withdrew to rejoin the Battalion, which ultimately came under command of the 50th (Northumbrian) Division which was holding the Gerawla area just east of Matruh.

The three companies, W, X and Z, were put under command of brigades. During the first afternoon in the Gerawla position, the 151st Infantry Brigade with Z Coy. under command was ordered to move out into the Desert to the south that night, and 'smash the enemy's L. of C.' as the enemy were rapidly by-passing the defences. This would have been a difficult enough task to accomplish in daytime but by night was even harder, since the L. of C. followed no definite line of country and was widely dispersed. June–July 1942

The Brigade moved off in transport at dusk, platoons with battalions, Company H.Q. with Brigade H.Q. The Brigade soon got split up in the darkness, and after driving for several hours and shooting up two enemy leaguers of transport, the signal was given to turn back to Gerawla. By this time enemy defences were alerted and a good deal of erratic fire was directed towards the Brigade's vehicles, which could not be seen but could certainly be heard. By skilful navigation, however, and a certain amount of luck, the Brigade returned to its defensive positions with few losses, having apparently achieved very little.

During the following day it became clear that the enemy in some strength had succeeded in getting behind the Division and had cut the coast road back to the east. Orders were therefore given for the Division to break out that night, drive south in the Desert for 30 miles and then swing north-east to aim at reaching the coast again, leaving the enemy to the west. The breakout was hindered, not so much by the enemy, who were in very scattered positions, but by a steep escarpment which could only be climbed by vehicles up the occasional spurs which had an easier slope. These spurs were hard to find in the dark and were covered with large boulders which wrecked many gearboxes. They were intersected by wadis which were also boulder-strewn and contained large patches of soft sand. Many vehicles went into these wadis by mistake and the noise of their furiously revving engines, in their efforts to get out, was appalling. Many vehicles had to be abandoned and their crews were busy with pick-axes wrecking them as best they could. Those vehicles which had found suitable ways up the escarpment had to carry the crews, weapons and ammunition of the less fortunate ones. What could be seen of the Division the following morning presented a sorry sight. Appallingly overladen vehicles were moving slowly along; many of them were towing others which had got to the top of the escarpment only to break down. Very little of the large force which had been in the Gerawla position seemed to have got clear. The rendezvous for Bn. H.Q. was Fuka, but on arrival there it was found to be already occupied by the enemy. This resulted in most of the Bn. H.Q. being captured, including the Adjutant, Captain H. Holmes. The Commanding Officer managed to get away on foot and was eventually picked up by No. 14 Platoon of Z Coy., who took him back to El Alamein, where a defensive line was already being prepared. Although Z Coy. lost a platoon during this breakout (it is believed they were trapped by soft sand in a wadi and could not get away before dawn, by which time they were surrounded), the Battalion as a whole had not fared too badly and, apart from lack of transport, they were in reasonable condition to fight.

By mid-July the general situation had become more stabilized and the Battalion (less Z Coy.) proceeded to Sidi-Bishr to refit, Z Coy. remaining under command of the 50th Division. It must be emphasized that during the operations just described the Battalion was not properly equipped for battle, and possessed only a fraction of the proper scale of transport. Since leaving Tobruk, six months before, they had been employed on guard duties. Active operations, without refitting, had not been contemplated and they were only sent to the Desert under the dire necessity resulting from Rommel's advance and the threat to Egypt.

July–Oct. 1942

For the next eight months the narrative must be divided—Z Coy. being separated from, and acting in a different role to, the rest of the Battalion, for the greater part of the time.

At Sidi-Bishr the Battalion (less Z Coy.) was reorganized. W, X and Y Coys. were amalgamated, but while this was in progress they became part of a special force called 'Martinforce,' which in addition comprised an Indian Mountain Battery, a troop of anti-tank guns, a section of Royal Engineers and two companies of the Argyll and Sutherland Highlanders. The task of this force was to site and construct various defended localities to the west and south of Alexandria. Some training was also carried out, W Coy. being later reconstituted as a training cadre. A welcome reinforcement consisted of some 220 officers and men from the 4th Battalion (the survivors from the Knightsbridge Battle in June).*

Meanwhile Z Coy. (plus a platoon from X Coy. to replace the lost one)—which had been involved in severe fighting on the Ruweisat Ridge, and elsewhere, with the 5th Indian Brigade—had been ordered to provide one platoon for a special mission. No. 14 Platoon, under Lieut. E. J. B. Raymond, was selected. The task proved to be a seaborne raid on the enemy-held coastline at Tobruk—in conjunction with other troops. The Platoon carried out training at Mustapha Barracks, Alexandria. The raiding party left Alexandria in motor torpedo boats on the 11th September and arrived off Tobruk on the 13th—after two very unpleasant days at sea. Surprise, essential to the success of the operation, was not effected. As a result, Sergt. Miller's section alone succeeded in landing. After evading capture for a considerable time, all but one of its members contracted dysentery and were compelled to surrender. The one man to escape, Cpl. Wilson, after many adventurous experiences in and around Tobruk, regained the British lines two months later after the Battle of El Alamein. The remainder of the Platoon had no alternative to returning to Alexandria, which, despite being heavily dive-bombed en route, they reached safely.

By mid-September 1942 the British Empire Forces based in Egypt had come under the command of General Sir Harold Alexander, with General Sir B. L. Montgomery in command of the Eighth Army. Rommel's final bid for victory at Alam Halfa had been defeated and preparations for the great Battle of El Alamein—the turning point of the war—were being made.

By early October the 1st Bn. Royal Northumberland Fusiliers was concentrated once again at Alexandria, the officer state being as follows:

Commanding Officer . .	Lieut.-Colonel E. O. Martin, D.S.O.
Second-in-Command . .	Major R. F. Forbes-Watson
Adjutant	Captain J. MacManners
Quartermaster . . .	Lieut. N. Rogers
Regimental Sergeant-Major .	R.S.M. G. Hughes, D.C.M.
O.C. W Coy. . . .	Major C. C. G. Milward
" X " . . .	Major T. F. C. Hamilton
" Y " . . .	Major R. H. S. M. Kent
" Z " . . .	Captain D. L. Lloyd, M.C.

* See Chapter 7.

16. 1st Battalion celebrating St. George's Day in Cairo, 1942—2/Lieut. W. Sanderson, C.S.M. P. Bell, M.M., 2/Lieut. F. Ward, M.C., Captain and Q.M. O. C. Dipper, M.B.E., D.C.M.

17. The colours being carried out of St. George's Cathedral, Cairo

18. Captain D. L. Lloyd, M.C., taken at the action at El Duda, November 1941

19. 1st Battalion machine-gun post in Italy (see chapter 10)

Oct. 1942–March 1943

The Battalion, although thoroughly reorganized and re-equipped, lacked final polish in training, as so many men who had recently joined from the temporarily disbanded 4th Battalion were unacquainted with the machine-gun role.

The Battle of El Alamein commenced on the 23rd October 1942. By the 3rd November the enemy was in full retreat. Tobruk was recaptured on the 13th November, Benghazi on the 20th and El Agheila on the 15th December. British troops entered Tripoli on the 23rd January 1943.

The original battle plan was changed, and this involved a great deal of movement for the Battalion but little fighting. Casualties were light, but W Coy. had the misfortune to lose a whole platoon during a night attack. Z was the only company to take part in the subsequent pursuit, and the narrative now turns to their activities when once again detached from the Battalion.

After being attached to a number of formations during the assault stage of the battle, Z Coy. finally came under command of the 1st Armoured Division for the pursuit. The Division moved forward on the night of the 4th/5th November. After some days of confused movement, in which the Company became much dispersed, they finally concentrated and moved back to join the rest of the Battalion at Barrani. The whole unit then moved forward to an area some 50 miles west of Tobruk, but soon after Z Coy. joined the King's Dragoon Guards. Later the Company moved with a squadron of the Greys to join the 7th Armoured Division—whom they reached on the 24th November. Here they came under the 22nd Armoured Brigade.

For the next four months this company was part of the spearhead of the comparatively small force (7th Armoured, New Zealand and 51st Highland Divisions) which continued the pursuit 1,500 miles to the Mareth Line. They played an active part in most of the engagement—including the capture of Tripoli, the 70-mile pursuit to Zuara which followed and Rommel's counter-attack in early March from the Mareth Line.

Before the capture of Tripoli Z Coy. played an unusual role for machine-guns. Tripoli was protected by a range of hills which ringed the town. The 7th Armoured Division, who had come up from the Desert to the south, could only find one way through these hills which was suitable for them to get their tanks and guns along. This route was blocked by a strong force of Germans. When the effect of the 51st Division's attack along the coast road from the east had made itself felt, it was feared that the force blocking the 7th Armoured Division's way might blow up the road, to render it impassable to armour, and withdraw. It was decided that the enemy should be encouraged to withdraw hastily, giving them no time to carry out any demolitions. To this end Z Coy., less one platoon, was ordered, together with a force of carriers armed with mortars and Bren guns, to try to get through the hills to the west of the road, come out on to the plain behind, and go into action. The country was very rocky and mountainous and the carriers were soon found to be unequal to it. Z Coy., who were in eleven jeeps, one for each gun and crew, and one each for company commander and platoon commanders (these also carried spare ammunition), found that they could get along slowly aided by a good deal of manhandling of the jeeps.

One platoon was eventually brought into action about halfway through the hills

March 1943 where an excellent position was found overlooking the enemy's forward elements and observation posts from a flank and slightly behind them. The other platoon managed to get right through the hills, but unfortunately could not see the enemy gun positions, which must have been among the hills. They did, however, find enemy infantry taking things very easily, and actually while they were mounting the guns a party of German staff cars drew up and several important-looking officers got out, brandishing large maps. They walked to the top of a hill, and by the time the guns were ready the staff officers were conveniently bunched together, silhouetted on the skyline. The platoon engaged these and the infantry with considerable effect. The other platoon had also been successful, having located a battery position which it had caused to cease fire. The Company withdrew into the hills that night. The enemy also withdrew hastily and without damaging the approaches for the 7th Armoured Division.

It is worth describing here the battle which took place at Medenine, some 15–20 miles south-east of Mareth. The three advanced divisions mentioned above had halted and taken up defence position. This was necessary from the administrative point of view, as the supply lines had been stretched to the limit, but the main reason was that intelligence reports showed that Rommel was concentrating his three armoured divisions, 10th, 15th and 21st Panzer, in the hills to the west of the coast road and the Medenine area.

Z Coy. were under the command of the 131st (Queen's) Lorried Infantry Brigade (the lorried infantry brigade of the 7th Armoured Division), which was commanded by Brigadier L. G. Whistler.

The defensive position held was in the shape of an inverted L. The 51st Division held a line from the coast, across the coast road, to some broken hills to the west. The line then swung south with the 131st Brigade in the hills covering a large wadi which afforded an excellent approach for the enemy. To their left were elements of the 201st Guards Brigade, who had been hastily brought up to thicken the defence. Finally came the redoubtable New Zealand Division, who had a large area to cover which included some steep rocky hills and a long stretch of open country.

The enemy attacked at dawn on the 7th March, under cover of a low-lying morning mist. The first thrust was made by lorried infantry against the 51st Division's left flank. This attack never got anywhere, although it was renewed at intervals during the day. Shortly after the enemy put in two strong armoured attacks, one against the New Zealanders and one against the 131st Brigade, in an effort to clear the wadi and so breach a hole in the defences to the rear of the 51st Division. Two sections of Z Coy.'s machine-guns had excellent defiladed positions covering the mouth of the wadi and afforded some protection to two 6-pr. anti-tank guns sited well forward. This was the first Desert battle in which 17-pr. anti-tank guns were deployed. In fact they were scarcely fired, as they were sited well back in depth, leaving the 6-prs. with the main task in the forward positions.

As the tanks advanced towards the wadi, the machine-guns sprayed them with bullets to force the tanks to close up their armoured panels and so reduce the drivers' visibility. When this had been achieved, the machine-guns switched to the lorries of infantry behind and caused complete disorganization and many casualties. In the meantime the anti-tank gunners of the Queen's, who had held their fire until the last

March 1943

moment, opened up as hard as they could. The effect was immediate: tanks halted and others caught fire. These two 6-pr. crews did gallant work and inflicted heavy damage before they themselves were knocked out. This initial blow caused the enemy to halt his attack and those tanks which were still mobile moved into the shelter of a side wadi, where they were still in full view of one machine-gun section. This section lay low and held their fire until the crews of the tanks, feeling they were safe, got out to survey the damage and hold a conference. The machine-guns dealt severely with this misunderstanding. At this time the artillery were given the map reference of the tanks by the machine-gun platoon commander and they concentrated a mass of shells into the small area. In the meantime some of the lorried infantry had been organized into an effective force and had infiltrated up into the hills round Lieut. D. Puleston's No. 13 Platoon. The country here was not suitable for machine-guns, so Lieut. Puleston sent out any men who could be spared from the guns, as small fighting patrols. These were most successful in driving the enemy off after inflicting many casualties. Fus. R. Graham, one of the platoon drivers, did gallant work with a rifle and was subsequently awarded the Military Medal.

The New Zealand Division, as was to be expected from a division of that calibre, inflicted heavy losses on the enemy who had attacked their positions, and in particular their 6-pr. anti-tank gunners had excelled themselves, of which the many derelict enemy tanks were proof.

As night fell the enemy withdrew, after having been soundly beaten in what was surely one of the shortest and most decisive battles of the war. It was Rommel's last attempt at large-scale offensive action in North Africa.

Before closing the brief description of this phase of operations tribute must be paid to Z Coy. and its commander, Captain D. L. Lloyd, M.C. They had experienced much more fighting than other companies of the Battalion. They gained a great reputation in the Eighth Army and worthily upheld the reputation of the Fighting Fifth in North Africa.

In December 1942 Lieut.-Colonel E. O. Martin, D.S.O., had vacated command on promotion and been succeeded by Lieut.-Colonel R. F. Forbes-Watson.

By early March the Eighth Army was facing Rommel's Afrika Korps defending the Mareth Line, and the 1st Bn. Royal Northumberland Fusiliers (less Z Coy., which was still with the 7th Armoured Division) were assembled in the forward area.

The battle for the Mareth Line commenced on the 21st March 1943. At that time the Battalion held a 'watching brief' on the left (or inland) flank facing the Medenine Hills, ready to deal with any enemy attempt at an outflanking movement.

This day was a sad one for the unit, as Major R. H. S. M. Kent, the enterprising commander of Y Coy., was killed, together with his driver, when his jeep was blown up by an enemy mine. Major Kent had only recently returned from a Staff appointment—a true Fifth Fusilier, whose death was a great loss to the Regiment.

The frontal attack on the Mareth Line—which had been heavily fortified by the French prior to their collapse in 1940—had failed, and General Sir B. L. Montgomery decided on a wide left hook to outflank the position. This movement was to be carried out by the New Zealand Division and the 1st Armoured Division, the whole force

March–April 1943

being under the command of the redoubtable Lieut.-General Sir B. C. Freyberg. The route lay from Medenine south through Foum Tatahouine, south again to a gap in the hills, thence north-west across desert country to El Hamma—a distance of about 200 miles. For this long and difficult move the Battalion was under command of the 1st Armoured Division, which led the advance.

See Map Page 103

The movement commenced on the 22nd March. The difficulties were almost indescribable! A hot desert wind blew continuously, lorries became bogged up to their axles, water was short (half a gallon per man per day for all purposes) and vehicle drivers were called upon to drive almost continuously. Progress was slow, but by the 24th the leading troops had reached a spot about 25 miles due south of El Hamma. To reach the town it was necessary to pass through a narrow valley about one mile wide with high hills on either side.

The New Zealanders attacked at 1600 hrs. on the 26th and by midnight all objectives had been taken and gaps made in an enemy minefield defending the pass. The next phase was to pass the 1st Armoured Division through the minefield, through the pass and on to El Hamma.

That night enemy shelling was heavy, but all went well with the Battalion until just after dawn on the 27th. At this time most of the Battalion had entered the pass; but Bn. H.Q. in rear was some 600 yards from the entrance, when eight very large enemy tanks appeared on the left flank, not more than 300 yards distant. The order was given to make for the pass at top speed, and although the tanks opened fire this movement was accomplished without casualties. Other troops in rear were, however, less fortunate and suffered heavily. Soon after this Y (Carrier) Coy., and some anti-tank gunners, wheeled about from higher up the column and engaged the tanks. In a short time the latter were all blazing wrecks.

The battle for El Hamma raged for three more days, when the enemy, realizing that this main position had been outflanked, withdrew and Commonwealth troops entered the town. The Battalion remained in the El Hamma oasis until the 1st April, and it proved to be a very delightful place.

The next operation was to force the passage of the Gabes Gap (known subsequently as the Battle of Wadi Akarit) at its eastern end and the Gafsa Pass—passages through a formidable range of mountains some 10 miles from El Hamma.

On the 2nd April Major T. V. H. Beamish joined the Battalion and assumed command of Y Coy.

The 1st Bn. Royal Northumberland Fusiliers took no part in the Battle of Wadi Akarit, but by the 7th April the 4th Indian Division had captured the Gafsa Pass and the Battalion moved through it. They had seen the last of the Desert: henceforth in Africa they were to fight among green hills and in green fields. That night was spent leaguered in a field of standing corn, preparatory to taking up the chase on the following day.

The pursuit continued until the 10th April, the Battalion covering about 70 miles to a position near Bou Thadi, 40 miles inland from the port of Sfax. A few casualties were suffered—among them the Padre, the Rev. James, C. F., whose vehicle was hit and destroyed and he himself severely wounded. This vehicle contained the St. George's Day roses which he had guarded so carefully and which were due to be worn in a fortnight's time. This was one of the rare occasions on which the 1st Bn. Royal Northumberland Fusiliers did not wear roses on St. George's Day. April 1943

The Battalion rested for six days at Bou Thadi, the chase being taken up by other units. During this period Z Coy. (Captain D. L. Lloyd), whose more recent exploits are described earlier in this chapter, rejoined the Battalion.

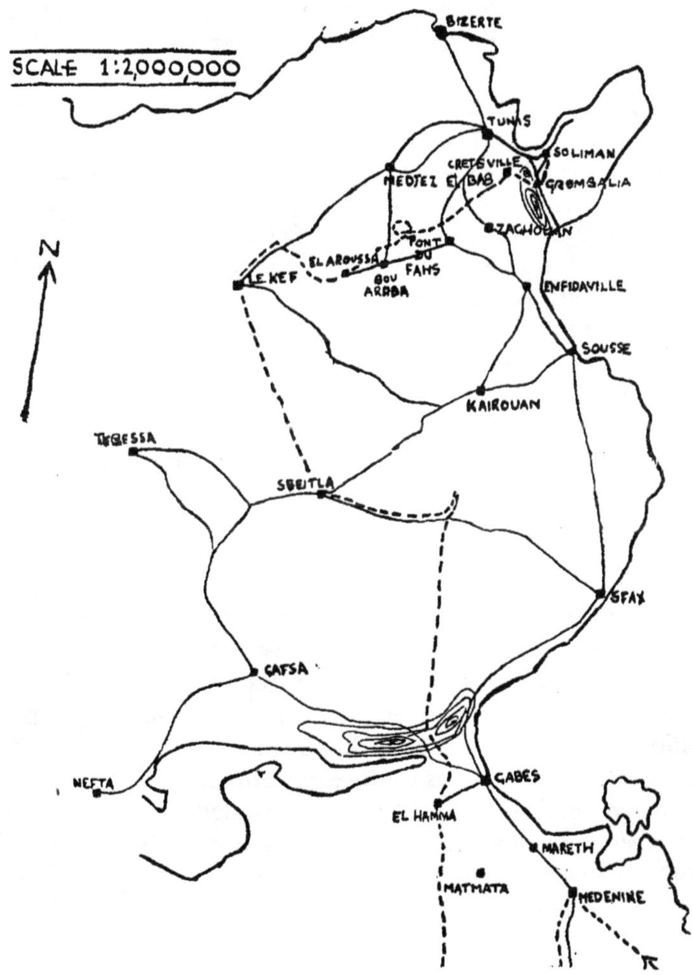

The advance of the Eighth Army from El Alamein to Tunisia had been carefully synchronized with Operation 'Torch,' the landing of Anglo-American forces at the western end of the North African coast. This landing took place in November 1942, and it had always been the intention that the two forces should join up and together drive the Germans and Italians out of Africa. The link-up of the Eighth Army with Lieut.-General Sir Kenneth Anderson's First British Army in Tunisia took place on the 7th April 1943.

April–May 1943

By the 16th April 1943 the 1st Bn. Royal Northumberland Fusiliers bore the signs and colours of the First Army, in anticipation of a change-over—the Eighth Army by this time having been cast for the role of invading Sicily and Italy.

Soon after midnight on the 16th/17th April the Battalion moved off in column, bound for Northern Tunisia. Passing through the Faid Pass to Sebetla they met American troops for the first time. A halt was made at this place for six hours, owing mainly to traffic congestion. Before nightfall the Battalion had reached Ebba Ksur, where on bright green turf they had a meal. Under a full moon they moved on, passing through Le Kef near the Algerian frontier, and halting for the night at Sidi Moussa. The distance covered in the twenty-four hours was 180 miles, entirely uninterrupted by enemy air action.

The move continued after dark on the 18th April, and the column arrived at its destination, El Aroussa, at 0200 hrs. on the 19th, where the troops bivouacked, for the first time, in the First Army area. On the following day exchanges of gossip took place with First Army troops, who were somewhat horrified at the battle-stained appearance of the Eighth Army men.

On the 21st the unit moved up some 8 miles to Bou Arada as a preliminary to a series of engagements in a confused mass of hills. The nearest, and most prominent, of these features was the Djebel Kournine, about 3,000 feet high. By St. George's Day this range had been captured and the 1st Battalion moved north across a low pass, in which the tail of the column was bombed and machine-gunned from the air.

The role of the Battalion for the next few days was to protect the left flank of an attack designed to pinch out the Pont-du-Fahs area. This type of role continued until the 16th May, positions being constantly moved, and new tasks being given to companies and platoons, according to the ever-changing situation. Casualties, although not heavy, mounted up and included Major H. J. Winn (W Coy.) wounded.

By this time the enemy had decided on the evacuation of North Africa, a task he was endeavouring to carry out mainly by air. The activities of the R.A.F. and American Air Force resulted in a high proportion of casualties, however, and it became clear that if the Allies could stage one more determined push a big 'bag' of prisoners was likely. On the 4th May Mateur was captured by American troops. The key to Tunis was now the Medjez-El-Bab Valley, which was strongly held by the enemy.

To assist in operations in this area Y Coy. was sent to join the 4th Division. The advance continued steadily along most of the front and by early May Allied forces were at the gates of Bizerta and Tunis; only the Cape Bon Peninsula remained to the enemy. Companies of the Battalion were continually going into, and coming out of, action.

By the 10th May the two great mountains of Rassas and Bou Kournine lay ahead of the Battalion. In the meantime the 6th British Armoured Division had cut across the base of the Peninsula from Hammam Lif to Hammammet, and this virtually sealed the fate of the German Afrika Korps.

On the morning of the 11th May, at first light, the Battalion moved to the village of La Cebela Du Mornag, under the shadow of Djebel Rassas. Here they suffered their last casualties of the campaign—fortunately none of them fatal. By midday they had moved to the area of the towns of Grombalia and Soliman at the base of the Cape

Bon Peninsula. Enemy resistance had now crumbled, and the mass surrenders indicative of the destruction of an army began. Germans were to be seen driving in long columns, in their own transport, to the prisoner-of-war cages. On the 13th May the enemy surrendered and all fighting ceased. May 1943

These highly successful operations brought the fighting in Africa to a close and liberated the entire continent. The campaign was typical of the growing power of the Allies. The meagre forces with which General Wavell commenced operations against the Italians in 1940 had grown, in less than three years, into a great Anglo-American force which, with detachments from other Allied nations, was shortly to follow its North African victories by invading Sicily and the Italian mainland.

CHAPTER 10

EGYPT, SYRIA, PALESTINE AND ITALY

May 1943 to May 1945

1st Battalion

(*See Maps Nos. IX and XI*)

May–June 1943 THE campaign in North Africa ended in mid-May 1943 with the surrender of the Axis forces in that theatre, and by then preparations for the Allied invasion of Sicily were well advanced. The 1st Bn. Royal Northumberland Fusiliers was not, however, destined to take part in that campaign. This chapter records their activities in Egypt, Syria, Palestine and Italy up to the close of the war with Germany in May 1945.

On the night of the 12th May—the day the Axis forces surrendered in Tunisia—the Battalion provided a machine-gun screen along the whole Divisional front as a precaution against possible treachery. This proved unnecessary, however, and the next few days were spent in directing individuals and parties of Germans and Italians to the prisoner-of-war cages. This was not a very strenuous task, and most of the time in the Grombalia area was devoted to rest, a measure of reorganization and sightseeing.

On the 20th May General Eisenhower took the salute at a victory parade in Tunis, the Battalion being represented by Captain H. I. A. Brown and C.S.M. Ambury—a warrant officer who had served as a boy and spent most of his life in the Regiment.

The Battalion still formed part of the 1st Armoured Division, and on the 21st May the Division commenced to move back to Tripoli. Moving via Kairouan, Mahares (a village south of Sfax), Wadi Akarit, Gabes, the Mareth Line and Medenine, the Battalion reached the small Italian settlement of Suani Ben Adam, situated in what is reputed to be the hottest bit of desert in North Africa (16 miles south of Tripoli), on the afternoon of the 24th May.

The Battalion remained in this area for six weeks. It was not a very pleasant stay owing to the intense heat; but by the end of the period much had been done to reorganize and re-equip the unit and repair vehicles. The 21st June was, however, a memorable occasion. On the morning of that day the whole of the 1st Armoured Division was drawn up on either side of the Suani–Ben Adem–Azizi road for inspection by His Majesty the King, who was on a visit to North Africa. It was the first time for over a quarter of a century that the 1st Bn. Royal Northumberland Fusiliers had been reviewed by their Sovereign. His Majesty was not unmindful of the unit's twelve years' service abroad and remarked, 'They would not recognize England now.'

Other visitors during this period were General Sir B. L. Montgomery and Leslie Henson.

Soon after His Majesty's inspection the Battalion left the 1st Armoured Division and joined the 7th Armoured Division, and on the 10th July moved to Homs. This was a very pleasant place, as the camp was a good one. On the 25th July they moved to Tripoli, where they embarked on two ships for Egypt. The voyage was uneventful and on the 31st July the Battalion arrived at Alexandria and moved to Sidi Bishr—a good station though a bad camp, as it was in a sea of soft sand. Life was pleasant here; some went on leave to Cairo, while others remained in camp, where they were entertained by Mrs. Barker's famous concert party, which had been performing to troops since the early days of the war.

No description of the Battalion's war years in the Middle East would be complete without mention of Lady Holmes, mother of Captain H. Holmes, and wife of Judge Sir Hugh Holmes, who lived and worked in Alexandria. She was indeed the Battalion's fairy-godmother. She kept open house for the officers and put up with all their vagaries when on leave from the Desert with a kindness and patience which was boundless. She worked unceasingly to provide comforts for the troops, and as each Christmas arrived every man would receive a Christmas parcel, subscribed for and wrapped by Lady Holmes and her family and friends. At the last of Mrs. Barker's concert parties given for the Battalion, Major K. O. N. Foster, who was commanding while Lieut.-Colonel Forbes-Watson was on leave in South Africa, presented Lady Holmes with a silver cigarette box on behalf of the Battalion, and Mrs. Barker with a large bouquet, for all the good work they had done.

Early in September rumours of another move were received and in the middle of the month the Battalion moved by road and rail to Syria. The destination was Qatana, near Damascus, where they came under command of the 10th Indian Division.

The period in Syria saw many comings and goings among all ranks. Reinforcements were received (including returning officers who had been wounded or sick) and many old soldiers left for the United Kingdom on completion of five or six years abroad.

By mid-November the Battalion was at Sidon, where they had moved in connection with the riots which occurred about this time, and which the French authorities had some difficulty in handling.

In December two moves were made, the first to a camp between Jaffa and Gaza, and then to Gaza itself. Christmas was spent in Gaza, and among the many Christmas cards received was one from 'Mrs. Whistance and Allen'—a touching tribute from the widow and infant son of Cpl. Whistance who had died of wounds received in Tunisia the previous April.

The early weeks of 1944 were uneventful, the only incident of real importance being the issue of 4·2-in. heavy mortars to the Battalion. Z Coy. then became a mortar company of four platoons, with an increased strength, which included no less than seventeen officers.

The invasion of Sicily had been successfully carried out in the summer of 1943, followed almost at once by the invasion of the Italian mainland. The latter event synchronized with the surrender of Italy, and after that the only enemy met in this theatre of operations were Germans. By the early days of March 1944 the Anglo-American forces (comprising the Fifth American and Eighth British Armies) had overrun Southern Italy and were established on a general line north of Foggia and Naples and with a bridgehead, formed by troops of the Fifth American Army, at

March–May 1944

Anzio, south of Rome. The Allied armies in Italy had, however, been considerably reduced in strength, three British and four American divisions having been diverted for the coming invasion of North-West Europe.

After a number of moves the Battalion embarked at Port Said and disembarked at Taranto in Italy at the end of March. The unit's return to an active theatre of operations, after nearly twelve months in the Nile Delta, Syria and Palestine, was not under the happiest conditions. The men were not trained in the use of the 4·2-in. mortar: previously only Y Coy. had been equipped with carrier vehicles, but now the other companies (except Z Coy., which retained its 15-cwt. trucks) were to be similarly equipped and this involved training many additional carrier drivers.

On arrival in Italy the organization and officer state was as follows:

Commanding Officer . .	Lieut.-Colonel R. F. Forbes-Watson
Second-in-Command . .	Major M. C. Speer
Adjutant	Captain M. H. Lassetter
Quartermaster . . .	Lieut. N. Rogers
Regimental Sergeant-Major .	R.S.M. G. Richardson
O.C. H.Q. Coy. . . .	Captain R. M. Newburn
„ W (M.G.) Coy. . .	Major A. Neilson
„ X „ „ . .	Major H. J. Winn
„ Y „ „ . .	Major T. V. H. Beamish, M.C.
„ Z (Mortar) Coy. . .	Major D. L. Lloyd, M.C.

Some little time was spent in camp outside Taranto drawing vehicles and kit. The difficulty of obtaining instructors for the 4·2-in. mortars was overcome by obtaining some from the 2nd Battalion, and the existing trained carrier drivers of Y Coy. were able to instruct men of the other companies.

The previous year's disaster to the St. George's Day roses was very nearly repeated in 1944—this time through the ineptitude of an Egyptian contractor. At the last minute the P.R.I. obtained a somewhat unorthodox collection from Naples; but every Fifth Fusilier wore a red and white flower of some kind on the national day.

By mid-April the Battalion had moved to Ortona, a coastal town on the Adriatic, just behind the front held by the 4th Indian Division, under whose command the Battalion had now come. The dispositions were as follows:

Y and Z Coys. had their headquarters at Ortona, with their platoons in the line along the Divisional front. Z Coy. had, attached to each platoon, a few Canadian N.C.Os. and Signallers from the Canadian company they had relieved.

Bn. H.Q. was about one mile back from Ortona, while H.Q. Coy. and B Echelon were some distance further back.

The town of Ortona was frequently shelled, but its substantial houses provided good protection and casualties were light. During May W (M.G.) and X (M.G.) Coys. moved into line, and Z (Mortar) Coy. were passed as fit by their Canadian instructors, who returned to their battalion. Thus by the end of the month the whole unit had gained useful battle experience under the new conditions.

These conditions, particularly at Ortona, were very different from those in the Desert. The Battalion had been used to a highly mobile war where they could drive right up to their positions in most cases and where they were normally independent of roads. In Ortona they were fighting a static war, and in Italy as a whole all vehicle movement was confined to the roads. At Ortona the Battalion was spread over a long front and platoons had their positions either in the ruins of houses and villages or they lived in dugouts built into the side of valleys. In the spring, fields of corn, sown before the war reached Ortona, were a vivid green, and wild flowers grew in profusion; there were no water problems and the NAAFI supplies were frequent and plentiful; numerous stray chickens found their way into platoon cookhouses; and last but not least, the Indians, who had an abundant daily ration of tea and sugar, were more than generous in supplying it to mortar and machine-gun platoons. Consequently the Battalion were very much alive to, and appreciative of, the new conditions under which they were to fight. It was not until the winter set in that they were to regret the days in the Desert. May–July 1944

During their year in Italy the Battalion, although it was kept fully occupied, was never able to play such a big part in the offensive battle as they had in the Desert, though when the Division was on the defensive the machine-guns came into their own. This was due partly to the terrain, which seldom offered good fields of fire for machine-guns, and also to the extreme shortage of ammunition, which was withheld from Italy for use in the Normandy invasion. The mortars, which were eminently suitable for the country, and could and did inflict great damage on the enemy, were often limited to as little as five rounds a mortar a day. Thus if a raid or attack required mortar support, the mortars had to keep silent for some days in order to save enough ammunition to make their contribution worth while. Ammunition was unrationed for the duration of major operations only.

By the end of May the Allied Armies had been regrouped and offensive operations were in progress along most of the front. The Eighth Army captured Cassino on the 18th May and in the west the forces in the Anzio beach-head had joined up with the main body of the Fifth Army advancing from the south. By the end of the month the enemy had given up the Gustav Line and was in full retreat.

On the 14th June the Allies occupied Rome, and a few days later the Battalion moved to Venafro, where they were to remain for a month. Here the time was spent in further training and on visits to the nearby battlefield of Cassino.

On the 25th preparations were made for the 4th Indian Division to relieve the 10th Indian Division. The frontage held by the latter ran from the hills just north of Assisi to a point a mile or two north of Ripa and thence back to the River Tiber near a road junction west of Santa Croce. The 10th Division was newly established in this area and the situation somewhat confused; mopping up of isolated pockets of German resistance was still in progress. See Map Page 110

By the last day of June the relief was complete, and the 4th Indian Division established in the new area. The task was to push forward as quickly as possible. On the 5th July Monte Acuto was captured and Umbertide occupied. During this advance No. 4 Platoon of X (M.G.) Coy. performed the first carrier shoot carried out by the Battalion.

On the 6th, Bn. H.Q. moved to Umbertide, and on the following day No. 4 Platoon again went into action in support of a successful attack on Montone. That

July 1944

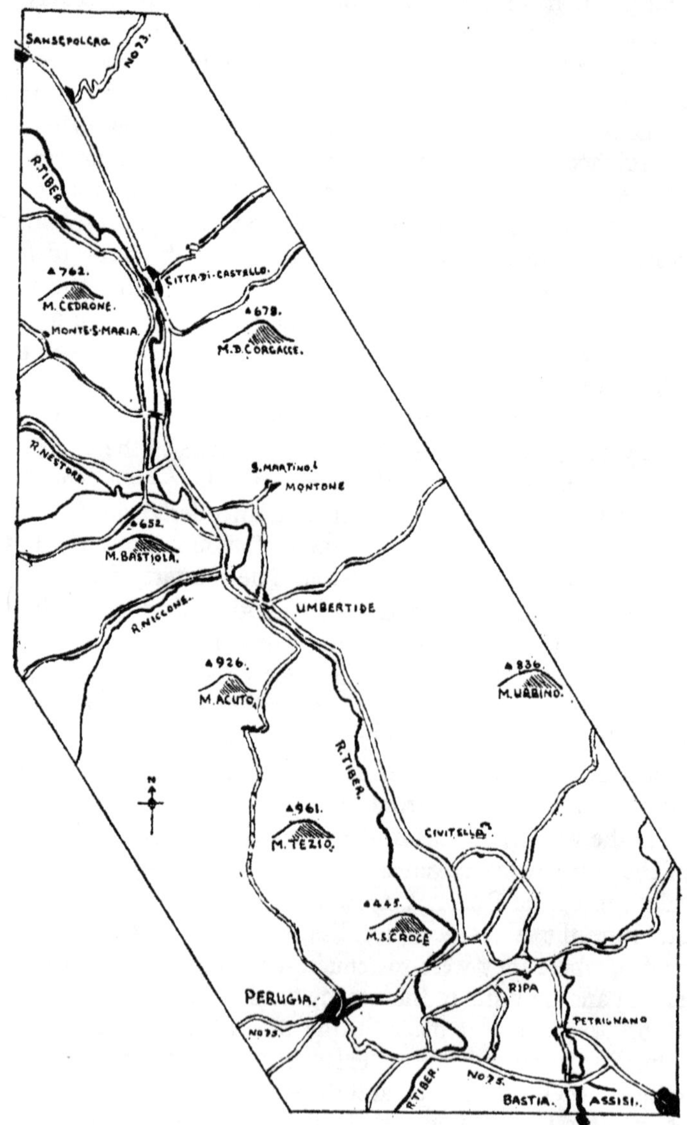

night Z (Mortar) Coy. had the misfortune to suffer eight casualties from a bomb dropped by a solitary German airplane.

On the 25th July Bn. H.Q. and Z Coy. (the only portions of the Battalion not actively engaged) were honoured by a second visit from His Majesty the King. On this occasion they provided a small Guard of Honour at a halt about a half-mile south of Umbertide.

See Map Page 112 By the end of the month the main body of the Division was advancing on Anghiari, with one brigade group in the area of the Citerna Ridge. The steady advance had now been in progress for nearly a month. All machine-gun companies had been actively engaged and carried out some good shoots, although there had been little opportunity for Z (Mortar) Coy. to employ their comparatively new weapons. July–Oct. 1944

On the 28th July Major T. V. H. Beamish was wounded by a shell splinter, his place as Y (M.G.) Coy. Commander being taken by Captain D. C. Jackson. Major Beamish returned to duty on the 16th September 1944.

The next phase of operations—from the 3rd to 7th August—was the attack on Monte Castello. This was a most desperate battle in which W (M.G.) Coy. were mainly in support of a Gurkha battalion. The feature changed hands three times, but finally remained in Gurkha hands. Nos. 1 and 3 Platoons suffered severe casualties during these operations. While this was in progress Nos. 6 (M.G) and 10 (Mortar) Platoons were engaged in the Monte Doglio area in support of patrol operations by a battalion of the Punjab Regiment.

These operations ended with the 4th Indian Division taking over a very extended front, to enable other troops to concentrate in preparation for a further advance. The Division was deployed in five groups, the dispositions of the 1st Bn. Royal Northumberland Fusiliers being as follows:

Colignola	Bn. HQ.
Anghiari Sector . . .	One platoon X (M.G.) Coy. One platoon Z (Mortar) Coy.
Alpi di Catenaia Sector . .	X (M.G.) Coy. less one platoon Two platoons Z (Mortar) Coy.
Subbiano (Centre) Sector .	One platoon W (M.G) Coy. One platoon Z (Mortar) Coy.
Subbiano to Castillion Sector	Y (M.G.) Coy. less one platoon
Monte di Loro Sector . .	One platoon Y Coy.

This front was approximately 33 miles long. On the left the Monte di Loro feature was occupied on the 13th, and other small advances continued to be made throughout August. By the middle of August Commonwealth forces had reached the Gothic Line.

It will now be as well to summarize the general situation in the Italian theatre. On the 11th August the front ran from north of Ancona, north of Arezzo, through Florence and Leghorn to the coast, a distance of some 150 miles. In the last week of August the Allies assaulted the Gothic Line and on the 31st broke through on a 20-mile front.

As the 4th Indian Division was not on the main front of attack, their role during the offensive to breech the Gothic Line was one of active defence. For the Battalion the period 1st to 17th September was one of routine defence. On the night of the 16th Fus. R. Burnett earned a Military Medal, to add to his previously won Distinguished Conduct Medal, by carrying a wounded comrade to safety over some 500 yards of bullet-swept ground.

The 28th September found the Battalion moving into a concentration area near the ruined village of Coriano, prior to coming into action under the 10th Indian Division. Here they were in close proximity to a portion of the 2nd Battalion of the Regiment and the opportunity was taken to celebrate the reunion.

On the 1st and 2nd October the 10th Indian Division relieved the left portion of

Oct. 1944

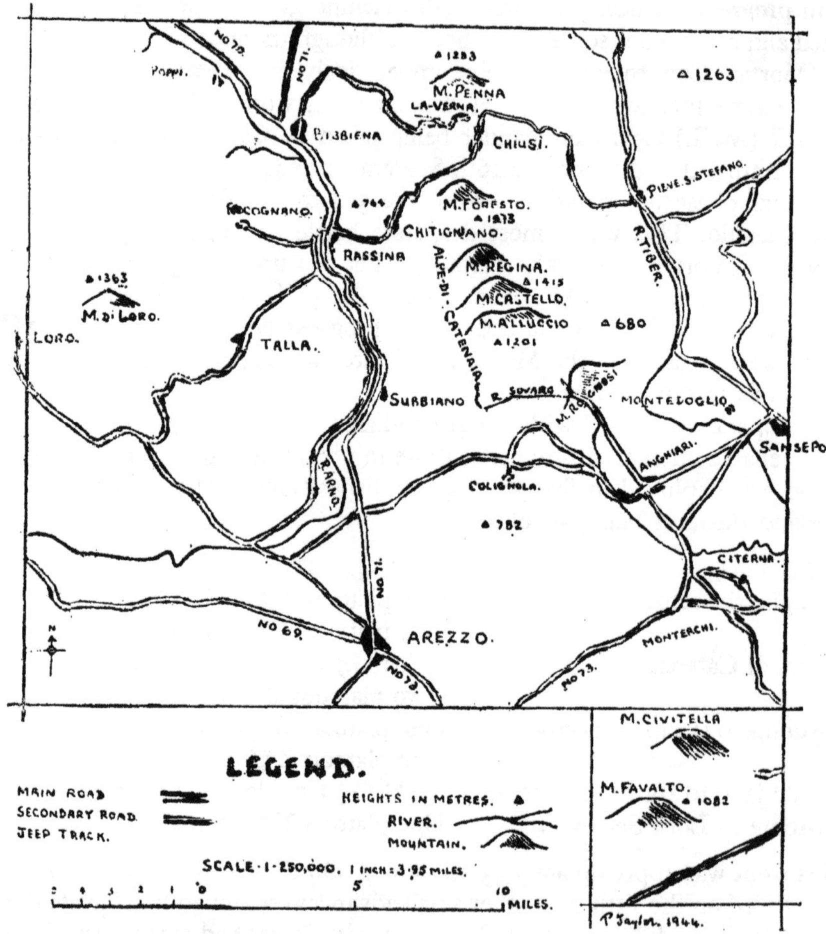

the 4th Indian Division's front and from the 3rd October to the 3rd November the Battalion—as part of the 10th Division—pressed on steadily, capturing many features and crossing many rivers and streams.

See Map Page 114 At the commencement of these operations on the 3rd October the dispositions were as follows:

Bn. H.Q.	near San Marino
X (M.G.) Coy. Nos. 10 and 12 Platoons of Z (Mortar) Coy.	with the 25th Indian Infantry Brigade on northern end of the Burghi ridge.
W (M.G.) Coy. Nos. 11 and 13 Platoons of Z (Mortar) Coy.	with the 20th Indian Infantry Brigade in the hills to the south-west.
Y (M.G.) Coy.	with the 10th Indian Infantry Brigade in reserve in the Scorticata area.

As a preliminary move the 25th Indian Infantry Brigade captured the south-west end of the Burghi feature and the 20th Indian Infantry Brigade captured Sogliano village and two bridges over the River Fiumicino. Oct.–Dec. 1944

From the night of the 6th/7th till the morning of the 10th October the 25th Indian Infantry Brigade battled hard, and eventually successfully, for the Roncofreddo–S. Lorenzo ridge. Nos. 5 and 6 Platoons and Nos. 10 and 12 Platoons fired respectively large quantities of small-arms ammunition and bombs in support of this operation. During the battle Lieut.-Colonel R. V. Clifford (Orby), commanding the 3/1st Punjab Regiment, was killed. He was the brother of Major W. R. M. Clifford of the Fifth and a son of Lieut.-Colonel W. Clifford, D.S.O., a Fifth Fusilier killed in France in 1917.

After this the 10th Indian Infantry Brigade participated in the further advance to a ridge south-east of the River Savio. The actual crossing of the river was carried out by the 20th Indian Infantry Brigade without opposition.

The whole of these operations, which had commenced early in October, were conducted in almost continuous rain.

This was followed by the advance to the River Ronco, in which Nos. 2 and 3 (M.G.) Platoons and Nos. 11 and 13 (Mortar) Platoons participated. By the 3rd November the Ronco had been crossed, and the 10th Indian Division was withdrawn to rest and refit.

The Battalion spent the period 4th to 18th November in reasonably comfortable Italian barracks at Cesena. While in this location news was received that Sgt. G. E. Charlton had been awarded the Military Medal for gallantry during the summer campaign and Captain D. C. McLeod and Sgt. Bean had been mentioned in despatches.

By the 19th November the 10th Indian Division was again in action—this time in the plains of the River Po. On the night of the 20th/21st the River Mentone was crossed, and by the 30th the enemy had been cleared from the area east of the River Lamone. In these operations sub-units of the Battalion fired huge quantities of ammunition—Nos. 11 and 13 (Mortar) Platoons reaching a combined total of 1,000 bombs per day on some occasions.

The first few days of December saw the 1st Canadian Division and other troops take the lead, and as a result the three machine-gun companies concentrated in billets at Forli, to be followed by Z (Mortar) Coy. a day or two later. Meanwhile Bn. HQ. had taken over accommodation in Forlimpopoli from the 2nd Bn. Royal Northumberland Fusiliers, who were about to proceed to Greece.

Early in this month the 25th Indian Infantry Brigade had come temporarily under the command of the 46th Division, which had been heavily engaged on the Pergola–Pideura ridge, south of Route 9. The enemy, observing the ensuing reliefs, and what he recognized as preparations for attack, reacted with exceptional violence. Since the nature of the country had necessitated the siting of supporting machine-guns in the F.D.Ls., the platoons of X Coy. furnishing these suffered severely—particularly from an enemy S.P. gun firing over open sights at a range of 1,000 yards. The O.P. party of Z (Mortar) Coy. also became involved. Despite three machine-guns being put out of action, and the constant need for rebuilding gun platforms, all demands

Feb. 1945 for fire were successfully met, but at the cost of five other ranks killed and two officers and six other ranks wounded. For their conduct during these operations, Lieut. V. G. S. Oehl (Middlesex Regiment) received the immediate award of the Military Cross and Sgt. L. Harland that of the Military Medal.

During the next few weeks sub-units of the Battalion in turn supported various offensive operations designed to stabilize a satisfactory winter line of defence. These

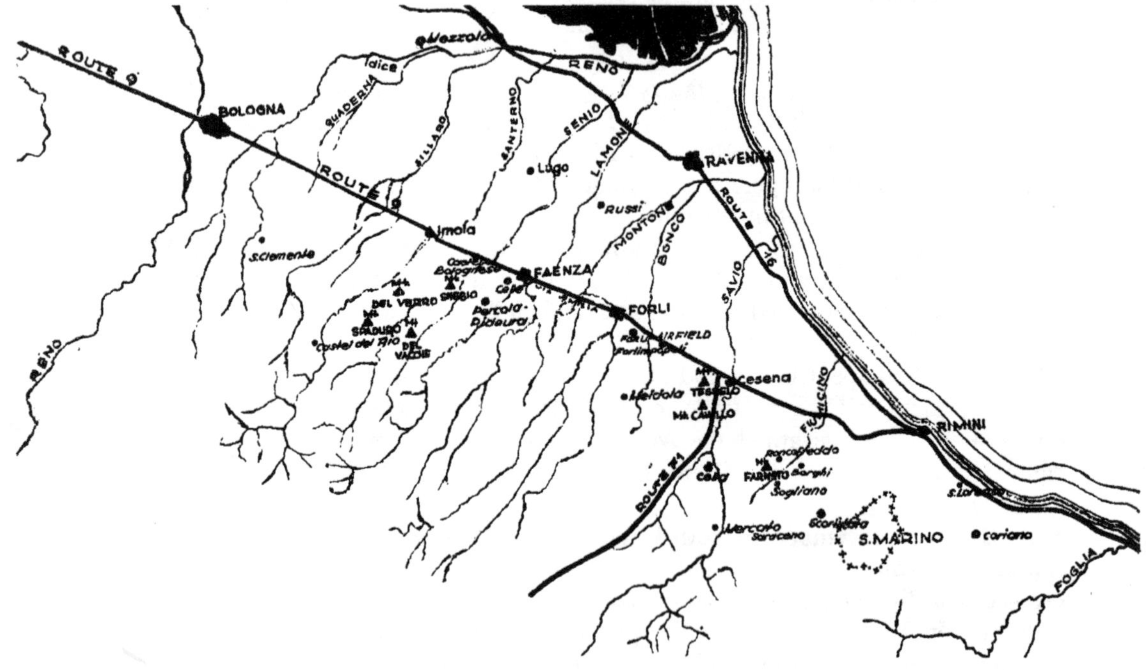

attacks carried some troops of the 25th Indian Infantry Brigade across the River Senio, but they were later withdrawn to the line of the river, which was not recrossed by Allied troops until April 1945.

The first snow of the season fell just before Christmas. Christmas Day found Y (M.G.) Coy. the only company in action, and the rest of the Battalion were able to enjoy the customary festivities—under reasonably good conditions.

The Battalion remained in this area, under conditions of semi-static warfare, until the first week in February 1945, when the 10th Indian Division was relieved by the 3rd Carpathian Division of the Polish Corps and in turn moved to relieve the 78th Division in the Castel Del Rio area. The latter relief was a most unpleasant one, involving a move through the mountains along a road in very bad condition. The actual position was, however, a good one tactically, as it dominated the German defences throughout its length. It was not so satisfactory from the point of view

20. Combining comfort with safety

21. 1st Battalion 4·2-in. mortar in action

22. Getting a 4·2-in. mortar in action

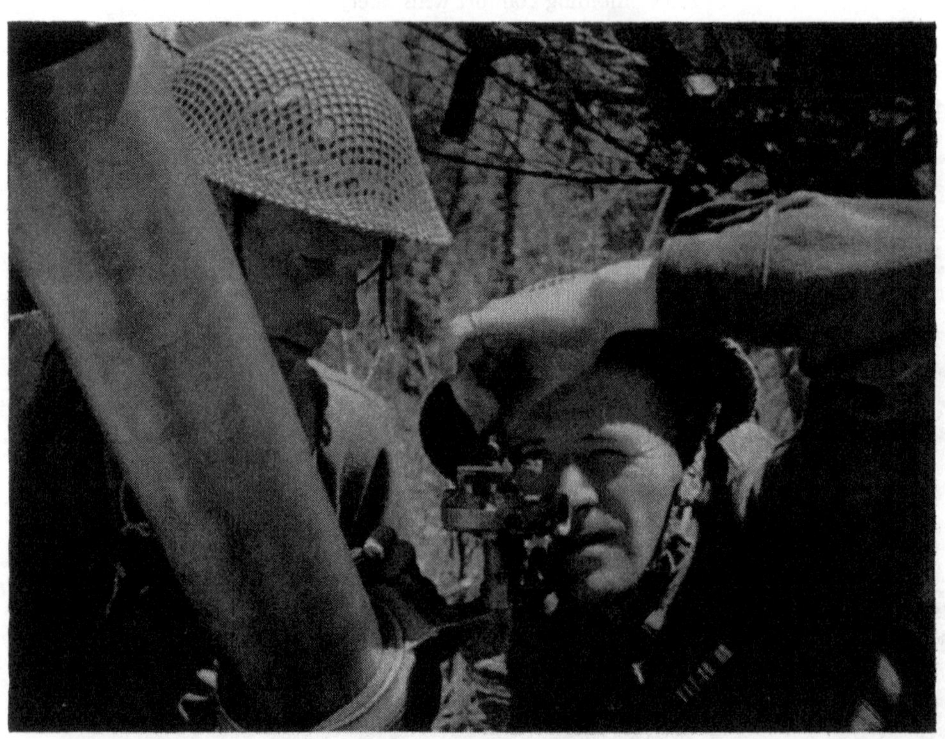

23. Fus. Hall and Cpl. Edwards, M.M., setting the sights of a 4·2-in. mortar

Feb.–March 1945

of comfort, being very wet and muddy. The Battalion dispositions were as follows:

Two platoons Y (M.G.) Coy. Nos. 12 and 13 Platoons of Z (Mortar) Coy.	On the right in support of the 10th Indian Infantry Brigade on the Monte Del Verro and Monte Spaduro features.
W (M.G.) Coy. (now temporarily reduced to two platoons) No. 11 Platoon of Z (Mortar) Coy.	On the left in support of the 20th Indian Infantry Brigade on the lower slopes of Monte Grande.
X (M.G.) Coy. No. 10 Platoon Z (Mortar) Coy.	With the 25th Indian Infantry Brigade in rear at Citta Di Castello in the Upper Tiber valley.

The only road leading to the front line ran for the last mile of its course by a long broad valley, which intersected the divisional front and opened to a plain. Through this valley the enemy could see right into the divisional area and obtain observation of the positions of two artillery regiments deployed just off the road on the flat ground to the rear. This necessitated a smoke-screen being maintained across the valley throughout the hours of daylight. When the wind blew from the east, No. 11 Platoon, sited near this smoke-screen, found themselves blanketed by a thick, suffocating fog with a strong chemical smell. They could, however, find comfort in being one of the few platoons which could maintain themselves by road.

Most of the Battalion could only be reached after a long walk over the hills, and were maintained by night by mule transport ran by the R.A.S.C.

During the previous months there had been several occasions when both machine-gun and mortar platoons had had to leave their normal transport behind and move on a mule basis. The mortars were especially difficult to load, since the baseplates were immensely heavy, as were the bombs, which required a great many mules to get a reasonable supply forward.

But the greatest difficulties came with winter, when for several weeks the whole front was deep in snow. Often the wretched mules would sink up to their bellies in this. Loads would then be removed and likewise sink into the snow. Having extricated the animals by heaving on ropes passed under their bellies, it would then be necessary to dig out the loads and proceed with reloading. All this in pitch darkness. Nor, with the melting of the snow in spring, when the low ground was converted to a sea of mud, were conditions easier for the mortar platoons, which were all sited in the valleys. Mud, worse even than snow, meant often that a mule having sunk deep could not be extricated.

The month of March saw a number of changes within the Battalion. Lieut.-Colonel R. F. Forbes-Watson vacated command and was succeeded by the Second-in-Command, Major M. C. Speer; Major D. L. Lloyd and Captain D. C. McLeod—partners in Z Coy. for over three years—returned to the United Kingdom; and Captain N. Rogers, the Quartermaster, left for an administrative appointment at Bari.

By this time events were shaping which were to bring victory to the Allies in Europe

March–May 1945

within two months. By the middle of March the Anglo-American armies were on the Rhine and preparations to cross the river and advance into the heart of Germany were in full swing. The Russian armies from the east were advancing on Berlin against diminishing resistance. In Italy preparations were afoot for the final offensive which was to result in the Germans opposed to Field-Marshal Sir Harold Alexander's force being the first to capitulate in any European theatre of operations.

By the 9th April 1945, when the spring offensive opened, the 10th Indian Infantry Brigade had been relieved by Italian troops, although the supporting arms, including platoons of the 1st Bn. Royal Northumberland Fusiliers, remained in action under Italian command—a situation which could hardly have been contemplated twelve or eighteen months before.

On the 13th and 14th April the 10th Indian Infantry Brigade with Y (M.G.) Coy. (now only two platoons strong) and two platoons of Z (Mortar) Coy. carried out a very hurried 60-mile move to positions near Lugo on the right of the New Zealand Division. The rest of the 10th Indian Division followed to Lugo, ready to participate in any advance made by the 10th Indian Infantry Brigade.

Events now moved quickly. The River Sillaro was crossed on the night of the 15th/16th, followed by the crossing of the Scolo Sillaro Canal. By the 19th the River Quadern had been crossed. These operations were carried out against comparatively weak opposition, although individuals and small groups of very brave Germans often remained behind and had to be mopped up.

The crossing of the River Idice was the 10th Indian Division's last battle. Attacking near the village of Mezzolaro at 1930 hrs. on the 21st April the 1/2nd Punjab Regiment were thrown back with heavy losses; but before dawn the next morning they had attacked again and by 0900 hrs. Mezzolaro was in their hands.

The chase was now taken up by the 6th American Armoured and 10th American Mountain Divisions, leaving the 10th Indian Division to mop up the numerous pockets of enemy resistance in rear. The 1st Bn. Royal Northumberland Fusiliers had fired their last shot in the Second World War—No. 8 Platoon of Y (M.G.) Coy., commanded by Lieut. Packer, claiming this honour whilst supporting the 20th Indian Infantry Brigade during the advance to the River Idice.

St. George's Day 1945 was marred by the sad death, due to a mine explosion, of Sgt. Wilson of Z (Mortar) Coy. This N.C.O.'s name will long be remembered for his walk, through enemy-held territory, from Tobruk back to the British lines 1942.*

On the 2nd May 1945 the German armies in Italy surrendered unconditionally. So hostilities ended for the senior Battalion of the Regiment, which fought almost continuously throughout the war—in the early victories in Africa under O'Connor, in the stubborn defence of Egypt in the days of adversity, in Montgomery's victorious advance to Tunisia and in the heavy fighting of the last thirteen months of the Italian campaign. They served in a variety of roles in many famous divisions—the 4th Indian, the 6th and 9th Australian, the 1st and 7th Armoured, the 50th Northumbrian and the 10th Indian.

* See page 98

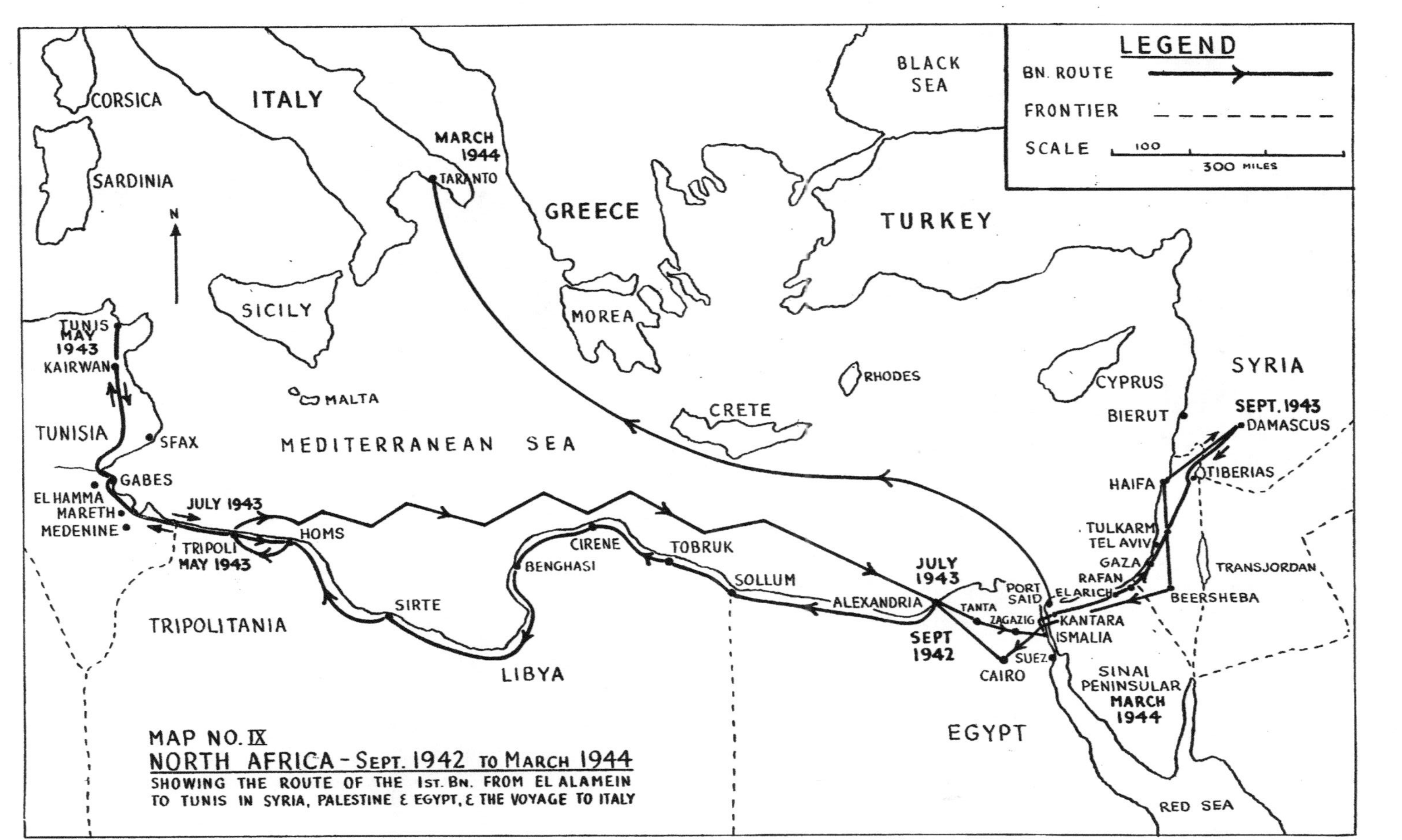

MAP NO. IX
NORTH AFRICA - SEPT. 1942 TO MARCH 1944
SHOWING THE ROUTE OF THE 1ST. BN. FROM EL ALAMEIN TO TUNIS IN SYRIA, PALESTINE & EGYPT, & THE VOYAGE TO ITALY

CHAPTER 11

NORTH AFRICA AND ITALY

June 1943 to May 1944

2nd Battalion

(*See Maps Nos. X and XI*)

As explained in Chapter 6, the 2nd Battalion—which had been in the United Kingdom June
since the Dunkirk evacuation—reorganized in the spring of 1943 into a small Battalion 1943
H.Q. and three Brigade Support Groups, each consisting of Group H.Q., one machine-gun company, one heavy (4·2-in.) mortar company and one A.A. company; with a total establishment (including 1st Reinforcements) of 80 officers and 1,237 other ranks. This reorganization had been completed by the 10th June 1943.

By this time the whole of Africa had been liberated from the enemy and preparations were afoot for the invasion of Sicily—to be followed by an assault on the Italian mainland.

The Battalion left St. Germans in Cornwall on the 16th June and embarked at Avonmouth on H.M.T. 'Tamaroa' the following day, bound for North Africa. It was a matter for congratulations that out of over 1,200 men granted embarkation leave only four failed to return at the proper time.

The Battalion's state was as follows:

	Battalion H.Q.
Commanding Officer . .	Lieut.-Colonel E. H. Butterfield
Second-in-Command .	Major S. Enderby, M.C.
Adjutant	Captain L. F. Hay
Quartermaster . . .	Captain W. R. E. Brown
Regimental Sergeant-Major	R.S.M. C. V. Caborn
	No. 1 Group
Group Commander . .	Major J. H. Cubbon, O.B.E. (Cheshire Regt.)
Second-in-Command .	Major J. A. Dewhurst (Cheshire Regt.)
O.C. A (Mortar) Coy. .	Captain E. R. Coutts-Deacon (Essex Regt.)
„ B (A.A.) Coy. . .	Captain G. H. Redfern (Manchester Regt.)
„ C (M.G.) Coy. . .	Major C. W. Summers (Middlesex Regt.)
	No. 2 Group
Group Commander . .	Major H. R. M. Wilkin
Second-in-Command .	Major A. E. Richards
O.C. D (Mortar) Coy. .	Captain R. M. Kershaw
„ E (A.A.) Coy. . .	Captain J. R. Bullock
„ F (M.G.) Coy. . .	Captain R. A. J. Cheffins, M.C. (Middlesex Regt.)

June–Sept. 1943

No. 3 Group

Group Commander .	. Major J. D. Buckle
Second-in-Command	. Major F. Gray
O.C. G (Mortar) Coy.	. Major E. H. Parkhurst
,, H (A.A.) Coy. .	. Captain A. W. Wilkins
,, K (M.G.) Coy. .	. Captain A. S. Oakes (Middlesex Regt.)

Of the junior officers no less than 26 had less than six months' commissioned service.

The voyage, made in convoy, was uneventful. Living conditions were very cramped and everybody was pleased to see the North African coast. Disembarkation took place at Algiers on the 27th June. Some disappointment was caused by the Battalion's reception. Officers and men had been led to believe that the unit had been asked for in connection with a special task. On arrival nobody appeared to know anything about them—a condition of affairs not unfamiliar to experienced campaigners. They disembarked at 1500 hrs. and after a long march arrived in camp at 2300 hrs.

After a week near Algiers the Battalion moved to a tented camp in the Forêt de St. Ferdinand, and intensive training commenced almost at once. A generous allotment of somewhat 'part-worn' vehicles was received for training purposes. After a short time the Battalion was attached to the 46th Division (Major-General H. A. Freeman-Atwood).

It soon became apparent that the 46th Division was not to take part in the invasion of Sicily, but had been earmarked for the assault on the mainland of Italy which was to take place later but which was already being planned. The Division was to form part of the Xth Corps (Lieut.-General B. G. Horrocks).

Normally Groups were to be allotted as follows:

No. 1 Group . . . 138th Infantry Brigade
6th Bn. York and Lancaster Regiment
6th Bn. Lincolnshire Regiment
2/4th Bn. King's Own Yorkshire Light Infantry

No. 2 Group . . . 128th Infantry Brigade
2nd Bn. Royal Hampshire Regiment
1/4th Bn. ,, ,,
5th Bn. ,, ,,

No. 3 Group . . . 139th Infantry Brigade
2/5th Bn. Leicestershire Regiment
5th Bn. The Sherwood Foresters
16th Bn. Durham Light Infantry

As will be seen, however, circumstances were to prevent a strict adherence to this allotment in the early days in Italy.

Plans for the initial landing in Italy were subject to many alterations, but by the 1st September the position, as far as the Battalion was concerned, was as follows: Nos. 1 and 3 Groups, who were to form part of the First Flight, were at Bizerta about to embark. Both Groups had been issued with a full complement of service vehicles. Bn. H.Q. and No. 2 Group were still in the Forêt de St. Ferdinand, being unable to take part in the early stages of the operation owing to a shortage of service vehicles and shipping space. Sept. 1943

The 46th Division (whose Commander by this time was Major-General J. L. I. Hawkesworth) landed at Salerno in the early hours of the 9th September 1943, as part of the United States Fifth Army (Lieut.-General Mark H. Clark). This landing, some distance up the west coast, was designed to cut off the enemy forces in the south opposing General Montgomery's Eighth British Army, which had landed on the toe of Italy a few days previously.

The A.A. guns of both Groups came into action during the sea voyage, and each claimed to have brought down one Focke-Wulf 190.

The assault on the Divisional sector was made by the 128th Infantry Brigade; supported by No. 3 Group, 2nd Bn. Royal Northumberland Fusiliers. No. 1 Group with the 138th Infantry Brigade landed with the second wave. One landing craft of No. 3 Group was hit before beaching and several casualties resulted. Soon after landing they also lost Lieuts. H. B. Dennison and J. H. G. Deighton, who stepped on mines whilst carrying out a reconnaissance.

During the early stages of the landing it is necessary to follow the fortunes of each Group separately. No. 3 Group, being the first in action, is taken first.

No. 3 Group

Some difficulty was experienced in collecting and organizing after landing on the 9th September. On the following day, however, the Group was in battle positions in its assembly area. On the 11th, under orders of the 139th Infantry Brigade, one M.G. platoon was in action and reconnaissances for mortar positions were carried out.

On the 12th September both mortars and machine-guns fired in support of an attack by the King's Own Yorkshire Light Infantry of the 138th Infantry Brigade.

By the 14th the battle for Salerno had reached a critical stage and all companies were heavily engaged. As there was little enemy air activity H Coy. (A.A.) was organized into two infantry platoons, and went into action in an infantry role on the night of the 17th/18th September. It reverted to the A.A. role on the 21st.

On the 20th the Group came under the 201st Guards Brigade, but on the 22nd they moved from Salerno to Vietri Sol Mare. Here they joined up with No. 1 Group to support an attack by the 138th Infantry Brigade. In this attack the Mortar Company fired 1,390 bombs over a period of forty minutes—an average of more than one bomb per mortar every thirty seconds. After a short rest both mortar and M.G. companies supported an attack on Cava.

Regrouping took place on the 28th and on the following day the whole Group, except one M.G. platoon, was withdrawn to rest.

No. 1 Group

This Group landed after the first shock of the assault, but encountered more shelling and mortar fire than No. 3. They went into action almost at once, their mortars and machine-guns being much in demand in support of the infantry.

Sept. 1943

By 1100 hrs. 10th September the Group was complete at assault scale, with H.Q. just west of Ponte Cagnano, in support of the 138th Infantry Brigade, Sub-units went into action as follows:

One mortar platoon, One M.G. platoon: In support of Commando troops in the Vietri Sul Mare area. (The mortars remained for two days in this role and the M.G. platoon for twelve.)

One M.G. platoon in support of the 6th Bn. York and Lancaster Regiment on the road Salerno–Avellino.

One M.G. platoon in support of the 6th Bn. Lincolnshire Regiment on the Alessia feature.

Two mortar platoons in support of No. 2 Commandos and 6th Bn. Lincolnshire Regiment, with whom they remained for five days.

There was stubborn fighting in these positions. Lieut. R. R. Gibson (Cheshire Regt.) greatly distinguished himself in the handling of his M.G. platoon and received an immediate award of the Military Cross.

On the 12th the enemy launched a determined counter-attack on the Dragone feature, where Lieut. Gibson's and Sgt. Spratt's M.G. platoons were in action. The latter was overrun and Sgt. Spratt with several others was reported missing. The enemy attack was renewed on the following day. Throughout this operation Lieut. Gibson's platoon was constantly in action and carried out some excellent shoots.

Although the infantry were relieved on the evening of the 13th September, the platoons of the Support Group remained in position and were in action continuously until the 22nd.

On the 13th Major C. W. Summers (O.C. C (M.G.) Coy.) was wounded and Major E. R. Coutts-Deacon (who had just been promoted and come from hospital in Bizerta) assumed command. His place as O.C. A (Mortar) Coy. had been taken by Captain R. M. Kershaw just prior to embarkation.

On the 25th/26th September there was a general advance on the Brigade front. On the 28th, Group H.Q. moved to Cava di Terreni, and the whole Group concentrated in the same area. The last days of the month were spent overhauling vehicles and equipment. Since landing 5,200 mortar bombs and 130,000 rounds of ·303 ammunition had been fired.

During these activities by Nos. 1 and 3 Groups the luckless Bn. H.Q. and No. 2 Group had remained inactive in their camp near Algiers.

At this stage it will be convenient to give a picture of the progress of operations as a whole. Italy had surrendered unconditionally on the 8th September 1943. This event, whilst being a move in the right direction, made little difference to the conduct of the campaign. It merely regularized the non-participation of Italian troops in the fighting—an event which had already taken place. As the front moved steadily up the leg of Italy the Italian people were to pay a terrible price—in the form of ruined cities and villages—for Mussolini's decision to join Germany in 1940.

Although the Fifth Army had encountered very heavy opposition in the Salerno bridgehead, the Eighth Army to the south had made rapid progress. By the 21st

September troops of the two armies were in contact. The difference in the degree of resistance on the two fronts was accounted for by the fact that Italian troops had been given the role of defending Southern Italy, whereas the Salerno landings were opposed by Germans, who reacted with their customary vigour. Sept.–Oct. 1943

For the next phase of operations it is possible to deal with the two Groups (Nos. 1 and 3) together.

On the 6th October both Groups moved to a new Divisional concentration area north-west of Literno on the coastal plain. The next few days were comparatively quiet while the Division made preparations for the crossing of the River Volturno. About this time the decision was made that, owing to the heavy casualties in infantry officers, each Support Group was to send three officers to infantry regiments—two being taken from the A.A. Company and one from the M.G. Company.

For the next operation, the crossing of the River Volturno, the detailed arrangements were as follows:

No. 1 Group. Under command of 128th Infantry Brigade, which was to make the assault. The Group moved into its concentration area during the night of the 11th/12th October and companies deployed to their battle positions on the evening of the 12th.

No. 3 Group. In support of the crossing of 139th Infantry Brigade, No. 10 (M.G.) Platoon being placed under command of the 16th Bn. Durham Light Infantry. The Group moved to its battle positions on the evening of the 12th October. On the previous day Major J. D. Buckle had been admitted to hospital and Major F. Gray assumed command of the Group.

The assault crossing carried out by the 128th Infantry Brigade commenced at 2100 hrs. on the 12th without any previous bombardment. Lieuts. C. F. James and A. D. Wood, mortar O.P. officers, with their O.P. parties, crossed with the leading infantry. C (M.G.) Coy. (Major E. R. Coutts-Deacon) also crossed at an early stage in support of the infantry. No. 1 Group A.A. Company was deployed in the area of Castel Volturno. Although the initial crossing was carried out with only minor opposition the 128th Infantry Brigade had great difficulty in extending their bridgehead, and were involved in much tough fighting.

On the 139th Infantry Brigade's front the 16th D.L.I. crossed successfully with its attached M.G. platoon of No. 3 Group under Lieut. J. C. Brown. At first light on the 13th October the 5th Foresters crossed with No. 11 (M.G.) Platoon under Lieut. J. A. Kysh, and a mortar O.P. under Lieut. R. B. Pares, in support. These troops ran into a tank ambush and were overrun. Lieut. Kysh was wounded and later became a prisoner of war. Several other ranks of the M.G. Coy. also became casualties. Lieut. Pares and his party escaped by swimming the river. The A.A. Coy. came into action at dawn on this day and claimed one German fighter aircraft.

Very bitter fighting continued in the bridgehead for several days along the whole Divisional front, and both Support Groups were in action almost continuously. By the 19th October, however, it could be said that the passage of the Volturno had been successfully accomplished and that the bridgehead was secure.

On the 18th Major J. D. Buckle returned from hospital and resumed command.

Oct.–Nov. 1943

The period 20th to 26th October was spent mostly out of action—training and reorganizing—although some platoons of No. 3 Group remained in their battle positions.

On the 25th, No. 3 Group (less G (Mortar) Coy., which remained near Villa Literno) moved to the area of Francolise, about eight miles north of the Volturno on the main Capua–Rome road.

No. 1 Group moved to an area north-west of Capua in the early hours of the 27th.

At this stage of operations 139th Infantry Brigade was holding the entire Divisional front in the Francolise area; 128th Infantry Brigade was in support and 138th Infantry Brigade in reserve.

In the assault on Italy, described in this narrative, Support Groups had been used for the first time and it will be of interest to summarize the extent to which they had been successful. As in the past the medium machine-gun had proved an invaluable weapon in all types of operations, but more particularly in defence. The fact that the weapon was now incorporated in a Support Group, with other weapons, in no way diminished its usefulness or the methods of its employment. The 4·2-in. mortars, with their long range and powerful moral—as well as material—effect, were an outstanding success. They were not very accurate and consequently not suitable for 'pin-point' targets: their chief value was for area shoots when extreme accuracy was not essential. Soon after Support Groups arrived in the Mediterranean theatre the Commander Xth Corps (Lieut.-General Sir Richard McCreery) said of them: 'The Brigade Support Groups in 46th Division, especially the 4·2-in. mortars, have been an outstanding success. There has been unanimous agreement amongst all prisoners that they fear above all other weapons the 4·2-in. mortars.' The light A.A. companies, although the weapon was effective, did not fit into the Support Group organization so well. It frequently happened that there was no useful role for them in the same area as the machine-guns and mortars, and they were often detached at some distance, out of proper control of Support Group H.Qs. Later, in some formations, light A.A. companies were removed from Support Groups and formed into a separate divisional unit under the C.R.A.

On the 28th October, No. 3 Group H.Q. moved to Pizzone and during the night of the 28th/29th all three M.G. platoons supported the 2/5th Leicesters and 16th D.L.I. in the crossing of the Savone di Teano. On the 30th, Group H.Q. moved back south of Francolise.

At the end of the month No. 1 Group was in reserve with 138th Infantry Brigade.

On the 30th October news was received of Captain R. R. Gibson's (attd. from Cheshire Regt.) award of the Military Cross, and at the same time notification was received of the award of the Military Medal to No. 4269064 Sgt. J. Dobson (No. 9 Platoon, K (M.G.) Coy.) for gallantry at Salerno early in the campaign. These were the first awards granted to personnel of the 2nd Battalion in Italy.

On the 31st October some much needed new transport vehicles arrived for No. 1 Group, and both Groups commenced preparations for an advance into the mountainous country north of the Volturno Plain.

By the 3rd November No. 3 Group had been withdrawn to a rest area near San Croce, where they carried out training and staged a number of M.G. demonstrations for the benefit of other troops. On the 4th November Major J. D. Buckle, the Group Commander was admitted to hospital, Major F. Gray assuming command. Nov.–Dec. 1943

Meanwhile No. 1 Group had moved forward on the 5th November in defensive support of the 138th Infantry Brigade. The detailed dispositions were as follows:

No. 1 Group H.Q.	West of Sessa Aurunca
A.A. Coy. . .	In action along the road Capua–Minturno, west of Sessa Aurunca
Mortar Coy. .	In action in 2/4th K.O.Y.L.I. area with defensive fire tasks covering the Brigade front
M.G. Coy. . .	No. 9 Platoon in support of 2/4th K.O.Y.L.I. No. 11 Platoon in support of 6th Lincolns No. 10 Platoon—not deployed

On the 12th November the Battalion lost one of its most capable officers, to whose energy and organizing ability it owed a great deal—Major J. H. Cubbon, O.B.E. (attd. from Cheshire Regiment), who left to become Second-in-Command of the 5th Bn. Royal Hampshire Regiment in 128th Infantry Brigade.

It will be as well at this point to digress from the narrative of events in Italy and follow the fortunes of Bn. H.Q. and No. 2 Group who were still in Algeria. By the 15th October they had received their full complement of service trucks and carriers, and the prospects of early departure for Italy seemed good. Shortly after this, however, No. 2 Group suffered an epidemic of sickness—mostly malaria and jaundice—which somewhat curtailed training with the new equipment. This misfortune added to the frustration of being left behind.

Towards the end of October they were employed constructing a large camp for the accommodation of troops in Algiers sub-district.

On the 4th November preliminary orders to proceed to Italy were received, and by the 12th November they had reached the Transit Area at Bizerta. Here they encountered a spell of very bad weather—rain, mud and severe gales. Embarkation took place on the 24th November on an American 'Liberty' ship the U.S.S. 'Joshua Seney.' She left port early the following morning and after calling at Augusta in Sicily, finally arrived at Naples at 0900 hrs. on 30th November 1943 after an exceptionally crowded and uncomfortable voyage. The troops arrived at the transit camp outside the city at about 1430 hrs.

With the whole of the 2nd Bn. Royal Northumberland Fusiliers now in Italy the activities of each Group are, for the time being, best followed separately.

No. 1 Group

On the 1st and 2nd December the 128th Infantry Brigade made final arrangements for an attack on the Monte Cammino area, which was to be supported by No. 1 Group. This operation, which commenced on the evening of the 2nd December, involved very bitter fighting and the Group continued in action until the 7th. By then all the infantry objectives had been captured and on the 9th the Group withdrew to rest.

On the 12th December Group H.Q. moved to San Clemente and A (Mortar) and C (M.G.) Coys. to La Marata, close by. B (A.A.) Coy. were made responsible for the

Dec. 1943 protection of the Brigade B Echelon area. A few days later M.G. platoons took up defensive positions in the Cocuruzzo and Rocca D'Evanbro areas.

This Group spent the rest of the month preparing to move to the Mignano area, and in planning to support an attack on Porchia and Cedro.

No. 3 Group

From the 1st to 5th December the Group was engaged in defensive and harassing fire tasks in support of the 139th Infantry Brigade. This was not a spectacular role, but a great deal of ammunition was fired—6,000 mortar bombs and 800 M.G. ammunition belts. An example of the crushing effect of 4·2-in. mortar fire was an attack by the 2/5th Leicesters (commanded by Lieut.-Colonel S. Enderby, M.C., recently promoted from the 2nd Bn. Royal Northumberland Fusiliers). This was supported by No. 3 Group, assisted by No. 1 Group. There was little organized resistance and many prisoners were taken—all of whom were stupified by the tremendous concentration of mortar fire. On the 9th December, following some minor readjustments in tasks and dispositions, the whole Group withdrew to rest.

On the 14th and 15th, Group H.Q. and the mortar and M.G. companies moved to the San Carlo area in support of the 128th Infantry Brigade. Here the task was to protect the left flank of the 46th Division on the River Garigliano—whilst, as related previously, No. 1 Group gave direct support to the Brigade's attack on Monte Cammino. The A.A. Coy., acting in an infantry role, provided the close defence of San Carlo village.

These dispositions, with minor modifications, were maintained until the end of the month.

Bn. H.Q. and No. 2 Group

On arrival in Italy this portion of the Battalion remained near Naples for two days and on the 3rd December moved to camp at Cardito about 10 miles distant. It should be explained that the unit transport had travelled in a different ship from the personnel, and had not yet joined up. However, on the morning of the 8th the transport ship docked at Naples, and by the evening of the 10th both personnel and transport were together at Cardito. Some inconvenience was caused by the necessity of isolating all transport personnel, owing to an outbreak of infectious disease on the ship by which they had travelled.

By the 20th December Bn. H.Q. and No. 2 Group had moved forward into the 46th Division area in the mountainous, and recently captured, Monte Cammino area—Bn. H.Q. to Friello and No. 2 Group to Vezzara and Vezzarola, all a few miles south of the River Garigliano. Here officers and men of No. 2 Group underwent a period of instruction in the form of attachments to the now highly trained No. 3 Group. With the Italian winter now at its worst, very hard living conditions were experienced in this inhospitable area.

It will be appropriate at this stage—the end of the year 1943—to give a general picture of the campaign as a whole. By this time the Allies had overrun Southern Italy, and were holding a line from north of Termoli on the Adriatic to the mouth of the River Garigliano, about 40 miles north of Naples, with the British Eighth Army

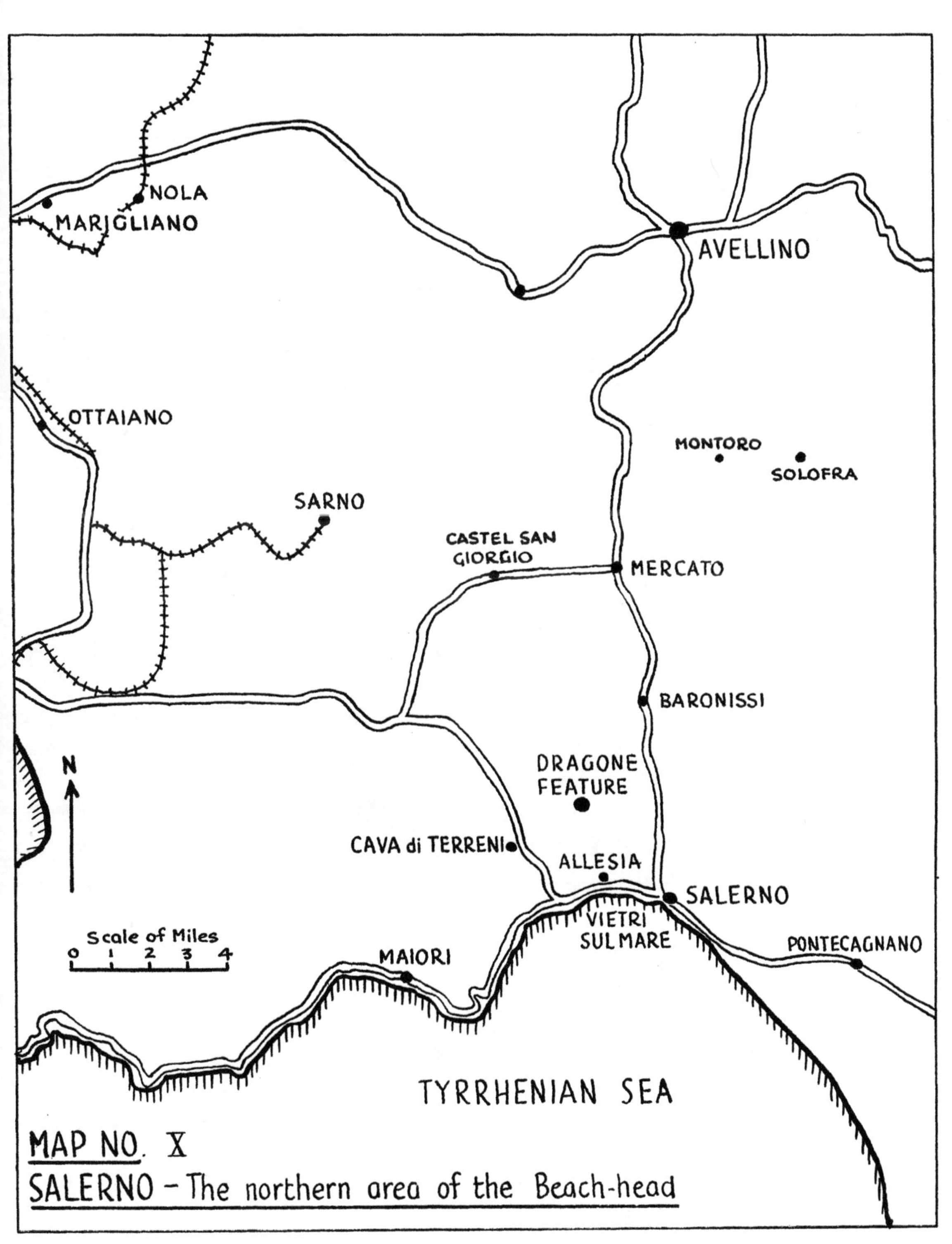

MAP NO. X
SALERNO – The northern area of the Beach-head

on the right and the American Fifth Army on the left. A substantial part of the country was, therefore, under Allied control and it was considered important to exploit this success as quickly as possible. There were, however, many factors which made it unlikely that a straightforward drive up the leg of Italy would lead to satisfactory results. The Germans had been reinforced and had now reorganized and redeployed their forces. The country favoured the defence: weather conditions were bad and likely to remain so for some weeks. Dec. 1943–Jan. 1944

It was therefore decided to carry out another landing up the west coast, and by mid-December a plan for this had taken shape. The Fifth and Eighth Armies were to carry out limited offensive operations to keep the Germans busy on their immediate fronts, and in order to gain suitable 'jumping off' areas for more ambitious operations later on.

The Fifth Army was also to carry out a seaborne landing at Anzio, south of Rome, with a force of approximately two divisions, with the object of capturing the Italian capital and cutting the communications of the enemy formations opposing the main body of the Fifth Army. The plan visualized a speedy link-up between the troops in the new bridgehead and the main forces—a condition which was not in fact brought about for many months and only after very fierce fighting.

As a preliminary to these events it was necessary to regroup the Fifth and Eighth Armies—reinforcing the former at the expense of the latter.

Christmas Day was spent by the Battalion in reasonably comfortable conditions—good food and drink being provided on an almost lavish scale.

The year 1943 ended with the 2nd Bn. Royal Northumberland Fusiliers disposed as follows:

Bn. H.Q.: Vezzarola.

No. 1 *Group*. In support of 138th Infantry Brigade, who were awaiting orders to attack Monte Cedro—an operation which had been planned some time before and postponed several times.

No. 2 *Group*. In support of 128th Infantry Brigade, who were also awaiting orders to carry out a previously planned assault over the River Garigliano—following the attack of the 138th Infantry Brigade.

No. 3 *Group*. In action in support of 139th Infantry Brigade, who were holding a defensive position. The A.A. Coy. was in an infantry role defending Brigade H.Q.

The New Year commenced with bad weather, including a very severe snowstorm, which greatly aggravated the supply position and did not promise well for the impending offensive.

The attack by the 138th Infantry Brigade (No. 1 Group in support) on Monte Cedro was launched on the 5th January 1944, but after a successful start the attack lost momentum—mainly due to an exposed right flank—and the troops were withdrawn to their original positions.

This lack of success automatically cancelled the operations of the 128th Infantry Brigade (No. 2 Group in support).

On the following day the 138th Infantry Brigade (No. 1 Group in support) relieved the 139th Infantry Brigade (No. 3 Group in support).

Jan. 1944

Meanwhile another operation for the crossing of the River Garigliano had been planned, the objective being the village of San Ambrogio on the far bank. During the planning of this operation some 90 reinforcements for the Battalion arrived. These brought the numbers up to approximately full strength, although there was still a shortage of specialists.

The attack, which was to be carried out by the 128th and 139th Infantry Brigades (supported by Nos. 1 and 3 Groups), involved a very complicated M.G. and mortar fire plan, including many feint shoots and bombardments. The date of the crossing was repeatedly postponed, owing to heavy rain and the swelling of the already fast-flowing river.

The assault took place on the morning of the 20th January, but was not successful, as the troops were unable to cross owing to the strength of the river's current. Further downstream, however, a brigade of the 56th Division succeeded in crossing and was subsequently relieved by the 138th Brigade of the 46th Division. In support of this movement No. 1 Group took up positions on the eastern bank of the river in order to give support to the Brigade on the western bank. On the 22nd January portions of this Group moved forward into positions on the western bank.

At the same time the 139th Infantry Brigade took over the defence of the whole Divisional front, thus relieving the 128th Infantry Brigade to support the 138th on the western bank.

Consequent on the establishment of a bridgehead west of the river, Groups of the Battalion were to some extent redeployed and their activities during the next few days were as follows:

No. 1 Group. On the 26th January the Group supported a considerable attack by 138th Infantry Brigade. In this engagement C (M.G.) Coy. under Captain R. R. Gibson, M.C., captured a number of prisoners of the 276th Panzer Grenadier Regt., and on the following day No. 11 Platoon had a particular good shoot at enemy in the Masse Valle di Sujo area. Both machine-guns and mortars remained in action until the 30th January.

No. 2 Group. On the 29th January this Group supported an attack by 128th Infantry Brigade on the Damiano feature, to the west of Castleforte, and continued in this role until the 30th. During the 'dumping' programme prior to this attack Cpl. Goodfellow (No. 2 Group) greatly distinguished himself by driving several lorries, loaded with 4·2-in. mortar bombs, past a fiercely burning vehicle in a narrow lane—an action for which he was mentioned in despatches.

No. 3 Group. In defensive support of 139th Infantry Brigade and disposed as follows:

H.Q. . . .	San Clemente
One M.G. platoon One mortar section	In the northern sector of the Divisional front
One M.G. platoon One mortar section	In the southern sector of the Divisional front
Remainder of Group	In B Echelon area

On the night of the 1st/2nd February 1944, No. 2 Group relieved No. 1 Group as part of a relief of 138th Infantry Brigade by 128th Infantry Brigade. Feb. 1944

The following statement shows the officers and other rank casualties which occurred in the Battalion between the 9th September 1943 and the 31st January 1944:

OFFICERS

No. 1 Group

Reported missing, later reported died of wounds as prisoner of war:	Lieut. D. R. Pollard (Manchester Regt.)
Wounded:	Major C. W. Summers (Middlesex Regt.)
	Lieut. D. A. Bloor (Rifle Brigade)
	2/Lieut. D. A. McRae
	Major R. M. Kershaw
	Captain S. J. Terblanche (U.D.F. South Africa)
	Lieut. J. Martin
	Lieut. G. H. Strutt (Cheshire) (twice)
	Lieut. W. J. Muir (remained at duty)
	Lieut. C. F. James (Manchester Regt.)

No. 2 Group

Wounded:	Lieut. F. St.J. C. Gore (remained at duty)
	Lieut. R. O. Hutton

No. 3 Group

Wounded:	Lieut. H. B. Dennison
	Lieut. J. H. G. Deighton
	Lieut. D. N. Martin
Missing:	Lieut. J. A. Kysh
Later reported prisoner of war, wounded and in hospital:	Lieut. J. A. Kysh

OTHER RANKS

	Killed or died of wounds	*Wounded*	*Missing and prisoners of war*
No. 1 Group	18	62	5
No. 2 Group	5	13	—
No. 3 Group	11	28	2
Totals	34	103	7

Earlier in the narrative it has been explained that Allied plans had been made for a further landing up the west coast at Anzio. This landing had taken place on the

Feb.–March 1944

morning of the 22nd January 1944, and met with considerable initial success. Later, however, the Anzio beachhead was to be the scene of much bitter fighting and a long casualty list. Moreover, the offensive by the Fifth and Eighth Armies on the main front met with stubborn opposition and, by the date of the Anzio assault, neither Army had reached the objectives assigned to them. It was, however, essential to maintain pressure on the main front during the early part of January in order to contain enemy forces which might be used against the troops assaulting Anzio. This accounts for the somewhat disjointed offensive operations of the 46th Division at that period and the fact that they were conducted in such unfavourable weather conditions. The link-up with the new beachhead, and the capture of Rome, was destined to be a long and painful process.

The months of February and March were without any major incidents from an operational point of view. The front remained more or less static. Normal reliefs took place, groups and companies of the Battalion spending most of the time supporting the infantry in the line with short periods of rest in rear areas.

The A.A. Coys. of Nos. 1 and 2 Groups spent a few days early in March attached to the 2nd Battalion Coldstream Guards holding a sector of the line in an infantry role.

On the 10th March a draft of 60 reinforcements joined the Battalion, this being only the second sizable draft received since December 1943.

On the same day an event of considerable importance to the Battalion took place. For some time it had been known that the 46th Division was to leave for another theatre of operations, and since mid-February the Division had been in process of handing over to the 4th Division (Major-General H. J. Hayman-Joyce). On the 10th March this process was completed and the 2nd Bn. Royal Northumberland Fusiliers became a unit of the 4th Division. The following message was received from Major-General J. L. I. Hawkesworth, commanding the 46th Division:

> 'I shall be grateful if you will tell all ranks how much I have appreciated their conduct since they came ashore straight into conflict at Salerno. The standard which was set there, and had been maintained since, is well worthy of their Regimental traditions. I have admired the steadfastness and cheerfulness of all ranks: the enemy knows to his cost the Machine Guns and Mortars of the Fighting Fifth: our own troops have cause to be grateful for them. I wish all ranks the best of luck in the future.'

The composition of the 4th Division was as follows:

10th Infantry Brigade:

- 1st Bn. Bedfordshire and Hertfordshire Regiment
- 2nd Bn. The Duke of Cornwall's Light Infantry
- 6 Bn. East Surrey Regiment

12th Infantry Brigade:

- 2nd Bn. Royal Fusiliers
- 1st Bn. Royal West Kent Regiment
- 6th Bn. The Black Watch

28th Infantry Brigade: March–April 1944

2nd Bn. The King's Regiment
2nd Bn. Somerset Light Infantry
2/4th Bn. Royal Hampshire Regiment

This change was followed by a period of reliefs, orders and counter-orders, moves and counter-moves.

On the 15th March the first attack on Cassino commenced. The Battalion had a grandstand view of the air bombardment—in which over 7,000 tons of bombs were dropped on Cassino town and the Monastery area—as a prelude to the assault. The Battalion's part in this operation was not a direct one, but took the form of simulating attacks by means of feint machine-gun shoots and mortar bombardments. The attack on Cassino was impeded by heavy snowfalls and the desperate resistance of the German garrison. Eventually our troops were forced to abandon the assault and withdrew to the line of the Rapido River.

On the 18th March plans were put into operation for the relief of the 4th Division by French troops and a move across Italy to the Foggia area on the Adriatic coast. As the relief was in progress this order was cancelled, and the Battalion eventually moved as follows:

Bn. H.Q.	Between the River Volturno and Venafro
No. 1 Group	To billets in Alvignano in the Volturno valley, where they arrived on the 24th March
No. 2 Group	To an area near the River Volturno near Ailano, arriving on the 27th March
No. 3 Group	To a bivouac area on the road Venafro–Isernia on the 22nd March

The Battalion remained in these locations until the end of the month—out of range of enemy artillery and engaged mainly on vehicle maintenance.

The next move was to positions on the Divisional front, taken over from French troops, in the Belvedere area, north of Cassino across the Rapido River. The forward positions were on the Terelle feature. The 10th Infantry Brigade (with No. 1 Group in support) took over first on Terelle, and later the 28th Infantry Brigade (with No. 2 Group in support) relieved the 10th Infantry Brigade and No. 1 Group. The position was very exposed, being under observation from the front, the right, right rear and the left. All positions were under constant mortar and artillery fire. This was a very mountainous area—served only by narrow mountain tracks, which made the supply problem a very real one. B Echelon, near Venafro, was more than 30 miles from the forward troops. The Battalion moved into this sector on the 3rd April. No incidents of special note occurred from an operational point of view; but on the 4th April one of considerable Regimental interest took place, when Lieut.-Colonel R. F. Forbes-Watson and Major T. V. H. Beamish of the 1st Battalion visited the 2nd Battalion.

Between the 12th and 15th April the greater portion of the Battalion was relieved, and moved to a very pleasant rest area—Venatro–Pietravairano–Latina. Here most

April 1944

of the Battalion spent St. George's Day, which was celebrated in the customary manner. This rest period was, however, somewhat interrupted by elements of No. 2 Group having to remain in the line, and the premature departure of part of No. 3 Group to Cassino in support of the 1st Guards Brigade.

On the 21st April Major-General A. D. Ward, D.S.O., took over command of the 4th Division—which was relieved by the New Zealand Division on the nights of the 21st/22nd and 22nd/23rd April. About the same time various proposals were made for modifications in the organization of support battalions, but it was decided that any major changes would be impracticable under the active battle conditions which were forecast for the near future. It was, however, decided to institute a 'counter-mortar' organization on the same lines as 'counter-battery' in the Royal Artillery.

The rest period continued, with exceptions in the cases of a few sub-units, until the end of April.

By this time the Italian winter was over and bright spring weather had commenced. The flooded rivers had subsided and conditions were becoming favourable for cross-country movement and operations on a more active scale. By May 1944 the Allies were about to commence the great offensive operations which they had been planning for so long, and which within the space of a year were to beat the life out of Nazi Germany. Within a few weeks landings of Allied troops were to take place in Normandy and in Southern France. Synchronized with these operations the Russian armies were to advance from the east and the Allied armies in Italy from the south.

Although Allied troops in the Italian theatre were to play a great part in these events—and the German armies opposed to them were to be the first to accept unconditional surrender—the opening of another Anglo-American battlefront in North-West Europe was, in a sense, a handicap to Field-Marshal Alexander's command. From henceforth Italy was no longer the main theatre of operations, and for the rest of the war it was frequently mulcted of its best formations and units in order to reinforce other fronts, and suffered shortages of trained reinforcements and equipment. The story of how these difficulties were overcome and the offensive pressed home to victory is told in the next chapter.

24. A long carry at Salerno

25. A Vickers medium machine-gun in action—Italy

26. A machine-gun of the 2nd Battalion observing ground in front of Monastery Hill, Cassino

27. The tragic fate of Cassino (see chapter 12)

CHAPTER 12

ITALY

May 1944 to December 1944
2nd Battalion

(See Map No. XI)

In May 1944 began the great offensive in Italy which was to be the forerunner of the Normandy landings and the Russian offensive from the east. May 1944

The 4th Division was given the most difficult and most important task in the opening stages of this operation, in which the 2nd Bn. Royal Northumberland Fusiliers were to play a distinguished part. The task of the Division (in conjunction with the 8th Indian Division) was to force the crossing of the Rapido-Gari River before Cassino—a defensive position of great natural strength held by the best German troops and heavily fortified. Hitherto this river line had defied all attempts to cross it.

Prior to the 1st May the Battalion was at rest at Pietravairano, but on that day No. 2 Group took over the front-line positions of the M.G. Battalion of the 8th Indian Division. Although they were in ignorance of the details it was clear to all, from the amount of supply and ammunition dumping in progress, and other activities, that great events were impending. On the 8th the Commanding Officer was informed that during the battle he was to be the Divisional Commander's personal liaison officer, which duty included the supervision of the Divisional traffic control organization.

The essence of operation 'Honker' (the code name given to the operation) was surprise, and secrecy in preparation; but by the second week in May all 'key' commanders had been given an outline of the plan.

The 4th Division's plan was as follows:

10th and 28th Infantry Brigades to carry out the assault crossing, after which the 10th was to turn right and together, with the 1st Guards Brigade (of the 6th Armoured Division),* clear Cassino.

12th Infantry Brigade was then to pass through and continue the advance alongside the 28th Infantry Brigade—linking up with the Polish Corps astride Route 6 several miles west of Cassino.

To support this operation the Battalion was deployed as follows:

Bn. H.Q. at Monte Lungo, with H.Q. 4th Division.

Nos. 1 and 2 Groups supported the 10th and 28th Infantry Brigades during the crossing.

---

* The 1st Guards Brigade was temporarily detached from the 6th Armoured Division, and under the 4th Division, for this operation.

May 1944

The machine-guns of No. 3 Group also supported the leading troops in the initial stages. Thereafter they were to be prepared to move forward with the rest of the Group in support of the 12th Infantry Brigade.

The opening bombardment commenced at 2300 hrs. on the 11th May. In this the mortars and machine-guns of Nos. 1 and 2 Groups participated to the maximum extent, firing huge quantities of ammunition. Later the mortar companies carried out 'counter-mortar' tasks.

At 0900 hrs. 12th May A (Mortar) and C (M.G.) Coys. assisted the 6th Bn. East Surrey Regiment (10th Infantry Brigade) in repelling a counter-attack on Point 36—a knoll some 300 yds. from the far bank of the river.

Meanwhile small detachments from the administrative portions of the Battalion—who had roles directing traffic and bringing back prisoners—were having an exciting time. In the confused fighting which followed the crossing some of these detachments became mixed up in the fighting in the most forward infantry areas. Lieuts. J. S. Ormston (Bn. Intelligence Officer) and I. E. Cockburn were wounded in the course of these duties. Sgt. M. Punton was later awarded the Military Medal for his fine work in connection with traffic control.

One mortar platoon and one machine-gun platoon of No. 2 Group crossed the river close behind the infantry, and came into action on the far side in support of the 28th Infantry Brigade. It is recorded that at one time the wireless set with Lieut. P. B. Gorst's mortar O.P. was the only link between the forward battalions and Brigade H.Q.

The fighting on the far bank had been very bitter, but by the evening of the 13th May the tide of battle had turned. The 26th Armoured Brigade, closely followed by the 12th Infantry Brigade, had crossed the river, passed through the other two brigades of the 4th Division, and were pushing on to the west.

On the afternoon of this day one mortar platoon (Lieut. G. L. Pearce) of No. 3 Group crossed the river in support of the 12th Infantry Brigade, the remainder of the Group continuing to give support from the east bank, between Monte Trocchio and Cassino town.

No. 10 (M.G.) Platoon (Lieut. G. H. Strutt) of No. 1 Group crossed at 1700 hrs. and was soon in action in support of the 10th Infantry Brigade. A section of this platoon captured 20 prisoners. Later three carriers were hit by shell-fire and Lieut. Strutt was slightly wounded—his fifth wound in eight months.

At 1800 hrs. No. 9 (M.G.) Platoon (Lieut. J. C. Brown) also crossed and came under orders of the 1st Bn. Royal West Kent Regiment.

On the 14th the mortars and No. 9 (M.G.) Platoon of No. 3 Group supported attacks by the 12th Infantry Brigade, and towards the evening Nos. 3 (Mortar) and 9 (M.G.) Platoons moved forward in order to give closer support.

Meanwhile the 78th Division, which had so far been in reserve, was moving forward to pass through the 4th Division and continue the pursuit.

By the 16th May the 28th Infantry Brigade had been withdrawn and No. 2 Group accompanied them to Ailano. Nos. 1 and 3 Groups, however, continued to give support to the forward troops, the mortars preparing to fire smoke on Monastery Hill in order to mask the advance of Polish troops to the north.

On this day orders were received to discontinue the use of Mark VIII Z ammunition and for the machine-guns to revert to the old short-range Mark VII. It was found that prolonged use of the former caused excessive wear to the barrels, and there was only a limited supply of spare barrels.

By the morning of the 18th the gallant Poles had occupied the famous Monastery and British tanks and infantry were in process of clearing the last remaining enemy from Cassino. By 1400 hrs. all organized resistance on the front of the 4th Division had ceased and the 78th Division began to pass through.

By the 21st the whole Battalion was concentrated at rest in the Piedimonte d'Alife area. The following figures give some idea of the ammunition expenditure between the 11th and 19th May:

Machine-guns: Over 500,000 rds.—an average of about 14,500 rds. per gun. Three guns of No. 11 Platoon (No. 1 Group) fired approximately 35,000 rds. each.

Mortars: 15,000 bombs—an average of 640 per mortar. No. 4 Platoon (No. 1 Group) fired an average of 1,412 per mortar.

The casualties in this battle were as follows:

Officers:

Wounded . . . . Lieut. J. S. Ormston
Lieut. I. E. Cockburn (60th Rifles)

Other ranks:

Killed and died of wounds 5
Wounded 23

On the 23rd May every officer in the Division attended an address given by the Divisional Commander. Afterwards they were entertained to lunch—a somewhat unique function in the wake of an advancing army.

On the 27th May an order was received for the Battalion to organize forthwith to the war establishment of a machine-gun battalion composed of:

Bn. Headquarters
Headquarter Coy.
Three Machine-gun Coys. (A, B and C Coys.)
One Mortar Coy. (D Coy.)

D (Mortar) Coy. was organized into two self-contained parts—a Right Half-Company and a Left Half-Company.

This was a formidable task which necessitated not only a decrease in numbers but the reduction in rank of some personnel. Moreover, time was an important factor, as the unit could not hope to remain at rest for more than one or two weeks.

A detailed account of the process of reorganization would make tedious reading. It will be sufficient to say that it was completed, and the Battalion on the move

June 1944 again, by the 6th June. The Battalion state under the new organization was as follows:

Commanding Officer . .	Lieut.-Colonel E. H. Butterfield
Second-in-Command .	Major J. A. Dewhurst
Adjutant	Captain L. F. Hay
Quartermaster . . .	Captain W. R. E. Brown
Regimental Sergeant-Major	R.S.M. C. V. Caborn
O.C. H.Q. Coy. . .	Captain A. W. Wilkins
„ A (M.G.) Coy. . .	Major A. E. Richards
„ B (M.G.) „ . .	Major H. R. M. Wilkin
„ C (M.G.) „ . .	Major J. D. Buckle
„ D (Mortar) Coy. .	Major E. H. Parkhurst

The programme of reorganization was suddenly upset during the first week in June by news that the 4th Division was to move forward again in pursuit of the now fast retreating enemy. By the 6th June the Division was advancing north of Rome with the object of cutting off three German divisions which were between the River Tiber and the sea.

The Battalion convoy of some 200 vehicles left the cornfields near Piedimonte d'Alife, which had seen the rebirth of the 2nd Bn. Royal Northumberland Fusiliers as a machine-gun battalion, at 1300 hrs. on the 6th and moved via Alife and Pietravairano along Route 6 to an area between Arce and Ceprano—a distance of 68 miles. By the time they arrived there, however, the 4th Division had pushed on a further 50 miles.

On the 7th June the advance continued, via Ceprano, Frosinone and Ferentino to Valmontone, about 15 miles south of Rome. This move of 48 miles was a very slow one, as there was much congestion of military traffic on the roads.

On arrival at Valmontone a small liaison party was sent to Divisional Headquarters, now only some 18 miles further forward. They returned with orders for a Tactical Bn. H.Q., and one mortar platoon each for the 10th and 12th Infantry Brigades, to move forward immediately. This move, which was into the recently relieved Anzio beachhead, was completed by 0100 hrs. 8th June. Bn. H.Q. was located at Corcolle, and the two mortar platoons moved out in support of their respective brigades.

At 1330 hrs. on this day (the 8th June) Bn. H.Q., moving immediately in rear of H.Q. 4th Division, left Corcolle for an area about 1½ miles south of Palombara Sabina. Meanwhile the rest of the Battalion was moving forward to Corcolle.

By the morning of the 10th, B Echelon had rejoined the Battalion from Ceprano. On the evening of this day B (M.G.) Coy. and a half-company of D (Mortar) Coy. (under Captain R. M. Kershaw) moved through Rome, to an area about 8 miles north-east of the city, where they came under command of 28th Infantry Brigade.

Later in the evening, but before dusk, the Battalion, less B (M.G.) Coy. and three mortar platoons already deployed with brigades, moved to a plateau 6 miles east of Rome. During this move the dome of St. Peter's and many other famous landmarks were clearly visible. As the descendants of the Northumbrians, whose country had been occupied by the Romans almost two thousand years before, drove their modern chariots through the heart of the old Roman Empire, one could not help feeling that this was a strange reversal of events. June–July 1944

On the night of the 11th/12th June another move was made to a locality in the marshy plains bordering the River Tiber, some 10 miles north of Rome, and near the area where B (M.G.) Coy. was already established. As there was every prospect that the stay here would be a prolonged one, and as the detached portions of the unit were not in action, it was arranged that B (M.G.) Coy. and the three mortar platoons should rejoin the Battalion.

On the 13th June Lieut.-Colonel R. F. Forbes-Watson, commanding the 1st Battalion, paid another visit to the 2nd Battalion.

The next few days were spent in maintenance, the calibration of the mortars of D Coy. and in rest.

On the 15th B Coy. moved to a forward concentration area north of Viterbo. On the 19th the rest of the Battalion moved to an adjoining area. On the 20th a party from the unit visited Rome and were received in audience by His Holiness the Pope.

Meanwhile the 4th Division remained in reserve, with the prospects of a fairly early return to the battlefront in the area of Lake Trasimeno and Chiusi.

The weather, which had been bad, cleared on the 21st June. Training had just commenced, when on the night of the 21st/22nd somewhat unexpected orders for an early move were received. B (M.G.) Coy. moved in advance, taking over positions from the 1st Kensingtons (Machine-Gun Battalion of the 78th Division), and on the 23rd the rest of the Battalion moved via Bagnoreggio–Orvieto–Ficulle and Monteleone to a very inaccessible area north-east of Citta Della Pieve—a total distance of about 50 miles. Here the sound of guns, heard for the first time for several weeks, welcomed their arrival on a ledge of ground, served only by a very narrow track.

On the 24th June B (M.G.) Coy. and the Right Half of D (Mortar) Coy. supported an attack by the 28th Infantry Brigade, in which 20,000 rds. and 220 mortar bombs were fired.

On the 26th A (M.G.) Coy. and the Right Half of D (Mortar) Coy, came under orders of the 10th Infantry Brigade when it relieved the 28th Infantry Brigade. On this day Captain J. J. Hinson, Lieut. F. St.J. C. Gore and three other ranks of B (M.G.) Coy. were wounded by shell-fire.

By the evening of the 29th all companies had been deployed in defensive support of the infantry along the Divisional front. It was a matter for satisfaction that this deployment worked smoothly so soon after the drastic reorganization which the Battalion had undergone, and which was, in some respects, still incomplete.

On the following day Bn. H.Q. moved to an area about one mile from Lake Chiusi near Strada. On the same day No. 15 (Mortar) Platoon suffered eight casualties (Cpls. McIntosh and Osborne and Fus. Herdson being killed) when a house occupied by a portion of the Platoon received a direct hit from a shell.

During the month of July the Division remained in the same area. The fighting was of a semi-static nature and there were no spectacular offensive operations. Nevertheless, every effort was made to push forward as opportunity offered and the aggregate amounted to a very substantial advance.

During this phase the 2nd Bn. Royal Northumberland Fusiliers carried out the

July 1944

normal tasks of a machine-gun battalion of those days, giving machine-gun and mortar support in the advance as required, harassing shoots and defensive fire tasks. It was rare for the whole unit to be committed at one time and reliefs between machine-gun companies and mortar platoons were frequent.

Two features characterized these operations—the activity of the artillery on both sides and the difficult nature of this hilly country. Gone were the days of two-way tarmac roads, which had now given place to narrow country lanes and hill tracks.

On the 2nd July while C (M.G.) Coy. was moving to the neighbourhood of Foian Della Chiana the platoon sergeant's carrier of No. 10 Platoon received a direct hit from a shell, which killed Sgt. Fox and wounded five Fusiliers. The loss of this experienced N.C.O., who had served the Regiment in peace and war for fifteen years, was a sad blow.

About this time a number of cases of dysentery and acute diarrhœa occurred. The highest incidence was among despatch riders and other motor-cyclists, which confirmed the belief that it was mainly due to dust from the roads.

On 3rd July Lieut. J. G. G. Dixon was reported missing from a visit to one of the infantry Bn. H.Qs.* On the following day Captain C. Hill (C (M.G.) Coy.), who had joined the Battalion in the Isle of Wight in 1940, was killed by a direct hit from a shell on his carrier.

On the 5th Bn. H.Q. and A (M.G.) Coy. moved forward up the Val Di Chiana, companies being in support of infantry brigades as follows:

A (M.G.) Coy.	10th Infantry Brigade
C (M.G.) Coy.	12th Infantry Brigade
D (Mortar) Coy. . . .	12th and 28th Infantry Brigade

B (M.G.) Coy., not being immediately required, remained behind at rest.

By the 8th July the methodical advance of the 4th Division had come to a standstill and orders were received for the Divisional front to be held with the minimum number of troops. Two platoons each of A (M.G.), C (M.G.) and D (Mortar) Coys. were deployed, the balance of the Battalion remaining in reserve at rest.

On the 11th July some mortars of the unit were 'shot,' for the first time, by an 'Air O.P.'—normally used by the artillery for spotting targets and directing fire. The results were acclaimed a great success.

On the night of the 15th/16th July the 6th Armoured Division (on the right) carried out an attack and the 4th Division took advantage of this digression to move forward up Route 69 towards Florence. The whole Battalion (less the Right Half of D (Mortar) Coy.) gave normal support during this operation. The advance progressed well and on the 16th Bn. H.Q. left Montevarchi and advanced via Monte San Savino–San Pancrazia and Capannole (a very difficult route) to Pogi to the west of the Arno valley.

On the 19th A (M.G.) Coy. moved to Mercatale some 8 miles distant. The other companies remained in the vicinity of Bn. H.Q.

On the 24th the Battalion moved to an area about Cavriglia. An unusual feature

* Lieut. Dixon was later reported to be a prisoner of war.

here was the fact that Bn. H.Q. was located much nearer the enemy than any other portion of the unit. About this time B (M.G.) Coy. was employed for some days assisting the Sappers in road maintenance and the construction of a bridge—subsequently named 'Northumberland Bridge,' in recognition of the company's work.

July–August 1944

On the 25th a party of 100 officers and men, under Major J. D. Buckle, lined part of the route in a rear area on the occasion of the visit of His Majesty the King to Italy.

By this time the foremost troops of the 4th Division were about 20 miles south of Florence. The country here was difficult. Some of the features were over 2,000 ft. high, and often densely wooded. The Divisional axis road was winding and in poor condition; the side roads were narrow, dusty and frequently very steep.

The advance was slow but steady. It was not until the 31st July that Bn. H.Q. moved again—to a field on a lateral road between Ponte and Dudda, about 15 miles from Florence.

During the months of June and July 1944 the Battalion casualties were as follows:

Officers:

Killed	Captain C. Hill
Wounded	Captain J. J. Hinson
	Lieut. F. St.J. G. Gore
	Lieut. P. B. Gorst
Prisoner of war	Lieut. J. G. G. Dixon

Other ranks:

Killed and died of wounds	10
Wounded	38

The 5th August found the Battalion only 4½ miles from Florence, with Bn. H.Q. in an orchard near La Brencola, beside a stream called the Ema.

The Division had been looking forward to occupying Florence—the city which it had been battling for for nearly two months—but this was not to be. Early in August orders were issued for the relief of the 4th Division by the 1st Division.

On the 8th the Battalion (less the fighting companies) moved via San Pola, Figline, Monte Varche, Arezzo, Fiorentino, Cortona, Riccio, Magione, Bastia and Assisi to an olive grove near Foligno. The rest of the Battalion followed at intervals, but by the evening of the 11th August all were concentrated in the Foligno area.

During the relief (and after the departure of Bn. H.Q. from the Florence area) some platoons were sharply engaged. Lieut. G. H. Strutt's and Sgt. Midcalf's platoons of A (M.G.) Coy. supported a local attack by the 2nd Bn. Duke of Cornwall's Light Infantry (10th Infantry Brigade) on the 8th August. The former, after knocking out several *Spandaus*,* inflicted heavy casualties on a party of Germans forming up for a counter-attack. Sgt. Midcalf, on being informed that the enemy were about to counter-attack, led his platoon in its carriers across country—firing on the move—and later took up positions from which they did great execution. For his part in this

* *Spandaus*—light German machine-guns.

August–Sept. 1944 action Sgt. Midcalf was awarded the Military Medal. Before leaving the area for Foligno the Company received congratulations from Brigadier S. N. Shoosmith, commanding the 10th Infantry Brigade.

The stay at Foligno lasted for one month, and was a period of real rest and relaxation. A Battalion rest camp was established at Lake Piediluco, and arrangements were made to send personnel on leave to Rome, to a winter sports hotel in the highest part of the Abruzzi and other places. For nearly four weeks 25 per cent. of the unit was always on leave. The remainder spent their time in maintenance, short cadre courses, calibrating mortars, zeroing machine-guns and other duties necessary to make the Battalion thoroughly battleworthy for the future.

On the 3rd September a warning order was received for the Battalion to be prepared to move on the night of the 5th/6th September to a destination on the Adriatic coast.

By this time preparations were well advanced for the new offensive which aimed at breaking the German defensive position known as the 'Gothic Line' and an advance into the industrial north of Italy. On arrival in the new area the 4th Division was to be in the Ist Canadian Corps. The offensive was to be launched by the 1st Canadian Division who, it was hoped, would break the crust of the German defences—after which the 4th Division was to pass through to exploit the success and pursue the retreating enemy.

The move was postponed for twenty-four hours, but at 2100 hrs. on the 6th the Battalion commenced its 100-mile journey to the Adriatic. The climb of 2,000 ft. over the Abruzzi was carried out in darkness. The route was through Fabriano and Sassoforrato, to an area near Senigallia. On arrival news was received that a further move would be made on the following day (the 8th) to the vicinity of Tombo Di Pesaro. The move started early in the morning, D (Mortar) Coy. leaving at 0400 hrs. and the rest of the unit at 0745 hrs. Very soon the rain, which had begun the previous day, developed into a storm. This flooded the roads and damaged the bridges so badly that it became necessary to halt. The whole Division spent the rest of the day bivouacked by the side of the road in pouring rain. Movement was resumed at midnight (8th/9th September) and the Battalion, moving through Fano and Pesaro, arrived at its destination, the village of Pieve, in time for breakfast.

On the 11th orders for the coming operation were issued. The plan was quite different from what had been anticipated. The 4th Division was to take part in the initial attack which visualized the capture of various features in succession—the Coriano ridge, bridgeheads across the Marano and Ausa rivers, the airfield at Rimini, the San Fortunato feature and finally a bridgehead over the River Marecchia which flows into the sea at Rimini.

C (M.G.) Coy. and the Left Half of D (Mortar) Coy. moved first into positions before Coriano, followed on the evening of the 14th by B (M.G.) Coy. and the Right Half of D (Mortar) Coy. A (M.G.) Coy. was placed under orders to move with the 10th Infantry Brigade. On the 16th, Bn. H.Q. moved across the River Conca to Bastella.

The operation went well. A (M.G.) Coy., although they made numerous moves, were not deployed and remained inactive until the end of the month. On the 16th, B (M.G.) Coy. fired 28,000 rds. in support of a successful attack by the 2/4th Royal

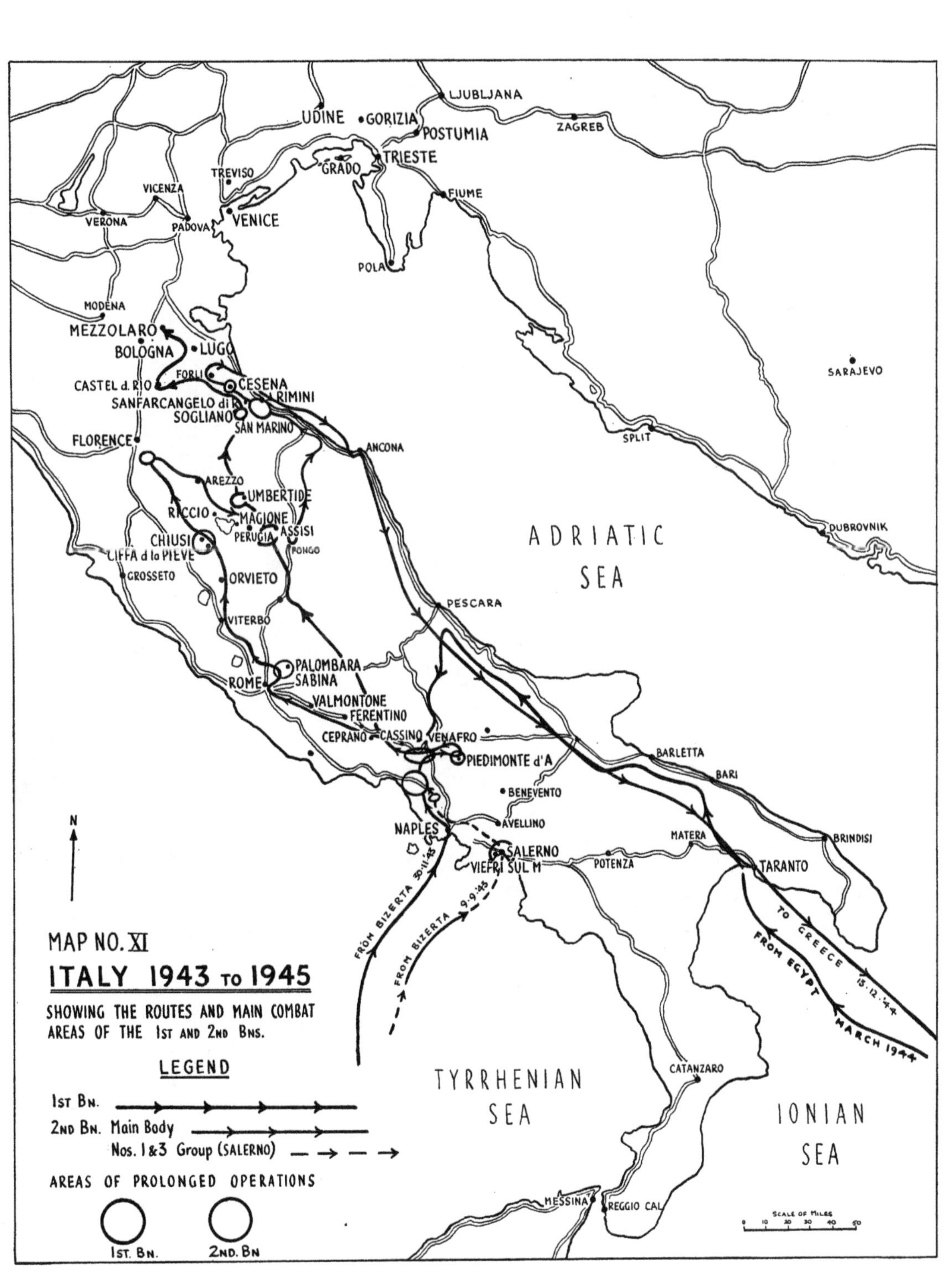
LJUBLJANA
UDINE
GORIZIA
POSTUMIA
ZAGREB
TREVISO
GRADO
TRIESTE
VICENZA
FIUME
VERONA
PADOVA
VENICE
POLA
MODENA
MEZZOLARO
BOLOGNA
LUGO
FORLI
CASTEL d. RIO
CESENA
SANFARCANGELO di R.
RIMINI
SOGLIANO
SAN MARINO
SARAJEVO
FLORENCE
ANCONA
SPLIT
AREZZO
UMBERTIDE
RICCIO
MAGIONE
DUBROVNIK
CHIUSI
PERUGIA
ASSISI
CIFFA d la PIEVE
PONGO
ADRIATIC
SEA
GROSSETO
ORVIETO
VITERBO
PESCARA
PALOMBARA
SABINA
ROME
VALMONTONE
FERENTINO
CEPRANO
CASSINO
VENAFRO
PIEDIMONTE d'A
BARLETTA
BARI
BENEVENTO
N
NAPLES
AVELLINO
MATERA
BRINDISI
SALERNO
VIEFRI SUL M
POTENZA
TARANTO
FROM BIZERTA 30·11·43
FROM BIZERTA 9·9·43
TO GREECE 15·12·44
FROM EGYPT MARCH 1944
MAP NO. XI
ITALY 1943 TO 1945
SHOWING THE ROUTES AND MAIN COMBAT AREAS OF THE 1ST AND 2ND BNS.
LEGEND
1ST BN.
2ND BN. Main Body
Nos. 1&3 Group (SALERNO)
AREAS OF PROLONGED OPERATIONS
1ST. BN.
2ND. BN
TYRRHENIAN
SEA
CATANZARO
IONIAN
SEA
MESSINA
REGGIO CAL
SCALE OF MILES
0 10 20 30 40 50

Hampshire Regt. (28th Infantry Brigade) on Cerasolo. After this they came out of action and remained near Misano under Battalion control. C (M.G.) Coy. supported attacks by the 12th and 28th Infantry Brigades on the 15th and 16th September and then moved out of action to near Coriano. During this operation enemy shelling and mortar fire was exceptionally heavy. B (M.G.) Coy. was subjected to considerable *Nebelwerfer* (7-barrelled heavy mortars) fire. Sept.–Oct. 1944

D (Mortar) Coy. continued to support the 12th and 28th Infantry Brigades until the 20th September, when they too came out of action.

The weather had been bad and the offensive which had started so well gradually lost momentum in the mud and floods. The operation resolved itself into a steady advance culminating in the crossing of the Marecchia and the capture of Rimini—opening the way to the plains of Northern Italy and the valley of the Po. It was the type of operation which became familiar in Italy, and elsewhere, during the latter stages of the war and known as 'passing the armour through.' During the latter part of September the rain and wind increased, however, making any spectacular advance by the waiting armour out of the question.

During this phase of the campaign the 10th Indian Division—in which the 1st Bn. Royal Northumberland Fusiliers was the Machine-Gun Battalion—was on the left of the 4th Division, and several interchanges of visits were arranged.

Early in October the 4th Division was transferred to the Vth Corps. On the 4th October D (Mortar) Coy. was placed under command of the 46th Division (Major-General J. L. I. Hawkesworth) and moved at once across the Marecchia and Rubicon rivers, where they immediately deployed for action. The rest of the Battalion, and the rest of the 4th Division, remained concentrated behind the line. D (Mortar) Coy. remained attached to the 46th Division until the 11th October, during which they fired nearly 4,000 bombs in support of the infantry—both in attack and defence. The following message was received from the Commander 46th Division:

> 'Will you please convey the thanks of the 46th Division to the Mortar Coy. of the Northumberland Fusiliers for the part they played in the battle of Montilgallo, and congratulate them most heartily on the way they co-operated.
>
> 'I know the Coy. had a very unpleasant time; they had to endure the most severe shelling and mortaring and ghastly weather. They triumphed, however, over all these difficulties.
>
> 'In particular the offensive spirit which they displayed was admirable; the only effect of the German shelling was to make the Northumberland Fusiliers send back more and more effective fire.
>
> 'Thank you very much for this co-operation.'

The period of inactivity for the rest of the Battalion was soon to end. The next operation was to be an advance by the 4th Division on Cesena—not directly by the main road along Route 9, but from the south-west, over the hills. This simplified the problem of D (Mortar) Coy. rejoining, as they could be 'picked up' from the 46th Division's area as the Battalion moved forward. The second week in October was favoured by a spell of fine weather.

Some days prior to the commencement of this operation machine-gun companies

Oct. 1944 moved into their respective infantry brigade areas—A Coy. to 10th Infantry Brigade, B Coy. to 28th Infantry Brigade and C Coy. to 12th Infantry Brigade.

On the 17th two platoons of D (Mortar) Coy. (which had rejoined on the 11th) moved to a concentration area in 12th Infantry Brigade area.

On the 19th, after a series of moves, Bn. H.Q. was established in a field near Santarcangelo just across the River Rubicon.

This battle, for Cesena and the River Savio, was fought more on a brigade group than on a divisional basis, and the various components of the Battalion were in consequence widely scattered. It is, therefore, considered best to record the activities of each company separately.

A (M.G.) Coy.

The Company went forward with 10th Infantry Brigade on the 19th October, but were not committed to action until they moved into Cesena on the night of the 23rd/24th after the town had been captured by troops of 139th Infantry Brigade (46th Division) and 12th Infantry Brigade. They then crossed the Savio, through 12th Infantry Brigade, to continue the advance.

On the 25th the Company moved up Route 9 with its platoons in support of their respective infantry battalions. No. 4 Platoon was the only one to take up positions, in support of the 2nd Bn. Duke of Cornwall's Light Infantry when they crossed the River Ronco; but they were not called upon to open fire. On the following day, however, all three platoons were in action.

On the 29th, the night of the 29th/30th and the 30th the Company was in action continuously, engaged on harassing fire tasks: 103 belts were expended during this period, mostly in a successful attempt—in which No. 3 Platoon (Lieut. J. Martin) played the leading part—to prevent the enemy destroying a vital bridge beyond the River Ronco. This action earned the Company Commander the name 'Horatius.' *

B (M.G.) Coy.

The Company moved into the Cesena area on the 24th October. They moved forward gradually with 28th Infantry Brigade, each platoon with the battalion to which it was affiliated. By the end of the month they had reached an area south-east of the Ronco, behind the 10th Infantry Brigade.

C (M.G.) Coy.

The Company came into action on the 17th October, each platoon with the battalion to which it was affiliated, but saw little action during the first two days.

By midnight on the 19th/20th the infantry of the 12th Infantry Brigade had advanced to the near bank of the River Savio, which runs through the north-west outskirts of Cesena. By dawn on the 20th all platoons were in action ready to support the infantry in their assault crossing. In these positions they were subjected to very heavy shelling and were lucky to escape casualties.

---

* 'How well Horatius kept the bridge.
In the brave days of old.'
[Macaulay's *Lays of Ancient Rome.*]

During the night of the 21st/22nd, on the 22nd and night of the 22nd/23rd 300 belts were fired in harassing tasks on enemy escape routes.

In the final stages of exploitation after this very successful river crossing Nos. 10 and 11 Platoons closely supported the infantry as they pressed the enemy back.

The Company finally came out of action on the 24th and concentrated in Cesena.

D (Mortar) Coy.

On the 19th October the Right Half-Coy. was in support of 12th Infantry Brigade and on the same day the Left Half-Coy. moved to a concentration area with 10th Infantry Brigade. Both half-companies supported their respective brigades in the early stages; but on the 24th the Right Half-Coy. came out of action and concentrated in Cesena. The same evening the Left Half-Coy. moved across the River Savio in support of 10th Infantry Brigade.

While these operations were going on the Battalion B Echelon had been located at Tomba Di Pesaro. As this was 60 miles in rear it caused very serious delays in moving supplies and ammunition forward.

During September and October the following casualties were suffered:

Officers:

Wounded	Lieut. H. Brittain
	Lieut. P. T. Grant
	Lieut. J. G. Scott

Other ranks:

Wounded	8

The last day of October 1944 found the Battalion disposed as follows:

Bn. H.Q. C (M.G.) Coy.	Cesena
A (M.G.) Coy. D (Mortar) Coy.	Supporting the infantry of the 4th Division on the line of the River Ronco
B (M.G.) Coy.	In reserve behind the River Ronco

On the 3rd November Bn. H.Q. moved to Forlimpopoli, where it was to remain until the Battalion came out of action. In this location they were continuously and heavily shelled.

Preparations were now being made for the Battle of Forli, in which the Commanding Officer—for the first time—found himself the Divisional Machine-Gun Commander. Hitherto machine-gun companies had always operated under the control of infantry brigades. D (Mortar) Coy. operated under the control of the Divisional Artillery in this operation.

The machine-gun fire programme commenced at 1600 hrs. on the 6th November, and continued throughout the night.

The attack on Forli was successful and by the 10th C (M.G.) Coy. had advanced with the forward troops of 12th Infantry Brigade, through Forli to the south-western

Nov. 1944

outskirts of the town. In this section some 4·2-in. mortars, directed by Captain P. B. Gorst, put down very heavy concentrations in support of an attack by the 6th Black Watch round the eastern outskirts of Forli. All objectives were captured with very few casualties and German prisoners testified to the crushing effect of the mortar fire. Captain Gorst was awarded the Military Cross for his part in this operation.

In this engagement A (M.G) Coy. fired 315,000 rds. and B (M.G.) Coy. 146,250 rds. —during the period 10th to 14th November when they were employed on harassing fire tasks.

Lieut. J. H. G. Deighton (C (M.G.) Coy.) was later awarded the Military Cross for his part in the Forli operations.

The next operation was the assault crossing of the River Montone and an adjoining canal which ran parallel to the river—both formidable obstacles with open, muddy approaches. All three machine-gun companies were committed to this operation.

On the 18th A (M.G.) Coy., with two platoons of C (M.G.) Coy. attached, supported an attack by 10th Infantry Brigade across the River Cosina, a southerly tributary of the Montone, south of Route 9.

On the nights of the 19th/20th and 20th/21st A (M.G.) Coy. was engaged in harassing fire tasks, as were B (M.G.) and C (M.G.) Coys. on the 21st.

The initial assault by the 10th Infantry Brigade—in support of which the Battalion fired 300,000 rds. of ammunition and 2,500 mortar bombs—was not successful and a new attack had to be staged, in a different manner, on the evening of the 21st, by the 28th Infantry Brigade. Elements of all companies supported this assault, which was successful.

On the 24th C (M.G.) Coy. concentrated in Forli, as did B (M.G.) Coy. and A (M.G.) Coy. on the 25th and 26th respectively.

Special mention must be made of D (Mortar) Coy. during this phase of operation, in which they were continuously in action in support of all three infantry brigades. They were actively engaged at the crossing of the River Ronco (4th to 7th November), the attack on Forli airfield (9th November) and later in the crossing of the River Montone. The Company received tributes and congratulatory messages from the Divisional Commander (Major-General A. D. Ward), and the Commanders 10th Infantry Brigade (Brigadier S. N. Shoosmith) and 12th Infantry Brigade (Brigadier A. G. W. Herber-Percy).

By the 26th November D (Mortar) Coy. had come out of action and joined the machine-gun companies in Forli.

It should be mentioned here that during November 1944 home leave was started. The number of vacancies allotted was three at any one time. On this scale it was estimated that the whole Battalion would complete one period of leave in the United Kingdom by the year 1957!

Casualties in these operations had not been unduly heavy—Lieut. M. L. F. Dibble wounded and two other ranks killed and 15 other ranks wounded.

During the Forli battle the Commanding Officer had been informed that the Division was shortly to be withdrawn from the line and sent to Palestine. There followed a period of orders and counter-orders, which caused much trouble and inconvenience. Moreover the move was shrouded in the greatest secrecy.

Nov.–Dec. 1944

The advance party left on the night of 20th/21st November under Major J. A. Dewhurst.

On the 26th the Battalion was given sixteen hours in which to move out of the line and embark on a 200-mile journey to Vasto.

On the 27th they left the battle area, for the first time for over three months, and moving down Routes 9 and 16, through Cesena, Rimini and the Adriatic port of Ancona, to Porto Chivitanova. Here they halted until the early hours of the 28th, when the journey was continued to the medieval fortress of Atri, where they went into billets.

Soon after arrival the startling news was received that the Battalion was likely to entrain for Taranto at very short notice, leaving a rear party to hand over the vehicles, surplus equipment, etc. Preparations to carry this out were put in hand at once. By the 1st December all vehicles and equipment had been handed over.

The Battalion entrained for Taranto on the 4th December and arrived at Narsisi Station on Taranto Bay at 2200 hrs. on the 5th. The rail journey was made in 'box wagons' (28 men to a wagon) and was an extremely uncomfortable one. On arrival a night march of about 5 miles was made to a tented camp outside Taranto. The duration of the stay was at that time unknown.

Meanwhile there were reports of activities in Greece; and when, on the 9th December, urgent orders were received for the Battalion to take over again all the vehicles and equipment it had just handed in, many predicted that the destination had been changed to Greece. This proved to be correct, and later information was received that the Battalion would be required to organize, and operate, as an infantry battalion.

While at Taranto Major J. D. Buckle—who had served with the 2nd Battalion continuously since 1934—left to attend a Staff course in the Middle East.

On the 13th December 1944 the 2nd Bn. Royal Northumberland Fusiliers embarked on H.M.T. 'Cameronia' in Taranto harbour. Thus 35 officers and 500 men of the unit sailed for Greece, with a large rear party and all their vehicles and most of their equipment and stores still in Italy, and with an advance party in Palestine.

CHAPTER 13

THE HOME FRONT

Preparations for the Invasion of Normandy—August 1943 to June 1944

7th and 8th Battalions and Nos. 1, 2 and 3 Independent Machine-Gun Companies (4th Battalion)

1. GENERAL

1943 BY the summer of 1943 the threat of invasion had passed and anti-invasion duties in the United Kingdom became largely nominal. As explained in Chapter 6, the decision had been made at the conference of Allied leaders at Quebec in August 1943 to launch an Anglo-American assault on North-West Europe in the spring or early summer of 1944. From then onwards the main task of all troops at home was to prepare for this operation.

By the early spring of 1944 the American General Eisenhower—whose great qualities had been proved in North Africa, Sicily and Italy—had been nominated as the Supreme Commander for operation 'Overlord,' the code name given for the Normandy invasion. This embraced command of all three services, British and American. General Sir Bernard Montgomery had been recalled from the Eighth Army in Italy to take command of the 21st Army Group at home, and had been designated as the commander of the Anglo-American land forces which were to carry out the initial assault. Combined-operations and other specialized training were in full swing and it was clear to all that great events were impending.

The following units of the Royal Northumberland Fusiliers were part of the 21st Army Group and participated in the training and other preparations for the assault on the Normandy coast:

4*th Battalion*—later disbanded as a battalion and formed into three Independent Machine-Gun Companies

No. 1 (Guards Armoured Division)

No. 2 (11th Armoured Division)

No. 3 (7th Armoured Division)

7*th Battalion* (Machine-Gun Battalion, 59th Division)

8*th Battalion* (Reconnaissance Regiment, 3rd Division)

(The 49th Bn. Royal Tank Regiment—which with the 43rd had been formed from the 6th Bn. Royal Northumberland Fusiliers—was not part of the original 21st Army Group, but joined it as part of the 1st Tank Brigade in August 1944. Its activities are described separately in Chapter 17.)

II. THE 4TH BATTALION

Dec. 1942–Jan. 1944

(NOTE: In the case of this unit the narrative commences at the beginning of 1943 when the Battalion was reformed.)

The story of the virtual destruction of the 4th Bn. Royal Northumberland Fusiliers during the Knightsbridge battle in North Africa, in June 1942, has been told in Chapter 7.

On the 26th December 1942 Lieut.-Colonel E. H. D. Grimley arrived at Headquarters, 15th (Scottish) Division at Morpeth, in Northumberland, charged with the task of reforming the Battalion as the Divisional Support Battalion. A few days later Major J. T. Lisle, Captain D. N. Clark-Lowes, and about 10 other rank survivors from the original Battalion in North Africa arrived to form the nucleus of the new unit.

The war establishment on which the Battalion reformed comprised Bn. H.Q. and two Support Groups, each consisting of a Vickers machine-gun company, a 4·2-in. mortar company and a light anti-aircraft (20-mm.) company.

In the early days the Battalion was located at Seaton House, near Ashington; but as numbers increased additional accommodation was taken over in Ashington town.

At first weapons, vehicles and other equipment arrived faster than trained men could be provided to handle them. On the other side of the border, however, where the 2nd Bn. Royal Northumberland Fusiliers were located around Selkirk, reverse conditions existed. The 2nd Battalion was rich in trained mortarmen, but lacked certain essentials of mortar equipment—of which the 4th Battalion possessed an abundance. Following a meeting on the moors on the Northumberland side of the border between representatives of the two Battalions, a satisfactory exchange of personnel and equipment was arranged to the advantage of both units.

The officer state of the reformed Battalion was as follows:

Commanding Officer . .	Lieut.-Colonel E. H. D. Grimley
Second-in-Command .	Major R. S. N. Clarke (joined later)
Adjutant	Lieut. A. N. Dyson
Quartermaster . . .	Lieut. (Q.M.) J. N. Chapman
Regimental Sergeant-Major	R.S.M. G. Hildrew
O.C. Y Support Group .	Major R. M. Pratt
,, Z ,, ,, .	Major J. T. Lisle

It is interesting to record that a base-plate for 4·2-in. mortars originally produced at the instigation of the 4th Battalion, and used by them on training in the spring of 1943, was later taken into general use throughout the Army.

By mid-winter 1943/44 the Battalion had made good progress and was rapidly becoming a fully trained unit, when it was suddenly replaced by the newly resuscitated 1st Bn. The Middlesex Regiment—the 4th Battalion being sent to the VIIIth Corps.

At that time the VIIIth Corps of the 21st Army Group was located in Yorkshire, in course of training and preparation for the invasion of Normandy. It consisted of the Guards Armoured Division (to which Y Support Group was assigned) and the 11th Armoured Division (to which Z Support Group was assigned). Bn. H.Q. was located at Corps H.Q.

Jan.– June 1944

Later instructions were received to form a third Support Group for the 7th Armoured Division, which was on its way from Italy to join the VIIIth Corps. Bn. H.Q. then moved to Skegness, where the formation of the new group proceeded. Later the new group moved to Norfolk, within the area earmarked for the 7th Armoured Division.

Soon after this Field-Marshal Sir Bernard Montgomery assumed command of the 21st Army Group. He had different views on the organization and role of Support Battalions, and orders were issued for light anti-aircraft companies to be disbanded, for an increase in the number of 4·2-in. mortars and for Support Battalions to be renamed Machine-Gun Battalions. This decision reduced the strength of the 4th Battalion considerably and entailed much reshuffling of officers and cross-posting of other ranks.

When the Battalion joined the VIIIth Corps there was much discussion on the functions of—and the necessity for—Battalion Headquarters. With only two Support Groups, attached to two different divisions, there was just a case for retaining Battalion Headquarters; but with the formation of a third Support Group it was decided that Headquarters had no useful operational role and should be disbanded.

On the 26th April 1944 the 4th Bn. Royal Northumberland Fusiliers went into 'abeyance' and its three companies (up to now known as Support Groups) became Nos. 1, 2 and 3 Independent Machine-Gun Companies, Royal Northumberland Fusiliers, forming part of the Guards, 11th and 7th Armoured Divisions respectively.

No. 1 Independent Machine-Gun Coy.

On the 5th May 1944 the Company, commanded by Major R. M. Pratt, left Malton, in Yorkshire, where it had been since reforming in its new guise, and moved to Glenleigh tented camp, near Eastbourne. This was the first stage of its move, as part of the Guards Armoured Division, to join the British liberating armies in the invasion of North-West Europe.

During the stay at Glenleigh the weather was generally good. Weapons and vehicles were finally overhauled, and 'waterproofing,' as well as some useful training, carried out. The afternoons were mostly devoted to games, in order to keep the men fit, and short periods of leave were granted freely. The last live ammunition practice was held on the 3rd June, when the mortars and machine-guns fired out to sea from the top of Beachy Head.

On the 9th June the Company was put at six hours' notice to move, but this was soon cancelled as bad weather held up the embarkation of the whole Guards Division.

On the morning of the 16th June the Company commenced to move to a Staging Group at Woodford, near London. This entailed going through the suburbs of London, which had been bombed that night, the destination being reached about 1030 hrs. The night of the 16th/17th June opened the 'flying bomb' attack on London and the Company witnessed the flight of many of these new missiles as they passed overhead.

Loading of vehicles took place at the Albert Docks on the 18th and on the afternoon of the following day the personnel boarded the 'San Pep,' an American Liberty ship. This ship anchored off Southend until the 23rd and the Company finally disembarked in France, at Le Hamel, on the night of the 25th/26th June.

28. A machine-gun of the 2nd Battalion in action under summer conditions in Italy. The man with the water bottle is an Italian volunteer (see chapter 12)

29. Mortars of D Company, 2nd Battalion, supporting an attack by 4th Infantry Division, Po Valley, Winter 1944 (see chapter 12)

30. Troops landing on the Normandy coast (see chapter 14)

31. Bridges at Nederweert (see chapter 14)

No. 2 Independent Machine-Gun Coy.

Feb.–June 1944

With the dispersion of the 4th Bn. Royal Northumberland Fusiliers in the winter of 1943/44, Z Support Group (later renamed No. 2 Independent Machine-Gun Coy., Royal Northumberland Fusiliers) spent several months in billets in Yorkshire, where they were attached to the 159th Brigade of the 11th Armoured Division. In February 1944 they were at Thorngumbald near Hull.

At the end of March they moved to Aldershot. By this time the Company, commanded by Major E. E. M. Williams, had completed the process of conversion to an independent machine-gun company and was an integral part of the 11th Armoured Division. Here intensive training took place, with the emphasis on waterproofing and other aspects of semi-amphibious warfare.

The 159th Brigade was due to land on D Day plus 13.

The Company moved to the Victoria Docks, London, in its own transport on the 9th June and embarked on L.S.T. 307 on the 12th. The ship lay off Southend for a few hours before making for the open sea. The voyage, although a rough one, was uneventful and the Company reached the Normandy coast, off Arromanches, shortly before nightfall on 14th June 1944. The ship lay offshore that night and beached the next morning, when disembarkation took place.

No. 3 Independent Machine-Gun Coy.

The circumstances in which No. 3 Coy. came into being were somewhat different from Nos. 1 and 2. It was not a successor to one of the original Support Groups of the 4th Battalion, although the third Support Group was in existence in skeleton—in anticipation of the arrival of the 7th Armoured Division from overseas. When, however, the Company was finally formed at Hingham in Norfolk, under Major H. B. Van der Gucht, a high proportion of its personnel were drawn from Y and Z Groups. They were also fortunate in getting a few experienced warrant officers and N.C.Os. with war service with the 1st Battalion.

With the arrival of the famous 7th Armoured Division (The 'Desert Rats') in England No. 3 Independent Machine-Gun Coy. was immediately attached to the 131st Brigade. They, however, remained at Hingham gathering equipment, training and getting to know the units of their new formation and their methods.

On the 9th May they, with the rest of the 7th Armoured Division, moved to a Marshalling Area, near Brentford, on the outskirts of London. Here the waterproofing of vehicles, initial briefing and other preparations were carried out. On the 4th June the Company moved to another camp near Tilbury. Embarkation (on three different ships) took place on the 5th, after which the convoy lay off Southend until the 7th, when it steamed through the Straits of Dover, arriving off Arromanches about midday on the 8th. Disembarkation took place during the evening of the same day.

III. THE 7TH BATTALION

By the autumn of 1943 the 7th Bn. Royal Northumberland Fusiliers had been organized into a Support Battalion consisting of three Brigade Support Groups, each of one machine-gun company, one 4·2-in. mortar company, and one light anti-aircraft company. This was not a very satisfactory organization, as it was intended that

Jan.– June 1944 each Support Group should be attached permanently to an Infantry Brigade, thus leaving Battalion Headquarters with no operational role. Early in 1944, before it had been fully implemented, this organization was changed and the unit reverted to the old organization (in a modified form) of Machine-Gun Battalion of the 59th Division. Under this organization the Battalion comprised three machine-gun and one 4·2-in. mortar companies, and had an approximate strength of 35 officers and 650 other ranks.

On the 1st January 1944 Lieut.-Colonel P. Earle assumed command in succession to Lieut.-Colonel R. W. H. Fryer, who was promoted to command the 176th Infantry Brigade.

Although no details were known it was apparent to all that the invasion of North-West Europe was to take place in the spring or early summer. Consequently training under the new organization was carried out with feverish enthusiasm. The Battalion was still at Shorncliffe, in close proximity to its ranges and field firing area, and much live ammunition practice was carried out between January and mid-April.

Another form of training introduced during this period was that of working by night and sleeping by day. On an 'exercise' between the 27th February and 5th March all training and other activities commenced in the evening and continued until daylight, when an 'evening' meal was served, after which all personnel retired to bed.

On the 14th April the Battalion moved to Charleton Park, near Canterbury—this being the first stage towards embarkation for Normandy. On arrival all surplus Regimental and personal property was disposed of, and thereafter the Battalion was prepared to move at short notice at full war scale.

During the first week of June the Colonel of the Regiment, Major-General W. N. Herbert, visited the Battalion for a few days and watched its final preparations for operation 'Overlord.'

The Battalion was not destined to take part in the initial assault on the Normandy coast, which took place on the 6th June. On the 19th June they moved to an embarkation camp just north of Tilbury, where they spent the next week. They embarked on the 27th and landed from landing craft on the beach at Arromanches on the morning of the 29th June, 1944.

IV. THE 8TH BATTALION

1943 The 3rd Division, of which the 8th Battalion was the Reconnaissance Regiment, had been selected as one of the two assault divisions for the Normandy landing. In the early planning stages the role of the Battalion had been uncertain and training for several roles was carried out. By the end of 1943, however, its task had been clarified and consisted of:

(*a*) The provision of a communications network among the assaulting forces, known as Contact Detachments, and

(*b*) The provision of a group of officers and other ranks for the specific task of ensuring the smooth flow of traffic through the exits from the beaches, commencing with the initial landing on D Day.*

---

* The organization for, and method of carrying out, the tasks outlined in (*a*) and (*b*) above are given in detail in Chapter 14, Section II.

These duties were, of course, entirely different from the normal tasks of a reconnaissance regiment. Their duration was uncertain; but it was made clear that the Battalion might be required to revert to its normal role at short notice. These special duties absorbed about 100 officers and men. The remainder of the Regiment was not included in the initial assault force, and it was planned to bring it into the beachhead on D Day plus 8. Jan.–June 1944

On the 1st January 1944 the Regiment was stationed in Scotland—B Sqn. near Inverness, and the remainder at Langholm. Normal training, and the training of the special detachments mentioned above, went on concurrently, and with increasing tempo until the end of April.

Several valuable exercises on a Divisional level were carried out during this period, including the amphibious Exercise 'Grab' and the dress rehearsal for the D Day landing, Exercise 'Fabius.' A special study was made of likely types of enemy mines.

Early in February the unit moved to the Banff–Dufftown area, and at the beginning of April to Blenheim Barracks, Aldershot, where they remained until embarkation.

The 6th June 1944 (D Day) was the culmination of four years' training and preparation for the assault on Europe, and the 8th Bn. Royal Northumberland Fusiliers went into battle with the knowledge that everything that human ingenuity could devise had been done to make the great enterprise a success.

In this manner the Battalions of the Royal Northumberland Fusiliers—in their varying roles and under different systems of organization—prepared for the greatest amphibious operation in military history. No armies had ever been more lavishly provided and equipped, better trained or more abundantly supported by warships and aircraft.

The high hopes with which the expedition set out were to be fully realized. Within eleven months France and the Low Countries were to be liberated, Germany invaded and Hitler's Germany brought to ruin.

CHAPTER 14

NORTH-WEST EUROPE

Normandy and the Low Countries—June 1944 to September 1944

8th and 7th Battalions and Nos. 1, 2 and 3 Independent Machine-Gun Companies (4th Battalion)

(See Maps Nos. XII, XIII and XIV)

I. GENERAL

June 1944 THE conditions under which the troops of 21st Army Group—and units of the Royal Northumberland Fusiliers in particular—prepared for the invasion of North-West Europe have been described in Chapter 13.

This and the following chapter give an account of operations by the 8th and 7th Battalions and the three Independent Machine-Gun Coys. formed from the 4th Battalion, during this campaign.

Operation 'Overlord' was launched on the 5th June 1944, and on the morning of the following day British and American troops landed by sea and air in Normandy. The operation was supported by many hundreds of Allied warships and by an overwhelming air force.

Although the overall command was vested in the American General Eisenhower, the command of the land forces, both British and American, was given to General Sir Bernard L. Montgomery, and this organization was retained until the tide of battle flowed through France towards Germany.

Summarized the plan was as follows:

(*a*) American troops on the right and the British 21st Army Group (First Canadian and Second British Armies) on the left were to make an assault on the Normandy coast on a wide front. American and British airborne forces were to fly in and protect the right and left flanks respectively.

(*b*) After securing a deep bridgehead a rapid build-up of strength was to take place. Meanwhile American troops were to prepare to thrust forward, cut off the Cherbourg Peninsula and seize the ports of Cherbourg and Brest.

(*c*) (*a*) and (*b*) above were to be followed by a great armoured drive by American armoured divisions, through Central France and directed on Paris.

With minor modification, but only after bitter fighting in the initial stages, this plan was carried through ahead of schedule.

June 1944

II. THE 8TH BATTALION

The Battalion—whose official designation was '3rd Reconnaissance Regt. (N.F.)'—was the Reconnaissance Regiment of the 3rd Division, comprising the 8th, 9th and 185th Infantry Brigades.

The Battalion state at the beginning of June 1944 was as follows:

Commanding Officer . .	Lieut.-Colonel H. H. Merriman, M.C.
Second-in-Command .	Major J. K. Warner, M.C.
Adjutant	Captain T. H. Greenall
Technical Adjutant . .	Captain C. F. P. Jewell
Regimental Sergeant-Major	R.S.M. Dawson
O.C. H.Q.Sqn. . . .	Major N. Gill
„ A „	Major K. T. Beck
„ B „	Major P. H. Gaskell
„ C „	Major G. W. T. Norton

The 3rd Division was on the left of the two assault divisions of the Ist Corps, and was directed on Caen—the scene of the most desperate fighting in the early days of the landing.

As the normal work of a reconnaissance regiment was not visualized for the first few days, the Battalion was, as previously explained, given the following tasks:

(*a*) By means of 'Contact Detachments' the provision of a network of communications among the assaulting forces.

(*b*) Traffic control forward from the exits of the beaches—commencing on D Day (6th June)

These duties absorbed about 100 officers and other ranks. It was planned that the remainder of the Battalion would land about D Day plus 8 (14th June).

The detailed organization of the two groups which took part in the first landings was as follows:

(*a*) *Contact Detachments*

	Det. No.	*Officer*	*H.Q. or unit with which operated*
Regtl. H.Q.	1	Major P. H. Gaskell	H.Q. 3rd Division
	2	Lieut W. J. Derbyshire	
A Sqn.	3	Captain A. S. Gardner	8th Infantry Brigade
	4	Lieut. D. H. Ennals	Suffolks
	5	Lieut. W. R. Dorrell	East Yorks
	6	Lieut. G. R. Robinson	South Lancs
B Sqn.	7	Lieut. J. S. Forrest	9th Inf. Bde.
	8	Lieut. A. J. Beck	R. Ulster Rifles
C Sqn.	9	Captain P. H. Symes	185th Inf. Bde.
	10	Lieut. J. Hamer	Warwicks
	11	Lieut. W. I. Davies	Royal Norfolks
	12	Lieut. D. G. Snelling	K.S.L.I.

June 1944

(b) Beach Traffic Control

Commander	Major N. Gill
Beach Exit Officers . .	Captain I. O. Stevens
	Lieut. W. L. Brough
	Lieut. J. Farnworth
	Lieut. W. G. St. S. Brogan

Both groups landed on D Day with the assaulting troops and assumed their duties immediately. The arrangements for communication and traffic control, which had been planned and rehearsed so carefully, worked splendidly. Unfortunately Major Gill was severely wounded soon after landing, and was one of the first casualties to be evacuated to England.

The Beach Traffic Group, having completed its tasks by D Day plus 4 (10th June), returned to England and rejoined the main body of the Regiment. The Contact Detachments, however, remained in their special role until the Regiment arrived in Normandy.

During this time the bulk of the Regiment was still at Aldershot awaiting orders to embark. These orders arrived on the 14th June, and on the 16th the Regiment (less C Sqn. which was to follow later) embarked at Tilbury on three L.S.Ts. (Landing Ships—Tank), and by the 18th had arrived off the Normandy coast. Two L.S.Ts. succeeded in disembarking their loads on the night of the 18th/19th June, but the third, for some reason, did not do so. Meanwhile a violent storm developed and this third ship was unable to beach until the afternoon of the 22nd. By that evening the Regiment (still less C Sqn.) was at Colville, except for B Sqn., which had been given the task of watching the big minefield running from Beuville to Gazelle. The Squadron continued in this role for ten days based on the village of Periers-sur-le-Dan. The Regiment remained in these dispositions until the 27th, out of actual contact with the enemy and subject only to shelling. These five days enabled all ranks to test the safety and comfort of slit trenches and in other ways become accustomed to active-service conditions.

On the 26th June A Sqn., with an anti-tank troop attached, took over a position on the extreme left flank of the Division, covering the Caen–Blainville road.

By the end of the month the position in the bridgehead had become more stabilized —the enemy making desperate efforts to drive the Anglo-American Armies into the sea; the Allies making equally determined efforts to hold their positions while they built up their strength and formed reserves of ammunition and supplies. The 3rd Division's front was hardly an ideal defensive position, as the Germans still held the village of Lebissey and the high ground round Epron and La Landel. These positions overlooked those of the Division and blocked the approaches to Caen. The enemy troops in this sector included the formidable 21st Panzer Division of North African fame and an S.S. formation.

Allied plans had included the early capture of Caen, but this was not realized, and for some time to come this town was to be the scene of some of the heaviest fighting of the whole war in Europe. It can be said, however, that the desperate battles fought by British and Canadian troops in this area were a major contribution to the success of the Normandy campaign. By easing the pressure on the Allies' western flank they enabled the Americans to make good progress, which eventually was to culminate in the break-out from the bridgehead and a great sweep through Central France by General Patton's Third American Army. June–July 1944

On the 27th June the Regiment (less B Sqn. at Blainville and C Sqn. which had still not arrived from England) moved to the Mathieu area. This move was in connection with operation 'Aberlour'—an attempt by the 3rd Division to open the way to Caen. The preliminary attack by the 8th Infantry Brigade was, however, unsuccessful and the rest of the operation was cancelled.

On the 5th July A Sqn., at Blainville, was relieved, and on the same day C Sqn., which had landed on the 3rd, joined up. Thus the whole Regiment was concentrated at Mathieu.

On the 6th orders were received for operation 'Charnwood'—the capture of Lebissey by 185th Infantry Brigade and the subsequent capture of Caen by 9th Infantry Brigade supported by other troops further to the west. The Regiment provided an extensive Contact Detachment net for this operation, but was otherwise in Divisional reserve. Consequent on this some minor readjustment of dispositions took place, Regtl. H.Q. moving back to Colville to be near Divisional H.Q. On the evening of the 7th July the Regiment witnessed the mass air attack on Caen by 450 Lancaster and Halifax aircraft of Bomber Command. The attack commenced in the early hours of the 8th July, and was completely successful. 185th Infantry Brigade captured Lebissey on that day and on the 9th the whole of Caen west of the River Orne was occupied.

This success resulted in a new and important role for the Regiment, which took over the defence of the whole Divisional front along the Orne, from inclusive Blainville to inclusive Herouville. Detailed dispositions were as follows:

Regtl. H.Q.	Blainville
B Sqn. (later relieved by C Sqn.)	Blainville and the Shipyard Island
A Sqn.	Herouville
C Sqn. (later relieved by B Sqn.)	Beauregard

Soon after these positions had been taken up the rest of the 3rd Division withdrew to rest. The Regiment remained in these dispositions for seven days. Apart from patrol activities, and a very successful mortar shoot on Colombelles, no incidents of note occurred.

The Regiment was relieved by the Derbyshire Yeomanry (51st Div. Reconnaissance Regt.) on the 17th July and, leaving B Sqn. at Norfolk Wood, concentrated for rest and maintenance in the Hermanville area.

Meanwhile preparations were being made for Operation 'Goodwood,' designed as a 'break-out' attack from the bridgehead east of the Orne, towards Falaise. The 3rd Division was given a secondary role in this operation—that of protecting the left flank by attacking Troarn and the villages between it and Escoville. The Regiment was not given an active task in the early stages of this battle.

During this period personnel of the Regiment made full use of the excellent Divisional Club at Luc-sur-Mer, where a bath, change of clothing, a meal and a

July–August 1944

drink could be obtained. In the early stages operation 'Goodwood,' which commenced on the 18th July, was very successful and on that day the Regiment received orders to cross the Orne and harbour in the Escoville area. This move was somewhat unexpected, as the unit was at 'long notice' and several parties of officers and men had been despatched to the Divisional Club. However, by the evening the destination had been reached, and proved to be a very unpleasant one—enemy defensive fire of every kind being directed on the area.

On the 19th, B Sqn. carried out a reconnaissance towards Emieville and the area south-west of Troarn. They soon met opposition and, after holding their ground for a time, were withdrawn. At the same time C Sqn. was given the task of holding Touffreville.

From the 20th to 27th July the Regiment held a support position behind the 8th and 9th Infantry Brigades, with squadrons at Touffreville and Sannerville and Regtl. H.Q. and a reserve squadron at Escoville. These locations were under constant artillery and mortar fire and in addition the area harboured a particularly unpleasant variety of mosquito. Moreover, bad weather was experienced for most of this period.

At the end of the month the 3rd Division came into Army Group reserve and the 8th Bn. Royal Northumberland Fusiliers recrossed to the west bank of the Orne.

The desperate land battles on the British front, combined with constant attacks from the air, had by this time effected a serious decline in German strength and morale, and enabled American troops on the right to make good progress. The British VIIIth Corps to the west were also advancing well in their drive through Caumont. It seemed that the great break-out from the beachhead—which had been planned so carefully and fought for so strenuously—was about to take place.

On the evening of the 2nd August the Regiment commenced a move which was to take them out of the eastern end of the beachhead to the more enclosed country to the west, where more fluid operations were anticipated. By the morning of the 3rd they were concentrated near Cahagnolles, ready to move south through Caumont. On the 5th a move to Carville was made, with C Sqn. further south holding a defensive position near Montisange, alongside troops of the 11th Armoured Division.

The 185th Infantry Brigade had recently come temporarily under command of the 11th Armoured Division, and on the 6th August it was decided that the rest of the 3rd Division should occupy some high ground east of Vire in preparation for a further advance on Tinchebrai and Flers. This ground was held by a German parachute formation, but it was confidently expected that they would withdraw, as their troops were extremely isolated and unsupported on their flanks. B and C Sqns. were therefore pushed ahead to seize this ground prior to its occupation by the 9th Infantry Brigade. This move was not successful, as the parachutists fought most tenaciously. Various attempts were made to outflank and infiltrate into the position, but by midnight 6th/7th August both squadrons were definitely held up and the enemy still in possession of the feature. Lieut. D. G. Snelling was later awarded the Military Cross for the handling of his armoured car troop (C Sqn.) in this engagement.

Meanwhile the Regiment had developed a close friendship, and liaison, with a nearby American unit—the 102nd Mechanized Cavalry Group, a reconnaissance unit with a similar role to that of the 8th Bn. Royal Northumberland Fusiliers.

Desultory fighting continued for the next few days, during which squadrons of the Regiment were given various protective tasks; but only minor advances were made. The optimism of the Higher Command at this time somewhat outstripped the German rate of withdrawal. During the period Lieut. H. S. Nundy (A Sqn.) gained a well-earned Military Cross.

While these events were taking place on the VIIIth Corps front American armour to the west was making rapid progress round the flanks and rear of the enemy opposed to the British. The battle of the Falaise 'pocket'—the graveyard of the German Armies of the West—was taking shape.

On the 15th August the break on the 3rd Division's front began. On the right C Sqn., after negotiating enemy mines, moved into Tinchebrai ten minutes ahead of their friends the 102nd (American) Mechanized Cavalry. They were, however, held up in the town by an enemy rearguard covering a demolished bridge.

B Sqn. also advanced rapidly to Montsecret, where they were similarly held up by the river and suffered casualties from heavy artillery and mortar fire. B Sqn. suffered a great blow on this day, its Commander, Major P. H. Gaskell, being mortally wounded.

Regimental Headquarters spent the night of the 15th/16th August just north of Tinchebrai in a deluge of rain.

By the morning of the 16th the leading infantry had lost touch with the enemy, who had withdrawn during the night. The 8th Bn. Royal Northumberland Fusiliers, with two squadrons of armoured cars attached, were ordered to pursue towards Flers. This was the Regiment's last, and most satisfactory, operation on French soil.

The two armoured car squadrons operated on the right flank and met little opposition. C Sqn. advanced down the Divisional centre-line (the road Tinchebrai–Flers), with A Sqn. on the left moving through Montsecret. B Sqn., in reserve, followed in rear of C Sqn.

The advance commenced at 1000 hrs. and progressed excellently. By the afternoon C Sqn., supported by an anti-tank troop, were in occupation of Flers. There was still resistance in the eastern outskirts, but the enemy withdrew at nightfall. Before then, however, elements of the 11th Armoured Division had arrived in the town.

On this day the Regiment advanced some 8 miles and captured nearly 100 prisoners. To celebrate the first truly mobile action of the campaign the Divisional Commander ordered the issue of a rum ration and sent the message 'Well done F.V.P." (the Regimental codesign). Late in the evening the Corps Commander, Lieut.-General Sir Richard N. O'Connor, visited the unit in Flers and congratulated them on their achievements.

The break-out of the Allied Armies from the bridgehead, coupled with the German High Command's persistence in holding on to positions far to the west, left the enemy only a narrow corridor for withdrawal. British and American troops closed in on this from almost every direction: the retreating columns were shot at from all sides and mercilessly bombed from the air. By the third week in August the Seventh German Army had been decimated. Roads leading east and west through Falaise presented a scene of almost unbelievable carnage, in which it was necessary to 'bulldoze'

August 1944 German vehicles, dead men and horses to the sides of the road, to make way for oncoming traffic. The Battle of France had been fought and won.

For the 3rd Division there followed a period of rest. The 8th Bn. Royal Northumberland Fusiliers moved a short distance from Flers to St. Paul, where they remained until the 2nd September: then to the Saussay La Campagne–Doudeaville area, just east of Andelys on the Seine, except for C Sqn., which was detached for duty for the protection of Headquarters, Second Army. It is interesting to record that although this squadron was for a time nearly 300 miles from Regtl. H.Q. they were in daily wireless communication with them—using the normal unit wireless equipment.

This rest period was spent in training—with special reference to the lessons of the Normandy campaign. At this time Humber armoured cars were exchanged for Daimlers—the latter being much superior vehicles.

The attitude of the French inhabitants is worthy to record. In some places, such as ruined Caen where the fighting was intense, they were stunned and, not unnaturally, thought that the price of liberation was a high one. In some country districts untouched by battle the troops were received with the greatest enthusiasm. Typical of the latter condition is the following message read out to the Commanding Officer, and others, at an official reception given by the mayor and parish priest of St. Paul on the 21st August:

'*Officers and Men of the British Army*

'I have been asked by the Civil Authorities, by the Parish Priest, a Knight of the Legion of Honour, and by the whole population to welcome you to this small village. Our first feeling is one of gratitude and happiness. You can be sure it has been a rare joy for us all to see the British troops arrive and drive the Germans away before them. This minute is a very stirring one chiefly for those, and I think there are many, who, in spite of everybody and everything, have remained the faithful friends of England and her Allies. This gathering seems to be like the meeting of old friends in the open air and sunshine, on going out of a dark and damp dungeon.

'For this ceremony no place could be fitter than this one. Here we stand near the grave of the valiant sons of this village who laid down their lives for their Fatherland and the freedom of the world, side by side with the gallant British and American soldiers. How happy they must be to see that their own children, brothers and sisters, can breathe freely again.

'For the last four years there have been many misunderstandings between our two nations. Of course the whole responsibility does not rest with you alone; we have had our own share of it, and it is a long one. But your sacrifices for the common cause, your present victories and the return of your armies on the French soil open the new era of comradeship and good understanding. Though you are a peace-loving people, you wage a war to liberate France and Europe, and to secure the freedom of the whole world. We feel sure that before long the sons of Normandy and Brittany, as well as those of the rest of France, will be proud to join in this crusade, and when they have been equipped with modern weapons, to fight with you for the final crushing of tyranny and the restoration of peace and freedom all over the world. Sept. 1944

Welcome to you all!!!
Long live England!!!
Long live France!!! '

By the middle of September 1944 the Allied Armies had swept through France and most of Belgium to near the Dutch border. The dispositions of the 21st Army Group at this time were as follows:

XXXth Corps. On the line of the Escaut Canal with a small bridgehead on the east bank south of Walkenswaard—in preparation for the advance north towards Eindhoven, Nijmegen and Arnhem in conjunction with Anglo-American airborne troops.

VIIIth and XIIth Corps. On the left and right respectively of XXXth Corps ready to cross the Escaut Canal in support of the drive north.

First Canadian Army. Employed 'mopping up' the German garrisons along the Channel coast.

On the 16th and 17th September the Regiment in two groups—one of wheeled and one of tracked transport—left the Saussay la Campagne–Doudeaville area for Peer in eastern Belgium, a distance of 285 miles. Each group staged in the middle of the journey south-west of Brussels. Movement was by night.

Having concentrated at Peer the Regiment's first task was to provide the traffic control organization for the assault crossing of the Escaut Canal by the 3rd Division. This assault was successful and the Traffic Control Group played a useful part in the build-up. By the 20th the bridgehead was secure and A Sqn. moved out into the Hamont area, where they soon ran into a screen of German protective troops. On this day the bulk of the Regiment crossed the frontier from Belgium to Holland. The Dutch inhabitants were very enthusiastic in their reception of the troops. The night of the 20th/21st September was spent in widely dispersed bivouacs, and preparations were made for a further move forward in the morning.

The 21st and 22nd were occupied by all squadrons in pushing forward into the angle made by the canals near Weert and Nederweert. C Sqn. moved towards Weert and then swung north towards Nieuw Parochie. B Sqn. followed C and moved through them to Nederweert. A Sqn., based on Dorplein, protected the southern face of the angle. Regtl. H.Q. moved to Maarheeze.

On the 22nd the 8th Infantry Brigade captured Weert and the 8th Bn. Royal Northumberland Fusiliers held the line of the canal until the 25th, on which day C Sqn., based on Nieuw Parochie, took over the whole front. The rest of the Regiment concentrated in the Sommeren area with A Sqn. on a protective role towards Helmond. Later this Squadron moved to Meisel to protect the right flank of 185th Infantry Brigade. Hostile troops were in considerable numbers in this area, and the Squadron spent an active few days.

By the 30th September the whole Regiment had been withdrawn from the forward area and concentrated at Bakel.

Sept. 1944 Meanwhile the Anglo-American airborne operation against Arnhem had taken place and, with the failure of this attempt to carry the war into Germany in 1944, the troops commenced preparations for holding their gains during the fast approaching winter—a winter which for some was reminiscent of those of 1914–18.

(The narrative of the 8th Battalion is continued in Section II of the next chapter.)

III. THE 7TH BATTALION (*See Map No. XII*)

June–July 1944 (NOTE: In this section the background of the general picture of the campaign has been kept to the minimum, consistent with a proper understanding of the narrative. A more comprehensive survey of the general situation, from time to time, has been given in Section II (The 8th Battalion) of this chapter.)

The 7th Bn. Royal Northumberland Fusiliers left Bishopsbourne in Kent on 19th June, embarked at Tilbury on an American Liberty Ship on the 27th, and landed in Normandy on the 29th.

The Battalion, organized into three machine-gun companies and one mortar company, was the Machine-Gun Battalion of the 59th Division (Major-General L. O. Lyne), consisting of the 176th, 177th and 197th Infantry Brigades.

The Battalion state was as follows:

Commanding Officer .	Lieut.-Colonel P. Earle
Second-in-Command .	Major C. C. G. Milward *
Adjutant . . .	Captain C. H. Ritzema
Quartermaster . . .	Captain (Q.M.) R. W. Harmer, M.B.E. (W. Yorks Regt.)
Regimental Sergeant-Major	R.S.M. Swyer
O.C. H.Q. Coy. . .	Captain R. D. Burnell (Rifle Brigade)
„ A (M.G.) Coy. . .	Major C. W. Dalby
„ B (M.G.) „ . .	Major J. R. Shields
„ C (M.G.) „ . .	Major W. P. S. Hastings
„ D (Mortar) Coy. .	Major A. J. H. Cramsie

On landing the Battalion moved at once to a very pleasant area near Bayeux, the rest of the 59th Division concentrating in the same locality. Here they remained for the next week.

On the 4th July the Battalion moved to the left flank of the British front, where the 59th Division was to take part in the attack on the town of Caen, which although scheduled for occupation on D Day (6th June) had so far defied all attempts to capture it. It was now to be attacked by three divisions—3rd (Canadian) Division right, 59th Division centre and 3rd Division left—supported by 450 heavy bombers based on England.†

The particular task of the 59th Division was the capture of the villages of Galmanche, La Bijude, St. Contest, Epron and Courf-chef (in that order), which covered Caen to the north.

---

* Major C. C. G. Milward was killed in action in Korea on the 3rd January 1951.

† See also Section II of this chapter.

By the evening of the 4th July the Battalion had reached Douvre, and preparations for the attack commenced on the following day. C (M.G.) Coy. were under command of 197th Infantry Brigade on the right, and A (M.G.) Coy. under 176th Infantry Brigade on the left. D (Mortar) Coy. was to be employed on Divisional tasks. B (M.G.) Coy. was in reserve. The country was very enclosed and observed shooting at long ranges almost impossible. July 1944

The attack commenced at 0420 hrs. on the 8th July. The 176th Infantry Brigade soon captured La Bijude, but were then held up. On the right 197th Infantry Brigade advanced for over a mile to capture St. Contest. A and C Coys. followed the assaulting infantry in carriers and took part in the close-quarter fighting with enemy S.S. troops who were holding this sector. These young Germans fought with fanatical determination, asking and giving no quarter. Much as our men disliked the regime for which these men fought, it was difficult not to admire their bravery and soldierly qualities.

The latter stages of the battle became very confused; but by midday on the 9th—the two flank divisions also having made good progress—the Commander Ist Corps launched his armour on the left, and with this support the 3rd Division moved into Caen and occupied the greater part of the town.

The Battalion casualties in this operation were two other ranks killed and one officer and 24 other ranks wounded.

The mortar company. fired 5,000 bombs in this engagement.

On all parts of the bridgehead the enemy was now being steadily pushed back. On the main road between Villers-Bocage and Caen lay the straggling village of Noyers, some two miles behind the enemy's foremost defences. This village was to be the 59th Division's next objective.

The Battalion moved forward to Loucelles on the 13th July and on the 16th the battle for Noyers began. This was a stubborn and bloody battle against determined infantry and dug-in Tiger tanks.

The attack commenced at 0530 hrs. with 197th Infantry Brigade on the right and 177th Infantry Brigade on the left, the first objectives being the Ferme de Guiberon spur and the villages of Brettevillette, Quedeville and Les Nouillons. All went well in the early stages, but at about 1400 hrs. an enemy battle group of six Tiger tanks and a strong company of infantry launched a counter-attack. This retained most of the Guiberon spur, caused much confusion and inflicted heavy casualties. The infantry also suffered casualties from mortar fire.

In the initial stages of this engagement the Battalion supported the assault by machine-gun fire on the flanks and by mortar fire.

After two days' fighting the enemy had been driven back nearly two miles, but Noyers remained in his hands. By the 20th July the assault had lost its momentum and further attempts at frontal attack were abandoned.

On the 18th the Battalion experienced practically the only hostile low-flying air attack of the Normandy campaign—along the line of the road east of Noyers—and A Coy. had one N.C.O. killed and several men wounded.

The next eight days were spent in harassing fire by the machine-guns and in counter-mortar tasks by the mortars. Owing to the difficulties of observation in this part of

July–August 1944

France most shoots were carried out from the 1 : 25,000 map, the mortars co-operating closely with the Divisional Artillery.

On the 29th July offensive operations were resumed by the 197th Infantry Brigade, supported by C (M.G.) and D (Mortar) Coys. This attack was designed to outflank Noyers from the west. Although the first objectives were captured, enemy resistance stiffened later and only a partial success ended in very bitter fighting.

On the 30th July a carrier containing Major W. P. S. Hastings and Lieut. A. Cooper (both of C (M.G.) Coy.) was blown up by a mine. Lieut. Cooper and the carrier crew were killed: Major Hastings was blown over a fence, but managed to continue at duty.

On the 3rd August Bn. H.Q. moved forward to Juvigny. Enemy morale and fighting capacity were now deteriorating fast under the relentless pressure of the Allied ground and air attacks. Prisoners included Russians, Poles and others from the occupied territories, with whom the Germans were diluting their depleted units.

On the 4th August 176th Infantry Brigade passed through 197th Infantry Brigade, and supported by A (M.G.) Coy. entered Villers-Bocage against only slight opposition. The village had by then been reduced to a heap of rubble, but was important as the junction of seven roads.

The enemy was now in full retreat and the British advance continued. Machine-gun companies were decentralized to infantry brigades, only D (Mortar) Coy. being retained under Battalion control. On the 6th August 176th Infantry Brigade advanced to the River Orne opposite the Forêt de Grimbosq, and 177th Infantry Brigade passed through ruined Noyers to an area on the right of 176th Infantry Brigade. The Orne at this point is a wide river and a set-piece crossing had been anticipated, but on the evening of the 6th August the 7th Bn. South Staffordshire Regt. (176th Infantry Brigade) discovered a ford beside a blown bridge and established a bridgehead on the far bank, near the village of Grimbosq.

Two days of desperate fighting followed, as the 12th S.S. Panzer Division, which had withdrawn from Caen, attacked the 59th Division's bridgehead with characteristic fury. By this time the 7th Bn. Royal Northumberland Fusiliers (less B Coy.) were again under centralized control and the whole firepower of the Battalion—machine-guns and mortars—together with the Divisional Artillery, was employed in support of the 176th Infantry Brigade. The enemy suffered terrible casualties, the bridgehead held firm and on the 8th August the enemy broke off the engagement and withdrew. The successful outcome of this battle was in no small measure due to the personal leadership of the Commander 176th Infantry Brigade, Brigadier R. W. H. Fryer—a Fifth Fusilier. This was a fine operation in which the Battalion played a worthy part. Between the 6th and 8th August the machine-guns fired 130,000 rds. and the mortars 4,000 bombs—mostly by observed fire at good targets.

Meanwhile 177th Infantry Brigade, with B (M.G.) Coy. in support, was carrying out a detached operation to the west. Here, in a gap between the rest of the 59th Division and a neighbouring formation, this Brigade pushed slowly southwards through difficult country towards Hamars.

On the 12th August infantry and armour, pushing south to clear the east bank of the Orne, were held up by a determined enemy detachment holding the small town of

Thury-Harcourt. The town was eventually captured under cover of a smoke-screen put down by the 4·2-in. mortars of D Coy. August 1944

On the 14th the enemy was again in full retreat towards Falaise, and the stage was set for the destruction of the Seventh German Army in that area. Machine-gun companies were again decentralized to brigades.

197th Infantry Brigade, with C Coy. in support, drove south through the Bois de St. Clair to Point d'Ouilly and up to the high ground along which runs the main road to Falaise. Here 177th Infantry Brigade, with B Coy. in support, took the lead and attacked southwards through the Isles de Bardel, against disorganized opposition.

At this stage the 59th Division was ordered to stand fast in order to relieve the congestion among the rapidly contracting circle of Allied divisions. From Bn. H.Q. on the ridge near Ouilly could be seen, and heard, the progress of this decisive phase of the battle—American shells falling to the south; to the east beyond Falaise the Canadian guns pounding the enemy columns retreating towards Chambois; to the west the 11th Armoured Division battling its way forward up the west bank of the Orne.

On the 19th August, when the spirits of all were at their peak, the officers and men of the 59th Division received a crushing blow. Orders were received to disband the Division at once and place all units in 'suspended animation.' * This decision commenced a policy which was continued until the end of the war. After five years of war British manpower was at a low ebb. Battle casualties and wastage, and the requirements of industry, made it essential to reduce the number of field formations in order to keep the remainder up to reasonable strengths. Naturally those formations which had fought the hardest, and consequently suffered the heaviest casualties, were often selected for disbandment. A few months later the famous 50th (Northumbrian) Division was to suffer the same fate.

Although, after explanation, the reason was fully understood by all ranks, the decision was, nevertheless, a hard one to bear. There can be no precedent for the disbandment of a whole division on the field of battle in the hour of victory—a victory which the 59th did so much to bring about.

Arrangements were made for as many officers and men as possible of the 7th Bn. Royal Northumberland Fusiliers to join the three independent machine-gun companies (which had been formed from the 4th Battalion) which were operating with armoured divisions—these being the only units of the Regiment in a machine-gun role in 21st Army Group; and that the remainder should join the Durham Light Infantry Battalions of the 50th (Northumbrian) Division.

On the 26th August the Battalion moved to an area near Thury-Harcourt, west of the Orne, where it set about the melancholy task of dispersing its personnel, vehicles and stores. This occupied until the 20th September 1944, on which date the 7th Bn. Royal Northumberland Fusiliers ceased to exist.†

* The term 'suspended animation' implies the temporary disbandment of a unit.

† The 7th Battalion was reformed again in 1947 as part of the post-war Territorial Army—under Lieut.-Colonel P. Earle, who had commanded it during the Normandy campaign.

August 1944 During the Normandy campaign the Battalion casualties were as follows:

	Killed	*Wounded*
Officers	2	3
Other ranks	17	69

IV. THE 4TH BATTALION

(Nos. 1, 2 and 3 Independent Machine-Gun Coys.)

June 1944 The breaking-up of the 4th Bn. Royal Northumberland Fusiliers, and its transformation into three Independent Machine-Gun Companies to form part of the three Armoured Divisions of the 21st Army Group, has been described in Chapter 13.

This Section (and Section III of the next Chapter) gives a brief account of the activities of the three Companies with their respective Armoured Divisions during operations in North-West Europe, from June 1944 to May 1945.

In the initial stages of the campaign the three Armoured Divisions—Guards (No. 1 Coy.), 7th (No. 3 Coy.) and 11th (No. 2 Coy.)—were grouped in the 8th Corps (Lieut.-General Sir Richard N. O'Connor). Later the VIIIth Corps ceased to consist entirely of armour and the Armoured Divisions were attached to other Corps as required by the situation.

The operations of all three Divisions followed much the same pattern:

(*a*) Hard fighting in the Normandy beachhead.
(*b*) The great armoured drive through France and Belgium into Holland.
(*c*) Participation in the airborne operations against Arnhem in September 1944.
(*d*) The winter campaign of 1944/45—holding the line and limited offensive operations.
(*e*) The crossing of the Rhine and the drive into the heart of Germany.

Of these phases (*b*) and (*e*) represented the true role of Armoured Divisions, for which they had been specially organized and trained.

Each Armoured Division included one Armoured Brigade and one Lorried Infantry Brigade organized on a special establishment. It was with the units of the latter that Nos. 1, 2 and 3 Independent Machine-Gun Coys. usually co-operated, although on occasions they supported units of the Armoured Brigades. The normal allotment was one M.G. platoon to each infantry battalion, the fourth platoon (mortars) usually being controlled by Company H.Q. on Divisional tasks, although here again there were occasional exceptions.

It will be seen, therefore, that an Independent Machine-Gun Company often covered a very wide front, with each platoon acting independently. Under these conditions the narrative of their activities in a regimental history of this kind can only be in mere outline. No attempt has been made to include more than a general picture of the moves and engagements of each company.

32. The village of St. Contest

33. The village of Bijude

32. The village of St. Contest

33. The village of Bijude

No. 1 *Independent Machine-Gun Coy.*

By the end of June 1944 a considerable beachhead had been established in Normandy; but the build-up had been delayed by exceptionally bad weather. The Guards Armoured Division (of which No. 1 Independent Machine-Gun Coy. formed part) was one of the formations whose embarkation was held up for several days. June–August 1944

Disembarking at Le Hamel on the night of the 25th/26th June the Company moved at once to a concentration area near Bayeux.

On the 29th June the 32nd Guards Brigade took over a comparatively quiet sector of the defences from the 43rd Division overlooking the airfield at Carpiquet, which was still held by the Germans. Sub-units of the Company were distributed as follows:

No. 3 (M.G.) Platoon . .	to 5th Bn. Coldstream Guards
" 4 (M.G.) " . .	to 3rd Bn. Irish Guards
" 5 (M.G.) " . .	to 1st Bn. Welsh Guards

The Mortar Platoon was directly under the control of the Company Commander (Major R. M. Pratt).

This distribution, with a few exceptions, remained in force throughout the campaign. The Company was 'blooded' in this area, by carrying out useful shoots with both machine-guns and mortars. On the 11th July it was withdrawn to a rest area near Bayeux—in company with the rest of the 32nd Guards Brigade.

On the 17th July the machine-gun platoons rejoined their battalions to take part in the Guards Armoured Division's first engagement as a division—the attempted break-out from Caen to Cagny. Bitter and confused fighting took place in this area, and the Company was continuously in demand for supporting fire. The operation was not entirely successful and the 32nd Guards Brigade lost heavily. On the 16th August the Company withdrew to rest at St. Charles de Percy, and this ended their fighting in Normandy.

They remained at St. Charles de Percy for a week, during which time General Patton's Third American Army had broken out from the bridgehead and, accompanied by French troops, reached Paris.

On the 24th August the Company moved with the Division to an area north-west of Flers, and on the 28th the great three-day 'run' through France to Brussels commenced. Laigle, the first stop, was reached on the afternoon of the 29th—a distance of 78 miles. Here machine-gun platoons rejoined their battalions. By 1700 hrs. on the 30th the Division had advanced another 50 miles to Vernon on the River Seine, and thence to Beauvais (60 miles) on the 31st, and Arras (another 60 miles) by the evening of the 1st September. On the following night the Company reached Douai and by the evening of the 3rd they had arrived at their final destination for the time being, Brussels, a day's run of 83 miles.

Since the 28th August there had been little contact with the enemy, as the German armies in France had disintegrated with their defeat at Falaise. The Company entered Brussels at 2000 hrs. The reception accorded to the liberating troops by the population was embarrassing in the extreme and considerably hampered the movement of convoys through the city.

Sept. 1944 On the 8th September the 32nd Guards Brigade forced the crossing of the Albert Canal at Beeringen against heavy opposition. All platoons of the Company were in action, No. 2 (Mortar) Platoon firing over 400 bombs in support of the assaulting troops.

Between the 9th and 12th September No. 1 Independent Machine-Gun Coy. again supported the 32nd Guards Brigade in a prolonged attack on Hechtel. It was not until the 12th that the village was finally captured—on which day the mortars fired 900 bombs and No. 5 (M.G.) Platoon 40,000 rds. in support of the 1st Bn. Welsh Guards.

After further fighting on the Escaut Canal the Guards were relieved by the 50th (Northumbrian) Division and the Company concentrated at Lindel on the 15th September. Here preparations began for co-operation with Allied airborne troops in the famous Arnhem operation. The Guards Armoured Division was to form part of the force which was to drive north and link up with the three airborne divisions which were to seize the vital river crossings—the 82nd (American) Division at Grave, the 101st (American) Division at Nijmegen and the 1st (British) Division at Arnhem.

The machine-gun platoons rejoined their battalions early on the 17th September. Nijmegen was reached and the river crossed on the 19th, after stubborn fighting; but all attempts to approach Arnhem were unsuccessful.

This bid to cross the Rhine, and enter Germany, before winter weather set in was not successful. Grave and Nijmegen were captured and held, but the 1st British Airborne Division was cut off at Arnhem and only a small number escaped.

By the 30th September the offensive had died down and No. 1 Independent Machine-Gun Coy. (less No. 4 (M.G.) Platoon, which remained at Grave with the 3rd Bn. Irish Guards) had been withdrawn to rest between Grave and Nijmegen—making a further short move to Maldon on the 10th October. Two days later No. 2 (Mortar) Platoon fired 100 bombs *into Germany* in support of the 82nd (American) Airborne Division.

No. 2 Independent Machine-Gun Coy.

June–July 1944 The Company, as part of the 11th Armoured Division, landed on the Normandy coast at Cainet on the 15th June 1944. Disembarkation was carried out under shell-fire and two casualties were suffered during the process.

The first engagement in which the Company was involved proved to be one of the most unpleasant. The 11th Armoured Division was to form a bridgehead over the River Odon with the 159th Brigade dug in on both sides of the river. The 1st Herefords were on the enemy side and the whole Brigade under direct observation. Both flanks were unprotected. Until the 6th July this position was held despite repeated attacks by enemy armour and infantry.

On the 5th July the Company Commander, Major E. E. M. Williams,* was severely wounded.

---

* Major Williams's father—Major E. E. Williams, D.S.O., of The Fifth—was killed in Gallipoli in 1915 while serving with the 8th (Service) Battalion of the Regiment.

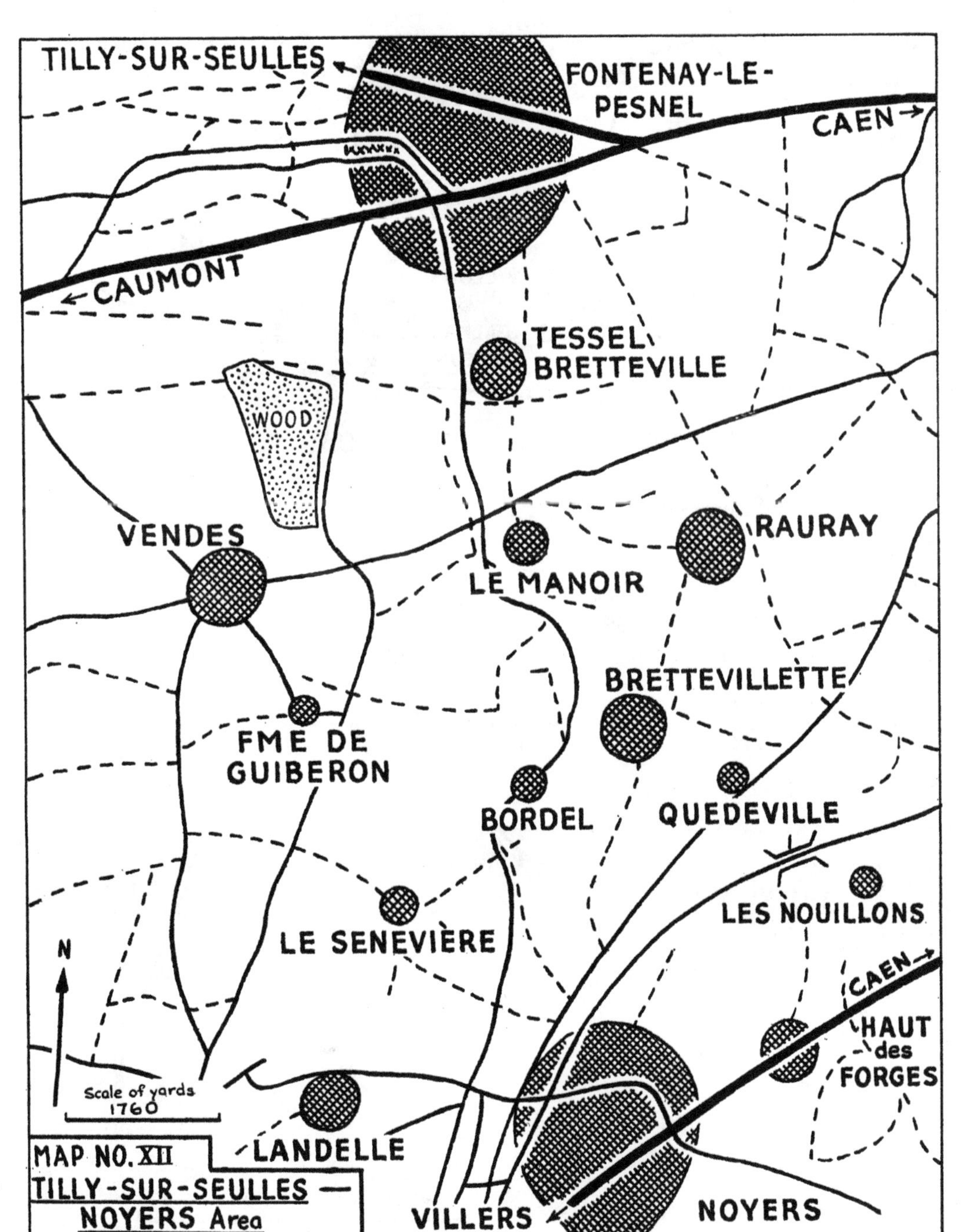

MAP NO. XII
TILLY-SUR-SEULLES — NOYERS Area

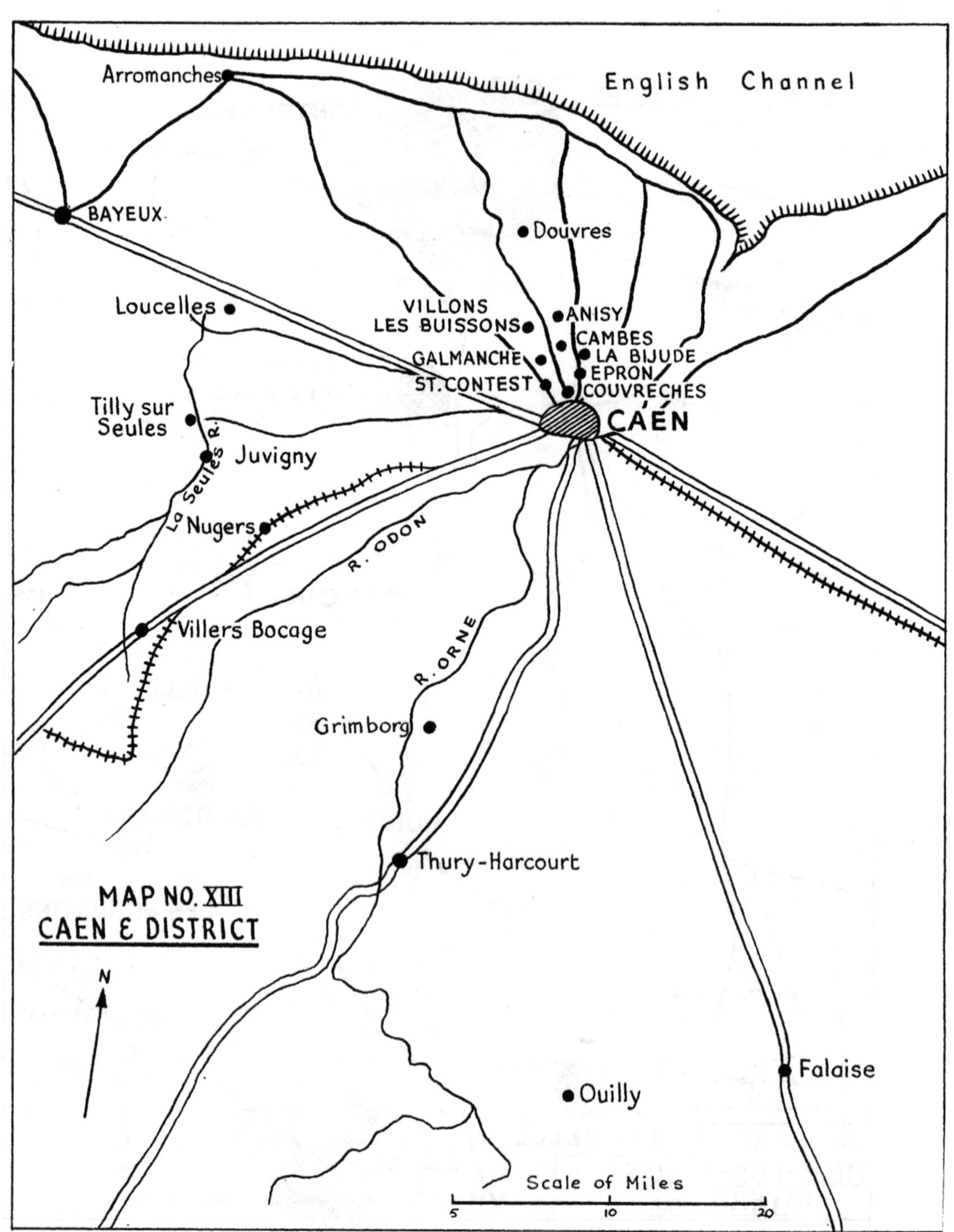
English Channel
Arromanches
BAYEUX
Douvres
Loucelles
VILLONS
LES BUISSONS
ANISY
CAMBES
LA BIJUDE
GALMANCHE
EPRON
ST. CONTEST
COUVRECHES
CAEN
Tilly sur
Seules
Juvigny
La Seules R.
Nugers
R. ODON
Villers Bocage
R. ORNE
Grimborg
Thury-Harcourt
MAP NO. XIII
CAEN & DISTRICT
N
Falaise
Ouilly
Scale of Miles
5
10
20

On 7th July the Brigade was relieved and the unit withdrew to Coulombs to refit. Here the new Company Commander, Major A. H. Bonham-Carter, joined the unit. On 17th July the Division was moved to the east of the front to break out of the bridgehead held by the airborne troops. The breakthrough was to be by three armoured divisions—the Guards Armoured Division on the left, 11th Armoured Division in centre and the 7th Armoured Division on the right. During the advance the machine-gun platoons were under command of infantry battalions with the role of protecting the flanks. Company H.Q. moved to Cuverville on July 18th and Ranville and thence to Mesnelfrementie on the same day and stayed in this area until 22nd July. The weather during this period was wet, and as the centre-line was largely on unmade roads the attack lost its momentum. On the 23rd July the Company moved back to Burow to refit. July–Sept. 1944

Up to this point the activities of the Company had not been spectacular, although much good work had been done in the support role, in both offensive and defensive operations. Large quantities of ammunition had been expended, some casualties suffered and many more inflicted. Operations were now about to take a different turn and the unit was about to play its part in the great Allied drive through France and Belgium into Holland.

By the 14th August they were at Montcamps, and moving via Ecouche and Gace crossed the River Seine at Chamenard on the 28th. Amiens was reached on the 1st September and Antwerp on the 6th. There had been no serious opposition during the advance, as the German Armies of the West were in a condition of disintegration and only isolated and unorganized resistance had been encountered. Such had been the haste and confusion of the German withdrawal that the great port had been abandoned with its docks and other facilities almost intact. Nevertheless, there had been a few sharp engagements, and it was never safe to relax local protection. From Antwerp onwards stiffer resistance was to be met.

On the 9th September the Company was in the area just south-west of Beeringen and by the 11th had reached Peer. On this day they suffered a great misfortune. Major Bonham-Carter,* the Company Commander, whilst driving in his jeep, ran into an enemy machine-gun post just south-east of Hechtel and he and four other ranks in the vehicle were killed. He was succeeded by Major D. L. Irwin, who, except for a brief period, continued in command until the end of 1945.

From the 13th to the 18th September the Company was at Wychmael: apart from defensive patrols the time was spent refitting.

The next operation was for the 11th Armoured Division to pass through the bridgehead established by the 3rd Division over the Escaut Canal, with the object of protecting the right flank of the Second Army's advance into Holland. For this operation No. 2 Platoon was under the command of the 1st Herefords, No. 4 Platoon under the command of the 4th K.S.L.I. and Nos. 1 and 3 Platoons under Company command. On the 21st the Company crossed the Dutch border. At 1700 hrs. H.Q. was established at Zomeren, and platoons were supporting the crossing of the

* Major Andrew Bonham-Carter was the son of Air-Commodore I. M. Bonham-Carter, C.B., O.B.E., a former Fifth Fusilier and Adjutant of the 1st Battalion.

Sept. 1944 Wilhelm Canal. During this action the foremost section of No. 2 Platoon fired almost continuously from 2200 hrs. on the 21st until 0600 hrs. 22nd September, expending 10,000 rds. Heavy casualties were inflicted on enemy infantry who counter-attacked during the hours of darkness.

The advance continued during the succeeding days, the Company moving forward via Uliordan to St. Anthonis. On the 26th September the Brigade took up defensive positions round St. Anthonis and Oploon.

No. 3 Independent Machine-Gun Coy.

June–July 1944 At about 2100 hrs. on the 8th June 1944 the Company—part of the 7th Armoured Division and under command of Major H. B. Van der Gucht—commenced disembarking at Arromanches. By this time a good beachhead had been established and although subjected to shelling the disembarkation area was not under small-arms fire. It had been arranged that the vehicle party and marching party, which had sailed in different ships, should join up at a rendezvous a few miles inland. These arrangements worked smoothly and by the 11th the Company was ready for action.

On the 12th the Company was called upon to support the 131st Infantry Brigade (7th Armoured Division) and No. 13 Platoon went into action with the 1/6th Queen's Royal Regiment. On the following day the Platoon Commander (Lieut. L. Byrne) narrowly escaped capture when on reconnaissance.

Immediately after this the 7th Armoured Division made the first serious attempt to enlarge the beachhead around Bayeux, in an attempt to capture Villers-Bocage, some 13 miles from the coast. For this operation machine-gun platoons joined the units with which they normally worked:

No. 13 Platoon	with the 1/5th Queen's Royal Regiment
,, 14 ,, ...	with the 1/6th Queen's Royal Regiment
,, 15 ,, ...	with the 1/7th Queen's Royal Regiment

Fighting was sharp and bitter. Leading elements of the Division entered Villers-Bocage, but were promptly counter-attacked and thrown back. Eventually they took up defensive positions north of the town about Briguessard. Here the Company remained in close contact with the enemy until the 1st July. During this period large amounts of ammunition were expended—the Mortar Platoon in particular firing a huge quantity of bombs. Numerous casualties were suffered. Lieut. J. Harrer (Mortar Platoon) was awarded the Military Cross for the efficient handling of his mortars in action after his carrier had received a direct hit and both his driver and wireless operator had been killed. Sgt. R. Chambers (No. 14 Platoon) was awarded the Distinguished Conduct Medal—to add to his Military Medal and bar.

On the 1st July the whole of the 7th Armoured Division moved to a rest area, where they remained until the 17th. A move to the east was then made and on the 21st July the Division came under command of the First Canadian Army in the Caen area. The 131st Brigade took up positions around St. Martin-de-Fontenay–Verrieres–Hubert-Folie, where in spite of fairly heavy shelling casualties were very light. On the 25th Major Van der Gucht was taken ill and evacuated to England. Captain (later Major) W. E. N. Davis assumed command of the Company.

On the 1st August the Division moved to the area of Caumont. On the following day the Mortar Platoon lost four vehicles from shelling. No. 14 Platoon also took part in heavy fighting when the unit they were supporting (1/6th Queen's) was heavily counter-attacked by the German 10th S.S. Division. On the 9th August the machine-guns of the Company fired 30,000 rds. from the slopes of Mount Pincon, at almost perfect targets. Very heavy casualties were inflicted on the enemy. August–Sept. 1944

By this time German resistance in Normandy was weakening and the Allied Armies were about to commence the great sweep through France and Belgium described earlier in this chapter.

For the 7th Armoured Division progress was slow at first, but in the latter stages it became a pursuit, limited only by the speed of the vehicles along the congested and damaged roads and the necessity for constructing, and repairing, bridges. The Company crossed the River Seine on the 31st August and the Somme on the following day. Here, at Frevent, they were given the task of defending the town while the rest of the Division passed through.

The halt here was a short one, as the Division received orders to press on and occupy Ghent, in Belgium. This involved an advance through country still occupied by bodies of disorganized enemy troops—attempting to get back to Germany, but still prepared to fight with characteristic German stubbornness. Units ran their vehicles to the limit, halting only at night for brief periods. The Division soon cleared most of Ghent, No. 3 Independent Coy. being given the task of mobile reserve in and around the town, with the frequent role of using their machine-guns mounted in carriers to 'spray' houses containing Germans who offered resistance. Some casualties were suffered in this role and others from shelling, which was often very heavy.

This long and arduous advance was followed by a short period for rest and refitting, the Company moving to an area just outside Malines. The amenities were good here, and included visits to Brussels, which had just been liberated.

By the middle of September the Allied Armies had cleared France, Belgium and part of Western Holland, and preparations were being made to cross the Rhine and enter Germany before the winter weather set in.

The 7th Armoured Division was not destined to play a leading part in the initial attempt to cross the river and capture Arnhem, but after a short spell of action on the Albert Canal, they moved into Holland. The attempt by the 1st British Airborne Division to seize Arnhem, and of the Second Army to join up with them, had failed. The 7th Armoured Division was now given the task of reopening the road from Oudenrode to Veghel, to permit the withdrawal of the Guards Armoured Division and the survivors of the 1st Airborne Division—whose escape route had been closed. The Company was not very heavily involved in this action but suffered some casualties.

About this time the first batch of reinforcements was received, mostly young soldiers, with a good proportion from Northumberland.

By the end of September the task of withdrawing from Arnhem had been completed and the Division was in a static role, No. 3 Coy. Headquarters being near Veghel with platoons deployed in support of their respective battalions.

The spectacular advance of the 21st Army Group had come to an end, and preparations for a semi-static winter campaign were now put in hand.

CHAPTER 15

NORTH-WEST EUROPE

The advance into Germany—October 1944 to May 1945
8th Battalion and Nos. 1, 2 and 3 Independent Machine-Gun Companies (4th Battalion)

(*See Map No. XIV*)

I. GENERAL

Oct. 1944 BY the beginning of October 1944 the Allied Armies had liberated practically the whole of France, the greater part of Belgium and a small portion of South-West Holland. The great port of Antwerp had been occupied almost unopposed, but was not in use as, owing to the Germans still being in occupation of the Dutch islands of Walcheren and South Beveland, the Scheldt was closed to Allied shipping. German troops continued to hold out in some of the Channel ports, and consequently much of the ammunition and supplies for the Allied troops were still being brought forward from ports in Western France. This situation was eased by the middle of November, by which time Canadian and British troops had assaulted and captured the Dutch islands, the Scheldt had been swept of mines and the port of Antwerp opened to Allied shipping.

By the autumn General Eisenhower had assumed direct control of the three Army Groups comprising the Allied land forces. Normally Field-Marshal Montgomery's command was confined to the 21st Army Group, although for particular phases of operations—such as during the critical period of the German counter-offensive and later the crossing of the Rhine—American troops were placed temporarily under his command.

Although in some sectors the winter campaign of 1944–45 was reminiscent of those in Flanders in the First World War, there were nevertheless many differences. The armies were not entirely immobilized by winter conditions as they had been thirty years previously. There were many reasons for this—the disparity between the fighting qualities of the contesting armies (the cream of the German Army had been destroyed in France); the six weeks of hard frost which provided excellent 'going' for tanks; and the offensive spirit of Anglo-American commanders and troops. The winter period was therefore one of considerable activity and included such large-scale operations as Field-Marshal von Rundstedt's offensive—the final German bid for victory—and 21st Army Group's operation 'Veritable,' in February 1945, to clear the area between the Rhine and the Meuse. For the majority, however, it was a period of 'holding the line' in waterlogged country or under severe conditions of frost.

II. THE 8TH BATTALION

The comparatively static conditions of the winter months were clearly not suited to operations by a reconnaissance regiment in its normal mobile role, and the 8th Bn. Royal Northumberland Fusiliers spent the period from October 1944 to early February 1945 in static tasks. There were no outstanding incidents, but much patrolling, ambushes and similar duties requiring constant alertness and involving a lot of hard work. Oct.–Dec. 1944

During the period 2nd to 13th October the Regiment, based on Haps, was employed holding a sector of the line of the River Meuse. On the 4th October the Commanding Officer (Lieut.-Colonel H. H. Merriman) was wounded when returning from the St. Agatha observation post. Fortunately the wound was slight and he was back at duty within ten days. The St. Agatha was an almost ideal O.P., giving perfect observation within our own lines and behind those of the enemy. From it officers of the Battalion watched the unsuccessful attack against Middelaar by American airborne troops, and the reactions of the Germans.

In the latter part of October the 3rd Division staged an attack on Overloon and Venray. For these operations the Regiment formed part of a mobile force with the task of protecting the left flank by holding the river line about Vierlingsbeek. As a preliminary to this B Sqn. captured the village of Vierlingsbeek, which they did with little difficulty.

As the winter increased in severity this portion of the front became stabilized. Here, in the Den Bosch area, the Germans held a small sector west of the Meuse. Patrol activity by both sides was a feature of this phase of the winter campaign. One night a German patrol, of about platoon strength, attempted to break into the Vierlingsbeek Station area—held by two carrier troops under Lieut. J. R. Rogerson. The attempt was frustrated and Lieut. Rogerson was later awarded the Military Cross for his part in the action.

From time to time organized shoots were arranged in which artillery, 4·2-in. mortars and machine-guns took part. These were greatly assisted by the excellence of the unit observation posts at Vierlingsbeek and Groeningen.

During this period Regimental H.Q. was first at Dormitory Farm, between Oploo and Overloon, and then at Lactaria, the latter being a very pleasant spot. Although in the battle area, many of the local inhabitants remained in residence, billets for H.Q. and reserve personnel being provided in a local monastery and also in a nearby convent. The reserve squadron was located at Lactaria in the monastery.

And so the routine of defensive warfare went on, in accordance with the well-established practices of both World Wars, until the early part of December, when the Regiment was withdrawn into Divisional reserve in the Meerselo–Venray area. Here they remained for four weeks, during which the time was spent in training and overhauling vehicles and weapons. Much excitement was caused at this time by periodical 'draws' for leave home. Christmas was well and truly celebrated, although B Sqn. were unlucky in being sent to hold a reserve position near Vierlingsbeek and did not have their Christmas dinner until relieved a few days after the 25th. A very successful party was held for the Dutch children of Meerselo.

Jan.– Feb. 1945

On the 2nd January the Regiment moved back for its last front-line spell in this area. The sector was a slightly different one to the previous occasion, as it included Sambeek, but not Vierlingsbeek. In reality it consisted of holding the villages of Groeningen, Vortum and Sambeek. To assist in this task the Regiment had under its command two companies of the Dutch Army of Resistance.

This position was held for five weeks, the first four being extremely cold with occasional snow. There was considerable competition between squadrons and the Dutch companies to capture a prisoner. The honours went to the Dutch holding Vortum, who ambushed a German patrol and captured one of them. C Sqn. later had a successful encounter with an enemy patrol in Groeningen.

Harassing fire, on an extensive scale, was a matter of almost daily routine.

On the 28th January a very successful patrol was carried out by men of A Sqn. under Major R. D. Wilson. The patrol consisted of a reconnaissance party under Lieut. D. Hodgetts, supported by a fighting patrol. After crossing the river in assault boats opposite Sambeek the reconnaissance portion killed two Germans between the river and the Afferden–Heijen road, and the fighting portion made one prisoner and inflicted casualties on an enemy party which approached them near some lock gates. The patrol then recrossed the river, under cover of smoke, and arrived back without casualties. This patrol was the first to cross the Maas successfully on the front of the 3rd Division. Major Wilson was awarded the Military Cross for his part in the operation. A very well organized and smart piece of work.

The thaw commenced in the first week of February and on the 7th the Division was relieved by the 52nd (Lowland) Division—the Regiment handing over its sector to the 52nd Reconnaissance Regt.

On relief the 8th Bn. Royal Northumberland Fusiliers moved far to the rear to Lubbeck, near Louvain. By midday on the 9th February the whole Regiment had reached its destination and commenced a period of maintenance, recreation and rest. So ended their watch on the Meuse, which coincided with large-scale preparations for the final offensive which was to bring victory in 1945.

The stay at Lubbeck was a busy but very pleasant one. Meanwhile the XXXth Corps operation 'Veritable'—planned to clear the country between the Rivers Maas and Rhine—was in full swing, and although not progressing as quickly as had been expected was making good headway. It was therefore thought that the Division's next task would be the crossing of the Rhine, and 185th Infantry Brigade had already gone to an area designed to practice and rehearse this operation. Consequently orders to move at short notice in an easterly direction came somewhat as a surprise.

The Regiment left Lubbeck at about noon on the 24th February bound for Goch. They stayed the first night at Tilburg, where the carrier troops of A and B Sqns. were sent forward, under Major R. D. Wilson, to assist the 8th Infantry Brigade who had taken over a somewhat extended line from the 15th (Scottish) Division. This force had an unpleasant time in wet wooded country, but was fortunate in suffering only slight casualties during the period of detachment.

In the meantime the remainder of the Regiment had left Tilburg during the night of the 26th/27th February, and moving via St. Hubert and Haps, crossed the Maas at Gennep.

March 1945

The 7th German Parachute Division was putting up a very stubborn resistance, while the Regiment waited for a chance to take part in the type of mobile operation for which a Divisional reconnaissance unit is trained but which so rarely occurs. It was not, however, until the 2nd March, when Kervenheim was captured, that the chance came. On the following day C Sqn. moved through Kevelaer and Wetten, captured two enemy demolition parties preparing charges, and was held up just short of Kapellan by a well-handled enemy S.P. (self-propelled) gun. The number of prisoners captured exceeded 100, but the day was marred by the death in action of Lieut. J. K. Ferguson, whose troop had played a prominent part in the Squadron's activities. Major G. W. T. Norton, the O.C. Sqn., was awarded the Military Cross for his conduct on this occasion.

Although the relentless British pressure had put the German withdrawal out of gear it had not resulted in a rout. On the 7th March the 3rd Division halted to allow the Guards Armoured Division to pass through. While one brigade of the 3rd Division was still employed assisting to compress the German bridgehead round Xanten, the rest (including the 8th Bn. Royal Northumberland Fusiliers who concentrated at Wetten) remained temporarily inactive.

The Regiment remained at Wetten until the 15th March. This, its first extensive inroad into German territory, had certain unforeseen features. They had expected to encounter a sullen and passively, if not openly, hostile people. On the contrary they sensed relief rather than enmity and the civil population gave little trouble—this being the general rule throughout the Allied advance into Germany. On the other hand, it was always necessary to be on the alert for 'booby traps' and mines, left behind by German troops in houses, in gateways and in other places.

On the 15th March the Regiment came under the command of the 6th Guards Tank Brigade for the crossing of the Rhine, and moved to Walbeck. Here the accommodation was far from lavish and much improvisation was resorted to—A Sqn. in particular building a remarkable collection of log huts. During this period the 3rd Division was holding a sector of the west bank of the Rhine, while immediately in rear an immense concentration of troops, guns, vehicles and stores was being built up for the crossing.

About this time Major J. K. Warner (Second-in-Command) left the Regiment. Major P. E. Nesbitt took his place and Major E. Rayer on joining the Regiment assumed command of B Sqn.

The outline plan for operation 'Plunder'—the crossing of the Rhine and subsequent advance into industrial Germany—had been prepared many months in advance. Consequently when the troops actually reached the river only the details were lacking and it was possible to schedule this formidable operation for a surprisingly early date.

The assault crossing was carried out by three divisions and the 5th Commando Brigade, on the night of the 23rd/24th March 1945. On the morning of the 24th the assaulting troops were supported by the 17th U.S.A. and 6th British Airborne Divisions, which 'flew in' from bases in England and dropped a few miles east of the river—a fantastic sight, which those who witnessed it will never forget.

The portion of the front with which the 8th Bn. Royal Northumberland Fusiliers were concerned was centred on the town of Wesel, on the right flank, which was to

March 1945

be assaulted by the 5th Commando Brigade. This was near the junction of the British right with the left of the Ninth American Army. It was anticipated that there would be much hard fighting in the bridgehead for three or four days, after which British and American armour would break out and advance at speed into Germany. In this phase the Regiment, as part of the 6th Guards Tank Brigade, was to advance from the area east of Wesel.

This forecast proved correct. The initial crossing was successful along the whole front and on the night of the 26th/27th the Regiment crossed the Rhine on an American rubber pontoon bridge and moved through, and beyond, shattered Wesel. By 0300 hrs. they were concentrated in a field just west of Peddenburg. By noon it had been disclosed that the Brigade objective was the much bombed city of Munster. The next eight days was to be a period of continuous activity, in which the Regiment was in almost constant contact with the enemy. An outstanding feature of these operations was the resistance offered by German S.P. guns, which were boldly and skilfully handled. A single gun was often sufficient to hold up a column for a considerable time.

In the initial advance on Munster A Sqn. was to lead, supported by the Scots Guards, who had an American parachute battalion mounted on their vehicles. At first movement was very slow owing to enemy S.P. guns and snipers. When darkness fell the Scots Guards were ordered to move across country to Dorsten, and A Sqn. was also moved to Schermbeck to assist the Coldstream Guards on the following morning. This move was opposed by the enemy, but as Dorsten had been captured the Coldstream Guards passed through the Scots Guards and B Sqn. moved out to protect them.

On the 28th good progress was made, both A and B Sqns. making contact with the enemy and taking prisoners. In the evening C Sqn. was brought forward to cover the northern flank. During the night the Coldstream Guards reached Haltern.

Up to this point the right flank had been protected by the Dortmund–Ems canal, all bridges over which had been destroyed by the retreating enemy. Beyond Haltern, however, both flanks were exposed, as the Ninth American Army on the right and the 6th British Airborne Division on the left were both some distance behind. In view of this B Sqn. passed through Haltern on the night of the 28th/29th March to protect the right flank. Similarly A and C Sqns. moved to the north, round Lavesum to protect the left. These two squadrons met considerable opposition, in the form of S.P. guns and infantry, which was not overcome until midday. By the afternoon of this day (the 29th) the Scots Guards had reached the outskirts of Dulmen, which was cleared that night by the 17th American Airborne Division.

The advance continued steadily, although not spectacularly. Every village and tactical feature was held by one or two S.P. guns and a few courageous infantry who fought stubbornly. On the 30th B and C Sqns. together captured Rorop. A Sqn., after a cross-country move, engaged enemy holding Darup and later occupied Nottoln, from which they moved forward and gained contact with enemy holding Schapdetten. Here a sharp engagement took place, which was brought to a successful conclusion by the co-operation of B Sqn., after gaining contact with the 6th Airborne Division.

This cleared the northern flank and as a result the whole Regiment moved over to

36. A car of A Squadron, 3rd Reconnaissance Regt., 8th Bn. Royal Northumberland Fusiliers, firing a Besa gun at Goch

37. Lieut.-Colonel H. H. Merriman being presented with the ribbon of the D.S.O. by Field-Marshal Montgomery

38. Machine-gun carrier of No. 2 Independent Machine-Gun Company in action

39. No. 3 Independent Machine-Gun Company entering Hamburg

March–April 1945

this route, through Havixbeek, leaving the Guards to battle forward along the main axis road.

On the 31st the Regiment made a determined effort to be the first unit to enter Munster. B Sqn. advanced on Nienberg, which was occupied at dawn, while A Sqn. struck south to Roxel. This was only some 3½ miles north-west of Munster and it was planned to pass C Sqn. through B into the town. This, however, was not to be, as a few stout-hearted S.P. gunners, supported by infantry, barred the way. In this engagement Major E. Rayer, commanding C Sqn., was wounded, Captain C. F. P. Jewell assuming command.

On the night of the 1st/2nd April C Sqn. made another attempt to enter the city, but after a cross-country move were again held up—this time by German anti-aircraft gunners and infantry. By this time the Scots Guards had reached Nienberg and on the 2nd April they and some American paratroopers put in attacks from the north and north-west. These were successful and so Munster fell.

On the 3rd April the Regiment concentrated just south of Greven, where a short period of much needed rest was enjoyed.

On the 6th April orders were received for the Regiment to rejoin the 3rd Division in the XXXth Corps to the north. Here progress had been much slower than on the VIIIth Corps front and the move meant a return to Holland. Accordingly the Regiment moved to Enschede, whence they immediately took part in the attack on Lingen. A fine action by A Sqn., clearing a bridgehead south of the town, resulted in Sgt. T. Cottrell being awarded the Distinguished Conduct Medal. On the 9th April the 3rd Division was transferred to the XIIth Corps, in order to relieve the 7th Armoured Division far to the west in the outskirts of Bremen. The move forward to Westercappeln was complicated by a damaged bridge and attempts to find an alternative route were frustrated at Rheine, where all the bridges were down. However, the Regiment (less A Sqn.) eventually concentrated at Lemforde. A Sqn. was left behind to guard a sector of the Ems–Weser Canal.

By the 11th April Regimental Headquarters was installed in a gin distillery at Heiligenloh, with B Sqn. close by. C Sqn., under command of 185th Infantry Brigade, was filling a gap on the right flank near Verden. Thus while the 3rd Division was gradually closing in on Bremen, the Regiment was spread out over some 50 miles of country. Nevertheless, communications worked well and the supply system operated smoothly.

The end was now in sight. Up to the 24th April the Regiment was employed on the left flank—with Regimental H.Q. first at Kirchseele and later at Gross Mackenstedt, A and B Sqns. operating around Ippener, and C Sqn. operating an improvised traffic control organization over a wide area. They were still in this role on the 24th April, when the attack on Bremen took place. This operation was a complete success and the whole town south of the Weser was soon occupied.

On the 26th the Regiment relieved the 154th Infantry Brigade of the 51st (Highland) Division—with Regimental H.Q. in a school at Varel, A Sqn. at Hutchting and B and C Sqns. at Iprump. Two days later they moved to the left flank of the 3rd Division, where they supported the 5th Canadian Infantry Brigade who were operating towards Oldenburg.

May 1945

On the 30th April the Regiment captured its last prisoner.

At 0800 hrs. on the 5th May 1945 came the 'Cease Fire'—and the end of the battle career of the 8th Bn. Royal Northumberland Fusiliers. The Regiment had been one of the very first to land on the Normandy coast on D Day, and had fought its way through France, Belgium, Holland and the Rhineland—into the heart of Germany.

During the campaign the Battalion's casualties included 6 officers and 87 other ranks killed. Its officers and men received the following decorations and awards: *

Distinguished Service Order	1
Distinguished Conduct Medal	1
Military Crosses	9
Military Medals	7
Mentions in Despatches	20

Much of the Battalion's success was due to the fine example and skill shown by its Commanding Officer, Lieut.-Colonel H. H. Merriman, who was awarded the Distinguished Service Order in March 1945.

III. THE 4TH BATTALION

(Nos. 1, 2 and 3 Independent Machine-Gun Companies)

No. 1 Independent Machine-Gun Coy.

Dec. 1944– March 1945

During the winter of 1944–45 the Company made many moves and co-operated in a number of minor engagements—too numerous to relate in this history.

On the 15th December Major H. B. Van der Gucht (who had joined some five weeks before) took over command of the Company from Major R. M. Pratt.

In January 1945 a Flame-throwing Platoon was added to the Company, consisting of: six Wasps (Bren carriers equipped for flame-throwing), one Jeep, two 15-cwt. trucks, one motor-cycle, 1 3-ton lorry (for carrying fuel), one No. 19 wireless set. This Platoon was commanded by Lieut. J. I. McLanachan and was ready to take part in Operation 'Veritable' early in February. This operation was designed to clear the area of the Rhineland between the Rivers Maas and Rhine prior to the assault crossing of the latter.

Platoons of the Company fired large quantities of ammunition in support of the Guards in this series of battles, which culminated in the Division eliminating the last German bridgehead west of the Rhine, round Xanten, on the 9th March. The Guards were then relieved by the 52nd (Lowland) Division and the Company moved back to Mook, near Nijmegen.

The assault crossing of the Rhine took place on the 24th March and by the 29th enemy resistance had deteriorated sufficiently to enable the armour to pass through.

At 1900 hrs. on Good Friday, the 30th March 1945, the Company moved across the Rhine and passed through the shattered town of Rees to commence the final phase of the campaign in North-West Europe. Progress was rapid, and on the 31st

* The names of some of these, including that of Lieut.-Colonel Merriman, will not be found in Appendix B, since they were attached from other regiments.

the 32nd Guards Brigade covered 40 miles towards Enschede without encountering opposition. Crossing the Dutch frontier the Company moved through North-East Holland, until entering Germany again when Nordhorn was captured on the 3rd April. April–May 1945

On the 4th the Mortar Platoon fired 430 bombs and Nos. 3 (M.G.) and 5 (M.G.) Platoons 18,000 rds. in support of an attack by the 3rd Division, near Lingen on the Dortmund–Ems Canal. On the following day the Company suffered a number of casualties from shelling.

The advance continued, against spasmodic opposition, until the 14th, when the Division moved to a rest area—No. 1 Coy. to very comfortable billets at Cappeln near Cloppenburg.

They moved again on the 17th, through Vechta, Diepholz and Sullingen to Walsrode.

On the 19th Lieut. J. I. McLanachan, commanding the Flame-throwing Platoon, had a narrow escape when he ran into a party of Germans in a lane and his carrier was hit by fire from a 'Bazooka.'

On St. George's Day the Company came under command of the 5th Guards Brigade, and supported them in an attack on Zeven on the 24th April, 60,000 rds. and 600 bombs being fired. This was followed by a series of sharp engagements, including those at Badenstadt (26th April) and Ostertimke (27th April).

On the 28th the Guards Division liberated the notorious concentration camps at Sandbostel and Belsen, and by the 7th May the 32nd Guards Brigade Group had entered Cuxhaven.

The German Armies in North-West Europe surrendered on the 8th May 1945 and on the following day No. 1 Independent Machine-Gun Coy. (Royal Northumberland Fusiliers) concentrated at Altenwalde.

(NOTE: A more detailed account of the operations of No. 1 Independent Company can be found in an excellent short history of the Company by Major H. B. Van der Gucht.)

No. 2 Independent Machine-Gun Coy.

The first week in October 1944 found No. 2 Coy. occupying various isolated farms round Coy. H.Q. at Gemert. Owing to casualties and wastage platoons were considerably under strength: some 30 reinforcements were, however, received. Oct. 1944

On the 7th October defensive positions were taken up in support of the 159th Infantry Brigade in the St. Anthonis area and on the 11th the Company supported an attack by the 3rd Division near Overloon. During this action Sgt. Sowerby (No. 2 Platoon) won the Military Medal for gallantry in rescuing under fire some men who had been wounded, and partially buried, by shell-fire.

This action was followed by short moves to Deurne and Usselstein, and on the 25th November they were withdrawn to Helmond for a short rest.

On the 30th the Company supported an attack on Kasteel. This area was heavily mined and enemy resistance was very stiff. After severe casualties the infantry succeeded in capturing the position. During this action 450 mortar bombs and large quantities of small-arms ammunition were fired.

Jan.– May 1945 By the 8th January 1945 the Company had moved to Weert in the Roermond area.

This was followed by a period devoted to training for operation 'Veritable,' which was to take place in February—first at Weert and then at Neertter and Weelde.

Operation 'Veritable,' launched on the 8th February, had as its object the clearing of the area between the Rivers Maas and Rhine by means of a drive south, between the two rivers, from Nijmegen. Weather conditions were most unfavourable. Heavy rain fell and the area became seriously waterlogged. Consequently progress was much slower than had been anticipated.

On the 24th February No. 2 Coy. moved to a concentration area in the Reichwald Forest, and from then until the 9th March was engaged with the 11th Armoured Division about Udem, clearing that part of the area between the Maas and Rhine.

With the successful conclusion of this hard-fought operation the way was paved for the crossing of the Rhine, and the 11th Armoured Division was withdrawn to plan and train for this next phase of the campaign. No. 2 Coy. moved to Lubeck.

Following the assault crossing of the Rhine by infantry formations in the early hours of the 24th March, supported by airborne landings a few hours later, the Company crossed the river on the 28th, and with the rest of the Division moved to a concentration area in and around Wesel. Here preparations were made for the break-out from the bridgehead and for the rest of the campaign movement, with an occasional sharp engagement, was to be the order.

Riessenbeck was reached on the 2nd April, Andensen on the 8th and Hebstorf on the 10th. On the 5th the Company Commander, Major D. L. Irwin, was slightly wounded and Captain P. M. Gordon assumed command until Major Irwin returned a short time later.

By the 12th April they had reached Bucholz, then Beckendorf (15th), Lindon near Uflzen (18th) and the River Elbe at Bardwick on the 20th. Here stiff resistance was met, and the Division had to await the arrival of infantry formations before a crossing could be effected.

On the 29th April the 15th (Scottish) Division forced the passage of the Elbe at Lunenburg and No. 2 Coy. crossed the river unopposed at Havekost on the 1st May.

When the German Armies of the West surrendered on the 7th May 1945 the Company was at Buhnsdorf.

No. 3 Independent Machine-Gun Coy.

Oct. 1944 The beginning of October 1944 found the Company in a static role near Veghel. Machine-gun platoons were with infantry battalions, the only activity being night harassing shoots by both machine-guns and mortars. They remained in these positions for the first three weeks of the month, after which they participated in local operations designed to clear the country south of the River Maas from about Veghel towards the coast. This was followed by further limited offensive operations around Roermond and Wessen, during which the weather was extremely bad and difficulty was often experienced in supplying forward platoons in the waterlogged country.

About this time the composition of the 131st Brigade (7th Armoured Division) was changed, the 9th Bn. Durham Light Infantry and 2nd Bn. Devonshire Regt. replacing the 1/6th Queen's and 1/7th Queen's respectively. Nov. 1944–March 1945

During November the Division held a line running from Sittard on the Dutch-German border, across the frontier to a point about 10 miles inside Germany. There was little activity in this area and on the 17th December No. 3 Coy. was relieved by its sister company—No. 1 (Guards Armoured Division).

On the 23rd the German Ardennes offensive started and the Company went back into the line, Coy. H.Q. being in a convent just south of Sittard. The Christmas period was spent in digging defensive positions—in frozen ground—against the possibilities of an extension of the German offensive to the Sittard area.

On the 1st January 1945 there was considerable enemy air activity and Fus. Bramwell (No. 14 Platoon) was credited with bringing down a Me.109 by Bren-gun fire.

On the 10th January the Division was relieved by the 52nd (Lowland) Division and moved to a concentration area in the north, the Company being located 15 miles north-west of Sittard.

The next task was Operation 'Blackcock,' an offensive designed to clear the whole area west of the River Ruhr. This proved a most bloody battle, involving stubborn fighting for every village and tactical feature, in country laced with canals and dykes. Machine-gun platoons remained with their infantry battalions throughout the operation and were almost continuously in action from the 17th January until the 4th February, by which time the operation had been brought to a successful conclusion by the capture of Heinsberg and the elimination of the last pockets of enemy resistance west of the Ruhr. The Company continued in a defensive role until the 21st February, when the Division was relieved and moved to a training area on the River Maas. Here preparations for the crossing of the Rhine commenced, the Company being located at Posterholt.

Meanwhile the XXXth Corps had begun operations for the clearing of the area between the Maas and the Rhine, preparatory to crossing the latter. By the second week in March troops of the 21st Army Group had fought their way to the west bank of the Rhine on a broad front—from Wesel to north of Rees—with American troops in a similar position on the right. The stage was set for the assault crossing of Germany's national river and the final offensive to end the war in Europe.

By the third week in March No. 3 Coy.—together with the rest of the 7th Armoured Division—had completed its training and reorganization on the Maas. Infantry formations crossed the Rhine on the night of the 23rd/24th March 1945, followed by British and American airborne troops after daylight on the 24th, and by the 27th a substantial bridgehead had been secured.

The Company crossed the river with the 7th Armoured Division on the 27th at 0030 hrs., and by the 28th had reached Raesfeld. Conditions were now ripe for the break-out from the bridgehead and the great advance into central Germany. Traversing the 'Dropping Zone' of the 6th British Airborne Division on the 28th, the Company passed through Borkem, Gemen, Weseke, Sudholn and Stadtholn in rapid succession, and opposed only by scattered and unorganized resistance. On the 1st April Major W. E. N. Davis vacated command of the Company and was succeeded by Captain L. W. Byrne.

April–May 1945

On the 2nd and 3rd April the Division was held up on the line of the Dortmund–Ems Canal, but by the 7th they had reached Diepholz. By the 11th they were occupied clearing the area south of Bremen, and on the 13th they crossed the River Weser at Nienbourg.

Meanwhile other troops were closing in on Bremen, which was attacked and finally captured on the 27th April.

On the 3rd May No. 3 Coy. moved into Hamburg, and were still there when the German Armies surrendered on the 7th May 1945.

40. A searchlight in action (see chapter 16)

41. Preparing a detachment site and manhandling a generator at Hamsterley, Co. Durham, Spring 1940 (see chapter 16)

43rd & 49th BATTALIONS, ROYAL TANK REGIMENT
(formerly 6th (CITY) BATTALION, R.N.F.)

42. Combined Officers Group at Waitwith Camp, Catterick, June, 1939, the last Territorial Army Camp before mobilization (see chapter 17)

Reading left to right throughout:

Top Row: 2/Lts. W. H. B. Swan, E. M. Brett, Lt. G. W. Robinson, 2/Lts. E. L. S. Gjemre, A. F. Studd, J. R. Herbertson, B. M. Rowe, D. H. Pybus, H. J. M. Scott, M. A. Pybus.

Middle Row: 2/Lts. W. H. Girling, P. R. Angus, W. E. Alvey, W. N. Greenwell, R. Atkinson, G. T. Swinney, Capts. P. Medd, P. Cooper, R. A. Rogers, Lt. D. C. McCoull, Capts. R. J. Clayton, S. B. Hewitt, Lts. E. I. Weidner, P. A. Boyns.

Front Row: Capt. and Q.M. G. Ouzeman, Capt. H. J. M. L. Criddle, Majors H. P. Bell, P. Gardner, S. G. March, G. L. A. France, Lt. S. Stibbard, Lt.-Col. C. B. Carrick, M.C., T.D., Lt.-Col. F. Dawson, M.C., T.D., Capt. T. R. Lovibond, Majors C. S. Graham, K. O. Potter, J. A. Crisp, R. Potter, A. Angus (M.O.), Lt. and Q.M. J. Moon.

43. A Churchill tank and crew of 43rd (Northumberland) Battalion, Royal Tank Regt., Sussex, Summer 1942 (see chapter 17)

Capt. D. A. Halahan, Sergt. T. Chisholm, L/cpl. F. Brookes, Tpr. G. Telford, Tpr J. Rayner

CHAPTER 16

THE HOME FRONT AND NORWAY

1939 to 1945
5th Battalion

THE 5th Bn. Royal Northumberland Fusiliers had, for most of its existence, the distinction of combining the county spirit of the Regiment with the technique of a Searchlight Regiment, Royal Artillery. 1939

On mobilization it was known as the 5th Bn. Royal Northumberland Fusiliers (53rd Searchlight Regiment). In August 1940 it changed its designation to 53rd Searchlight Regiment R.A. (5th Bn. Royal Northumberland Fusiliers), T.A. In January 1945 it became a Garrison Regiment under the new title of 638th Regiment R.A. (R.N.F.), T.A. In March 1945 its role—but not its title—was again altered and it became a 'B Type' Infantry Battalion. In spite of these changes the unit remained intensely proud of its Royal Northumberland Fusilier connection and its personnel always wore the Regimental cap badge.

Many units forming part of the Air Defence of Great Britain saw little of the enemy and rarely came into action. The 5th Battalion were more fortunate in frequently being located in areas selected by the German Air Force for special attention. After the German collapse they were sent to Norway to assist in disarming and repatriating the very large German Army quartered in Norway at the time of the capitulation.

The Regiment * mobilized on the 24th August 1939 as a Searchlight Regiment of three companies and deployed immediately as follows:

408 Coy. . . .	Newcastle-on-Tyne, in a light A.A. role.
409 " . . .	Hartlepool } in a searchlight role
410 " . . .	Darlington } in a searchlight role

At the time of mobilization the Regimental state was as follows:

Commanding Officer .	Lieut.-Colonel W. H. Leete, O.B.E., D.F.C., T.D.
Adjutant . . .	Captain H. S. Flower
Quartermaster . .	Captain S. Tyrell, M.M.
O.C. 408 Coy. . .	Major G. M. I. Stanley
" 409 " . .	Major H. Phillips
" 410 " . .	Major A. E. B. Plummer, M.C.

* In view of its unusual designation the unit is referred to as Regiment in the rest of this chapter.

1939–1944 In December 1939 408 Coy. moved from Newcastle and deployed in the Durham area in a searchlight role.

Before proceeding further with the narrative of the Regiment's activities it will perhaps be as well to give a summary of the progressive improvement in searchlight equipment which took place during the war. Up to the end of 1940 the standard equipment was the 90-cm. projector; but about this time the 150-cm. projector made its appearance. This was a much more powerful and efficient equipment. By the end of the war about 90 per cent. of all lights were of 150-cm. calibre. The most marked improvements were, however, in the methods of 'picking up' hostile planes. With the hand-controlled sound locators with which searchlight units mobilized, the illumination of a hostile plane was a rare occurrence—and if achieved led to almost embarrassing congratulations from many quarters. Later when radar control was introduced and as the type and pattern of this equipment improved it led to a marked increase in efficiency. By 1942 the 'picking up' of hostile planes within range became almost automatic, and failure to do so invariably called for an explanation.

Searchlight duties are exceptionally exacting on morale. Fighter aircraft, A.A. artillery units and even units armed with small-bore weapons can often claim a 'kill'; but searchlight personnel, whose role is to illuminate enemy aircraft, were never in a position to do so—although often instrumental in destroying hostile planes.

After Dunkirk in June 1940 enemy air attacks became very heavy. Regimental personnel were continuously on duty and often in action. In addition, the threat of invasion made it necessary for them to train in a ground role as infantry.

In January 1941 the Regiment moved to Northumberland, where it deployed in a wide screen as an integral part of the defences of Glasgow, and cluster sites were instituted as a new experiment. As there were at this time practically no A.A. guns in the area action was mainly confined to co-operation with fighter aircraft. The cessation of raids on Glasgow which followed these dispositions seemed to testify to their value.

In November 1941 a newly formed battery,* the 565th, joined the Regiment, which then moved south to stations on the East Coast between Morpeth in the north and Whitby in the south. They remained in this area for over two years and took their full share in dealing with enemy raids on numerous vital points in the locality. In addition many exercises, in co-operation with the R.A.F. and heavy A.A. units, took place.

In August 1942 Lieut.-Colonel W. H. Leete vacated command of the Regiment and was succeeded by Lieut.-Colonel J. Preece, O.B.E.—who was in turn succeeded by Lieut.-Colonel L. N. Side, O.B.E., T.D., in December 1943.

Early in 1944 a number of A.A. formations and units moved south to thicken up the defences in preparation for the Allied invasion of the Continent. The 5th Battalion moved in February and was given the important task of participation in the defence of Portsmouth and Southampton—two batteries being deployed on the Isle of Wight and one on the mainland.

* With the change of designation in August 1940 Searchlight Companies became known as Batteries.

Following this move information was received concerning the possibilities of the Germans using pilotless aircraft, and practice and experiment in counter-measures were undertaken. This early practice proved most useful when later the enemy commenced using this new type of weapon. 1944–1945

Raids on the Portsmouth–Southampton area took place frequently in March, April and May; but, contrary to expectations, there was no enemy air activity immediately prior to, or after, the Normandy D Day (6th June 1944).

At the end of August the Regiment undertook the training of personnel in an infantry role, for which officers and N.C.Os. had already attended courses. For this purpose a Regimental Infantry Training School was opened at Golden Hill Fort, Isle of Wight.

About this time Lieut.-Colonel W. O. N. Hammond, O.B.E., T.D., assumed command of the Regiment in succession to Lieut.-Colonel L. N. Side.

In the middle of June 1944 the Germans commenced an attack on London and Southern England with their new pilotless aircraft (known variously as 'flying bomb,' 'doodle bug' and 'V.1'). The first of these was launched on the 13th June and for some weeks the attacks increased in severity. A.A. Command countered this by deploying a large number of A.A. guns (mostly 3·7-in.) in a strip along the South Coast covering the line of attack. In a short time—assisted by the R.A.F., and the new American V.T.98 proximity fuse (known as 'Bonzo') *—a considerable measure of success was attained and only a small proportion of the missiles got through to their targets. As the Allied liberating armies advanced through North-West Europe they overran the launching sites and the attacks gradually declined and eventually ceased. Later, however, the Germans started launching the bombs from Heinkel aircraft over the North Sea. This required a new deployment of A.A. artillery on the East Coast, between Yarmouth and the Thames Estuary, and eventually some 500 3·7-in. A.A. guns were deployed on this strip.

In December 1944, all enemy activity having ended in the Portsmouth–Southampton area, the Regiment deployed on the East Coast with batteries at Ipswich, Harwich and Colchester. Personnel were employed solely in building gun sites.

By January 1945 the counter-measures, coupled with the further advance of the Allied Armies, had proved successful and the Regiment moved back to the Southampton area and was converted to a Garrison Regiment with the title of 638th Regiment R.A. (R.N.F.), T.A. The remainder of the A1 men under thirty-five were withdrawn and sent to other units, and in March the role of the Regiment was again altered to that of a 'B-Type' Infantry Battalion. Training in the new role continued at Southampton and later in the New Forest until June.

SERVICE IN NORWAY

(Note: Although a departure from the chronological order of this book, it has been thought best to include this account of the 5th Battalion's short period of service

* This fuse detonated itself automatically on arrival within 60 feet of the target. It was not, however, self-destroying and could therefore only be fired out to sea.

1945 in Norway in the chapter, thus preserving continuity in the narrative of the unit's activities.)

For some time prior to the German surrender anxiety was felt as to the likely attitude of the German troops garrisoning Norway. These numbered over 200,000. They were remote from the theatre of operations and unlikely to feel the same sense of defeat as their countrymen nearer home. It was thought possible that they might not accept the surrender terms, or even that the Nazi leaders might fly to Norway and make a last stand there. These fears proved groundless; but nevertheless a force was organized in the United Kingdom to proceed to Norway as soon as possible after the capitulation of Germany. This force consisted of British troops and Norwegian units which had been training in Scotland since 1940.

The 5th Bn. Royal Northumberland Fusiliers formed part of the 304th Infantry Brigade of this force, which proceeded to Norway early in June 1945.

The Regiment landed at Tromso in Finnmark on the 12th June. This port is well within the Arctic Circle and they were therefore the most northerly British troops in the world. The Commanding Officer, Lieut.-Colonel W. O. N. Hammond, became the Sub-Area Commander, with responsibility over an area of country measuring some 150 by 50 miles. The three batteries were widely separated.

The duties at Tromso consisted of:

(*a*) The immediate collection and disarming of the German garrison, followed later by 'screening,' the arrest of those required for trial as war criminals and arrangements for the repatriation of the remainder to Germany.

(*b*) The collection and repatriation of Russian prisoners of war (of whom there were about 40,000 in Norway) and displaced persons of various other nationalities.

(*c*) Assistance to the Norwegian inhabitants.

These duties had been completed by the beginning of October and the Regiment then moved south to Oslo. Before leaving Tromso they constructed a monument, in the form of a mosaic of the Regimental cap badge, in the ex-German camp which they occupied—a permanent reminder to the inhabitants of the unit's service in the Arctic Circle. On completion of the move they took over guard and other duties in the capital. By this time, however, demobilization had started and the first eighteen release groups had left for home. It became necessary to merge the three regiments of the Brigade into two. As the number of officers in the 638th Regiment was reduced to 7, and the Commanding Officer was to leave shortly, it was decided that they should merge into the 630th and 637th Regiments.

On Monday, the 29th October 1945, the 638th Regiment R.A. (R.N.F.), T.A., held its last ceremonial parade at Frogner Stadium, Oslo, when they were addressed by, and marched past, the Brigade Commander—Brigadier F. W. Sandars, D.S.O. A few days later the unit was placed in 'suspended animation.' *

* The term 'suspended animation' implied the temporary disbandment of a unit.

Throughout its long vigil in the defence of the United Kingdom, and in Norway 1945 after the German surrender, the Regiment performed its tasks in the manner to be expected of a unit of the Royal Northumberland Fusiliers. Its duties were never spectacular and officers and men were denied much of the glamour which comes to soldiers who fight the enemy at closer quarters.

Finally it may be said that they gained a reputation second to none among the Searchlight Regiments of Anti-Aircraft Command.

CHAPTER 17

THE HOME FRONT, INDIA AND NORTH-WEST EUROPE

1939 to 1945

6th Battalion

1939–1940 The story of the 6th Bn. Royal Northumberland Fusiliers in the Second World War cannot be made to follow the chronological sequence in which this book is mostly written. The history of the two Tank Battalions—to which it was converted prior to hostilities—has therefore been confined to this one chapter. Despite their role during the war years the question of their exclusion from the history was never considered, as they always maintained a very close link, and many of the traditions and customs, of their parent Infantry Regiment.

When, in 1938, the Territorial Army was reorganized on mechanized lines the 6th Bn. Royal Northumberland Fusiliers was converted as an armoured unit and became the 43rd (Northumberland) Bn. Royal Tank Regiment. In the spring of 1939, when all Territorial Army units were duplicated, a second-line battalion was formed under the title of 49th (Northumberland) Bn. Royal Tank Regiment. These two units remained in an armoured role throughout most of the period 1939–45.*

Both units were embodied in September 1939 as part of the 25th Army Tank Brigade, the officer states being as follows:

	43rd Bn.	*49th Bn.*
Commanding Officer	Lieut.-Colonel F. Dawson, M.C., T.D.	Lieut.-Colonel C. B. Carrick, M.C., T.D.
Second-in-Command	Major G. S. Graham	Major G. L. A. France
Adjutant . .	Captain E. Martin	Captain S. Stibbard
Quartermaster .	Lieut. D. Blakey	Captain G. Ouzman
Sqn. Commanders .	Major K. O. Potter	Major P. Gardner
	Major J. A. Crisp	Major S. G. March
	Major R. Potter	Major H. P. Bell
	Captain T. R. Lovibond	Major H. J. M. L. Criddle

The 25th Army Tank Brigade continued to train in a tank role in the United Kingdom until the middle of 1940, when, owing to developments which followed the Dunkirk evacuation, it was converted into a motor machine-gun brigade, with an anti-invasion role.

* From the autumn of 1940 to the autumn of 1941 the 43rd Bn. R.T.R. was temporarily in a motor machine-gun role—as part of the 25th Army Tank Brigade.

In the autumn of 1940 the 49th R.T.R. left the 25th and joined the 1st Tank Brigade. From this juncture the activities of the two units must be described separately. 1940–1945

THE 43RD ROYAL TANK REGIMENT

In the autumn of 1941 the Battalion reverted to its normal tank role and became part of the 21st Army Tank Brigade, which mobilized almost at once for service in the Middle East. Eventually only one regiment of the Brigade sailed and the 43rd, with the rest of the Brigade, remained in England on Home Defence duties.

In the winter of 1941 the unit was transferred to the 33rd Army Tank Brigade, which was just forming—the two other regiments being converted infantry battalions. For some considerable time the 43rd's experience was utilized helping in the conversion of these two units.

In January 1942 the Brigade became part of the 3rd Division—then known as a 'Model' (or experimental) Division—which included the 33rd Army Tank Brigade. With this formation they again mobilized to take part in the assault on Sicily. Again it proved to be a false alarm, as at the last moment a Canadian tank formation was substituted for the 33rd Army Tank Brigade.

Immediately after this the Brigade joined the 79th Armoured Division which was in process of forming. In this Division were concentrated all the experimental armoured vehicles, known later as 'funnies,' which were hitherto being developed separately for special purposes—amphibious tanks and armoured troop carriers, 'Kangaroos,' 'Buffaloes,' 'Flails,' 'D.D. tanks' and many others.* At first the Division was in reality an experimental establishment, but later took part in the Normandy landings and the subsequent campaign in North-West Europe. It never operated as a division, but was responsible for advice on, and the allocation of, its 'funnies' to other formations for particular tasks. Its commander, Major-General P. C. S. Hobart, was a tank enthusiast whose progressive views, and impatience of orthodox methods, had not always found favour. His selection to command an armoured division was due to Mr. Churchill's personal representations on his behalf.† The appointment was a particularly fortunate one, and much of the success of the 'funnies' was due to his energy and flair for novel ideas.

The Regiment served in the 79th Division from June 1943 until the Normandy invasion in June 1944, carrying out experimental work on the various equipments and instructing other units in their use. As a result of this specialized role they did not proceed to France with the Division, but remained at home engaged in the same kind of work, until the formation of the Assault Training and Development Centre which took over the responsibility.

In the summer of 1945 the 43rd Royal Tank Regiment was re-equipped with another type of specialized tank—the C.D.L.,‡ which was to be used against the Japanese. It sailed for the Far East in June 1945. On arrival in India it became part

* For explanation of these terms see Glossary on pages xxi and xxii.
† See *The Second World War*, Volume II, by Winston S. Churchill—page 602.
‡ For explanation of term 'C.D.L. Tanks' see Glossary on page xxi.

1945 of the Allied land forces in South-East Asia who were preparing for the invasion of Malaya. Soon after arrival, however, the war with Japan came to an end, and the Regiment suffered its final disappointment in not being operationally employed.

The Regiment then reverted to the command of Army Headquarters, India, and squadrons were dispersed to various parts of India on internal security duties. They did valuable work maintaining order in Bombay and Calcutta during a period when riots were not infrequent.

THE 49TH ROYAL TANK REGIMENT

1940–1945 When the 49th R.T.R. joined the 1st Tank Brigade, in the autumn of 1940, that formation was preparing for service in the Middle East; but just prior to its departure the Regiment was removed from the Brigade and sent to the South-East Coast in an anti-invasion role. Its stay there was only a short one and it very soon moved north to Penrith, the experimental training centre for C.D.L. tanks.

For over two years the Battalion was engaged in tank development work—first as an independent unit, then in the 35th Tank Brigade and finally again in the 1st Tank Brigade, which had returned from the Middle East to become the C.D.L. Brigade for the campaign in North-West Europe.

The unit proceeded to France with the 1st Tank Brigade in early August 1944, but was not actively employed for a considerable time. In the autumn of 1944 the C.D.L. Brigade was disbanded and the 49th R.T.R. was converted into an Armoured Personnel Carrier Regiment—their vehicles being familiarly known as 'Kangaroos.'

The 'Kangaroo' was a Sherman tank with the turret removed, and was used to convey infantry (and sometimes Sappers, Signal personnel and others) forward in the assault. It was proof against small-arms fire, shell splinters and direct hits from shells of small calibre.

In this new role the Battalion was in great demand, and the Squadrons were almost continuously in action, or preparing for action, from the end of October 1944 until the cessation of hostilities in Europe in May 1945.

During the winter the strength of 49th R.T.R. was increased by inclusion of the 52nd Independent Tank Sqn., a unit which had been helping to invest Dunkirk, and which became F Sqn. of the 49th R.T.R.

Prior to the crossing of the Rhine (end of March 1945) one squadron of C.D.L. tanks was brought out from England and placed under command of the Battalion. This with the three squadrons of 'Kangaroos' made a total of approximately 200 armoured vehicles.

The Battalion participated in all the main battles from October 1944 onwards—the crossing of the River Maas, the capture of Blerick, the Ardennes, the engagements round Goch and Cleve in the Rhineland and in the final break-through after the crossing of the Rhine. In this last drive into the heart of Germany the three 'Kangaroo' squadrons played a leading part. A Sqn. was attached to the 7th Armoured Division and C and F Sqns. at various stages to the 15th (Scottish), 43rd, 49th, 51st (Highland) and 52nd (Lowland) Divisions. The C.D.L. Squadron took part in the actual crossings of the Rhine and Elbe.

These two Tank Battalions, who represented the 6th Bn. Royal Northumberland 1945
Fusiliers, were in a sense unfortunate in their war experiences. The 43rd Battalion remained in Great Britain until it proceeded to India after the German surrender, but arrived too late to participate in the war against Japan. The 49th Battalion was more fortunate in seeing service in North-West Europe, and was employed operationally in a very active capacity from October 1944 to May 1945.

Both Battalions, however, played an important part in the country's war effort. The highly specialized experimental work on which they were engaged for most of the war contributed, in no small measure, to the successful assault on 'Fortress Europe' and the victory which followed. It was their high standard of efficiency that gave them that instructional value which so repeatedly forbade their being spared for active operations.

CHAPTER 18

GREECE

December 1944 to May 1945
2nd Battalion

Dec. 1944 EARLY in October 1944 British airborne forces landed in Greece, and by the 12th Athens had been cleared of the enemy by Greek partisans. By the 8th November the whole of Greece had been freed of the invaders. Meanwhile the Greek Government, headed by M. Papandreou, had returned to Athens on the 18th October. On the 14th December this Government fell and on the same day a provisional Government under a Regent—Archbishop Damaskinos—was established, pending the return of the King and the holding of elections.

With the departure of the Germans the Greeks, in true Balkan style, fell to fighting among themselves. Almost immediately the Edes, or right-wing party, which supported the Government, found themselves opposed by the Communist-dominated Elas, who attempted to occupy Athens and seize the reins of Government. It was the policy of the Allies to support the Regent's Government, and in order to help uphold it additional British troops were sent to Greece. This resulted in the 4th Division, which was about to move from Italy to Palestine, being diverted to Greece. H.M.T. 'Cameronia,' the ship which conveyed the 2nd Bn. Royal Northumberland Fusiliers, arrived off Piraeus, the port of Athens, on the morning of the 16th December 1944 and anchored in the harbour. Some gun and small-arms fire could be heard on shore and an occasional airplane flew overhead. A little later the ship was ordered to stand further offshore to permit some destroyers to bombard hostile positions on the outskirts of the town. It transpired that British troops and the rival Greek factions were having a spirited battle for control of the Greek capital.

H.Q. and some troops of the 4th Division had already landed and were in action. Soon after midday a Divisional Staff Officer came aboard and took the Commanding Officer, Adjutant and a representative from each company ashore in a landing craft. The situation was very confused, but it appeared that three British brigades were holding a narrow strip of coast and a small portion of Athens. Small detachments were reported to be cut off by Elas troops, who were difficult to identify, as only a few wore any form of uniform. The task of the Battalion was to take over the defences of the nearby Kalamaki airfield from the 10th Infantry Brigade by nightfall 17th/18th December. To assist in this three companies of infantry (improvised from the Divisional Artillery), one parachute company (formed from R.A.F. personnel) and two squadrons of the R.A.F. Regiment were placed under the Commanding Officer's orders.

By the evening of the 16th the Battalion had landed and moved to the airfield,

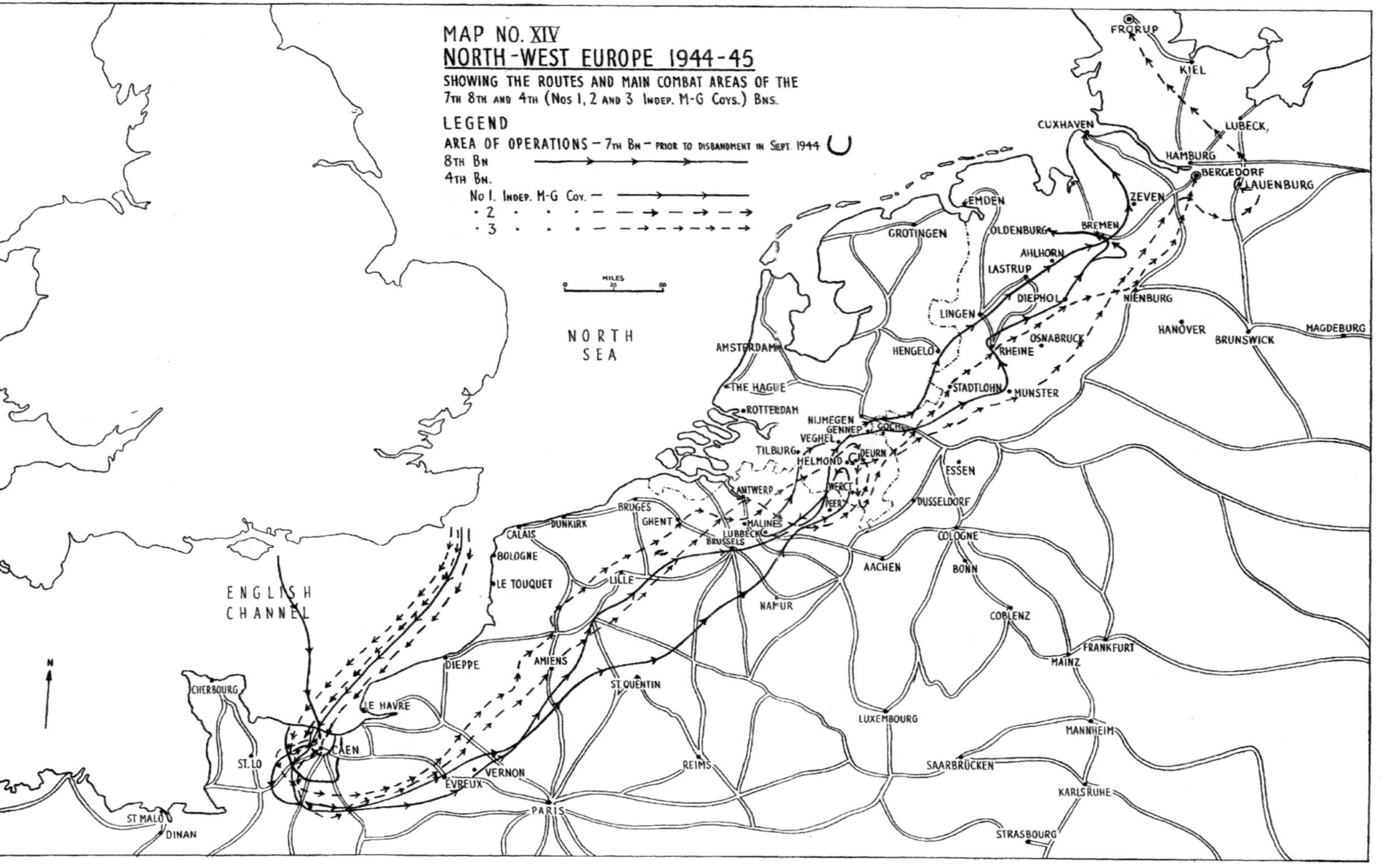
MAP NO. XIV
NORTH-WEST EUROPE 1944-45
SHOWING THE ROUTES AND MAIN COMBAT AREAS OF THE 7TH 8TH AND 4TH (NOS 1, 2 AND 3 INDEP. M-G COYS.) BNS.
LEGEND
AREA OF OPERATIONS – 7TH BN – PRIOR TO DISBANDMENT IN SEPT. 1944
8TH BN
4TH BN.
No 1. INDEP. M-G COY.
2
3
MILES
0
25
50
NORTH SEA
ENGLISH CHANNEL
N
FRORUP
KIEL
LUBECK,
CUXHAVEN
HAMBURG
BERGEDORF
LAUENBURG
EMDEN
ZEVEN
BREMEN
OLDENBURG
GROTINGEN
AHLHORN
LASTRUP
DIEPHOL
NIENBURG
LINGEN
HANOVER
BRUNSWICK
MAGDEBURG
OSNABRUCK
RHEINE
HENGELO
AMSTERDAM
THE HAGUE
STADTLOHN
MUNSTER
ROTTERDAM
NIJMEGEN
GENNEP
GOCH
VEGHEL
TILBURG
HELMOND
DEURN
ESSEN
ANTWERP
WERCT
PEER
DUSSELDORF
BRUGES
GHENT
MALINES
DUNKIRK
CALAIS
LUBBECK
BRUSSELS
COLOGNE
BOLOGNE
AACHEN
BONN
LE TOUQUET
LILLE
NAMUR
COBLENZ
FRANKFURT
MAINZ
DIEPPE
AMIENS
ST. QUENTIN
CHERBOURG
LE HAVRE
LUXEMBOURG
MANNHEIM
CAEN
ST. LO
REIMS
SAARBRÜCKEN
EVREUX
VERNON
KARLSRUHE
PARIS
ST MALO
DINAN
STRASBOURG

where they 'doubled up' with units of the 10th Infantry Brigade in various huts and buildings. Bn. H.Q. was established with the H.Qs. of the 2nd Bn. Bedfordshire and Hertfordshire Regt. in the centre of the airfield. Dec. 1944

On the following morning arrangements to take over commenced. The Kalamaki airfield—which was to be the home of the Battalion for some weeks to come—covered some four square miles and had a perimeter about five miles long. To the south of Athens lies the coastal suburb of Faliron. The airfield was located on an expanse of sand between Faliron and the southern tip of the semicircle of hills which encloses Athens from the sea. On the Athens side it was joined to the houses of Faliron and to the south the residential village of Glifadha encroached almost to the landing ground. To the east were the foothills of Mount Imettos, some 2,500 feet high; on the west a coastal road running parallel to, and near, the beach.

The air forces operating from this airfield consisted of five British and three Greek operational squadrons, together with numerous ground personnel.

The initial dispositions, which were taken up on the afternoon of the 17th, were as follows:

A Coy. . . .	Area of knolls at north-east corner of airfield
B „ . . .	Among a group of buildings at the south-east corner
Three Royal Artillery Coys. . . .	South-west corner and in the village of Glifadha
R.A.F. Parachute Coy.	Between B Coy. and the Royal Artillery Coys.

The remainder were kept in reserve, and to assist in maintaining the landing-ground and roads.

Thus 'Butterforce' was born, consisting at that time of some 1,500 men; but which later reached a strength of 5,000. Its duties while at Kalamaki were not all strictly military, but of a kind not unfamiliar to British troops in foreign parts—the reception and despatch of distinguished visitors travelling by air; guarding prisoners of war; dealing with refugees from Athens who clamoured for admittance at the barricades; the 'screening' of suspects and continuous vigilance, by means of guards and patrols, to prevent sabotage, pilfering and penetration of the perimeter by unauthorized persons. These and many other irksome and monotonous tasks—such as running soup-kitchens for the distressed local populace—continued day after day.

On the morning of the 18th December the Battalion received a welcome addition to its strength by the arrival of the original advance party from Palestine. This included the Second-in-Command (Major J. A. Dewhurst), the Signalling Officer (Captain L. J. Holloway), the Transport Officer (Lieut. B. C. Clements), R.Q.M.S. Cook and some 35 other 'key' personnel.

By the 20th the 4th Division had liberated most of Athens and a considerable stretch of the hinterland. This enabled the authorities to form those of the local inhabitants with military experience into battalions of what became known as the Greek National Guard. Each unit had a British liaison officer, who in actual practice performed most of the duties of commanding officer, adjutant and quartermaster. These battalions were raised, equipped and organized at Glifadha and while there were under command of 'Butterforce.'

Jan.–March 1945

The Battalion was too busy to celebrate Christmas or the New Year. By the first week in January Athens and its suburbs had been cleared of militant Elas, who had been driven into the hills. The Division thereupon left Athens and disposed itself across the ring of mountains to the north, between Khalkis and Corinth. The Battalion was called upon to provide only one mortar platoon and the rest settled down to training in the neighbourhood of Athens. The only incidents of note were the participation of the Battalion in the relief of some R.E.M.E. personnel in an Athen's factory and the holding of the south and south-eastern exits from Athens to prevent the movement of Elas troops during a round-up of the city by the 10th Infantry Brigade. With the departure of the Division further afield 'Butterforce' became enlarged to include all troops in the area of the capital, among them the 166th Bn. Greek National Guard, a total of about 3,000. On the 14th the Force attained its 'peak' strength of 5,000, when the 4th Greek Brigade was added to the order of battle.

On the 15th January 'Butterforce' came under direct control of H.Q. Military Command, Athens (Lieut.-General J. L. I. Hawkesworth). On the 18th the Battalion moved from the airfield into good billets in Kalamaki village, and periodical visits to Athens were permitted.

On the last day of January the 2nd Bn. Royal Northumberland Fusiliers provided a platoon, under Lieut. F. St.J. C. Gore, as guard and escort for two rival political delegations, which came from the north for discussions with the Regent, Archbishop Damaskinos.

The month of February was mostly uneventful. On the 11th the Battalion reverted to command of the 4th Division, and on the 14th Mr. Churchill, Mr. Eden and Field-Marshal Alexander landed on the Kalamaki airfield for a brief visit to Athens.

On the 2nd March the Battalion left the Athens area and moved via the shores of the Gulf of Elevsis to Mandra, Thebes and thence over the bridge joining the mainland of Greece to Khalkis, the capital of Euboea. Khalkis is a fishing town of about 18,000 inhabitants: billets were found partly in the centre of the town and partly in the outskirts. The main activities here were training and assisting the Greek civil authorities to re-establish some semblance of orderly local government.

The stay in Khalkis was a short one and on the 17th March the Battalion recrossed to the mainland, bound for Volos. This move took two days, the night of the 17th/18th being spent in bivouac in an olive grove between Lamia and Stilis. Volos was reached on the afternoon of the 18th. Here they were accommodated in a somewhat uncomfortable Greek barracks. Each company was given an area of surrounding country in which it was responsible for distributing Red Cross supplies to the inhabitants, most of whom were in a pitiful condition. Otherwise the duties were very much the same as at Khalkis.

The 25th March was one of the frequent Greek days of national celebration—on this occasion Independence Day. These always caused some anxiety, as they were liable to result in disorders between rival military parties and political factions. In order to meet this a similar policy to previous occasions was adopted. The streets of Volos were paraded by carriers with machine-guns mounted. This routine was carried out before and on the actual day. It proved entirely satisfactory, and no serious disorders occurred.

March–May 1945

By the end of the month Captain P. Bulman and the rear party from Taranto had arrived at Athens, and after a three-day journey by road rejoined the Battalion on the 28th.

On the 29th March the new Commander of the Greek forces, General Christos Avramidis and his British liaison officer, Major W. Christie-Miller (Royal Ulster Rifles), moved to the area and became members of the Bn. Headquarter Mess—as did Commander Pool, R.N., the Vice-Consul.

St. George's Day 1945 was celebrated in the traditional manner. The ceremonial parade was attended by many distinguished guests, including Archbishop Joachim of Volos, the officers commanding the Greek National Guard battalions; the senior Greek naval officer; the British Vice-Consul, Commander Pool, R.N.; and many others both British and Greek. The new Divisional Commander, Major-General C. B. Callander, who had succeeded Major-General A. D. Ward on the 20th April, was unfortunately unable to attend.

It will perhaps be appropriate to give the names of the officers on parade on this occasion—the last of its kind held by the 2nd Bn. Royal Northumberland Fusiliers in the Second World War. They were as follows:

Commanding Officer . .	Lieut.-Colonel E. H. Butterfield
Second-in-Command .	Major J. A. Dewhurst
Adjutant	Captain L. F. Hay
Regimental Sergeant-Major	R.S.M. C. V. Caborn
No. 1 Coy. . . .	Major A. E. Richards
	Captain R. R. Gibson, M.C.
	Captain R. V. Luther-Smith
	Lieut. G. H. Hulme
No. 2 Coy. . . .	Major H. R. M. Wilkin
	Captain J. J. Hinson
	Lieut. F. W. Little
	Lieut. D. S. Dumbreck
No. 3 Coy. . . .	Major R. D. Brook
	Lieut. L. C. G. Gilling
	Lieut. C. W. Brierley
	Lieut. J. C. Brown
No. 4 Coy. . . .	Major E. H. Parkhurst
	Captain E. R. Coutts-Deacon
	Lieut. A. D. Wood
	Lieut. A. H. Hobson

The ceremonial parade was followed by a sports meeting in the afternoon.

While all these events were taking place heartening news had been received from the battlefronts in Germany and Italy. It was clear that the end of the war with Germany was in sight, and there was naturally much speculation as to how this would affect the troops in Greece. When the news of Victory came it was a matter for satisfaction that the first large-scale German surrender was made to Field-Marshal

May 1945 Alexander and his Allied Armies in Italy—in which theatre of operations the 2nd Bn. Royal Northumberland Fusiliers had played a prominent part.

Victory in Europe Day—the 8th May 1945—was celebrated in Greece by British troops and Greek inhabitants alike. A Thanksgiving Service held by the Battalion was spontaneously attended by the Archbishop, the Prefect, General Avramidis and many other Greeks. At the end of the service the Archbishop gave an address—in Greek.

(NOTE: The final phase of the 2nd Battalion's service in Greece is recorded in Chapter 20: Aftermath of War, together with the activities of other units of the Regiment in the immediate post-war months.)

CHAPTER 19

MISCELLANY

THIS book is mainly concerned with the records of the Field Force Battalions of the Regiment, mostly during the war years—1939 to 1945. There are, however, certain activities, incidents and aspects of Regimental life which do not fit into the narratives of the preceding chapters—either because they are non-operational, or because they affect the Regiment as a whole, rather than any particular battalion.

These miscellaneous matters are dealt with in this chapter.

1. NON-FIELD FORCE UNITS

The Depot

No history of the Royal Northumberland Fusiliers would be complete without mention of the Depot at Fenham Barracks, Newcastle-on-Tyne—the Headquarters, and 'home,' of the Regiment.

Very little of note in Depot affairs occurred during the inter-war period. The introduction of the machine-gun role in 1936 made little difference to the basic purpose of the Depot and the principles on which it was organized and run. Up to 1939 the Officers' Mess had been shared with the Durham Light Infantry, the removal of whose depot from Fenham Barracks at this time ended a close association which had existed for many years between the two regiments. In that year the old block was pulled down and the new Sandhurst Block built. This did not include a Mess, and various buildings were used for the purpose until a proper Mess was finally established in the south end of the block, where it still remains.

On the outbreak of war in September 1939 the Depot (commanded by Major H. F. Attwater) became a machine-gun training centre. In August 1941 it was decided to amalgamate the regimental training centres of all machine-gun regiments—Royal Northumberland Fusiliers, Cheshire Regiment, Middlesex Regiment and Manchester Regiment—into a combined centre, known as the '24th Machine-Gun Training Centre,' at the Depot of the Cheshire Regiment, at Chester. Consequent on this move most of the Regimental property was stored in the Tower of Fenham Barracks, and a small 'Depot Party' (under Major D. C. Bucknall) remained there to represent Regimental interests.

By December 1942 the 24th Machine-Gun Training Centre had outgrown the available accommodation in Chester. It was therefore decided to form another centre at the nearby Blacon Camp—to be known as the '26th Machine-Gun Training Centre,' and commanded by Lieut.-Colonel T. C. L. Redwood. Accordingly, early in 1943, the Depots of the Royal Northumberland Fusiliers and the Middlesex Regiment moved to Blacon to form the new centre—together with all men under training for their respective regiments. This organization continued until the end of the war. In December 1946 No. 5 Primary Training Centre (under command of Lieut.-Colonel B. Tarleton—and later Lieut.-Colonel S. Enderby) was formed at Fenham Barracks, and later the Regimental Depot was re-established under Major R. H. Yorke. In April 1949 No. 5 Primary Training Centre closed down, and the Depot took on its immediate post-war form. In October 1951 it was re-organized and expanded to train infantry recruits.

The 10th Battalion (renumbered the 30th Battalion)

In October 1939 the 10th (Home Defence) Battalion of the Regiment was formed from No. 40 Group National Defence Coy.—under the command of Lieut.-Colonel R. Allen.

In December 1941 the unit was redesignated '30th (H.D.) Bn. Royal Northumberland Fusiliers' and was for a time attached to the 15th (Scottish) Division. During its period at home the unit was based on Gosforth, with many smaller detachments distributed on guard, and similar duties, throughout the North of England.

In May 1942 Lieut.-Colonel R. Allen was succeeded by Lieut.-Colonel R. H. Rohde.

In August 1943, although styled 'Home Defence,' the Battalion was ordered overseas, and sailed from Glasgow in S.S. 'Duchess of Richmond,' disembarking at Algiers at the end of the month. This move necessitated a considerable change in personnel, many of the older men and those unfit for overseas service being left at home. The Battalion continued to serve as a garrison unit in this part of North Africa until May 1944, when it moved to Malta—making a short stay at Naples in Italy en route.

In June 1944 Lieut.-Colonel J. Blenkinsop succeeded to the command of the Battalion.

The unit was still in Malta at the end of 1945—much reduced in strength and changed in composition, owing to the despatch home of men due for release.

Throughout the war this unit performed unspectacular and often very monotonous duties—but always in the same spirit of service as the more fortunate Field Force Battalions of the Regiment.

The 70th Battalion

The 70th Battalion of the Regiment was formed in the Gosforth and Benwell areas of Newcastle-on-Tyne on the 19th September 1940, for the purpose of absorbing the young soldiers of three Home Defence battalions—namely the 10th (or 30th) (H.D.) Bn. Royal Northumberland Fusiliers, 30th (H.D.) Bn. Green Howards and 30th (H.D.) Bn. Durham Light Infantry—who on transfer all became Royal Northumberland Fusiliers.

Key appointments in the Battalion were as follows:

Commanding Officer .	. Lieut.-Colonel J. O. Byrne, M.C. (succeeded by Lieut.-Colonel C. E. Beckwith in April 1942)
Second-in-Command	. Major T. H. J. Gillam (succeeded by Major A. D. Bryant)
Adjutant	. Captain D. Keith-Shaw (succeeded by Captain F. Howe)

44. The 2nd Battalion, marching through Volos

45. The 30th Battalion being inspected, 19th October 1944, by Lieut.-General Sir Edward Schreiber, Governor of Malta

46. Lieut.-Colonel T. C. L. Redwood, commanding 26th M.G.T.C., with Major-General W. N. Herbert, C.B., C.M.G., D.S.O., and Lieut.-General D. G. Watson, C.B., C.B.E., M.C., St. George's Day, Chester, 1945

47. 26th M.G.T.C.—Young soldiers of the Fifth Fusiliers and Middlesex Regiment celebrating the action of El Bodon, at which the 2/Fifth and 77th Regiment, on the 25th September 1811, having formed square

On formation the unit was some 1,400 strong. Bn. H.Q. remained at Gosforth, but very soon companies were spread out, up to a distance of 50 miles from Newcastle, on airfield defence. Except for a period of one month in the early part of 1942, when it carried out intensive training in the area Nunnykirk–Netherwitton (west of Morpeth), the Battalion continued in this role until the autumn of 1942.

In November 1942, when the Battalion was at North Seaton Hall, Newbiggin, it was converted into No. 98 Primary Training Centre, all surplus officers and men being posted to other units.

II. ALLIED REGIMENTS

In December 1928 *The Northumberland Regiment Non-Permanent Active Militia of Canada* became allied to the *Royal Northumberland Fusiliers*. Since then this Canadian regiment has changed its designation and now consists of two units as follows:

The Midland Regiment (Northumberland and Durham)

The Elgin Regiment
Les Fusiliers du St. Laurent

Since January 1930 the Regiment has also had an Australian allied regiment—the 35th Battalion (Newcastle's Own Regiment) Australian Infantry.

III. THE COLONELS OF THE REGIMENT

During the whole period under review the Regiment had only two Colonels—Major-General Sir Percival S. Wilkinson, K.C.M.G., C.B., who had been appointed in 1915, and Major-General W. N. Herbert, C.B., C.M.G., D.S.O., D.C.L., who succeeded him in 1935. Apart from the obvious advantages of continuity the Regiment was indeed fortunate in having two officers of such distinction, and with such a truly Regimental spirit, at the head of its domestic affairs. Moreover, the command of the 50th (Northumbrian) Division, which fell to both alike, brought them into close association with the territorial battalions of the Regiment. During his twenty years' tenure of the appointment the wellbeing of his Regiment never ceased to be the constant concern of Sir Percival Wilkinson.

Major-General Herbert spent most of his military life in, or in close association with, the Regiment. Adjutant of the 1st Battalion on the outbreak of war in 1914, he was appointed in October 1916 to its command, which he held, except for a brief interval, till appointed to brigade command in September 1918; and he again commanded it from November 1925 for a further four years. In 1939 he was recalled from retirement to form the 23rd in second line to the 50th (Northumbrian) Division, and commanded this Division, of which the 8th and 9th Battalions formed part, during the Dunkirk campaign of 1940. He was succeeded by the present Colonel of the Regiment—Major-General H. de R. Morgan, D.S.O.—on 1st January 1947. The value of General Herbert's services would be difficult to exaggerate, and his death on the 25th April 1949 was a grievous loss to the Regiment and his many friends.

IV. OTHER REGIMENTAL PERSONALITIES

There are many Fifth Fusiliers, of all ranks, whose service during the years 1919–45 was entirely, or mostly, outside the Regiment, and consequently their activities are not recorded or are recorded only briefly in the accounts of the various units. For reasons of space only the most distinguished can be mentioned; but there were many others who played more humble, but nevertheless worthy, roles in various parts of the world, and thereby contributed indirectly to the fame of the Royal Northumberland Fusiliers.

General Sir William Platt, G.B.E., K.C.B., D.S.O., joined the Regiment in 1905. He was awarded the D.S.O. for gallantry whilst serving with the 1st Battalion in the Mohmand campaign of 1908. As a General Officer he commanded the troops in the Sudan, and the Sudan Defence Force, from 1938 to 1941. From 1941 to 1945 he was G.O.C.-in-C. East African Command, and the defeat of the Italians, in that part of the world, was due very largely to his generalship and organizing ability. He retired from the Army in 1945.

Lieut.-General J. G. des R. Swayne, K.C.B., C.B.E., was originally in the Somerset Light Infantry, but became a Fifth Fusilier in 1935, when he assumed command of the 1st Battalion. He left the Battalion in 1937 to become an instructor at the Staff College. This short period in command was, however, sufficient to establish him in the Regiment as an officer of exceptional character and efficiency. His subsequent career was a distinguished one and, among others, he held the appointments of Head of the British Military Mission to French G.Q.G. 1939–40; Commander 4th Division 1940–42; C.G.S. Home Forces 1942; G.O.C.-in-C. South-East Command 1942–44; and C.G.S. India 1944–46. He retired from the Army in 1946.

Major-General H. de R. Morgan, D.S.O., took over command of the 2nd Battalion on the troopship at Southampton in September 1936, when they were under orders for Palestine—having previously served in The Buffs. The extent to which he identified himself with his new regiment may be judged from the fact that just over ten years later he became its Colonel. He returned to Bordon with the Battalion in 1937 and on the outbreak of war in September 1939 took it to France with the B.E.F. In March 1940 he was promoted to command the 148th Infantry Brigade, which he took to Norway in April and, after many adventures, embarked for England on the 1st May. From June 1941 to March 1943 he commanded the 45th Division in the United Kingdom, after which he was appointed President of the Regular Commissions Board, in which capacity he served for over three years. He retired from the Army on the 27th July 1946.

Major-General L. C. Thomas, C.B., C.B.E., D.S.O., M.C., joined the Fifth Fusiliers from the Indian Army in 1921. He served with the King's African Rifles from 1925 to 1927 and with the Sudan Defence Force from 1927 to 1929. He commanded the 9th Battalion at Dunkirk in 1940 and also at Singapore in 1942. He was among the officers specifically ordered to leave Singapore shortly before the garrison surrendered. Subsequently he commanded the 88th Indian Infantry Brigade (1942–43) and the 36th Indian Infantry Brigade (1943–45) in Burma. Following the appointment of B.G.S. in India in 1945 he became Inspector-General of the Burma Army (1945–47) and retired from the service in 1948.

V. ST. GEORGE'S DAY

Generally speaking the English do not observe their National Day with the same enthusiasm as the Scots, Welsh and Irish, and some are probably even ignorant of the date on which it falls. To a reader not closely associated with The Fifth it may therefore seem remarkable to have found it recorded that on one occasion only during the war years, when the vehicle containing them was destroyed by enemy action, did a unit of the Regiment fail to wear its St. George's Day roses on the 23rd April. From time immemorial it has been customary for The Fifth or Royal Northumberland Fusiliers to wear red and white roses, troop the colours and hold high festival on the day of their Patron Saint. For the Regiment, even in war, to be without its roses would always be regarded as something more than a minor tragedy.

VI. THE 'ROYAL' PREFIX

The prefix 'Royal' is a personal award by the Sovereign to a Regiment, or Corps, as a special mark of distinction and appreciation of its services. Up to 1935 the title of the Regiment was 'The Northumberland Fusiliers'; but in that year—on the occasion of his Silver Jubilee—His Majesty King George V conferred this privilege on the Regiment, which then became known as 'The Royal Northumberland Fusiliers,' * and which was at the same time permitted to retain its historic gosling green facings.

VII. THE 'ST. GEORGE'S GAZETTE'

Since the institution of the *St. George's Gazette* in 1883 the Regiment has owed much to the editors of its Regimental journal, but to none more than to Major B. T. St. John. In 1939, after twenty-three years in the editorial chair, Major St. John was on the point of retiring. Though alive from previous experience to the war-time difficulties of censorship and paper shortages, he generously consented on the outbreak of war to continue as editor. Special credit is due, too, to Messrs. G. W. Grigg & Son of the St. George's Press, Dover, who, despite severe damage to their premises through enemy action, maintained from 1939 to 1945 the record of the *St. George's Gazette* of never missing a monthly issue. Information contained in the journal has been of great value in compiling this history, and future generations will be indebted to those who found time amid the distractions of war to contribute to its pages.

---

* It will be noticed that in this book the title 'Royal Northumberland Fusiliers' has been used when recording events prior to 1935. Historically this is incorrect; but it was thought best to use throughout the volume the title by which the Regiment is now familiarly known. [Author.]

CHAPTER 20

AFTERMATH OF WAR

I. GENERAL

1945 HOSTILITIES with Germany ended on the 7th May 1945 and little more than three months later, on the 14th August, the Allies accepted the unconditional surrender of Japan.

The defeat of Germany, although it did not end the war, lessened the tempo and strain in most Commonwealth countries—except for those troops actually engaged with the Japanese in South-East Asia and the Pacific. Nevertheless, a very considerable effort was still required, as we were in duty bound to give the fullest support to America against Japan. Most people expected that the Japanese would fight on to the last. There were very few who thought the end would come without an Allied invasion of Japan, followed by a long period of bitter fighting and perhaps guerrilla operations which might go on for years. Indeed, it is now known that these anticipations might well have been realized, but for the dropping of two atom bombs on Japan. As it was, on the 10th August, within less than fourteen weeks of victory in Europe the welcome news came that Japan had broadcast her surrender offer on the radio.

Experience of the years following 1918 acted as a warning against over-optimism. Everybody realized that the economic road was likely to be a difficult one. Disturbances in India, Palestine and elsewhere were to be expected for a time; but these were no more than policing problems, to which we had been accustomed for many generations.

One thing seemed certain. We could expect a long era of freedom from the fear of another World War. Demobilization could start with a good flow at once, and in a short time we should be able to give up conscription.

As we now know, none of these hopes have been realized. A war-time ally has become a 'cold' war enemy; our economy has been ruined by the need for a new rearmament programme on a huge scale; and the United Nations Organization—although an improvement on the old League of Nations—has fallen short of expectations.

It was, however, in a spirit of sober confidence that British fighting men, at home and abroad, stood relaxed in the late summer of 1945, awaiting early demobilization and a return to a new, if somewhat different, life as civilians.

It is unnecessary to give precise details of the system of demobilization, which had been devised with much care and thought, and was ready some time before the cessation of hostilities. Under this system officers and other ranks were divided into groups according to age and service—known as 'Age/Service Groups'—these being numbered in order of priority. Periodically, as circumstances permitted, one or more

48. Major-General H. de R. Morgan, D.S.O., Colonel of the Regiment, 1947

age/service groups were 'called forward' for demobilization. Occasionally the release of specialists and 'key' personnel had to be deferred in the interests of the Army, these exceptions to the general rule being mostly confined to officers, warrant officers and senior N.C.Os. Personnel who volunteered to remain on for a period after the release of their groups were mostly allowed to do so, but the numbers were very small. 1945

In an undertaking so vast there were inevitably some cases of hardship and unfairness, but on the whole the system worked extremely well. Many consider that the process was too fast and for the few Regular soldiers and others who remained it was a sad sight to see famous units—which a few months before had fought our enemies to a standstill—reduced to skeleton strengths and, through lack of numbers, no longer operationally efficient.

It will be remembered that the 9th Battalion had not been reformed after the capitulation of the Singapore garrison in February 1942, and that the 7th Battalion had been disbanded in North-West Europe in September 1944. For convenience, and continuity of sequence, the narratives of the 5th and 6th Battalions in the post-war months have been included in the chapters devoted to the war-time activities of these two units.*

This chapter is therefore confined to a brief account of the 1st, 2nd, 4th (Nos. 1, 2 and 3 Independent M.G. Coys.) and 8th Battalions, during the period from the German surrender to the end of 1945.†

II. THE 1ST BATTALION

When hostilities in Italy ended the Battalion, under the command of Lieut.-Colonel M. C. Speer, was at rest in the village of Vigarano, near Ferrara—where they celebrated Victory in Europe Day.

Soon after this the Battalion moved to Venezia Giulia, and were destined to spend the next four months in the vicinity of Gorizia and the much disputed Port of Trieste and its surrounding territory. From here leave and recreation parties were sent to Venice, Austria, Trieste and Grado (a local 'Lido'). Eventually two houses were taken in Grado, and one company at a time sent to the comparatively comfortable quarters which they provided.

In August 1945 the Battalion moved into an Italian barracks situated in the centre of Gorizia. This accommodation, although not ideal, provided welcome shelter from the coming autumn weather. By this time the ranks had been seriously depleted by the departure of many officers and other ranks for release, and by transfers home and to other units.

By the end of September they were on the move again, the whole of the 10th Indian Division going to an area south of Milan—the 1st Bn. Royal Northumberland

---

* For the story of the 5th Battalion see Chapter 16, and for the 6th Battalion Chapter 17.

† In one or two cases the narrative has been carried beyond the 31st December 1945 in order to complete a phase or round off an incident.

1945 Fusiliers being located in barracks at Piacenza. These were taken over in an indescribably filthy condition, and even when cleaned up proved most uncomfortable quarters. The barracks consisted of large stone-flagged halls without doors or furniture, and with glassless windows.

Fortunately the stay at Piacenza was a short one, and very soon the Battalion moved to Merano in the disputed South Tyrol, some 40 miles south of the Brenner Pass. This was followed by the break-up of the British contingent of the 10th Indian Division, with which the Battalion had been associated for over a year. In the new area they came under command of No. 60 Sub-Area of No. 2 District, Milan.

Merano was an excellent place. It had been developed by the Italians as a spa and used by the Germans as a hospital centre. The inhabitants were mostly friendly and the accommodation first-class. It was, however, infested with ex-Nazis and ex-Fascists in hiding, and a centre for black-market activities.

The duties consisted of guarding German hospitals and stores and escorting convicted and suspected persons to and from various prisons and internment camps. These duties were frequent and very exacting, as by this time the Battalion strength was much depleted. Later Merano was found to offer excellent ski-ing and other forms of winter sport.

The last days of the Victory Year of the Second World War were occupied with the customary festivities—in exceptionally bad weather.

NOTE: Although beyond the period covered by this volume of the Regimental history, it is perhaps permissible to record in outline the drastic changes which were to follow—in the constitution of the Regiment as a whole, and the Regular battalions in particular.

In the autumn of 1946 the Army Council decided to abolish machine-gun battalions as such, and the Royal Northumberland Fusiliers reverted to their old role of an infantry regiment (except the 6th Battalion, which is still a tank battalion).

In January 1947 came the sad news that the 1st Battalion was to be placed in 'suspended animation,' following the decision that all infantry regiments were to be reduced to one Regular battalion each. This decision was implemented a few months later when the cadre of the Battalion landed at Liverpool (on the 15th May 1947) for final dispersal.

The detailed story of how, by the simple expedient of changing the numerical designation of the 2nd Battalion to 1st Battalion, the customs and traditions of the Regiment were preserved will be the task of another historian in a subsequent volume of the history of the Royal Northumberland Fusiliers.

III. THE 2ND BATTALION

The German surrender found the 2nd Battalion Royal Northumberland Fusiliers engaged in the unenviable task of keeping the peace in Greece, where years of German occupation had undermined the morale of the people and resulted in most bitter hostility between rival political factions.

The Battalion was quartered at Volos. Victory in Europe Day (8th May 1945) was followed by the Greek Labour Day (10th May) and a National Day of Prayer (13th May). These, and similar occasions, were likely to result in disorders, but violence was prevented by the system of patrolling organized by the Battalion in Volos and the surrounding villages. 1945

On the 3rd June Lieut.-Colonel E. H. Butterfield left the Battalion on promotion. This popular Commanding Officer had assumed command in the Dumfries area of Scotland in February 1943. In the two years and four months which followed he witnessed many changes in organization and led the Battalion in many lands, under an infinite variety of conditions. His part in the Battalion's successes was a very great one.

On Lieut.-Colonel Butterfield's departure Major J. A. Dewhurst took over for 10 days, when he left on release. He was followed by Major H. R. M. Wilkin, who was in turn succeeded by Major J. B. Buckle on the 2nd August.

Meanwhile the departure of many familiar faces, on release and transfer, was going on apace, and the main preoccupation of those who remained became the training of personnel to fill key appointments vacated by the departed and those about to depart.

About this time a considerable 'slump' in Greek currency occurred. This caused some consternation at first, but as the bulk of the Regimental Funds had been transferred to a home bank account, and individual funds were recouped at the new rate of exchange, no undue hardship resulted.

After a number of farewell parties the Battalion left Volos on the 15th August for a camp near the small coastal town of Stilis. Victory in Japan Day took place during the move, but was celebrated later by two days' holiday on the 24th and 25th August.

On the 18th October Lieut.-Colonel J. A. Sperling, D.S.O., arrived and assumed command of the Battalion.

By the middle of November the Battalion had moved to Khalkis, where it was quartered in a barracks which was stated to be the pride of the Greek Army. Here they celebrated Christmas and ushered in the New Year—1946.

IV. THE 4TH BATTALION

(Nos. 1, 2 and 3 Independent Machine-Gun Coys.)

No. 1 Independent Machine-Gun Coy.

On the 7th May 1945 the Company, as part of the 32nd Brigade Group (Guards Armoured Division), moved to Cuxhaven to receive the surrender of the 7th German Paratroop Division. Here they remained until the 19th when, with the rest of the Division, they commenced moving to the Rotenburg area. This was followed on the 17th June by a move to Refrath, near Bensberg, where they remained until the end of the year.

The early weeks were spent in disarming German troops, rounding up suspects, collecting and assisting displaced persons (mostly Russians) and on guard duties. The scene was somewhat enlivened at first by some Russian D.Ps. who formed themselves into bands of 'brigands,' carrying out night raids on villages and numerous

1945 acts of highway robbery. As the tempo of this work slackened more time was devoted to sport and recreation—combined with demobilization, as the various age/service groups came forward for release. The Company remained at Refrath until the end of the year.

No. 2 Independent Machine-Gun Coy.

The Company had crossed the River Elbe on the 1st May 1945 and when the German Armies surrendered on the 7th was in the vicinity of Buhnsdorf.

On the 11th they moved to Frorup (south of Flensburg on the Danish-German border). On the following day No. 3 Platoon moved to Krusaa, and this commenced a series of frontier control duties which were to be the Company's main preoccupation for the remainder of the year.

On the 17th May the O.C. Coy., Major D. L. Irwin, who had been slightly wounded on the 5th April, returned to duty.

On the 23rd May No. 3 Platoon had the experience of guarding a number of high German commanders and officials, who had surrendered to or been arrested by the Allies. Among these was Grand Admiral Doenitz, who was for a time Hitler's deputy and had been nominated by him as his successor.

By the end of May the unit had moved to permanent quarters in Harrisfeld. Here the duties consisted mainly of frontier control over a wide area, but also responsibility for the supervision of displaced persons and searching the area for suspects.

On the 13th August orders were received for conversion to an Independent Rifle Company on a special establishment; but these were cancelled a week later and the Company reverted to the machine-gun role.

The following four months were uneventful and the end of 1945 found the Company still at Harrisfeld engaged in frontier control, and in training to the machine-gun role newly joined personnel who had replaced the many who had departed on release.

No. 3 Independent Machine-Gun Coy.

When hostilities ended the Company—part of the 7th Armoured Division—was near Hamburg. After short periods at Draage, Mulhenbarbeck and Brunswick, they moved on the 4th July 1945 to Berlin, where they took part in the great Victory Parade attended by the Prime Minister, Mr. Winston Churchill. Once they had been cleaned up and repaired the quarters in Berlin were very good.

In September a second victory parade was held, and 50 members of the Company marched past the celebrated Russian general, Marshal Khukov.

In October and November the band of the 2nd Bn. Royal Northumberland Fusiliers visited Berlin, and played once a week in No. 3 Coy. lines, as well as at dances and concerts.

The Company was the only unit of the Regiment to be located in Berlin in the months immediately following the German surrender and was still there at the end of the year. Sgt. O'Neill of the Company had the distinction of broadcasting a message of greetings to those at home on the North Regional programme of the B.B.C. on Christmas Day.

V. THE 8TH BATTALION

The end of hostilities with Germany found the 8th Battalion with the 3rd Division in Western Germany, where they had been operating towards Oldenburg, south of Kiel. 1945

For some weeks they remained in the Lubeck area, engaged in collecting displaced persons, rounding up suspects and disarming German troops; but occasionally enjoying the amenities of the Regimental Club, the 'George and Dragon,' which had been opened by the Divisional Commander (Major-General L. G. Whistler, C.B., D.S.O.) shortly after hostilities ended.

In June a move was made to Freckenhorst, in Westphalia, and another in September to Bensberg. Here the Battalion said good-bye to its Commanding Officer, Lieut.-Colonel H. H. Merriman, D.S.O., M.C., who had led them in battle, with such conspicuous success, from the Normandy beaches, through France, Belgium and Holland into Western Germany. He was succeeded by Lieut.-Colonel J. K. Warner, M.C.

In October the 8th Battalion moved again, this time to Menden. Here they had a strenuous time—organizing Polish D.P. camps and checking their inmates, supervising the curfew regulations and in guard and other occupational duties. The task was not made easier by the continuous drain on officers and men as successive age/service groups departed on release.

By December 1945 the unit had left the famous 3rd Division, with whom they had served so long, and joined the 49th (West Riding) Division.

On the 29th December they had the satisfaction of winning the final of the Divisional Football Cup, defeating the 111th Heavy A.A. Regiment R.A. by 9 goals to 2.

The 8th Bn. Royal Northumberland Fusiliers were still at Menden at the end of the year.

NOTE: The story of the reforming of the Territorial Army Battalions of the Regiment on a post-war footing must await the publication of another volume of the history. It will suffice to give a statement of the units as they exist at the time of writing (October 1951):

Royal Northumberland Fusiliers—T.A. Battalions

4/5th Bn. (Infantry) .	Based on Newcastle and the Tyne area.
6th Bn. (Tanks) .	Known officially as '43rd Bn. Royal Tank Regiment (6th City Bn. Royal Northumberland Fusiliers).'
7th Bn. (Infantry) .	Based on Alnwick, with Drill Halls at Alnwick, Morpeth, Berwick and Ashington.

There are also six Cadet Battalions, known as '1st, 2nd, etc., Cadet Bn. Royal Northumberland Fusiliers.'

CONCLUSION

THIS chapter is the epilogue to the story of the Royal Northumberland Fusiliers in, perhaps, the most momentous years of the Regiment's long and honourable career in the service of King and Country.

The book records the uphill struggle of Regular and Territorial peace-time soldiers during the lean years from 1919 to 1933; the period of rearmament, commencing in 1933, but still incomplete when hostilities commenced; and the years of struggle between 1939 and 1945 when men from many walks of life fought with the various Battalions of the Fighting Fifth.

The Regiment has always had a very strong county connection and tradition. The men from Northumberland have ever been its backbone. Nevertheless, during the war years it absorbed men from most parts of the United Kingdom and from many Commonwealth countries of British stock. Representatives from almost every Christian denomination were to be found in its ranks. Whatever their stock or creed they soon assimilated the traditions and spirit of the Fighting Fifth and contributed to its fame.

The Regiment was represented in almost every theatre of operations—the 2nd, 4th, 7th, 8th and 9th Battalions at Dunkirk; the 1st Battalion throughout the North Africa campaign and the 4th in the epic stand at Knightsbridge; the 1st and 2nd Battalions in Italy; the 9th at Singapore, followed by their staunch and dignified conduct as prisoners in Japanese hands; the 7th and 8th Battalions and the three Independent Companies (formed from the 4th Battalion) in North-West Europe. This is a record of battle service of which the people of Northumberland may well be proud.

The nature of the machine-gun and reconnaissance role of most Battalions resulted in wide dispersion, and heavy responsibility falling on Company and Platoon Commanders and other junior leaders. They were not found wanting in these conditions. The episode which earned a posthumous Victoria Cross for Captain J. J. B. Jackman of Z Company of the 1st Battalion in North Africa on the 25th November 1941 is as fine an example of heroism and initiative as can be found in the history of our Army.

Now the Regiment—represented by the 1st Battalion, the amalgamated 4/5th Battalion and the 7th Battalion—is once again in its traditional character of an Infantry Regiment of the Line; while the 43rd Bn. Royal Tank Regiment is still the 6th City Battalion Royal Northumberland Fusiliers, and as such retains its old associations as a member of the family of The Fifth.

At the time of writing the 1st Battalion, with a high proportion of National Servicemen in its ranks, is again on active service in Korea, fighting in the old cause of liberty. Its Commanding Officer, Lieut.-Colonel K. O. N. Foster, and many others have fallen in battle. The full story of Korea has yet to be written, but who can doubt that present and future generations of the Fighting Fifth will acquit themselves as nobly as their predecessors.*

Let all who read this history remember the men to whom the book is dedicated—those soldiers of the Royal Northumberland Fusiliers who, in the years 1939–45, marched to war and did not come back.

GOD SAVE THE QUEEN.

---

* How well this forecast has been fulfilled can be judged from the Roll of Honour and List of Awards for Korea which have been added as Appendix E to this volume.

APPENDIX A

THE VOYAGE OF THE 'PUSH-ME-PULLU'

A short record of the adventures of a party of the 9th Bn. Royal Northumberland Fusiliers who escaped from Singapore Island at the time of its surrender in February 1942

THE party of the 9th Battalion ordered, together with 500 representatives of other units and formations, to attempt escape from Singapore consisted of Major B. J. Leech, R.S.M. Johnson, C.S.M. McQuade, A/S/Sgt. Rides (R.A.O.C. attached), Cpl. Sidey and Fusiliers Bennett and Casey. All were volunteers for the enterprise, though at first believing that it was to be a 'cutting out' expedition against the Japanese base on the Island.

At 7 p.m. on the 14th February, the date fixed for departure, Major Leech was informed that the only three craft available to the C.R.E., who had been made responsible for the embarkation, had been filled to capacity and had left; and that those who still remained unprovided for should be given the option of returning to their units or of making an individual effort to leave the Island. Major Leech explained to his party the danger and hardship likely to be involved in the latter choice, but all elected to go through with the venture.

To search for a boat the Regimental party, shortly after dark, left for the docks, which were being intermittently shelled. There, providentially, they came into touch with Captain T. V. H. Beamish (of The Fifth and G.S. 18th Division), who had acquired an 18-foot rowing-boat and had located a second dinghy. Captain Beamish and Mr. J. R. Miller of the Federated Malay States Volunteer Force, whose knowledge of the Malay people and their language was to prove invaluable, joined the party.

Here space allows only the barest outline of the remarkable voyage that started the same night from island to island of the Rhio Archipelago, but of which all should read the full account which appeared in the *St. George's Gazette*.*

The boat, by rowing, was brought at 3.30 a.m. on the 15th to St. John's Island, where the party was joined by Bombardier Chambers, R.A., who had swum over from a neighbouring island. Later in the day, the second dinghy having been abandoned, the voyage was continued, with some brief help of a tow by a junk, to Palau Samboe. On the following day a bamboo mast and some 'home-made' sails were obtained from a village on a nearby island, and the 'Push-me-Pullu,' as the boat had been christened, became a sailing ship.

Leech, as skipper, was assisted by Beamish as navigation officer. Johnson, selected as doctor for 'his soothing bedside manner,' had, as it was to prove, no sinecure. Other appointments were McQuade as quartermaster and sailmaker; Rides, assisted by Casey and Bennett, as cook; while without Miller as liaison officer with friendly islanders, the expedition might have suffered sadly from lack of provisions and necessary tackle. And so this strange craft, under the shadow of occasional Japanese airplanes and receiving constant reports of enemy occupation of neighbouring islands, without keel or centreboard, with a small broken oar as

---

* *St. George's Gazette* of June 1942.

rudder, and manned by soldiers, gained the east coast of Sumatra on the 21st February after a voyage of some 80 miles and countless adventures—an achievement surely in accord with the privilege so long enjoyed by The Fifth of playing 'Rule Britannia' in conjunction with their Regimental march!

Though this was the end of the 'Push-me-Pullu,' it was not the last of the adventure. A journey of over 200 miles to Padang on the west coast of Sumatra, where other escaping personnel were assembling, still lay before the party. This was made along the line of the River Indragiri, partly by boat, partly on foot, also by lorry, and lastly by rail. Padang was reached on the 28th February, but the prospect of a ship arriving to take off the 700 British civilians and soldiers there assembled seemed doubtful. At 4 p.m. on the 1st March a man-of-war was reported lying off Padang which could take 400 troops to Colombo. Within a half-hour this number was aboard and had left—but it had not included Leech's party. For them the last hope of escape seemed gone. The Japanese were known to be approaching, and they resigned themselves to fighting it out. Then, at 5 p.m., the astonishing news was received of the arrival of no fewer than *five* ships. In complete ignorance of the situation at Padang, these had only called in at the small port on account of having been unable to refuel at Batavia. An hour later the party was filing up the gangway of a British destroyer, and in two hours more, having been transferred to another man-of-war, they were heading north-west for Ceylon and safety.

The view at the outset, that the escape was being embarked upon as something in the nature of a forlorn hope, was justified by the fate which overtook too many of the others who attempted it. But though fortune had favoured them, Leech's party could not have succeeded in the enterprise had they not been inspired by the same spirit which carried their less fortunate comrades of the 9th Battalion through the horrors of the captivity which they had so providentially escaped.

APPENDIX B

ROLL OF COMMANDING OFFICERS OF UNITS OF THE ROYAL NORTHUMBERLAND FUSILIERS—1919–1945

Unit	*Commanding Officer*	*Month and year of appointment*
Colonels of the Regiment	Major-General Sir Percival S. Wilkinson, K.C.M.G., C.B.	20th January 1915
	Major-General W. N. Herbert,* C.B., C.M.G., D.S.O., D.C.L.	5th July 1935
Regtl. Depot and Training Centre	Major R. Auld	March 1919
	Major B. Cruddas, D.S.O.	September 1919
	Major R. M. St.J. Booth, D.S.O.	September 1922
	Bt. Lieut.-Colonel W. Platt, D.S.O.	April 1926
	Major J. F. Chenevix-Trench, D.S.O.	December 1927
	Major H. I. Powell	January 1931
	Major E. G. M. Buckley	January 1934
	Major J. H. Hogshaw, M.C.	January 1937
	Major H. F. Attwater	January 1938
	Major D. C. Bucknall } Depot Party	November 1941
	Major D. V. Redhead } Depot Party	June 1942
	Major R. H. Yorke } Depot Party	April 1946
1st Battalion	Lieut.-Colonel B. Cruddas, D.S.O.	September 1918
	Bt. Colonel C. Yatman, C.M.G., D.S.O.	July 1919
	Lieut.-Colonel A. C. L. Hardman-Jones	November 1921
	Lieut.-Colonel W. N. Herbert, C.M.G., D.S.O.	November 1925
	Lieut.-Colonel R. M. Booth, D.S.O.	November 1929
	Lieut.-Colonel J. F. Chenevix-Trench, D.S.O.	November 1933
	Lieut.-Colonel J. G. des R. Swayne	September 1935
	Lieut.-Colonel E. E. Dorman-Smith, M.C.	April 1937
	Lieut.-Colonel J. H. Hogshaw, M.C.	May 1938
	Lieut.-Colonel E. O. Martin	May 1941
	Lieut.-Colonel R. F. Forbes-Watson	December 1943
	Lieut.-Colonel M. C. Speer	March 1945
2nd Battalion	Lieut.-Colonel A. C. L. Hardman Jones	October 1915
	Lieut.-Colonel E. M. Moulton-Barrett, D.S.O.	June 1919
	Lieut.-Colonel H. R. Sandilands, C.M.G., D.S.O.	November 1921
	Lieut.-Colonel S. H. Kershaw, D.S.O.	September 1925
	Lieut.-Colonel O. B. Foster, M.C.	September 1929
	Lieut.-Colonel A. P. Garnier, M.B.E., M.C.	September 1933
	Lieut.-Colonel H. de R. Morgan, D.S.O.	September 1936
	Lieut.-Colonel T. C. L. Redwood	February 1940
	Lieut.-Colonel F. H. Butterfield	February 1943

* Major-General Herbert was succeeded by the present Colonel of the Regiment, Major-General H. de R. Morgan, D.S.O., on 1st January 1947.

Unit	*Commanding Officer*	*Month and year of appointment*
4th Battalion later formed into ↓	Lieut.-Colonel J. R. Robb	June 1920
	Lieut.-Colonel C. O. P. Gibson, M.C.	May 1922
	Lieut.-Colonel B. Cruddas, D.S.O.	May 1927
	Lieut.-Colonel A. B. Hare, M.C.	May 1932
	Lieut.-Colonel R. Wood, T.D.	November 1936
	Lieut.-Colonel E. P. A. des Graz	April 1941
	Lieut.-Colonel E. H. D. Grimley	December 1942
Independent M.G. Coys. No. 1	Major R. M. Pratt	April 1944
	Major H. B. van der Gucht	December 1944
No. 2	Major E. E. M. Williams	April 1944
	Major A. M. Bonham-Carter	July 1944
	Major D. L. Irwin	September 1944
No. 3	Major H. B. van der Gucht	April 1944
	Major W. E. N. Davis	July 1944
	Captain L. W. Byrne	April 1945
	Major G. D. Paterson	June 1945
5th Battalion	Lieut.-Colonel A. Irwin, D.S.O., T.D.	May 1920
	Lieut.-Colonel W. Anderson, D.S.O., M.C.	February 1926
	Lieut.-Colonel B. Peatfield, M.C.	December 1931
	Lieut.-Colonel W. H. Leete, D.F.C., T.D.	December 1937
	Lieut.-Colonel L. N. Side, O.B.E., T.D.	December 1943
	Lieut.-Colonel W. O. N. Hammond, O.B.E., T.D.	August 1944
6th Battalion later formed into ↓	Lieut.-Colonel E. Temperley	February 1920
	Lieut.-Colonel A. D. S. Rogers, T.D.	March 1924
	Lieut.-Colonel G. E. Wilkinson, M.C.	March 1928
	Lieut.-Colonel G. F. Bell	March 1932
	Lieut.-Colonel F. Dawson, M.C., T.D.	March 1936
No. 43 R.T.R.	Lieut.-Colonel F. Dawson, M.C., T.D.	September 1939
No. 49 R.T.R.	Lieut.-Colonel C. B. Carrick, M.C., T.D.	September 1939
7th Battalion	Lieut.-Colonel N. I. Wright, D.S.O., T.D.	February 1920
	Lieut.-Colonel Hon. H. B. Robson	February 1927
	Lieut.-Colonel A. J. K. Todd, M.P.	August 1932
	Lieut.-Colonel G. E. Fenwicke-Clennell	August 1936
	Lieut.-Colonel R. W. H. Fryer, M.C.	September 1940
	Lieut.-Colonel P. Earle	January 1944

Unit	*Commanding Officer*	*Month and year of appointment*
8th Battalion	Lieut.-Colonel F. B. Clarke, T.D. Lieut.-Colonel J. L. Challoner Lieut.-Colonel E. H. D. Grimley Lieut.-Colonel E. C. Bols Lieut.-Colonel H. H. Merriman	May 1939 May 1940 July 1940 April 1942 November 1942
9th Battalion	Lieut.-Colonel S. H. Gallon Lieut.-Colonel L. C. Thomas	May 1939 April 1940
10th Battalion later renumbered 30th Battalion	Lieut.-Colonel R. Allen Lieut.-Colonel H. A. Macpherson Lieut.-Colonel P. Allen Lieut.-Colonel R. H. Rohde Lieut.-Colonel J. Blenkinsop	October 1939 June 1941 October 1941 May 1942 June 1944
70th Battalion	Lieut.-Colonel J. O. Byrne, M.C.	September 1940 (until disbandment in November 1942)

APPENDIX C

HONOURS AND AWARDS

Summary of awards conferred on officers and other ranks during the period 3rd September 1939 to 26th January 1946

Theatre of operations	*V.C.*	*C.B.E.*	*O.B.E.*	*M.B.E.*	*B.E.M.*	*Bar to D.S.O.*	*D.S.O.*	*Second Bar to M.C.*	*Bar to M.C.*	*M.C.*	*D.C.M.*	*Bar to M.M.*	*M.M.*	*Mention in Despatches*	*Total*
Middle East . . .	1	—	—	3	1	—	1	—	2	9	3	1	31	59	111
B.E.F. 1940 . . .	—	—	1	2	—	—	1	—	—	9	5	—	14	37	69
Italy	—	—	3	4	—	1	2	—	—	6	—	—	8	47	71
Burma	—	1	1	—	—	—	1	—	—	1	—	—	—	8	12
North-West Europe .	1	—	—	1	—	—	1	—	—	7	2	—	5	28	45
Escaped prisoners of war	—	—	—	—	—	—	—	—	—	2	1	—	7	9	19
Half-yearly awards .	—	—	2	1	1	—	—	—	—	—	—	—	—	—	4
Miscellaneous operations	—	1	—	—	—	—	—	1	—	8	—	—	2	19	31
Total . .	2	2	7	11	2	1	6	1	2	42	11	1	67	207	362

Detailed statement of awards

V.C.

Major R. H. Cain
Capt. J. J. B. Jackman

C.B.E.

Col. G. C. Humphreys
Brig. L. C. Thomas, D.S.O., O.B.E., M.C.

O.B.E.

Major G. H. Bolster
Lt.-Col. F. H. Butterfield
Lt.-Col. H. S. Flower
Capt. H. O. Murton
Lt.-Col. F. G. A. Parsons

M.B.E.

C.S.M. R. Babington
Capt. C. R. I. Besley
Capt. W. R. E. Brown
Major W. A. C. Collingwood
Major W. J. P. Croft
Capt. O. C. Dipper, D.C.M.
Major E. A. Gutteridge
Capt. L. F. Hay
Major G. P. Hobbs
W.O. A. Hollick, A.R.C.M.
Lt. J. W. M. Purcell

British Empire Medal

L/Cpl. F. H. Dixon
C.Q.M.S. J. A. Dixon

Bar to D.S.O.

Lt.-Col. L. C. Thomas, D.S.O., O.B.E., M.C.

D.S.O.

Lt.-Col. S. Enderby, M.C.
Brig. R. W. H. Fryer, M.C.
Col. B. J. Leech
Lt.-Col. E. O. Martin
Lt.-Col. J. A. Sperling
Lt.-Col. L. C. Thomas, O.B.E., M.C.

2nd Bar to M.C.

Capt. D. C. McCreath, M.C.

Bar to M.C.

Capt. D. L. Lloyd, M.C.
Capt. D. C. McCreath, M.C.

M.C.

2/Lt. G. W. Anderson
Capt. T. V. H. Beamish
Lt. E. M. H. Beckingham
Capt. C. R. I. Besley, M.B.E.
Capt. B. Fitz G. Blood
2/Lt. H. E. W. G. Brown
Lt. H. W. G. G. Brown
Capt. H. B. Burn
Lt. J. H. G. Deighton
Capt. T. F. Ellison
Lt. H. G. Ferguson
Capt. P. B. Gorst
Lt. D. J. Graham
Major T. F. G. Hamilton
Lt. A. W. Harper
Lt. W. V. Hart
Capt. A. E. Hedley, M.B.E.
Lt. E. M. Hill
2/Lt. A. W. R. Leinster
Capt. D. L. Lloyd
Lt. C. K. Lockerby
Capt. D. C. McCreath
Lt. H. Marsh
2/Lt. J. S. W. Meikle
Capt. R. Mitchell
Capt. J. S. Moore
Lt. J. F. Nixon
Capt. R. E. Orr
Major W. C. W. Potts
Lt. D. F. Puleston
Lt. E. J. B. Raymond
Lt. M. M. Roberts
2/Lt. A. D. W. Ross
Major R. E. T. St. John
Lt. D. W. W. Selby
Lt. H. J. Sweeney
Capt. J. E. Tonkin
Capt. J. Turland
Major H. B. Van der Gucht
2/Lt. F. Ward
Major R. D. Wilson
Major H. J. Winn

U.S.A. Bronze Star Medal

Lt.-Col. M. Robson

Belgium Croix de Guerre 1940 *with Palm*

Fus. H. R. Calvert
Lt. E. P. Garland
Fus. P. Spreckley

D.C.M.

S.M. J. W. Brooks
Fus. R. Burnett
Sgt. R. Chambers, M.M.
Sgt. T. Cottrell
C.S.M. G. Hughes
Cpl. J. McCloy
Sgt. D. McKay
Sgt. J. A. Palfreeman
Fus. J. Purvis
P.S.M. J. Sanlon
Sgt. J. F. Thompson

Bar to M.M.

L/Sgt. R. Chambers, M.M.

M.M.

L/Sgt. T. W. Addinall
Fus. J. W. Barnes
Cpl. P. F. Baxter
Sgt. G. Bell
C.S.M. P. W. Bell
C.S.M. T. C. Boyle
Fus. R. Burnett, D.C.M.
Sgt. J. Campbell
Cpl. A. Cardwell
L/Sgt. R. Chambers
Sgt. G. E. Charlton
Fus. F. Chrystal
Fus. R. R. Clark
Fus. J. F. Clarke
L/Sgt. J. E. Coates
A/Sgt. J. Dobson
Fus. E. Edwards
Sgt. W. Elliott
Cpl. S. Fram
Fus. R. Graham
Fus. R. A. Hall

M.M.—contd.
Cpl. H. Hanlon
Cpl. J. R. Harbottle
Sgt. L. Harland
Fus. J. Higgins
C.Q.M.S. T. A. Hughes
L/Cpl. J. Jones
Fus. J. W. Kay
Sgt. R. Kenning
Cpl. P. B. Kirby
L/Cpl. H. Lamb
L/Cpl. F. Lloyd
Fus. E. McCann
Sgt. W. McCracken
Fus. W. McDonald
Sgt. R. McGregor
Fus. J. R. Marley
Sgt. E. Midcalf
Sgt. R. Miller
Sgt. S. B. Mitchell
Fus. E. G. Moore
Fus. J. Murray
Cpl. R. Myers
Fus. F. A. D. Peary
L/Cpl. E. Prady
Fus. T. E. Preston
Sgt. M. Punton
Sgt. R. Ramsay
Cpl. H. Ratcliffe
Cpl. N. R. Reed
Fus. A. Ridley
C.S.M. R. Riley
Fus. A. Robinson
Fus. G. W. Ryles
C.Q.M.S. H. Sanderson
L/Cpl. G. Scott
Sgt. W. Shaftoe
Sgt. A. E. Sheppard
Fus. H. Slaughter
L/Cpl. C. A. Sleight
Sgt. J. Smith
Sgt. D. Sowerby
Sgt. J. Spratt
Fus. W. Taylor
Fus. J. F. B. Watson
Fus. W. D. H. Williams
Fus. C. Wilson
W.O. F. W. Wool

NOTE: The above list does not include awards conferred on officers of other units attached to the Royal Northumberland Fusiliers during the operations recorded in this history. On the other hand, certain of the officers of the Regiment whose names are given received the awards shown when detached to the staff or to other units. Among the latter is Major R. H. Cain, V.C., whose citation for the Victoria Cross is given below.

Citation for the Victoria Cross

Captain (temporary Major) Robert Henry Cain (129484), *The Royal Northumberland Fusiliers (attached 2nd Battalion The South Staffordshire Regiment)* (*1st Airborne Division*)

In Holland on 19th September 1944, Major Cain was commanding a rifle company of the South Staffordshire Regiment during the Battle of Arnhem when his company was cut off from the rest of the battalion and during the next six days was closely engaged with enemy tanks, self-propelled guns and infantry. The Germans made repeated attempts to break into the company position by infiltration and had they succeeded in doing so the whole situation of the Airborne troops would have been jeopardized.

Major Cain, by his outstanding devotion to duty and remarkable powers of leadership, was to a large extent personally responsible for saving a vital sector from falling into the hands of the enemy.

On 20th September, a Tiger tank approached the area held by this company and Major Cain went out alone to deal with it armed with a Piat. Taking up a position he held his fire until the tank was only 20 yards away when he opened up. The tank immediately halted and turned its guns on him, shooting away a corner of the house near where this officer was lying. Although wounded by machine-gun bullets and falling masonry, Major Cain continued firing until he had scored several direct hits, immobilized the tank and supervised the bringing up of a 75-mm. howitzer which completely destroyed it. Only then would he consent to have his wounds dressed.

The next morning this officer drove off three more tanks by the fearless use of his Piat, on each occasion leaving cover and taking up position in open ground with complete disregard for his personal safety.

During the following days, Major Cain was everywhere where danger threatened, moving amongst his men and encouraging them by his fearless example to hold out. He refused rest and medical attention in spite of the fact that his hearing had been seriously impaired because of a perforated eardrum and he was suffering from multiple wounds.

On the 25th September the enemy made a concerted attack on Major Cain's position, using self-propelled guns, flame-throwers and infantry. By this time the last Piat had been put out of action and Major Cain was armed with only a 2-in. mortar. However, by a skilful use of this weapon and his daring leadership of the few men still under his command, he completely demoralized the enemy who, after an engagement lasting more than three hours, withdrew in disorder.

Throughout the whole course of the Battle of Arnhem, Major Cain showed superb gallantry. His powers of endurance and leadership were the admiration of all his fellow officers and stories of his valour were being constantly exchanged amongst the troops. His coolness and courage under incessant fire could not be surpassed.

APPENDIX D

ROLL OF HONOUR, 1939 TO 1945

Killed in action, died of wounds and died

10602656 Tpr. Adam, R. F.
4448902 Fus. Adams, G.
4267371 Fus. Adams, J. R.
4269384 Fus. Aisbitt, J. S.
4271826 L/Cpl. Aiston, H.
14328825 Fus. Aitchison, J.
4274062 Fus. Alexander, L.
4271887 Fus. Allan, F. E.
4272112 Fus. Almond, J.
4263441 Sgt. Amos, R.
4265416 W.O.I Anderson, J.
4269972 Fus. Anderson, J. B.
13071310 Cpl. Angus, G.
4274120 Fus. Angus, S.
4278354 Tpr. Appleby, A.
4270130 Sgt. Appleby, W. A. S.
4274239 Cpl. Aries, S.
4273537 Sgt. Armstrong, A.
4272979 Cpl. Armstrong, F.
4277002 Fus. Armstrong, J.
Capt. Armstrong, R. W.
6918366 Tpr. Ascott, P. H.
4275277 Fus. Atkinson, A.
Lt.-Col. Attwater, H. F.
6214017 Tpr. Austin, W. A.
6210695 Tpr. Bainbridge, E. D.
4607797 Fus. Bamford, B.
14347060 Fus. Barker, H.
4275682 Sgt. Barlow, A. J.
4270543 Fus. Barnes, J. W.
5512073 Fus. Bartlett, L. J.
4279175 Fus. Baxter, D.
4276185 Sgt. Bell, A.
4274122 Fus. Bell, G. R. H.
4267892 Fus. Bell, J. R. P.
4276625 Fus. Bell, N.
6847822 Sgt. Bell, R.
4276384 L/Cpl. Bell, T. F.
4268862 Tpr. Bell, W.
4397265 Fus. Bennet, L.
Major Bennett, T., M.C.
4127854 Fus. Bensley, W. H.
6916300 Fus. Berwick, W. T.
Major Besley, C. R. I., M.C., M.B.E.
4270109 Cpl. Beveridge, J.
6473631 Tpr. Bewley, W. C.
4127756 L/Cpl. Bishop, T. H.
4267620 Fus. Black, D.
4125605 Cpl. Blain, C. W.
6215416 Fus. Blair, J. R.
4270964 Fus. Blake, T.
4269432 Fus. Blakey, T. L.
2/Lt. Bland, T. B.
6216875 Fus. Blavins, H.
14600159 Tpr. Bloomfield, L. S.
5118084 Fus. Blount, F. W.
6921002 Fus. Blunden, T. H. G.
6353385 Fus. Bodley, G.
Lt.-Col. Bolster, G. H., O.B.E.
3531240 Fus. Bolton, G.
4265849 L/Sgt. Bond, E.
4278076 Fus. Bond, L.
Major Bonham-Carter, A. M.
4278184 Cpl. Bootland, W.
4274155 Fus. Borthwick, A.
4273903 L/Sgt. Boswell, D. G.
4447835 Fus. Bowen, J. J.
4266681 Sgt. Bowles, P. D. S.
3443179 Tpr. Boyson, T.
4608901 Sgt. Bradbury, A.
Major Braddell, W. H.
3185669 L/Sgt. Bradley, T. J.
4273230 Fus. Brady, M.
4611436 Fus. Brain, J. J.
4257334 W.O.II Bramley, L. R.
4276628 Fus. Bramwell, J. G.
5889155 Fus. Branson, H. L.
6211222 Fus. Brent, V. I.
6915237 Cpl. Brinkley, J. B.
4270112 W.O.II Brooks, A.
14217470 Fus. Brooks, A. L.
6207629 Cpl. Brown, A.
4274207 L/Cpl. Brown, F.
4269030 Fus. Brown, G. M.
Lieut. Brown, H. E. W. G., M.C.

4273357 L/Cpl. Brown, J.
4263885 Fus. Brown, J. A.
6214882 Fus. Brown, J. E.
4264268 Fus. Brown, N. L.
4273303 Sgt. Brown, R. R.
4275420 Fus. Brown, W. H.
4278538 Fus. Brownbridge, H. G.
4394782 Cpl. Bruce, W.
6212449 Fus. Brunt, B.
6920679 Fus. Bryant, W. J.
4275149 Sgt. Brydon, S.
4274914 Fus. Bryson, J. J.
6914296 Fus. Buck, S.
Major Buckley, E. G. M.
7662455 L/Cpl. Buie, J. W. B.
14440008 Tpr. Bulmanory, C.
Lieut. Burdes, T. N.
7918675 Fus. Burgess, F. C.
4271358 Fus. Burgon, J.
4133445 Tpr. Burke, T.
4278376 Fus. Burn, N.
4274209 Fus. Burnett, A.
4277223 Fus. Burton, F.
4275233 L/Sgt. Byrne, R.
4277015 Fus. Bywater, J.
4275792 Fus. Cable, J. S.
29358 Fus. Caddle, R. H.
4277224 Fus. Cain, S.
4273542 Fus. Caisley, C. S.
4275793 Fus. Calvert, A. J.
6470926 Tpr. Cambridge, J.
6914299 Fus. Campbell, R.
5733741 L/Cpl. Capper, G. L.
4543111 Tpr. Capper, H.
4272852 Fus. Carnall, A.
3527635 Sgt. Carr, A.
4461259 Tpr. Carr, B.
4267592 Sgt. Carrott, D.
4127738 Fus. Carsley, G.
14238437 Tpr. Carter, J. W. G.
4463406 Tpr. Carter, T.
4273543 Fus. Carter, W.
4275988 Fus. Cartwright, W. E.
4275798 Fus. Castle, J.
14331538 Fus. Caswell, A. E.
4274068 Fus. Chapman, J.
6202681 Cpl. Chapman, S. J.
4275800 Fus. Charleson, O.
4265606 Cpl. Charlton, G. T.
4278380 Fus. Charlton, T.
4269616 Fus. Chipchase, F. W.
4273974 Fus. Chisholm, T. W.
4265871 Cpl. Chitty, T. O.
14668857 Fus. Clague, G.
4272761 Fus. Clark, A.
4273813 Fus. Clark, J. W.
4272750 Sgt. Clark, R.
4273726 L/Sgt. Clark, R.
6915442 Fus. Clark, S. L.
4276638 Fus. Clark, T.
4275626 Fus. Clarke, J.
4279265 Fus. Clarkson, E.
4275278 Fus. Clayton, A. W.
6914595 Fus. Clements, A.
5619676 Fus. Cloke, H.
6412189 Fus. Cobby, R. C.
16224 Fus. Cochrane, H.
4273306 Fus. Coffey, J.
4274935 Fus. Collier, J. H.
6914309 Fus. Collings, F. J.
4270942 Fus. Collins, T. L.
4536857 Sgt. Collinson, J.
21966 Fus. Combs, J. W.
4273723 Fus. Conway, F.
4273724 Fus. Cook, J. P.
4273814 Fus. Cook, J. R.
4267471 Fus. Cooke, A. W.
Lieut. Cooper, A.
6297409 Fus. Cooper, D. J.
3537014 Fus. Cooper, J.
10601810 Tpr. Cooper, R.
4278197 Fus. Corr, B.
14296524 L/Cpl. Corry, E.
4275390 Fus. Coskin, C.
4268105 Fus. Coulson, L.
4271203 Fus. Coutts, J.
3185292 Cpl. Cowan, H.
4276641 Fus. Cowan, J. R.
4270931 Fus. Cowen, W. H.
4276776 Fus. Crampton, K. G.
4276403 Fus. Craven, C.
4279309 Fus. Cree, N. A.
14741537 Fus. Cree, W. G.
4278386 Fus. Critchley, E.
4276896 Fus. Crowther, T.
4273872 Fus. Crozier, A.
4276642 Fus. Cummings, J. G.
4272051 Fus. Cummings, W. W.
4459635 Sgt. Curry, H. W.
4277030 Sgt. Curry, W.
Lieut. Curtis, S. G.
14245426 Cpl. Dadswell, P. J.
4278033 Sgt. Dakin, A. H.
4275007 Fus. Dale, C. G. N.
6210435 Fus. Daniels, R. H.
6475044 Cpl. Davidge, E. C. L.
4121529 Fus. Davies, W. H.
6210007 Fus. Davis, E. G.

4268519 Cpl. Davison, F. A.
4273982 Fus. Davison, G.
14531484 Fus. Dawson, S. W.
3663209 Fus. Deakins, K.
6923683 Fus. Dean, G. F.
4268264 Fus. Dean, W.
14661055 Tpr. Debney, T.
4274961 Fus. Dees, James B.
6915455 Fus. Dellow, A. J.
4265878 L/Cpl. Derbyshire, J.
4277111 L/Sgt. De Roux, M. E.
13021650 Tpr. Deville, L.
7947287 Fus. Dewhurst, E. W.
4271470 Fus. Dirom, G.
4612503 Fus. Dishman, R. J.
4270192 Fus. Dixon, E.
10601821 L/Sgt. Dixon, F. W.
4278978 Fus. Dixon, R. P.
4278543 Fus. Dodd, J. T.
4272044 Sgt. Dodd, T.
4278713 Tpr. Dodds, A. L.
4278202 Tpr. Dodds, A. M.
4275666 L/Cpl. Dodds, R.
14590755 Tpr. Doherty, T. P.
4278525 Fus. Doherty, T. W.
14262792 Tpr. Doncom, M. G.
4271379 Fus. Donnelly, J.
4276646 Fus. Doran, J. G.
4273547 Fus. Douglas, W.
4275043 Fus. Douthwaite, L.
4271693 Fus. Dowie, A.
Lieut. Dowie, D. A.
4271189 Fus. Dowson, R. W.
3387422 Sgt. Duffy, C.
4273273 Fus. Dunbar, A.
2/Lt. Duncan, S.
4274124 Fus. Dunlop, J.
4268129 Fus. Dunn, J. C.
4270994 Fus. Durkin, J.
4127820 L/Cpl. Eagleton, G.
Major Eardley, W. A.
4267024 Cpl. Eastlake, G.
4271561 Tpr. Eddy, R. R.
4200984 Tpr. Edwards, R. N.
4133506 Fus. Edwards, S.
4278397 Fus. Egdell, T.
4270120 L/Cpl. Eley, A.
4269335 Cpl. Elliot, J.
4273911 Fus. Elliot, R. D.
4273988 Fus. Elliot, S.
6290699 Fus. Elliott, C. G.
4273336 Fus. Elliott, P.
14300560 Fus. Ellis, R. E.
4279057 Fus. Ellis, R. P.
4275821 Fus. Ellis, W.
4133625 Tpr. Elson, S. C.
4274806 Fus. Emerson, J. A.
20552 Cpl. Emery, W.
4275284 Fus. Errington, G.
4275669 L/Cpl. Eyton, C.
6918710 Tpr. Fairhall, T. C.
2818461 Fus. Falcus, J. A.
4126733 Fus. Farrington, C.
14400272 Fus. Farthing, E. B.
4444571 Cpl. Fawcett, R.
3776908 L/Sgt. Fay, J. J.
30446 Fus. Fearon, P.
4268498 Fus. Fell, M. S.
14587305 L/Cpl. Ferguson, R.
4279270 Fus. Finlinson, J. R.
4273993 Fus. Fleming, A.
4272024 Cpl. Fletcher, A.
4279111 Fus. Flynn, J.
4270111 L/Sgt. Flynn, J. H.
Lieut. Flynn, W. T.
4271162 Fus. Ford, E.
4275825 Cpl. Ford, J. A.
4271537 L/Cpl. Foreman, G. A.
4270798 W.O.II Forster, D.
4273913 Cpl. Forster, J. A.
4278208 Fus. Foster, W.
4268853 Fus. Fowler, N. J.
4266604 Sgt. Fox, F. W.
3607179 Tpr. Fox, G. W.
14555585 Tpr. France, R.
4275361 Fus. Fraser, S. J.
4274908 Fus. Fromson, T. M.
4276064 Cpl. Gair, G.
4268612 Fus. Gair, W.
4276066 L/Cpl. Gallagher, V. W.
4277417 Fus. Gardner, J.
4275066 Fus. Garside, H.
Lieut. Gatfield, D. H.
4266584 Fus. Geddes, J.
4271190 L/Cpl. Gee, W.
4278051 Sgt. Gibbins, R. F.
6921574 Cpl. Gibbs, W. W.
4271803 Fus. Gilbert, F.
14219726 Fus. Gillan, F. G.
Lieut. Gillinder, A. F.
4275834 Fus. Glancey, F.
4275178 Cpl. Goodwill, H. C.
4269416 L/Cpl. Goundry, L. J.
4263171 Fus. Graham, G.
4273368 Tpr. Graham, W. J.
4277490 Fus. Granville, J. E.
4461747 Sgt. Gray, P.
6214395 Fus. Greene, M.

4270068 Fus. Gregg, R. B.
6210596 Fus. Gregson, H.
4273690 Fus. Grey, J.
4274505 Fus. Grey, William
4270785 Cpl. Grieve, T. B.
4263609 L/Cpl. Griffen, P. E.
553906 L/Sgt. Griffiths, J.
4279571 Fus. Griffiths, R. R.
4122540 Sgt. Grimmer, J.
140583 2/Lt. Grocott, H. W.
4127724 Fus. Grundy, H.
4122579 Sgt. Gunning, J.
14888173 Fus. Gwilliam, H.
4278615 Fus. Hadden, W. J.
4279679 Tpr. Hall, G. A.
4277075 Fus. Hall, J.
4279329 Fus. Hall, J.
4277071 Fus. Hall, J. H.
4275395 Fus. Hall, R.
4270556 Fus. Hall, W.
4264979 L/Sgt. Hall, W. F.
4271168 Fus. Hamlet, J. E.
3534822 Cpl. Hammond, A.
10603609 Cpl. Hand, J. T.
4126886 Fus. Hanlon, D.
4269844 Cpl. Hanlon, H., M.M.
4271423 Fus. Hannay, C. B.
4607211 Sgt. Hardiment, W. J.
14257501 Fus. Harding, B.
4272818 Fus. Hardwick, C. E.
4267956 Sgt. Hardy, E.
4269945 Fus. Hardy, H.
4266869 Sgt. Hardy, W. M.
4442619 Fus. Harper, W. M.
2089473 Cpl. Harris, A.
14353968 Fus. Harris, E. R.
4267544 Cpl. Harrison, J. H.
Capt. Hart, E. B. L.
4273428 Cpl. Hart, R.
4256659 Sgt. Harvey, T. H.
4276414 Fus. Harwood, J.
14628114 Tpr. Hastings, T. N.
4273735 Tpr. Hawkins, F.
4276168 Fus. Hay, L.
14401769 Fus. Hayes, W. G.
6914862 L/Cpl. Heard, L. W.
4270972 Sgt. Hedley, A. G.
4269381 Fus. Hedley, T. M.
4127779 Fus. Hemmings, S.
4268552 Fus. Hemshall, J. E.
4274079 Fus. Henderson, J. W.
4276521 Fus. Henderson, S. G.
7343768 Fus. Henricks, F.
3455370 Fus. Herdson, J.
4273733 Sgt. Hetherington, M.
10600521 Tpr. Hewlett, F. A.
Capt. Hill, C.
4273692 Fus. Hill, N. F.
Capt. Hillman, W.
4275565 Fus. Hine, G.
5834106 Tpr. Hipsey, A.
4695004 Tpr. Hird, J. E.
4267800 Fus. Hirst, J. T. A.
38073 Fus. Hodgkinson, J. C.
6215409 Tpr. Hodgson, A. H.
14579680 Fus. Hodgson, J.
4272286 Fus. Hodgson, R. W.
4274966 Fus. Hogarth, J. R.
4268899 Fus. Hogg, J.
14339276 Fus. Holland, J. E.
4273555 Fus. Holleywell, E.
4273556 Fus. Holleywell, J.
4458910 Fus. Holmes, J.
14405897 Cpl. Hookings, D. S.
4627067 Fus. Horsley, J. R.
4271905 Fus. Howarth, T.
4270195 Fus. Howe, Wilfred
14320118 Fus. Hoy, S.
3963454 Tpr. Hughes, E. I.
4273373 Fus. Hughes, F.
14311897 L/Sgt. Hull, H.
4275592 Fus. Hume, J.
6925243 Fus. Humphreys, W. J.
10601491 Tpr. Humphries, H. J.
4264905 Cpl. Humpish, J.
4275359 Fus. Hunter, G.
4273651 Fus. Hunter, H.
4266780 Fus. Hunter, T.
4278232 Fus. Hunton, J. J.
14272491 Fus. Hutchinson, J.
4272702 L/Cpl. Hutchinson, J. G.
4273596 Fus. Hutton, J.
15452 Fus. Igo, W.
14234848 Tpr. Inman, R. M.
4268576 L/Cpl. Insall, H. G.
4449243 Fus. Ions, H.
4273339 Fus. Ions, W. T.
4277206 Fus. Irving, D.
14407126 Fus. Jackaman, R. J.
Capt. Jackman, J. J. B., V.C.
4278501 Tpr. Jackson, J.
4460161 L/Cpl. Jackson, W.
4444058 Cpl. James, T.
6916113 Tpr. Jarman, A.
14711753 Fus. Jarman, W. A.
5949191 Fus. Jarrett, G. A.
14237328 Tpr. Jeffries, W. G.
Lieut. Jenkins, J. I.

4545346 Fus. Jenkinson, W. L.
5831815 Fus. Jinks, G. C.
4446378 Cpl. Jobson, R. N.
4271909 Fus. Joel, H. C.
4268727 Fus. John, J. S.
4273318 Tpr. Johnson, D. G.
4274569 Fus. Johnson, G. W.
4272099 Fus. Johnson, H.
326252 Tpr. Johnson, H. R.
4271769 Fus. Johnson, J.
4273695 Tpr. Johnson, J.
4278447 Fus. Johnson, L.
Capt. Johnson, L.
4274179 Fus. Johnston, T.
6211087 L/Cpl. Jones, G.
14371396 L/Cpl. Jones, G. C. W.
4272854 Fus. Jones, J.
4257411 S/Sgt. Jones, W. R.
14302992 Tpr. Jowett, J. A.
14287726 Fus. Joyner, G. A.
4272284 Cpl. Keating, C. W.
6916995 Sgt. Kelly, J. J.
4271150 Fus. Kenneally, T.
4276090 Sgt. Kent, E.
Major Kent, R. H. S. M.
6917353 L/Cpl. Kentfield, G. P.
4274183 Fus. Kerr, J.
14336249 Tpr. Kidd, A. E.
14658689 Tpr. Kellington, A.
6915232 Tpr. Kingsland, T. W.
4389620 Fus. Kirby, H. W. B.
6921070 Fus. Kite, C.
4273514 Fus. Knight, W. D.
4278712 Fus. Knowles, S.
4273835 Fus. Laidler, R.
14618095 Fus. La Marsh, W. R.
6848498 Fus. Lane, L. P.
11264272 Fus. Langdon, S. T.
Lieut. Larkman, W.
4451361 L/Cpl. Laverick, T. L.
4270296 Fus. Lawlor, T. A.
10601853 Cpl. Lawrence, S.
10601854 Tpr. Lawson, H.
3455984 Fus. Leary, J.
4274184 Fus. Leck, J. R.
4272415 Fus. Lee, J.
6914356 Fus. Legg, J. W.
4277789 Fus. Leighton, G.
6917377 Tpr. Leith, R.
10603029 L/Cpl. Leslie, A. D.
14329537 Fus. Lewis, L.
6848499 Fus. Light, S. T.
4274111 Tpr. Lillico, R.
4451129 Fus. Litherland, R. J.
6917387 Tpr. Logan, D. W. G.
4277516 L/Cpl. Logan, E.
4275862 Fus. Long, J. R.
4273260 Fus. Longstaff, W.
4271691 Fus. Loraine, R. C.
4272955 Fus. Lowe, J.
4271915 Fus. Lowther, G.
14428271 Fus. Luckett, D.
4273283 Fus. Lundy, F.
4270747 Fus. Luscombe, G.
4273936 Fus. Mabon, J. B.
2933151 Sgt. Macdonald, D. D.
2871729 Fus. Mackenzie, G.
4261451 Fus. Madden, J. S.
4279855 Cpl. Mainswhite, J. L.
4125621 Cpl. Mair, T. E.
Lieut. Maitland, M. C. D.
4275531 Tpr. Major, H. A.
Lieut. Manser, R. W.
27518 Fus. Marr, H.
4389455 Sgt. Marshall, C. R.
24 Fus. Marshall, J.
4271127 Fus. Marshall, K.
4129594 Cpl. Marsland, J.
4268880 Fus. Martin, R. P. J.
4127170 Fus. Mason, A.
4275559 L/Cpl. Mason, F.
4275495 Fus. Mason, H. L.
4273602 Tpr. Mason, J. S.
4274515 Fus. Mason, N.
4271129 Fus. Maule, S.
4273294 Fus. May, T.
6210710 Fus. McCabe, H.
14522605 Fus. McCahill, T.
4265808 W.O.II McCente, J. J.
4128862 L/Cpl. McDonald, J.
4271924 Fus. McDonald, R. W.
3456100 Fus. McHugh, H. A.
4274018 Fus. McGregor, W. G.
14741994 Fus. McIntosh, A. H.
4265691 Cpl. McIntosh, G. M.
4270941 Fus. McIntyre, R.
Lieut. McKay, A.
2983630 Cpl. McKerracher, J.
4277117 Fus. McKie, J.
4448268 Fus. McKie, J.
4270156 Sgt. McLean, A.
4133883 Fus. McLoughlin, J.
2980548 Fus. McManus, M.
4275695 Fus. Meighan, C. L. F.
4269957 Sgt. Merry, C. A.
4273522 Fus. Metcalf, J.
4276377 Fus. Metcalfe, T.
4267133 Cpl. Middlemiss, A.

4275182 Fus. Midgley, L.
4278465 Fus. Milburn, W.
4971254 Fus. Miller, E.
4275868 Fus. Miller, E. C.
4276301 Fus. Miller, G.
4273699 Tpr. Miller, R.
4272872 Fus. Mills, G. W.
4275698 Cpl. Mills, L. V.
12247 Fus. Mills, T.
6210447 Fus. Mills, W.
Capt. Milne, J. E.
4273746 Fus. Mitcheson, E. R.
Capt. Mitchell, R. O.
6847895 Tpr. Mitchelmore, R. W.
4269643 Sgt. Mogie, H. G.
4273561 Fus. Mole, J.
4272137 Fus. Moon, T. C.
6210440 Fus. Moore, T.
6914682 Tpr. Moran, G. W.
4277397 L/Cpl. Morris, H.
14239780 Tpr. Morrison, N.
4275760 Fus. Morton, D.
6848505 Tpr. Morton, H.
4273505 Fus. Morton, R.
4267841 Cpl. Mowat, F. E.
3536637 Fus. Mulhern, P.
7075022 Fus. Mulligan, E., M.M.
4272857 Fus. Mulligan, J. E.
7010789 Sgt. Mulvey, T.
4269850 Sgt. Munro, G. N.
4273515 Fus. Murdie, H.
4277813 Fus. Murphy, F.
6214997 Tpr. Murray, G.
4269961 Fus. Murray, J. L.
4273388 Tpr. Murray, R.
4273884 Sgt. Murray, W.
2036163 Fus. Neary, A. E.
Lieut. Nelson, I. G.
4449361 Sgt. Neville, F. R.
6107495 Fus. Newman, F. W.
4271542 Fus. Newton, C.
4274091 Fus. Newton, M.
6210474 Fus. Newton, S.
4265053 Fus. Nichol, W.
4273658 Fus. Nicholl, A.
6923179 Fus. Nicholson, E. G.
4278673 Tpr. Nicholson, J.
6914371 Fus. Nicholson, J. A.
4273666 Cpl. Nicholson, P. J.
4384764 Sgt. Nixon, E.
14338612 Cpl. Nixon, G. W.
4273278 Cpl. Nixon, R.
4272696 L/Cpl. Noble, W. B.
4274854 Fus. Nockels, D.
14209570 Fus. Nolan, R. L.
4273937 Fus. Nutman, J. W.
4265255 Fus. Oakes, M.
4267095 Fus. O'Connor, J. D.
4273563 L/Cpl. O'Hare, J. R.
6924636 Fus. Olive, H. J.
4273940 Fus. Oliver, G. W.
4274026 Fus. Oliver, J. R.
4273442 Tpr. Oliver, R. W.
4278473 Fus. Oliver, W. J.
4271273 Tpr. O'Neill, C. E.
14207563 Fus. O'Neill, J.
4273393 Tpr. Opie, J. W.
6917461 Tpr. Oriel, A. K.
4273564 L/Sgt. Ormston, J.
4273322 Fus. Ormston, J. W.
4273525 Fus. Ormston, T. W.
4278781 Fus. Orr, J. J.
4272123 Cpl. Osborne, A.
14332748 Fus. Overton, R. S.
4274858 Fus. Padgett, J.
Lieut. Page, J. C.
4278782 Fus. Page, T. D.
4278783 Fus. Palmer, P.
4277935 Fus. Panter, J. E.
14587760 Fus. Park, C. G. M.
6925138 Fus. Park, J. D.
4275510 Fus. Park, T. H.
4268379 Fus. Parker, E.
4608628 Fus. Parker, F.
4273702 Tpr. Parker, J.
4275585 Fus. Parker, J. G.
14404421 Fus. Parker, J. L.
4276101 Fus. Parkin, A.
4257045 W.O.II Parkin, J. W.
4276484 Fus. Parkinson, N.
4273844 Tpr. Parry, F. E.
14291797 Fus. Patience, H.
4278559 L/Cpl. Patterson, L.
2982871 Fus. Patterson, R.
4276459 Cpl. Patterson, T.
4269818 Fus. Pattie, C. H.
4273395 Fus. Pattison, R. W. D.
4273700 Tpr. Pearson, A.
4273701 Tpr. Pearson, A.
4273941 L/Cpl. Pearson, J.
4272142 Cpl. Pearson, R. H.
4269017 Sgt. Pennock, G. E.
5827674 Cpl. Pepper, F. D. O.
14408957 Fus. Perkins, W. O.
Lieut. Phillips, E.
4266974 Sgt. Pick, J. S.
4271363 Fus. Pickavance, T. H. L.
4277321 Fus. Pickering, J.

6203467 Fus. Piper, W. J.
Lieut. Pitchford, O. W.
14332730 Tpr. Plowman, C.
4275293 Fus. Poll, J. E.
Capt. Pollock, J. A.
6915538 Fus. Pomphrett, E.
14742052 Fus. Porteous, G.
10601880 Tpr. Pottage, W. H.
6847863 Tpr. Pratt, A. O.
14401635 Tpr. Prentis, G.
4276461 L/Sgt. Price, J. H.
14384627 Tpr. Purvis, J.
4278261 Fus. Purvis, J. R.
6848427 Tpr. Quinton, G. R.
14516322 Fus. Radford, T.
4275313 Fus. Raffle, G.
4269447 Fus. Railton, A.
4270891 Fus. Rankin, J. P.
6917494 Sgt. Raxworthy, E. W.
3181078 Fus. Ray, J.
6917495 Fus. Raybould, W.
4269426 Sgt. Reay, E.
4270210 Fus. Redfearn, C.
4268588 Fus. Redpath, J. E.
4266359 Fus. Redpath, N.
10601885 Cpl. Reed, C. H.
2657821 Sgt. Reed, F. T.
4269364 Cpl. Reed, G. T.
4276545 Fus. Reed, J.
6923967 Fus. Reeve, J. K.
4274136 Fus. Reilly, J.
3457723 Cpl. Rennie, A. M.
4274031 Fus. Rice, R.
4272293 Fus. Richardson, A.
4275309 Fus. Richardson, R. A.
4387502 W.O.II Richings, N.
Capt. Ridings, J. V.
6915547 Tpr. Rigg, F. H.
4275457 Fus. Riley, D. H.
4278264 Fus. Riley, S. J.
4271100 Cpl. Rivers, J. W.
Lieut. Robertson, N.
4274099 Fus. Robertson, R.
5827335 Tpr. Robinson, B. D.
4269803 L/Cpl. Robinson, F.
2649264 L/Sgt. Robinson, H.
4270512 Fus. Robinson, J.
4275590 Fus. Robinson, J. A.
7952238 Tpr. Robinson, J. G.
4278480 Tpr. Robinson, J. R.
4278970 Tpr. Robinson, T.
4276224 L/Cpl. Robson, A. R. R.
4275762 L/Cpl. Robson, L.
5512838 Fus. Rollason, D.
4264510 Sgt. Rosemurgey, N.
4276225 Fus. Rounding, T. L.
4272832 Fus. Routledge, R.
4276334 Fus. Rowland, T. A.
14505656 Fus. Rushton, W. G.
4271570 Fus. Russell, J.
4269593 Fus. Rutherford, W. W.
4274138 Fus. Rutter, T. R.
4132924 Fus. Ryan, J.
4274096 Fus. Ryan, J. H.
6914941 Fus. Sams, I.
4268998 Sgt. Sanders, P. F.
3859703 Fus. Satterthwaite, J.
4270101 Fus. Scott, A.
4277329 Fus. Scott, C.
4273857 L/Cpl. Scott, G.
4273951 Fus. Scott, J. A.
4273855 Cpl. Scott, J. L.
4278276 Fus. Scott, M.
4273486 Fus. Scott, R.
Lieut. Scott, R. K. G.
4273707 L/Cpl. Scott, W. F.
22598 Fus. Self, G. T.
10601892 Tpr. Sellers, J. A.
4268564 Fus. Shanks, R.
4278890 Fus. Sharp, J. W. C.
4131468 Fus. Sharples, J.
6920651 Fus. Sheehan, E. W.
5388349 Tpr. Shelton, G.
4270952 Fus. Shepherd, L. S.
6915560 Fus. Sheppard, R. J.
7011208 Sgt. Shiels, P. J.
4275160 Fus. Short, L. J.
3537164 Fus. Sidebotham, J.
4273757 Fus. Simm, J.
4278486 Fus. Simmons, M. F.
31143 Fus. Simon, F. P.
4275976 Fus. Simpson, C.
4275727 Fus. Simpson, C. W.
4276549 Fus. Simpson, J. R.
35505 Fus. Simpson, T.
4270526 Fus. Sissons, E. W.
14331498 Cpl. Slater, R. J.
4275766 Cpl. Smeaton, J.
2/Lt. Smith, A. M.
4273438 Tpr. Smith, A. M.
4269244 Fus. Smith, D. R.
4277334 Fus. Smith, G.
5768858 Fus. Smith, G. W.
4271474 Fus. Smith, J. A. E. S.
4270864 Fus. Smith, J. P.
14508639 Tpr. Smith, L.
4266645 W.O.II Smith, P.
2616706 Sgt. Smith, S. W.

6916257 Fus. Smith, W. G.
4270525 Fus. Smithson, E. H.
4266022 Fus. Snowball, J. W.
4624465 L/Cpl. Spall, W. T. J.
4267540 Fus. Spellman, J.
14527271 Tpr. Spencer, R.
4279395 Fus. Spencer, W. J.
4270227 Fus. Stagg, J.
4275759 Fus. Stanbury, F.
6211295 Fus. Stanton, J. W.
6352429 Tpr. Starkey, A. J.
5724410 Fus. Startin, C.
4278815 Fus. Stayman W. F.
4272957 Fus. Steele, A. P.
14332512 Fus. Steele, W. K.
4276229 Fus. Stephenson, J. J.
4449673 Fus. Stephenson, T.
4277861 Cpl. Stevenson, W. M.
4271536 Fus. Stewart, J.
4275572 Fus. Stewart, J.
4273617 Fus. Stewart, T.
Lieut. Stockdale, A.
Lt.-Col. Stockley, R. C.
4276272 Fus. Stokes, H.
4273854 Fus. Stone, N.
10601901 Tpr. Storah, H.
4277338 Fus. Storey, T.
4457477 Fus. Stouph, W. F.
Capt. Strachan, A. M.
23118 Fus. Strathern, A.
7341816 Fus. Street, E. G.
13230 Fus. Strong, R. W. D.
4449406 Fus. Stuart, C.
3782633 Fus. Stubbs, G.
4276736 Fus. Suggett, H.
5626890 Fus. Surridge, F. E.
Lieut. Sutherland, J. W. F.
4133583 L/Cpl. Sutton, A.
4276943 Fus. Sweeney, T.
4279387 Fus. Sweeting, C. S. W.
4268038 Sgt. Sword, J. M.
4271077 Fus. Tait, J.
4271073 Fus. Tait, W.
Lieut. Taylor, H. N.
4275924 Fus. Teale, N.
4270531 Cpl. Terry, R.
6847856 Cpl. Tew, F.
6911296 Tpr. Theobald, F. H.
4271946 Fus. Thomas, B.
3606771 Tpr. Thomason, E.
4273444 Fus. Thompson, A.
4446698 Sgt. Thompson, A.
4274234 Fus. Thompson, A. H.
4278291 L/Cpl. Thompson, A. W.
4277869 Sgt. Thompson, F.
4271609 Fus. Thompson, G. E.
4266138 Fus. Thompson, T.
Lieut. Thomson, A.
Capt. Threlfall, C. R. M.
4270119 Fus. Tiffany, A.
14312072 Tpr. Tiffin, R.
4269047 Cpl. Timney, F.
Lieut. Tittle, J. M.
4278917 Fus. Tonkinson, S.
4606933 Cpl. Topps, H.
4265967 Sgt. Townsley, A.
6916976 L/Cpl. Tucker, A. G.
2028713 L/Cpl. Turley, C. H.
4278298 Tpr. Turnbull, G.
4270953 Fus. Turnbull, J. W.
4273570 Fus. Turnbull, J. W.
14248630 Fus. Turner, A. T.
4271030 Fus. Twitchin, G.
14355050 Fus. Unsworth, R.
Lieut. Varlow, E. R.
2616188 Sgt. Vernon, R. E.
6214948 Tpr. Vincent, D.
6922003 Fus. Vipont, W.
4273895 Fus. Wait, T.
4273893 Fus. Wait, W.
4274057 Fus. Waldie, J. D.
4276373 Fus. Walker, G. A.
4269625 Sgt. Walker, J.
4279733 Fus. Walker, J. A.
14375764 Tpr. Walker, R.
4270454 Fus. Walker, W.
4270214 Fus. Walker, W. L.
4276560 Fus. Wallace, R. A.
7948847 Fus. Wallace, W.
4608929 Sgt. Walsh, W.
4268300 Fus. Wanless, F. W.
4271505 Fus. Wanless, L.
4272350 Fus. Wanty, L. W.
4273675 Tpr. Ward, D.
4276159 Fus. Ward, J.
4278303 Cpl. Ward, J.
6911221 L/Cpl. Ward, L.
Lieut. Ward, M.
Capt. Warren, D. a la T.
6917615 Fus. Watling, J.
14655304 Fus. Watson, F.
4272932 Fus. Watson, H. G.
6847857 Tpr. Watson, H. L.
4277373 Fus. Watson, J. G.
Capt. Watson, R.
4265159 Fus. Watson, R. J.
4279600 L/Sgt. Watson, S. H.
4273861 Fus. Waugh, R.

6917622 Tpr. Weald, A. W.
4273894 Cpl. Weatherburn, J.
4275931 Fus. Weavers, G. F.
2653961 L/Sgt. Webster, J. E.
6215436 Tpr. Wells, G. E.
6921088 Fus. West, D. K.
14242112 Tpr. Wheeler, P.
Major Whelan, R. P.
4267158 L/Cpl. Whistance, J. H.
3321119 Tpr. Whitaker, J.
4276753 Fus. White, C.
4273349 Fus. White, G.
4277903 Fus. White, H.
4546206 Fus. White, H. S.
555590 Fus. White, J.
4264929 Cpl. White, J. R.
4275307 Fus. White, R.
4278508 Fus. White, W.
4275750 L/Cpl. Whiting, F. R. C.
6916283 L/Cpl. Wicks, J.
14231326 Fus. Wigington, H. J.
4395450 Tpr. Wilkinson, A.
4627254 Fus. Wilkinson, N.
4272916 Sgt. Wilkinson, T. A.
4264668 Fus. Willcox, H.
14233838 Fus. Willett, W. H.
14201895 Tpr. Williams, C.
14320170 Fus. Williams, E.
4081212 Tpr. Williams, G.
4271466 Cpl. Williams, H. S.
14322972 Tpr. Williams, K.
6204653 Sgt. Williams, R. G. H.
4273961 Fus. Williamson, A. B.
2/Lt. Willis, G. B.
6205113 Tpr. Willison, W. J.
5120476 Cpl. Wills, D. G.
4272108 Fus. Wilson, A. J.
14670226 Fus. Wilson, A. M. H.
4266058 Fus. Wilson, C. E.
14522113 Tpr. Wilson, H.
4268534 Fus. Wilson, N.
22261 Fus. Wilson, R.
4132606 L/Sgt. Wilson, S.
3537141 Fus. Wilson, W. F.
4275367 Fus. Wiltshire, W. H.
4447864 L/Cpl. Windle, S.
19336 Fus. Witty, M.
4274053 Fus. Wood, J. E.
4395242 Fus. Wood, J. H.
6917130 Tpr. Wood, N.
4394211 Fus. Worton, H.
4542644 Cpl. Wright, E.
14392775 Tpr. Wright, J.
4274525 Fus. Young, W.
4273863 Fus. Young, W. H.

APPENDIX E

1st BATTALION

Operations in Korea

January to October 1951

ROLL OF HONOUR

Killed in action, died of wounds and died

2/Lieut. G. M. Fitzgibbon
Lieut.-Colonel K. O. N. Foster, O.B.E.
Lieut. L. D. Foxton (York and Lancaster Regt., attd.)
Lieut. B. Millington (Royal Leicester Regt., attd.)
Major C. C. G. Milward
Lieut. D. Rudge (Cheshire Regt., attd.)
Lieut. D. A. White (East Yorkshire Regt., attd.)

22299115 Fus. Angus, P.
14470531 Cpl. Bailey, C.
4268914 Sgt. Bates, J.
4279234 Fus. Batey, J. W.
4803744 Fus. Blow, H. H. D.
19036708 Pte. Briggs, W. R. (S.F., attd. 1st Bn. R.N.F.)
19047035 Fus. Broadhead, D.
22539087 Fus. Broadway, S. D.
22337627 Fus. Brotherston, A.
6914196 Fus. Browne, A. R.
22525965 Fus. Buckthorpe, C. H.
22547909 Fus. Burn, J. N. (R.N.F., attd. 1st Bn. R. Leics.)
14453026 Fus. Clark, C.
22320888 Fus. Cooper, G.
4279053 Fus. Corbett, I.
5500178 Fus. Cox, B. L.
4747425 Fus. Cue, R.
4271177 Fus. Curry, F. A.
22432734 Fus. Dutton, P.
19037048 Fus. Eardley, R. J. (R.N.F., attd. 1st Bn. R. Leics.)
4272098 Fus. Eke, A.
19042432 Fus. Fail, F.
19044102 Pte. Fitzpatrick, F. (S.F., attd. 1st Bn. R.N.F.)
21036239 Fus. Ford, R. G.
19031259 Fus. Foster, K.
4391781 Fus. Gavillet, C. F.
4127360 Fus. Gerard, J.
14418676 Cpl. Green, E. J.
4615187 L/Cpl. Hamer, H.
21023603 Fus. Hodgson, G.
4449805 Sgt. Jackson, D.
4976158 Fus. Jackson, R. E.
19107599 Fus. Keenan, R. M.
14454933 L/Cpl. Leach, L. G.
22538101 Fus. Ludlow, S.
14475391 Cpl. McAleese, E.
22238679 Cpl. McIntosh, A.
4271957 Fus. McNally, T. H.
23336162 Fus. Marshall, W. H.
4453530 Cpl. Martin, T. W.
21072543 L/Cpl. Oldfield, D.
4747494 Fus. Pedley, J. H.
4747464 Fus. Phillips, J. W.
4272842 Fus. Pickering, H.
22525246 Fus. Roomes, E.
22348750 Fus. Sadler, C.

49. Lieut.-Colonel K. O. N. Foster, D.S.O., O.B.E., killed in action in Korea, 25th April 1951.

4344180 Fus. Seaman, J. A.
5949689 Fus. Sharp, T.
4976407 L/Cpl. Sharpe, C.
22309872 Fus. Shepherd, D. H. (R.N.F., attd. 1st Bn. R. Leics.)
19034425 Sgt. Smith, K.
14459274 Pte. Smith, R. H. (R. Warwicks, attd. 1st Bn. R.N.F.)
22347060 Fus. South, R.
22331471 Fus. Sugden, R.
22540096 Fus. Tamblyn, D. E.
19041759 Cpl. Thirkettle, D.
21187157 Fus. Vickers, F.
22267850 Fus. Walker, L.
22525966 L/Cpl. Walls, G. V.
4269659 Sgt. Williamson, J.
22328907 Fus. Wintersgill, K.
22188644 Fus. Winterton, R.

	Officers	*Other Ranks*
Wounded or injured in action	18	238
Missing	1	21
Prisoners of war	4	37

N.B.—The above particulars are derived from official lists compiled on 17th April 1952, on which date four of the other ranks reported missing were believed to have been killed and one known to have been wounded.

HONOURS AWARDED

Distinguished Service Order

Lt.-Col. K. O. N. Foster, O.B.E.
Major C. H. Mitchell
Major R. M. Pratt
Major H. J. Winn, M.C.

Distinguished Conduct Medal

22525874 Fus. R. Crooks, M.M.
4269977 W.O.II E. J. Radcliffe

Military Cross

2/Lt. L. S. Adams-Acton
Capt. C. W. Bowen (R.A.M.C., attd.)
Major R. D. Brook
Lt. J. M. Cubiss (W. Yorks Regt., attd.)
Major R. Leith-MacGregor, D.F.C.
2/Lt. W. P. Sheppard (E. Yorks Regt., attd.)
2/Lt. J. A. Yeo (E. Yorks Regt., attd.)
2/Lt. M. D. Young

Military Medal

7265498 Sgt. B. Baker (R.A.M.C., attd.)
4690537 Fus. J. B. Barker
19037566 Cpl. J. D. Thompson
4390499 Cpl. L. Hadfield
1427036 L/Cpl. J. Oven
4397370 Sgt. J. Pilcher
Fus. W. Wappett

The citations in respect of the above awards were given in full in the *St. George's Gazette* of 29th February 1952.

INDEX

NOTE: This index is applicable only to the body of the volume—not to the Foreword, Preface, Glossary and Appendices. It contains names of individuals (in the highest rank in which they are mentioned), place names, names of ships, formations and units.

A

B

D

H

N

www.ingramcontent.com/pod-product-compliance
Lightning Source LLC
Chambersburg PA
CBHW050402110426
42812CB00006BA/1779

* 9 7 8 1 8 4 7 3 4 1 5 6 3 *